SUPPLEMENTARY MATERIALS ON
ELECTRONIC DISCOVERY
For Use in Civil Procedure Courses

. . .

By
Shira A. Scheindlin
United States District Judge
Southern District of New York

Daniel J. Capra
Philip Reed Professor of Law
Fordham Law School

The Sedona Conference®

With an Introduction by Professor Richard L. Marcus

AMERICAN CASEBOOK SERIES®

WEST®
A Thomson Reuters business

Mat #40828538

© 2009 Thomson Reuters

    610 Opperman Drive
    St. Paul, MN 55123
    1–800–313–9378

Printed in the United States of America

ISBN: 978–0–314–20522–3

TEXT IS PRINTED ON 10% POST CONSUMER RECYCLED PAPER

PREFACE

Civil litigation is primarily about discovery practice. The information that parties obtain during discovery from each other or from third parties will affect whether a case is tried, settled, or resolved by motion. Today, the vast majority of records are created and maintained electronically. Thus, "paper" discovery is a thing of the past and "e-discovery" is the present and the future. The creation and storage of electronic records, and the almost incomprehensible volume of such records, create new challenges regarding preservation and production. Today, any course on civil procedure will include a segment on the many intriguing issues surrounding the discovery of electronic records. This Supplement is designed to meet that need: to help students and their professors with materials organized to address many, if not all of these issues. As you will see, this short volume provides leading cases and commentary in this critical and developing area of law.[1]

To set the stage, we begin with an overview in the Introduction by Professor Richard Marcus. Then we turn to a chapter (I) on the explosion of electronic information and how it is stored and retrieved. We turn then to a chapter (II) on the preservation of electronic information covering such questions as when the duty to preserve attaches and what records must be preserved. We move on to a chapter (III) covering the required meeting between counsel at the outset of litigation, when counsel must address issues surrounding the discovery of electronic information. When the discovery process gets into full swing the parties must produce the relevant information after conducting a privilege review (Chapter IV), and if the parties fail to produce relevant information the court must consider the imposition of sanctions based on the spoliation of evidence (Chapter V). Finally, when producing the equivalent of millions of documents, attorneys must carefully safeguard the client's privileges and protections (Chapter VI).[2]

There are three co-authors of this Supplement. Judge Shira A. Scheindlin was a member of the Advisory Committee on Civil Rules and a member of the Discovery Subcommittee that drafted the 2006 amendments addressing the discovery of electronically stored informa-

---

1. To make the cases easier to read, we have generally deleted the internal citations and footnotes in the cases. When we leave internal citations and footnotes in the cases, we do so in the belief that they make a specific contribution to the understanding of the case. When we retain a footnote in a case, we retain its original number.

2. For a fuller treatment of these issues, as well as chapters on data collection, ethical issues and the admissibility of digital evidence, see Scheindlin, Capra, and The Sedona Conference®, *ELECTRONIC DISCOVERY AND DIGITAL EVIDENCE: CASES AND MATERIALS* (2008).

tion. She is also the author of the landmark *Zubulake* opinions. Professor Daniel Capra of Fordham Law School is the Reporter to the Advisory Committee on Evidence Rules and the principal draftsman of Rule 502 on waiver of privilege. Finally, The Sedona Conference® has been the leading voice of the legal profession in addressing all of the concerns surrounding electronic discovery. Sedona has issued the most oft-cited publications in this area including the "The Sedona Principles: Best Practices Recommendations & Principles for Addressing Electronic Document Production" and "The Sedona Conference® Guidelines for Managing Information and Records in the Electronic Age." Because Sedona is made up of various sectors of the bench, bar, academy and private industry, we take this opportunity to thank those individual members of Sedona who contributed to the preparation of this Supplement.

Most importantly, we wish to give special thanks to Kenneth J. Withers, Sedona's Director of Judicial Education and Content, who, when it comes to the topic of e-discovery, is the personification of The Sedona Conference®, and one of the most knowledgeable people in the world.

And to the individual contributors, who assisted in the preparation of the following chapters we extend our deepest thanks: Chapter I: Jason R. Baron and John H. Jessen; Chapter II: Adam Cohen, William P. Butterfield, Jason R. Baron, William F. Hamilton, John H. Jessen, and Laura E. Ellsworth; Chapter III: Ariana J. Tadler; Chapter IV: Ariana J. Tadler, Jason R. Baron, John H. Jessen, Scott A. Carlson, Jay E. Grenig, William F. Hamilton, William P. Butterfield, and M. James Daley; Chapter V: Paul E. Burns, Adam Cohen, Ronald J. Hedges, and Jay E. Grenig.

We hope that the students and professors who use this Supplement will find it useful, versatile, and well organized. It has been our privilege and pleasure to create what we believe will be a unique and useful Supplement to ensure that this important topic is easily and comprehensively included in many Civil Procedure courses.

SHIRA A. SCHEINDLIN
NEW YORK, N.Y.

DANIEL CAPRA
NEW YORK, N.Y.

THE SEDONA CONFERENCE®
    BY: KENNETH J. WITHERS
PHOENIX, ARIZONA

Summary of Contents

TABLE OF CONTENTS

TABLE OF CASES

The principal cases are in bold type. Cases cited or discussed in the text are in roman type. References are to pages. Cases cited in principal cases and within other quoted materials are not included.

TABLE OF STATUTES

SUPPLEMENTARY MATERIALS ON
ELECTRONIC DISCOVERY

For Use in Civil Procedure Courses

*

INTRODUCTION

THE 2006 AMENDMENTS TO THE FEDERAL RULES OF CIVIL PROCEDURE GOVERNING DISCOVERY OF ELECTRONICALLY STORED INFORMATION: FITTING ELECTRONIC DISCOVERY INTO THE OVERALL DISCOVERY MIX

■ ■ ■

Richard L. Marcus, Horace O. Coil ('57) Chair in Litigation, University of California, Hastings College of the Law, Special Reporter, Advisory Committee on Civil Rules[1]

Electronic discovery is the hottest topic in litigation today. Some suggest that it might be "considered a specialized substantive expertise in the same vein as, for example, patent law," and argue that mishandling such discovery could become a fertile source of malpractice claims.[2] Partly to address such concerns, an electronic discovery industry has emerged that is anticipated to generate over four billion dollars in revenues in 2009. Within law firms, the advent of electronic discovery has prompted the creation of special departments and staff attorney positions to handle the activity. The costs of this form of discovery have mounted quickly; some lawyers now find that the cost of preparing a privilege log identifying electronically stored information ("ESI") withheld on grounds of privilege routinely exceeds one million dollars. Given the rising centrality of electronic discovery to litigation, it is understandable that you have chosen to study the topics covered in this book. This Introduction sets the scene for what follows.

---

1. As Special Reporter to the Advisory Committee, I was a primary drafter of the 2006 amendments to the Federal Rules to deal with the challenges of electronic discovery. In this Introduction, I speak only for myself and not for the Committee or anyone else.

2. Janet H. Kwuon & Karen Wan, *High Stakes for Missteps in EDD*, N.J. L.J., Dec. 31, 2007, at E2.

Although electronic discovery emerged as central only in the 21st century, American discovery has been a source of controversy for decades. Beginning in the mid 1970s, Federal Rule changes sought to contain and constrain American discovery. As electronic discovery appeared, a crucial question was whether additional rule changes were needed to handle its challenges. The eventual conclusion was that rule changes were needed, but it is important to appreciate from the outset how those changes fit into the broader framework developed for paper discovery. I begin, therefore, with those background developments.

A.   The Discovery "Revolution"

American discovery has long been distinctive. For example, in the 1870s American discovery efforts provoked German protests, and various countries have more recently adopted "blocking" statutes designed to prevent American discovery on their shores.[3] Until the 1930s, however, discovery was available in American courts only on a spotty basis. As late as 1911, for example, the Supreme Court inveighed against a "fishing bill" by which a party sought "to pry into the case of his adversary to learn its strength or weakness."[4]

The adoption of the Federal Rules in 1938 produced a revolution because it vastly expanded discovery:

> If one adds up all of the types of discovery permitted in individual state courts, one finds some precursors to what later became discovery under the Federal Rules, but ... no one state allowed the total panoply of devices. Moreover, the Federal Rules, as they became law in 1938, eliminated features of discovery that in some states had curtailed the scope of discovery and the breadth of its use.[5]

And the courts rapidly came to favor the broad discovery. The Supreme Court—which had denounced "fishing expeditions" in 1911—changed its tune by 1947: "No longer can the time-honored cry of 'fishing expedition' serve to preclude a party from inquiring into the facts underlying his opponent's case. Mutual knowledge of all the relevant facts gathered by both parties is essential to proper litigation."[6]

The rulemakers contributed further to expanding discovery. The 1938 rules had continued some constraints on discovery. In 1946, Rule 26(b)(1) was amended to make clear that information need not be admissible to be discoverable, and Rule 34(a) was amended to clarify that there was no need to specify each document that was sought; categorical requests were valid. In the 1960s, the Civil Rules Advisory Committee conducted a broad empirical study of discovery that led to the conclusion that "[d]iscovery

---

3.   Gary Born, *International Civil Litigation in United States Courts* 849, 856–71 (3d ed. 1996).

4.   *Carpenter v. Winn*, 221 U.S. 533, 540 (1911).

5.   Stephen N. Subrin, *Fishing Expeditions Allowed: The Historical Background of the 1938 Federal Discovery Rules*, 39 B.C. L. Rev. 691, 719 (1998).

6.   *Hickman v. Taylor*, 329 U.S. 495, 507 (1947).

has become an integral part of litigation."[7] On the strength of this conclusion, rule amendments that became effective in 1970 removed some remaining constraints. Most significantly, Rule 34 was amended so that a prior judicial order based on a showing of good cause was no longer needed for a document request; after that, document requests could be made without numerical limitations or prior judicial scrutiny. With the 1970 amendments, American discovery reached its high water mark.

At this point, American discovery also took its place as a feature of the "litigation boom" that many decried. In part, this controversy resulted from the American reliance on private enforcement of legal norms, which prompted resistance in some quarters. Discovery was central to this growth. As a leading federal judge put it:

> Congress has elected to use the private suit, private attorney-general as an enforcing mechanism for the antitrust laws, the securities laws, environmental laws, civil rights and more. In the main, the plaintiff in these suits must discover his evidence from the defendant. Calibration of discovery is calibration of the level of enforcement of the social policy set by Congress.[8]

Some said that broad discovery itself prompted expansion in several of these substantive areas.[9] "Broad discovery is thus not a mere procedural rule. Rather it has become, at least for our era, a procedural institution perhaps of virtually constitutional foundation."[10] Those who deal with discovery—including electronic discovery—must have this background in mind.

B. The Containment Effort: Rule Amendments to Constrain Overbroad Discovery

Nonetheless, growing clamor about the burdens and intrusiveness of discovery fueled efforts to constrain it. Beginning in the 1970s, many strong voices—some, perhaps, motivated by opposition to private enforcement of public law—urged that American discovery produced too much cost and not enough benefit.[11] Discovery remained a central feature of the Advisory Committee's agenda throughout the last quarter of the 20th century. The importance of this history is that this clamor resulted in adoption of a variety of rule changes that are relevant to the handling of electronic discovery.[12] The recent rule changes for electronic discovery

---

7. William A. Glaser, *Pretrial Discovery and the Adversary System* 51 (1968).

8. Patrick Higginbotham, *Foreword*, 49 Ala. L. Rev. 1, 4–5 (1997).

9. *See* Jack H. Friedenthal, *A Divided Supreme Court Adopts Discovery Amendments to the Federal Rules of Civil Procedure*, 69 Cal. L. Rev. 806, 818 (1981) (arguing that discovery itself had fueled growth in the substantive law of products liability, employment discrimination, and consumer protection).

10. Geoffrey C. Hazard, *From Whom No Secrets Are Hid*, 76 Tex. L. Rev. 1665, 1694 (1998).

11. For a contemporary catalogue of these objections, see *Addresses Delivered at the National Conference on the Causes of Popular Dissatisfaction with the Administration of Justice* (Apr. 7–9, 1976), 70 F.R.D. 79–246; *Proceedings of the National Conference on Discovery Reform*, 3 Rev. Litig. 1–221 (1982).

12. For a discussion of many of these amendments, see Richard L. Marcus, *Discovery Containment Redux*, 39 B.C. L. Rev. 747 (1998).

were designed to fit within this broader framework.

One key point to appreciate about this clamor from the 1970s to the 1990s is that it resembled much of the current clamor about electronic discovery, particularly in relation to paper discovery under Rule 34. Thus, lawyers that frequently had to respond to discovery requests (often representing defendants) asserted that their opponents were abusing discovery for tactical purposes. They said that dragnet discovery requests produced huge response costs but little or no actual evidence of importance; overbroad discovery could become a club to extract nuisance settlements. Lawyers that frequently sought information through discovery (often representing plaintiffs) reported that they had to make broad requests to obtain the information they really needed, and that responding parties often resisted proper discovery unjustifiably and/or resorted to "dump truck" practices, delivering enormous quantities of worthless material through which they had to sift to find the important information.

The quarter century of Federal Rules discovery reform did not change the basic American commitment to access to necessary information, but it did produce rule amendments that went into effect in 1980, 1983, 1993, and 2000. Among these many amendments,[13] several stand out as important to the issues covered in this book:

Conference regarding discovery plan and judicial review of the plan: Rule 26(f) was added in 1993 to require the parties to confer before formal discovery began to develop a discovery plan, and to deliver that plan to the judge before the Rule 16(b) scheduling order was entered. At the time of their conference or soon thereafter, under Rule 26(a)(1) the parties are to exchange basic information about the witnesses and documents they may rely upon in support of their respective cases. These provisions in part build upon the growing commitment of the federal judiciary to manage and supervise the cases before them.[14] As part of that managerial orientation, judges came to expect lawyers to cooperate and act in a more forthcoming way.[15] This orientation has become crucial to handling electronic discovery.

Proportionality in discovery: One of the recurrent concerns about paper discovery was that extremely broad discovery requests were easy to draft, extremely burdensome to satisfy, and often produced little or nothing of importance to the case. In 1983, the "proportionality" provisions now contained in Rule 26(b)(2)(C) were added to address these concerns. According to the Advisory Committee's Reporter at the time, the addition of the proportionality provisions represented a "180 degree shift"

---

13.   Others included a slight modification of the scope of discovery under Rule 26(b)(1), setting numerical limits on interrogatories and depositions, setting a time limit on depositions, and adding Rule 26(a)(1) requirements of disclosure without the need for a formal discovery request.

14.   *See* Richard L. Marcus, *Reining in the American Lawyer: The New Role of American Judges*, 27 Hast. Int'l & Compar. L. Rev. 3 (2003); Judith Resnik, *Managerial Judges*, 96 Harv. L. Rev. 374 (1982).

15.   *See generally* Robert Peckham, *The Federal Judge as Case Manager: The New Role in Guiding a Case from Filing to Disposition*, 69 Cal. L. Rev. 770 (1981) (describing the expectations of the judge).

in attitude toward overbroad discovery.[16] But a decade later, it was reported that the addition of these provisions "seems to have created only a ripple in the caselaw."[17] With the emergence of electronic discovery, this proportionality provision may gain added importance.

Certification of compliance with discovery obligations: In 1983, Rule 26(g) was added, directing that an attorney signing a discovery request or response thereby certified that it was proper and justified under the rules. This certification requirement was adopted at the same time Rule 11's certification requirements were strengthened, and the drafters thought that the changes to Rule 26 would have equal importance. But as any first-year civil procedure student learns, the two provisions did not initially pack a similar wallop. The 1983 amendments to Rule 11 caused widespread effects and concern, eventually leading to amendments in 1993 to reformulate that certification requirement. The Rule 26(g) provisions, in contrast, attracted little attention until the advent of electronic discovery, which heightened attention to the responsibilities of counsel.

Supplementation of disclosures and discovery responses, and sanctions including exclusion of materials not disclosed: Until 1993, Rule 26(e) was fairly lax regarding the need to supplement or correct incomplete or incorrect discovery responses. Now it is quite demanding. Rule 26(e)(1)(A) requires timely supplementation whenever a discovery response or disclosure "is incomplete or incorrect." Rule 37(c)(1) directs that a party may not use any information not provided initially or by supplementation, creating a relatively routine bar to presentation of evidence unless it is promptly revealed and raising the possibility of further sanctions.

C. The Rulemaking Response to Electronic Discovery

In a sense, electronic discovery came to the rule amendment process late in the game. To be sure, something of the sort had been there for some time. The far-sighted rulemakers of the 1960s foresaw the need to deal with discovery of computerized materials, and Rule 34 was amended then to permit discovery of "data compilations from which information can be obtained." In 1985, a district judge wrote that "[c]omputers have become so commonplace that most court battles now involve discovery of some type of computer-stored information."[18] The third edition of the Manual for Complex Litigation, in 1995, said that "[c]omputerized data have become commonplace in litigation."[19]

But what we now know as electronic discovery really did not emerge until later. In 1996, the Advisory Committee embarked on its Discovery Project, which was designed to survey the entire array of discovery issues

---

16. Arthur R. Miller, *The August 1983 Amendments to the Federal Rules of Civil Procedure: Promoting Effective Case Management and Lawyer Responsibility,* Federal Judicial Center, 32–33 (1984).

17. 8 Charles A. Wright, Arthur R. Miller & Richard L. Marcus, *Federal Practice & Procedure* § 2008.1, at 121 (2d ed. 1994).

18. *Bills v. Kennecott Corp.,* 108 F.R.D. 459, 462 (D. Utah 1985).

19. *Manual for Complex Litigation (Third)* § 21.446 (1995).

and determine whether further rule revisions were needed to control discovery. Many lawyers told the Committee that it was "fighting the last war" because the real issues regarding discovery had to do with e-mail and the like. The headlines soon confirmed these reports; the government's antitrust suit against Microsoft, featuring Bill Gates' e-mail statements, was "the first major E-mail trial."[20] Since then we have become familiar with the idea that "[c]orporate investigations used to mean following the paper trail, but these days many follow an electronic one."[21] Discovery seeking such materials was clearly a growing field.

The problems generated by electronic discovery sounded very familiar, however—volume, burden, and intrusiveness. By the time electronic discovery emerged, the Advisory Committee had spent two decades dealing with these very problems and developed a variety of rule amendments to address them. Moreover, it seemed that—in contrast to paper discovery— using computers might actually reduce the burden of responding to discovery. In 1978, the Supreme Court had recognized that

> although it may be expensive to retrieve information stored in computers when no program yet exists for the particular job, there is no reason to think that the same information could be extracted any less expensively if the records were kept in less modern forms. Indeed, one would expect the reverse to be true, for otherwise computers would not have gained such widespread use in the storing and handling of information.[22]

By the mid 1990s, others had recognized that the use of computers might make discovery manageable where it would have been too burdensome with paper materials.[23] And creating a new set of rules due to a technological development seemed dubious; although the photocopier dramatically increased the amount of material subject to discovery no rule changes were made as a result.

With the passage of time, however, it became clear that electronic discovery involved issues not presented by paper discovery that justified attention in the rules. A detailed description of the magnitude and nature of ESI is found in Chapter I. But the nature of those distinctive issues serves as the backdrop for a number of specific topics addressed by rule amendment in 2006.[24]

---

20. Steve Lohr, *Antitrust Case Is Highlighting Role of E-mail*, N.Y. Times, Nov. 2, 1998, at C1.

21. Ellen Byron, *Computer Forensics Sleuths Help Find Fraud*, Wall St. J., Mar. 18, 2003, at B1.

22. *Oppenheimer Fund, Inc. v. Sanders*, 437 U.S. 340, 362 (1978).

23. *See* William W. Schwarzer *et al.*, *Civil Discovery and Mandatory Disclosure: A Guide to Effective Practice* I–23 (2d ed. 1994) (noting that "[d]iscovery that otherwise might be impermissibly burdensome, such as requiring detailed identification of all known documents referring to relevant issues, may not be burdensome if the computerized system is able to generate the identifications.").

24. For further discussion of these issues, see Richard L. Marcus, *E–Discovery and Beyond: Toward* Brave New World *or* 1984?, 236 F.R.D. 598, 610–17 (2006).

Recognizing "ESI" as a separate object of discovery: Rule 34(a)(1)(A) now confirms that a party may seek discovery of documents or ESI. As the Committee Note emphasizes, this term is defined broadly to encompass all sorts of information stored in any medium including future developments in computer technology. The Rule also specifically authorizes testing or sampling of such materials. As the Committee Note recognizes, this additional opportunity may be important for electronic discovery, but it is "not meant to create a routine right of direct access to a party's electronic information system," and therefore "[c]ourts should guard against undue intrusiveness resulting from inspecting or testing such systems." Past experience showed that direct access to another party's computer system could do harm,[25] and the proper handling of such access presents challenges.

Directing the parties to discuss issues relating to electronic discovery: A recurrent phenomenon in the early days of electronic discovery seemed to be that problems arose well into the litigation because the parties had not thought about these issues in advance. One sort of problem could arise when production of ESI proceeded before the parties had discussed the format to be used; the receiving party might report that it was unable to use what it got, while the producing party might object to providing the information in a substitute format. Another sort of problem involved loss of ESI that was available when the suit was filed but was not preserved.[26] Rule 26(f) addresses these issues by directing that during their initial conference the parties discuss preservation of discoverable evidence (of whatever sort) and discuss any issues about electronic discovery, including specifically the form for production of ESI.

Although preservation and form of production are required topics of the Rule 26(f) conference, it is expected that a range of other issues will be discussed. As you cover the topics in this book, reflect on how counsel should approach them in the discovery conference. In order to discuss such issues intelligently, as the Committee Note recognizes, counsel will often need to become well acquainted with the client's electronic information systems, for only with that knowledge can counsel make meaningful commitments. The parties are to report to the court on their discovery plan, and Rule 16(b)(3)(B)(iii) provides for including provisions regarding electronic discovery in the court's scheduling order. Courts engaged in this judicial management activity are likely to expect counsel to be cooperative in developing the electronic discovery plan, and to regard the provisions of the resulting order as binding. This means that much is at stake for lawyers approaching this conference. Those who make commitments they cannot meet will likely suffer later on.

---

25. *See, e.g., Gates Rubber Co. v. Bando Chem. Indus.*, 167 F.R.D. 90, 111–12 (D. Colo. 1996) (discovering party's "expert" loaded software onto the responding party's drives that overwrote the existing data).

26. *See, e.g., GTFM, Inc. v. Wal–Mart Stores, Inc.*, No. 98 Civ. 7724, 2000 WL 335558 (S.D.N.Y. Mar. 30, 2000) (deposition of an IT representative of defendant revealed that information defendant had initially failed to produce during discovery on the ground it no longer existed had existed at the time of the discovery but had been deleted since then).

Addressing form of production: Form of production is normally not an issue with paper information, but with ESI there is a range of possible forms for production, as anyone who has ever received an electronic file that cannot be opened understands. Obviously, a file that won't open is not usable. And equally obviously, different kinds of ESI come in different forms—a word processing file and a video can't easily be compared. The problems are easy to imagine.

The problems are not easy to solve in a global way by rulemaking. A rule could direct that a specific form of production be used, but that would not work for all kinds of ESI, and would likely become outdated rapidly given the evolution of technology. The rules therefore don't attempt to provide a specific template for litigants, but to provide a process for tailoring the form of production to the given case. Form of production is one of those things that the parties should discuss during their Rule 26(f) conference, and it may be possible then to adopt a protocol for the case and include that protocol in the court's Rule 16(b) order. Beyond that, they can exchange information during that conference that would assist them in making sensible decisions about form of production later on. The spirit of reasonable cooperation should prevail.

The same attitude explains Rule 34's provisions on form of production. Rule 34(b)(1)(C) permits the party requesting discovery to specify the form for production. If the requesting party does so, the responding party may object under Rule 34(b)(2)(D). If the requesting party does not specify a form, under Rule 34(b)(2)(E)(ii) the responding party must produce in a form in which the information is ordinarily maintained or in a reasonably usable form. The possible use of a form in which the information is ordinarily maintained is often said to refer to "native format." A given party might have the same information in more than one native format; choice of any one of those formats would satisfy the Rule. In any event, the responding party need not produce the ESI in more than one form providing that it gave sufficient notice of the form it intended to use.[27]

One consideration in choosing a form of production is whether it is important to obtain "metadata" or "embedded data." These terms will be defined later in this book; the point here is that there is no transcendental answer to this question. In many cases neither metadata nor embedded data may matter. Indeed, sometimes the parties may prefer to have ESI produced in paper. But in other cases it is important that the information be delivered in a form that permits the requesting party to analyze or otherwise manipulate it. For this purpose some electronic formats— possibly including TIFF or PDF—may not suffice.

---

27. As noted below, the Rule also requires the producing party to notify its adversary as to what form it will use before production. The Committee Note observes: "A party that responds to a discovery request by simply producing electronically stored information in a form of its choice, without identifying that form in advance of the production . . . runs a risk that the requesting party can show that the produced form is not reasonably usable and that it is entitled to production of some or all of the information in an additional form."

Rather than prescribe a specific form, the Rules' goal is to provide a process that minimizes disputes about form. The worst sort of dispute arises when production has already occurred and the receiving party says that the form used does not work but the producing party responds "That's too bad, but you've had your one chance and I won't give the material to you in another form." To guard against this eventuality, Rule 34(b)(2)(D) directs that—whether or not the request specified a form for production—the responding party must state the form it intends to use before it produces the information. The goal throughout is to identify and crystallize the dispute before the costs of solving it spiral out of control. Ultimately, if the parties cannot agree on form the court must decide what form should be used.

The Rules don't tell the judge how to choose a form when the parties cannot agree. Presumably the judge is not limited to the forms preferred by the parties. (The judge's latitude might sometimes provide the parties with an incentive to agree on a form.) One concern would focus on how the requesting party intends to use the information it obtains. Another might focus on how the producing party uses the information in its business; if it regularly provides information in a given form to others in that business it may be difficult to refuse to provide information in that form through discovery.[28]

Problems of accessibility: Almost by definition, discovery requests seek to compel a party to retrieve and assemble materials that it would not otherwise retrieve and assemble. With paper materials, that gathering process can be very cumbersome. For decades, parties have dealt with this problem by rough-and-ready "proportionality" measures like refusing to search all offices worldwide when relatively complete documentation should be located in certain offices.

With ESI, these accessibility problems can be compounded. This information is so portable that it may be located in myriad places including such diverse items as hand-held devices and home computers of employees. Some may be on hard drives in space not used for purposes listed on the directory. The "delete" key does not delete information, but

---

28. The Freedom of Information Act provides an analogy. Its regulations regarding form for production by governmental agencies call for a "business as usual" attitude focusing on what format the agency uses in its ordinary business activities. Notwithstanding, the Department of Defense once refused to provide materials in a zipped format in response to an FOIA request despite evidence that it would provide information in zipped format to its contractors. The Department argued that the "business as usual" approach should be limited to its usual practice in responding to FOIA requests. In *TPS, Inc. v. United States Department of Defense*, 330 F.3d 1191, 1195 (9th Cir. 2003), the court rejected this argument:

The language of the FOIA does not support a reading that distinguishes between "business as usual" for FOIA requests and "business as usual" for activities that are part of the agency's business. . . . When an agency already creates or converts documents in a certain format—be it for FOIA requestors, under a contract, or in the ordinary course of business—requiring that it provide documents in that format to others does not impose an unnecessarily harsh burden.

Similarly with form of production in electronic discovery, one presumably should not accept the argument that the only referent is what form the party ordinarily uses to respond to discovery. Of course, there may be confidentiality issues that affect the analogy, but this case does provide a starting point.

only releases the space for further use; until that space is overwritten the information remains where it was, albeit often in fragmentary form and no longer easy to locate. Another source of information is the collection of "backup tapes" that almost every organization acquires as part of its disaster-recovery system. These records are made on a regular basis and include an undifferentiated collection of all data on the captured system at the moment the backup was made. They may be usable only after being "restored," a process that can be costly and take considerable time. Finally, many organizations continue to possess data that were generated by computer systems they no longer use, often called "legacy data." The organizations may have no present way to access the data.

Early on, it appeared that nobody really expected that the initial response to a discovery request would include searching out or unearthing all these kinds of data. The question is now addressed in Rule 26(b)(2)(B), which builds on the proportionality provisions already in the rules and specifies that a party need not produce information from "sources" it identifies as "not reasonably accessible." One premise of this exemption from initial production of responsive data is that "accessible" data will be voluminous and sufficient; ordinarily one would press for more only after first examining what has been produced. But if a party seeking discovery presses for more, the burden remains on the producing party to show that the sources not searched are genuinely not reasonably accessible, and it must do so in terms of the "undue burden or cost" that gathering the data would entail in comparison to its likely value to the litigation. One method for determining whether that cost is undue is sampling. Even if the producing party shows that the sources are not reasonably accessible, the court may order production for good cause, but it may also shift some or all of the cost of retrieving the data to the party insisting that it be retrieved.

Preservation and sanctions: As with the problem of form of production, Rule 26(f) now directs the parties to confer at the outset about preserving all types of discoverable information, including ESI. This will hopefully often yield agreements about what should be preserved, a great improvement over a dispute years after the litigation began about things that were not preserved. The value of such agreements is one reason why lawyers must become acquainted with their clients' computer systems; only an informed lawyer can negotiate an appropriate agreement. In the same vein, if the preservation issues cannot be resolved by agreement, a well-prepared lawyer will be able to present the client's position to the judge in connection with the Rule 16(b) report should the adversary seek an early order regarding preservation. And if the adversary does not seek an order and the party does what the lawyer proposed, it will probably be difficult for the adversary to persuade the judge later that a reasonable preservation regime is inadequate.

But the Rules themselves contain no provisions regarding preservation, and special problems attend preservation of ESI. For one thing, the operation of computers can alter information without intentional intervention by the person using the computer. For another, many computer systems are set up—for good reasons—to remove certain information after the passage of specified periods of time. And some storage media—such as backup tapes—are regularly reused, thereby removing information that was on them. Finally, in many companies an employee's computer hard drive is wiped clean when the employee leaves the company, and whatever discoverable data was on that drive is lost (unless recoverable through expensive forensic methods).

Although the Rules do not contain preservation provisions, they do contain sanction provisions, and one goal of some urging electronic discovery rule changes was to create a "safe harbor" for those who comply with reasonable procedures in preserving ESI. Rule 37(e) provides limited protections against sanctions "under these rules."[29] The protections apply only to data lost due to "routine" "operation of an electronic information system."[30] And the routine operation must be in "good faith." This requirement introduces the possible need for a litigation hold, as the Committee Note recognizes:

> The good faith requirement . . . means that a party is not permitted to exploit the routine operation of an information system to thwart discovery obligations by allowing that operation to continue in order to destroy specific stored information that it is required to preserve. When a party is under a duty to preserve information because of pending or reasonably anticipated litigation, intervention in the routine operation of an information system is one aspect of what is often called a "litigation hold."

One recurrent question may be whether there is any duty to preserve sources of ESI that are not reasonably accessible. The key point is that Rule 26(b)(2)(B) does not place such sources entirely off limits for discovery, but only exempts the responding party from searching them in completing its initial discovery response. Given that the court could later order discovery from those sources even if they are shown not to be reasonably accessible, good faith may require that they be retained, as the Committee Note confirms.[31]

Privilege waiver: "The inadvertent production of a privileged documents is a specter that haunts every document intensive case."[32] As a consequence, the Advisory Committee has long sought solutions to the

---

29. Other adverse consequences, not based on the Federal Rules, might result. For example, the rules do not purport to limit the authority of regulators such as the SEC to impose sanctions for failure to preserve materials.

30. This is not limited to a party's system; if the party has retained vendors or outsiders to store the party's ESI losses of information on the vendor's system could be covered.

31. The Committee Note to Rule 37(e) explains: "Whether good faith would call for steps to prevent the loss of information on sources that the party believes are not reasonably accessible under Rule 26(b)(2) depends on the circumstances of each case. One factor is whether the party reasonably believes that the information on such sources is likely to be discoverable and not available from reasonably accessible sources."

32. *FDIC v. Marine Midland Realty Credit Corp.*, 138 F.R.D. 479, 479–80 (E.D. Va. 1991). *See also* Richard L. Marcus, *The Perils of Privilege: Waiver and the Litigator*, 84 Mich. L. Rev. 1605 (1986).

problems created by inadvertent production of privileged material, and the costly and time-consuming review process necessary to minimize that risk.

Volume and search issues can compound these concerns when discovery of ESI is sought. Identifying privileged materials is always a challenge, and the possibility that embedded data eligible for protection may be hard to review exacerbates the problems, particularly in a world where the amount of electronic data to be reviewed is enormous. But there is a statutory obstacle to solving this problem by rule.[33] However, Federal Rule of Evidence 502 now addresses these issues.

Rule 26(b)(5)(B) does not directly address privilege waiver, but it does provide a process for preserving the issue for a court ruling for all forms of discovery material. Rule 26(f), beyond that, permits the parties to discuss additional arrangements for dealing with problems of privilege waiver, and Rule 16(b)(3)(B)(iv) authorizes the court to embody such agreements in a court order.

Discovery from nonparties: Rule 45, dealing with discovery from nonparties, has been amended to include electronic discovery provisions parallel to those added to Rules 26–37 for party discovery. In particular, Rule 45 now addresses not reasonably accessible sources of ESI, sanctions for loss of discoverable information, and privilege waiver.

Judicial interpretation and application: Many (maybe all) of these rule provisions call for interpretation and application by judges; they depend on the circumstances of the given case and not on absolute imperatives about what form of production, for example, is appropriate in all cases. The Rules are written in a way that should enable judges applying them to take account of technological change. For example, the determination whether a given source of ESI is "reasonably accessible" could change as new technology facilitates accessing the information. As you work through the materials in this book, therefore, keep in mind that judges tailoring the procedures to specific cases are doing what the rules intended, and that lawyers must therefore tailor their arguments to the specifics of their cases. As an attorney writing about the amended Federal Rules put it shortly before the amendments came into effect: "I wish I could say take two aspirin and call me in the morning, but solving the technological headaches attorneys will undoubtedly grapple with under the framework of the new Federal Rules of Civil Procedure will require a much stronger dose of medicine, not to mention a dose of reality."[34]

D. The Future of Electronic Discovery

The future of electronic discovery is largely in your hands, as you are the lawyers and judges of tomorrow, and you will be making the arguments and decisions about interpreting the rules in the courts of tomor-

---

33. *See* 28 U.S.C. § 2074(b) (providing that a rule "creating, abolishing, or modifying an evidentiary privilege" is ineffective unless approved by act of Congress).

34. Matthew D. Nelson, *Easing the Pain of E–Discovery: New Discovery Rules Giving You a Headache? Follow These Tips to Keep Costs Down and Make the Process Smooth and Efficient*, S.F. Recorder, Aug. 23, 2006, at 5.

row. A few parting observations may be useful, however, before you launch into the body of this book:

Electronic discovery in state court: This Introduction has focused almost entirely on the rules that apply in federal court, and so does this book. But most cases are in state court, and there is no reason to think that electronic discovery will not occur in state courts. What rules will apply there? Obviously that varies from state to state. But there may be considerable reason to expect that the state courts will generally adhere to the sorts of solutions the Federal Rules have adopted. For one thing, the amendments to the Federal Rules generally preceded adoption of parallel provisions for state courts.[35] The Federal Rules apply in the federal courts in every state, so the lawyers in your state will have to know about them to go to federal court and may carry that experience over to their state court cases. For another, the Federal Rules provisions are prominently followed in two sets of proposed rules for state court that have been developed.[36] Thus, you are likely to find that state courts follow rules very much like the ones that apply in federal court.[37]

More knowledgeable lawyers and judges: As the lawyers and judges of tomorrow, you who are products of the first digital generation are likely to be more familiar with the computer issues covered in the book and thus better able than those in my generation to deal with them.

Electronic discovery issues affect plaintiffs as well as defendants: Consider the extent to which defendants in personal injury cases may want discovery of any e-mail messages the plaintiff sent after the injury (*e.g.*, "Don't worry Mom, I wasn't really hurt"). Thus, a plaintiff's lawyer has made the following recommendations:

> To effectively represent a client now, you need to be well aware of the types of evidence that he or she—or family members, friends, and so on—has posted on the Internet. More and more, defendants request production of the client's personal computer, giving rise to legal issues such as relevance, the client's privacy, and third-party privacy. If the computer was used to post information online, protecting that information will be difficult. Moreover, if it was posted publicly on an [Online Social Network] site or blog, it may already be in defense counsel's hands before you even get to the fight.
>
> Accordingly, you need to ask your client—at intake or shortly after— for any information about him or her that exists online. Ask about both quantity and content. Of course, you can conduct your own

---

35. That's not entirely true. Texas adopted a rule dealing with electronic discovery in 1998. *See* Tex. R. Civ. P. 196.4.

36. *See* Guidelines for State Trial Courts Regarding Discovery of Electronically–Stored Information of the Conference of Chief Justices and Uniform Rules Relating to the Discovery of Electronically Stored Information of the National Conference of Commissioners of Uniform State Laws.

37. *See also* Richard L. Marcus, *E–Discovery Beyond the Federal Rules*, 37 U. Balt. L. Rev. 321, 333–37 (2008).

Internet search, but keep in mind that many people use pseudonyms on the Web.[38]

Preservation, accessibility, and form of production issues will likely affect plaintiffs in a way similar to the way in which they affect defendants.

The role of vendors: I began this Introduction by citing the projected revenues for electronic discovery vendors during 2009, and noting that some say mishandling such discovery may lead to malpractice claims. The vendor phenomenon results from understandable worries that lawyers may be unable to handle this process without expert help.

> E-discovery has brought about a kind of role reversal in the legal profession: Now it's the lawyers who find themselves surrounded by circling sharks. Once an e-discovery vendor identifies an attorney or law firm as a potential client, there's often no end to the sales pitches, product demos, complimentary mouse pads, and follow-up emails from perky PR reps.[39]

As you cover the materials in this book, think about when (and whether) you will need the assistance of a vendor in handling the many problems presented.

International constraints: I have stressed the broad American attitude toward discovery. The reality is, however, that the rest of the world looks at American discovery and has a response something like "Are they nuts?"[40] The Continental attitude toward electronic discovery is similar; data confidentiality laws in many countries may be important to application of American electronic discovery.[41]

Enduring importance of electronic discovery: Whatever the constraints, electronic discovery is not going away. Three decades ago, an American judge noted that "the heart of any American antitrust case is the discovery of business documents. Without them, there is virtually no case."[42] That is true of most suits, not just antitrust cases; as investigators have learned to "follow the e-mail trail," lawyers will continue to pursue ESI to prove their cases. As one lawyer put it: "What I've found is that when you've got the e-mails, people remember lots and lots of things."[43] I began by stressing the American "revolution" in discovery. Although more recent rule amendments have constrained the most aggressive forms of discovery and stressed the proportionality principle, the basic American commitment to finding the crucial evidence has endured. The

---

38. Karen Barth Menzies, *Perils and Possibilities of Online Social Networks*, Trial, July, 2008, at 58.

39. Tom McNichol, *The E–Vendors Cometh*, Cal. Law., Feb. 2008, at 37.

40. *See* Stephen N. Subrin, *Discovery in Global Perspective: Are We Nuts?*, 52 DePaul L. Rev. 299 (2002).

41. *See* Richard L. Marcus, *E–Discovery Beyond the Federal Rules*, 37 U. Balt. L. Rev. 321, 339–40 (2008).

42. *In re Uranium Antitrust Lit.*, 480 F.Supp. 1138, 1155 (N.D. Ill. 1979).

43. Peter Geier, *A Defense Win in "Enron Country,"* Nat. L.J., Jan. 23, 2006, at 6.

rest of the world rejects "fishing expeditions" and tolerates decisions based on limited information in a way we do not.[44] Armed with the information in this book, you will be prepared to continue this American tradition in the Brave New World of electronic discovery.

---

44. *See, e.g.,* Mirjan Damaska, *The Uncertain Fate of Evidentiary Transplants: Anglo–American and Continental Experiments*, 45 Am. J. Comp. L. 839, 843 (1997) (noting that Continental civil procedure exhibits "a considerable degree of tolerance—almost an insouciance, to common law eyes—for the incompleteness of evidentiary material").

I

The Effect of Electronic Information on Discovery Practice

■ ■ ■

A. EXPLOSION OF INFORMATION AND INCREASED SOURCES OF INFORMATION

What makes "e-discovery" different from traditional discovery practice? In what ways has the world changed since 1938, when the Federal Rules of Civil Procedure took effect?

EXCERPT FROM James N. Dertouzos, *et al.*, *The Legal and Economic Implications of E–Discovery: Options for Future Research*, RAND Institute for Civil Justice 1–2 (2008), available at http://www.rand.org/pubs/occasional_papers/OP183.

> Today, virtually all information is in electronic form. Electronically stored information grew at the rate of 30 percent annually from 1999 through 2002. * * * The sheer volume is astounding. A data processing center for a major corporation can contain 10,000 tapes or more. One tape can store as much as a 1 trillion bytes (1 terabyte) of information or even more. If converted to hard copies, information contained on a single tape would be the equivalent of a 200–mile-high stack of paper. The types of "discoverable" data in electronic form are also proliferating. Many are similar to previous hard-copy documents such as might be found in the printed output of Microsoft Word files and Excel spreadsheets. But discovery also includes more transitory forms that were never found in the pre-electronic world, with the primary example being email messages.
>
> A 2002 estimate put the number of emails sent worldwide at over 30 billion and predicted that that number would double by 2006. In addition, companies retain vast relational databases that are continuously updated. These systems contain payroll, sales, manufacturing, and supplier transactions and provide a snapshot of an entire enterprise, something not possible with hard-copy ledgers. A vast amount of information is stored on data recovery systems or "backup" tapes.

Historical information is retained on decades-old legacy systems that are now difficult to access and read. Data that have supposedly been deleted from computers may still in fact exist in "slack memory" and the various nooks and crannies of hard drives. Most application and system files maintain a myriad of bookmark files, activity logs, and temporary files, potentially leaving a detailed audit trail of internal corporate processes that was never imaginable before. Additionally, many application files (such as a Microsoft Word document) also have embedded "metadata" that provide details about the author or the history of edits or other activities. And to complicate matters even more, the stand-alone desktop computer is now only one source of data, given the explosion of various platforms capable of holding electronically stored information. These include personal digital assistants (PDAs), laptops, thumb drives, telephone calls that are placed through the internet (via voice over Internet Protocol, [VoIP]), smart cards, and cell phones.

EXCERPT FROM George L. Paul & Jason R. Baron, *Information Inflation: Can the Legal System Adapt?*, 13 Rich. J.L. & Tech. 10 (2007).

A. THE LEGAL PROFESSION CONFRONTS AN INFLATIONARY EPOCH

Probably close to 100 billion e-mails are sent daily, with approximately 30 billion e-mails created or received by federal government agencies each year. The amount of stored information continues to grow exponentially.

Perhaps more easily grasped, the amount of information in business has increased by thousands, if not tens of thousands of times in the last few years. In a small business, whereas formerly there was usually one four-drawer file cabinet full of paper records, now there is the equivalent of two thousand four-drawer file cabinets full of such records, all contained in a cubic foot or so in the form of electronically stored information. This is a sea change.

* * *

Take then, for example, litigation in which the universe subject to search stands at one billion e-mail records, at least 25% of which have one or more attachments of varying length (1 to 300 pages). Generously assume further that a model "reviewer" (junior lawyer, legal assistant, or contract professional) is able to review an average of fifty e-mails, including attachments, per hour. Without employing *any* automated computer process to generate potentially responsive documents, the review effort for this litigation would take 100 people, working ten hours a day, seven days a week, fifty-two weeks a year, over fifty-four *years* to complete. And the cost of such a review, at an assumed average billing of $100/hour, would be $2 billion. Even, however, if present-day search methods (such as in the tobacco litigation example) are used to initially reduce the e-mail universe to

1% of its size (i.e., 10 million documents out of 1 billion), the case would still cost $20 million for a first pass review conducted by 100 people over 28 weeks, without accounting for any additional privilege review.

When one considers all of the ESI that a given organization may have in its possession, the types and quantities can be staggering. In the three year period from 2004 to 2007, the average amount of data in a Fortune 1000 corporation grew from 190 terabytes to one thousand terabytes (one petabyte). Over the same time period, the average data sets at 9,000 American, midsize companies grew from two terabytes to 100 terabytes. Overall, the global data set grew from five exabytes (five billion gigabytes) in 2003 to 161 exabytes in 2006. It is estimated that in 2007 the amount of information created and replicated globally surpassed 255 exabytes.

Given the amount of ESI that exists within the average organization, the ability to quickly and efficiently identify, locate, retrieve, and preserve the targeted set of ESI most likely to be responsive to the matter at hand becomes essential. Understanding what types of data are likely to play a role in e-discovery, the possible storage locations of such data, and the likely ways in which the targeted data may be organized have all become important factors in designing a discovery effort that will be focused and productive.

1. How Much New Information Is Created Each Year?

EXCERPT FROM Peter Lyman & Hal R. Varian, *How Much Information? 2003,* available at http://www2.sims.berkeley.edu/research/projects/how-much-info–2003/execsum.htm.

1. **Print, film, magnetic, and optical storage media produced about 5 exabytes of new information in 2002. Ninety-two percent of the new information was stored on magnetic media, mostly in hard disks.**

- *How big is five exabytes?* If digitized with full formatting, the seventeen million books in the Library of Congress contain about 136 terabytes of information; five exabytes of information is equivalent in size to the information contained in 37,000 new libraries the size of the Library of Congress book collections.

- *Hard disks store most new information.* Ninety-two percent of new information is stored on magnetic media, primarily hard disks. Film represents 7% of the total, paper 0.01%, and optical media 0.002%.

- *The United States produces about 40% of the world's new stored information,* including 33% of the world's new printed information, 30% of the world's new film titles, 40% of the world's information stored on optical media, and about 50% of the information stored on magnetic media.

- *How much new information per person?* According to the Population Reference Bureau, the world population is 6.3 billion, thus almost 800 MB of recorded information is produced per person each year. It would take about 30 feet of books to store the equivalent of 800 MB of information on paper.

2. **We estimate that the amount of new information stored on paper, film, magnetic, and optical media has about doubled in the last three years.**

- *Information explosion?* We estimate that new stored information grew about 30% a year between 1999 and 2002.

- *Paperless society?* The amount of information printed on paper is still increasing, but the vast majority of original information on paper is produced by individuals in office documents and postal mail, not in formally published titles such as books, newspapers and journals.

2. What Makes "E–Discovery" Different From Traditional Discovery?

"Broad discovery is a cornerstone of the litigation process contemplated by the Federal Rules of Civil Procedure."[1] Arguably, how lawyers propounded and responded to discovery requests did not materially change between the 1930s and the 1990s, until the advent of office automation and the growth of the Internet. Document requests were propounded with the expectation that the receiving party, at counsel's direction, would devote sufficient resources to perform a reasonably diligent search for records found in hard-copy repositories including central file room areas and among work papers stored in offices.

Recognition that the volume of ESI presented different challenges for the practitioner occurred years before the 2006 amendments to the Federal Rules of Civil Procedure.[2]

3. How Electronic Information Is Stored and Retrieved

When considering the discovery of ESI, it is useful to review the various types of ESI that can be created, the physical ways in which such ESI can be stored, and the typical organizational schemas under which it can be organized. These various metrics can be used to target that ESI most likely to provide useful information.

a. Types of ESI

There are potentially thousands of different types of data that could exist within an enterprise data set. Typically, however, most organizations have a limited set of potential data types on a limited number of applications that create ESI. Thus, an important component of an ESI discovery plan is to identify the types of data that may yield responsive information.

---

1. *Jones v. Goord*, No. 95 Civ. 8026, 2002 WL 1007614, at *1 (S.D.N.Y. May 16, 2002).

2. *See* Kenneth J. Withers, *Computer–Based Discovery in Federal Civil Litigation*, 2000 Fed. Cts. L. Rev. 2, 3–4 (2000) ("Potentially discoverable records are stored according to computer logic, as opposed to 'business-record' logic, and can be difficult to locate and untangle from irrelevant and privileged records. The combination of multiple locations, tremendous volume, and arcane or non-existent records management practices is potentially explosive for defending counsel.").

Interviews with key players and with an organization's computer staff are two ways to determine which data types are worth focusing on.

From the perspective of creating a discovery plan, there are two fundamental categories, or types, of ESI: (1) data created by individual custodians using local applications; and, (2) data created by individual custodians using an enterprise application and/or which is automatically created and/or captured by an enterprise application.

i. Custodian–Based ESI

Custodian-based ESI is familiar to anyone who uses a computer, as it is the data that is created when using application programs on personal computers or through the use of personal digital devices such as cell phones and personal digital assistants. The key to custodian-based ESI from the discovery perspective is not necessarily what the application is or where the application is based, but rather that the custodian controls the creation, content, storage, and disposition of the data file created.

ii. Application Data

An application program, often referred to simply as an application, is any program that is designed to perform a specific function directly for a custodian or, in some cases, for another application program. For the purposes of discovery, key features of application programs are that they are initiated by the custodian, the custodian creates the content (data) by directly interacting with the application (whether personal-computer-based, a network application, or even an internet-based application,) and the custodian determines where the resulting application data file will be stored, what it is going to be named, its usage, and how long it will remain in existence. Examples of application programs include: word processors, spreadsheet programs, database programs, web browsers, software development tools, graphical publishing programs, document scanning and storage programs, voice-to-text conversion programs, printed-text to digital-text conversion programs, draw, paint and image editing programs, financial management programs, music management programs, and text and other instant messaging-type programs.

iii. Personal Digital Devices

A personal digital device is an electronic device operated by a custodian that is capable of creating ESI. These devices can be very specific in the types of data they hold, such as a photograph in a camera, or multi-purpose in the sense that they can hold specific types of ESI and act as a storage device for non-device-specific types of data. For example, an iPod is fundamentally a hard drive that has a music-playing application program (iTunes) on it. It can hold digitized music that is used by the application and/or it can be used to hold virtually any other type of data file. Examples of common personal digital devices include: cell phones, blackberries, pda's (personal digital assistants), cameras, and iPods or other similar devices.

iv. Messaging Systems

Messaging systems are a special form of application in that they share characteristics of both custodian-based applications and enterprise applications. Most messaging systems, especially those within organizations, are enterprise-wide and enterprise-hosted applications, meaning that the messaging program itself is maintained in a central location and is available for use by all those with an authorized account. Furthermore, the messaging system typically stores some custodian-specific messaging data at this central location. Like a custodian-based application, however, most messaging systems also allow the individual custodian to maintain some portion of her messaging data locally on her personal computer or at some other location she may designate.

When targeting ESI in a messaging system during discovery, one must consider both the enterprise and the individual nature of the system. Inquiry must be made to both the enterprise staff charged with the housing and operation of the messaging system and the individual custodian using the system in order to determine the location, quantity, scope and usage characteristics of the ESI sought. Examples of common messaging systems include: e-mail, voice-mail and instant messaging.

v. Enterprise–Based ESI

Enterprise-based ESI is data that has been created by individual custodians using an enterprise application which has been automatically created and/or captured by an enterprise application. An enterprise application is typically a system where the application and its associated data reside in a central location within the organization. The application is generally one that is used by many custodians across various units within the organization, all of whom need access to all or part of the application data set.

For purposes of discovery, the key aspect of an enterprise application is that the custodian using the application does not have control over the application, its general interface, or where or how the associated data is stored or managed. Accordingly, when considering enterprise data, it is important to involve the organization's computer management staff responsible for the operation of the targeted enterprise application.

vi. Databases

Most organizations utilize database applications to organize their products and business workflow. Databases often serve as the "backroom" for other application programs, holding the information that is created in an organized fashion. Enterprise databases tend to be central stores of large volumes of structured data relating to a particular business activity or business function (i.e. product inventory). As with organization-specific applications, it is important to identify their structure and their content.

vii. Generic Enterprise Applications

In addition to customized organization-specific applications, many organizations employ standardized enterprise applications that have been designed and built to solve a particular business need. Because these applications are generally available in the marketplace, it is relatively easy to find information about the application and about the data files that the application supports. Common examples of generic enterprise applications include: accounting, customer relationship management, electronic document and record management, enterprise resource planning (integrating the data needed for a variety of business functions such as manufacturing, supply, human resources and customer relations), product lifecycle management (from conception, through design and manufacture, to service and disposal), supply chain management (tracking raw materials, work-in-process inventory and finished goods), systems development life cycle (methodologies for developing computer systems), and supplier relationship management (tracking purchasing of in-house supplies, raw materials for manufacturing and goods for inventory).

viii. Internet

From a discovery perspective, the information presented by an organization's web pages, and the information gathered from visitors to those web pages, comprises a set of ESI that can be investigated. Increasingly, organizations are connecting their internet access points to databases and other application systems in an attempt to provide a low cost, single point of access to customers and prospective customers.

ix. Intranet

An intranet is a private computer network established by an organization that uses Internet protocols and network connectivity to create a private, in-house version of the Internet. Intranets are typically used to provide a secure forum for the organization to share information with its employees. Utilizing a familiar web browser interface, employees can access employee manuals, corporate calendars, updates on corporate events and milestones, records management policies, employee blogs, sales and marketing materials, stock quotations, and the like. Increasingly, intranets are being tied into corporate applications, legacy systems, and databases in an attempt to provide a single-source interface to the company.

x. Extranet

An extranet is a private network established by an organization that uses Internet protocols, and network connectivity to create a private, in-house version of the Internet that is then shared with selected extra-organizational parties, such as vendors, suppliers, clients, and business partners. Utilizing a familiar web browser interface, those granted access to the organization's extranet can gain access to sales materials, catalogs, production updates, account information, electronic mail, instant messaging, and blogs. Increasingly, extranets are being used to create virtual business communities where business partners come together to share information.

b.   How ESI Is Stored

i.   *Online Storage of ESI*

When ESI is stored online, the information is available to a user, on a computer system, in virtually real-time. The definition of online as established by the United States General Services Administration calls for an online system to be available for immediate use on demand without human intervention, in operation, functional and ready for service.

ESI stored online is the most familiar form of data to users of computer systems. When a computer user sits at her computer or workstation, creates a data file using an application program, and then stores that file on the computer or on the corporate network, she has created ESI stored online. When a computer user sits at her computer or workstation and retrieves a file from the local hard drive or from a networked drive, she is retrieving ESI stored online.

Online storage devices are primarily hard drives, whether singly in a personal computer or connected together in an array in a networked system. Hard drives allow fast access to data without any form of human intervention. As online storage provides the fastest retrieval time for ESI, it is typically used for those files that need to be immediately available at all times, which includes virtually all enterprise applications. Given the relatively low cost of online storage, most custodians choose to store their personal data files online as well.

From a discovery perspective, online data is relatively easy to identify, locate, search, retrieve and preserve.

ii.   *Near–Line Storage of ESI*

Near-line storage is the storage of data on direct access removable media. When a near-line storage device is re-attached to a computer system, the ESI stored thereon becomes available to the user online. Near-line storage provides inexpensive, reliable, and virtually unlimited data storage, but with less accessibility than with online storage, as it requires the step of reintegrating the storage device with the computer system.

Near-line storage is often used for the portability of, and/or to make a backup copy of, ESI. Near-line storage is a convenient way to store ESI that is used periodically, such as music on a CD disk, or to transport ESI from one location to another.The major categories of near-line storage include: magnetic disks, compact disks, solid state storage (flash memory data storage device), removable direct access storage device (hard drives, iPods), remote online backups, disk-based backups, printers with storage capability, fax machines with storage capability, and copy machines with storage capability.

From a discovery perspective, the portability of near-line storage can create identification and location problems. Additionally, while retrieval of ESI from a given near-line source is rarely an issue, retrieval from numerous near-line sources can create logistical and cost issues associated with the requirement for re-integrating the near-line storage device with the computer system before information can be retrieved.

iii.   Offline Storage of ESI

Off-line storage maintains ESI on a medium or a device that is not under the control of a processing unit and which is not available for immediate use on demand by the system without human intervention. Compared with online and near-line storage, off-line storage is very slow. The advantage of off-line storage is that it is relatively inexpensive, easily transported, and protects the data from alteration and/or infection. Because of the benefits provided by off-line storage, it is often integral to an organization's backup, or disaster recovery, program. The primary form of off-line storage is magnetic tape. When used as a backup medium, online ESI is written to (stored on) a magnetic tape. The recorded magnetic tape is typically then taken off-site from the organization and stored in a secure and controlled environment to protect it from natural disaster. If all or part of the ESI recorded on the magnetic tape is lost or damaged on the online system, the magnetic tape can be used to return a copy of the ESI to the online system. The time and cost associated with restoring ESI from a magnetic tape is substantial compared with the cost of online or near-line access, and backup tapes are therefore used as a last resort.

From a discovery perspective, backup tapes are a difficult and expensive environment in which to search for ESI. They must be retrieved, mounted and restored to the online system before any of the ESI on those tapes can be accessed. Given that backup tapes are used for backup, however, magnetic tape may be the only location that particular data exists if it has been removed from all other online and near-line sources.

4.   Records Management as a Solution

A report from a leading private records consulting firm, Cohasset Associates, supports the view that electronic records management policies are still not well understood and are otherwise underutilized.[3] How would implementing electronic records management solutions help solve or reduce the problem of information overload?

Are there ways to employ filtering and de-duplication techniques so as to significantly reduce the volume of data that must be culled and collected as part of the e-discovery process, prior to the later, more labor-intensive review stage (which still necessarily requires manual review, at least in part)?

---

3. *See* Electronic Records Management Survey—2007: A Call for Collaboration, *available at* http://www.cohasset.com/survey_research.html.

5. How Well Do Lawyers Understand the Technical Aspects of ESI?

In *Alexander v. Federal Bureau of Investigation*,[4] otherwise known as the "Filegate" case, plaintiffs filed a claim under the Privacy Act alleging that White House officials in the Clinton Administration violated the privacy rights of individuals by continuing to possess and access certain FBI files containing highly sensitive reports of interviews taken in connection with those individuals being nominated to positions requiring security clearances. Filed in 1996, the case bogged down in evidentiary proceedings related to the alleged loss of White House e-mail due to technical defects in the operation of the White House e-mail archiving system. A White House technician submitted a declaration stating that "all" e-mail had been preserved on the "ARMS" system (Automated Records Management System). Plaintiffs alleged that this technician knew or should have known that glitches had occurred resulting in the failure of the ARMS system to capture a significant portion of e-mail. Two million e-mails were eventually restored from backup tapes as a result of the lawsuit. After holding over fifty days of hearings on the subject of missing White House e-mail, the judge eventually concluded that there had been misunderstandings on the part of high level officials and counsel, but no deliberate misconduct or wrongdoing in the filing of declarations or in making representations to the court.

> The Court has concluded that the essential errors made by the White House Counsel's Office were caused by a lack of familiarity with computer terminology and language and workings by the lawyers involved. Mr. Barry, the computer expert, simply talked a different language, and the lawyers he dealt with did not fully appreciate the significance of some of the information that he gave them, and the information he didn't give them. All of this occurred long before development of current sophisticated ways that lawyers have had to learn to deal with computer experts. It calls to the Court's mind its own experience in dealing with intelligence officials, *i.e.*, if you don't use the right words in your question, you won't get the right answer. You have to learn to ask the question in a number of ways, and probe and examine and get into the nitty-gritty to understand what the truth is. None of the White House lawyers involved in this matter did that. But plaintiffs produced no evidence whatsoever that any of those lawyers deliberately obstructed justice, or deliberately provided what turned out to be false information to the Court. Not only is the evidence not "clear and convincing," as would be required for this Court to rule for plaintiffs on their contempt motion, but there is simply no evidence of any deliberate effort to conceal the truth. Plaintiffs would have the Court infer that some grand conspiracy existed to deprive them of necessary information. Plaintiffs simply have no such evidence.

---

4.   541 F. Supp. 2d 274 (D.D.C. 2008).

Writing in 2008 about events of many years earlier, the court noted that "[a]ll of this occurred long before development of current sophisticated ways that lawyers have had to learn to deal with computer experts." How confident are you that this type of misunderstanding couldn't happen again?

B.   RETRIEVING BACKUP INFORMATION

1.   Backups

Organizations typically make backups for three reasons:

First, a backup protects the organization from losing its valuable data in case of a disaster (natural or manmade) or in case of a computer system failure that results in data loss. *Second*, a backup can be used to restore specific data files that have been accidentally deleted, modified, or corrupted. *Third*, many organizations use backups as a generic form of long-term data archiving. In this capacity, backups are made and are held by the organization as a central repository of data over time.

2.   Typical Categories of Backups

While a backup is technically any process that moves a file from its on-line storage location to another on-line, near-line or off-line storage location, there are some typical ways in which backups are created by custodians and within organizations. In terms of discovery, it is important to understand the various ways in which both the client and the adversary conduct and organize their backup systems. This involves discussions with both individual custodians to determine how they back up data, as well as with the organization's computer staff to determine how organizational backups are conducted.

There are two different types of backups, unstructured and structured.

a.   Unstructured Backups

An unstructured backup is typically an ad-hoc copying of a small number of custodian-selected files to some form of on-line, near-line, or off-line repository. Unstructured backups are typically placed onto near-line stores like CD–R, DVD–R, or USB thumb-drive-type media. Unstructured backups typically have little or no information about what was backed up or when the backup took place, and there is typically little consistency to the frequency and/or content of such backups. Unstructured backups are probably the easiest to implement by the custodian, but they are the least managed and are prone to dispersal and loss.

From a discovery perspective, unstructured backups are usually very difficult to deal with. They require in-depth inquiry to identify, locate, and retrieve and, once retrieved, are costly to integrate into the discovery process due to the resources needed to identify the backup method, the types and quantities of data, and the inefficiencies associated with loading a relatively small amount of data.

b. Structured Backups

A structured backup is a backup of a predictable target set of data that occurs on a set timetable. Structured backups occur most frequently within organizations and they account for the vast majority of data stored within backups. Structured backups, and especially those conducted systematically by an organization's computer services department, typically have detailed descriptions about what was backed up, when it was backed up, and how it was backed up. From a discovery perspective, structured backups are generally easier to identify, locate, and retrieve, and a greater level of analysis can generally be conducted as to the types and quantities of data contained thereon.

c. Local Backup

Local backups are typically backups of data files conducted by custodians through the use of devices contained within, or attached directly to, their personal computer workstation. From a discovery perspective, local backups are usually sporadic in nature, stored in various locations, inconsistent in terms of types and quantities of data stored, and difficult to restore. Typical local backup schemas include: magnetic disks (floppy, zip or Syquest-type removable disks), compact disks (recordable disks CD–R, rewriteable disks (CD–RW), digital rewriteable disks (DVD–RW), solid state storage (flash drives, memory sticks), and removable hard drives such as iPods or portable hard drives).

d. Internet Backup

As high-speed Internet service has become more widely available and more robust, backup methodologies utilizing the Internet to create remote backup stores is growing in popularity. These remote sites can simply be other personal or organizational sites that the custodian can access, or they can be sites created by companies providing backup and storage services.

As remote Internet backup sites are organizationally and, typically, geographically removed, backing data up to the Internet can provide protection against geographically clustered disasters that could affect backup data stored in the same region as the host data. Even with high-speed Internet capability, Internet backups are substantially slower than backups to local disk storage or to backup tape. This speed issue generally limits the amount of data that a custodian chooses to send to a remote Internet site. Some organizations also feel uncomfortable placing their data into the hands of third-parties to hold and manage, fearing that sensitive data may be compromised.

From a discovery perspective, it is important to understand that the custodian typically determines the frequency of, and the composition of, the backup set that is sent over the Internet. Care must be taken to fully understand the extent to which a given custodian uses Internet backup, the frequency of such backups, the manner in which data is selected for backup, and the details of the remote site at which the data is stored.

e. Enterprise Backup

Perhaps the most common form of backup in a corporation or other organization is the enterprise backup. An enterprise backup is conducted by an organization's computer services staff involving business unit-level or organization-wide computer systems. A backup of an organization's e-mail system on a daily basis is an example of an enterprise backup. Because they are conducted by the organization's computer services staff for the purpose of providing a disaster recovery copy of the organization's data, enterprise backups tend to be the most structured in terms of the scope of the data targeted, the frequency of the backup, the consistency of the media onto which the backup is made, the recoverability of the backed up data, and the length of time the backup is maintained before disposal.

From a discovery perspective, enterprise backups are often the easiest to identify, locate, and retrieve, although the volume of backup sets that often exist within an organization can make the logistics of the discovery very difficult. It is also important to keep in mind that magnetic tapes can fail, thereby compromising the entire backup set to which that tape belonged. There may also be difficulties associated with interpreting the many types of data files that are often co-mingled on enterprise backups.

3. Types of Backup Schemas

Within categories of backups there are different backup schemas that can be employed. Understanding the schema chosen for a given backup is an important component in developing a proper model for restoring a backed up set of data, especially when restoring multiple backups to obtain data from a targeted time period.

Typical backup schemas include:

a. Full Backup

A full backup is a backup of every file on the targeted computer system, whether or not that file has changed since the previous backup. Because a full backup copies every file on the targeted system to the backup media, it takes the longest to accomplish and requires the most storage space on the backup media. In terms of restoration, however, a full backup provides the fastest restoration time when restoring the full data set.

Due to the time and tape space required, full backups are generally conducted on a periodic basis as part of a hybrid backup schema. For example, a full backup may be conducted every Sunday night, while an incremental backup is conducted on the days in between. Full backups are also typically performed on systems that are about to undergo hardware and/or software changes as a means to protect against data loss in case the changes do not work or damage the file storage systems.

b.   Incremental Backup

An incremental backup is a backup of every file on the targeted computer system that has changed since the last backup took place, regardless of whether the last backup was a full backup or an incremental backup. Because an incremental backup only targets those files that have changed since the last backup, which is typically a fraction of the total data set, it is usually the fastest type of backup and the one that requires the least storage space on the backup media. However, incremental backups also require the longest time and the most tapes to restore.

Due to the inefficiencies associated with restoring an incremental-only backup schema, it is rare to see an incremental-only backup schema. In most organizations, an incremental backup schema is used in conjunction with a full backup.

c.   Differential Backup

A differential backup is a backup of every file on the targeted computer system that has changed since the last full backup. While a differential backup is not as fast as an incremental backup, it is faster than a full backup as it does not copy every file. Correspondingly, a differential backup requires more storage space than an incremental backup, but less than a full backup. When used in combination with a full backup, differential backups can provide an effective and efficient backup process.

d.   Continuous Data Backup

A continuous backup is a real-time backup that immediately logs every change on the targeted computer system to a secondary system. This is often done by saving byte or block-level differences rather than file-level differences, which fully utilizes the real-time nature of the system. Effectively, pieces of files are saved as they are changed. If restoration is needed, the management system knows how to piece every-thing back together in proper form. With a continuing decrease in hard disk storage costs, continuous backup, sometimes referred to as mirroring, may become more popular.

4.   Backup Rotation

A backup rotation schema is the method chosen for managing backup sets when multiple media are used in the backup process. The rotation schema determines how and when each magnetic tape is used in a backup and for how long it is retained once it has backup data stored on it. The most common backup rotation schema is referred to as the Grandfather–Father–Son model, which defines three sets of backups—daily, weekly and monthly. The daily (Son) backups are rotated on a daily basis with one set graduating to Weekly (Father) status each week. The weekly backups are rotated on a weekly basis with one graduating to Monthly (Grandfather) status each month. Many organizations add to this model by removing one or more monthly tapes to an annual or multi-year storage.

Another common rotation schema is to use a rolling set of magnetic tapes over and over again. This incremental model defines a pool of backup media and, once the entire pool has been used, re-writes to the oldest set. For example, with a daily backup onto a set of ten tape sets, you would have ten days worth of individual daily backups. When all of the tape sets are used, the oldest one is inserted and re-used.

Tape rotation schemas can get very complicated based upon the needs of the organization. In terms of discovery, it is important to determine what tape rotation model is used and how it is implemented. With any rotation model there will be gaps in the tape sets due to human, machine, or tape failures. There may also be other models that have been created for a special purpose.

5. How ESI Is Stored From a Custodian/Records Management Point of View

From a technology standpoint, ESI can be stored on a variety of magnetic, optical, and solid-state media. The manner in which ESI is stored by the custodian onto these media can vary greatly, however, and has to do with both the organization's records management plan and the custodian's own desires regarding the naming and storage location of his or her data.

When considering what ESI may relate to a given discovery matter, it is important to consider where such data may have been placed by a custodian or, indeed, whether such data was ever under the direct control of the custodian.

There are five typical ways in which ESI can be stored:

a. Custodian–Centric Data Storage: Much of the ESI used by a custodian on a day-to-day basis, especially application data, is under the direct control of the custodian. It is the custodian who creates the content associated with a given data file, names it, and determines where the file will be saved. The custodian is also the default "records manager" for her data in the sense that she determines how long data will survive before being deleted. In terms of discovery, the custodian is often the best source of information about her data set, including: types of data created, quantity of data created, file naming conventions, data storage locations, types of backup created, and use of e-mail and attachments.

b. Virtual Workgroup–Centric Data Storage: A virtual workgroup is a group of individuals who work on a common project using digital technologies such as e-mail, instant messaging, shared application programs and databases, calendaring, and file management. Many virtual workgroups share a common data file through the use of applications that support such use. While the custodian creates some of the content for the application data file, she may have little or no say in how the data file is named, where it is stored, how it is ultimately used, or how long it remains in existence. Many times these issues are handled either by organization rules or by a custodian named as the workgroup leader.

As networking and the Internet become more pervasive, and as application software providers enable workgroup features into their software, the concept of virtual workgroups is likely to grow. Rather than sending a file to a number of individuals and then integrating their suggestions and changes, the data file remains in a central location and the users modify it directly, with each person's edits and/or notations identified by name.

In terms of discovery, the custodian is often the best source of information about his or her participation in a virtual workgroup.

c. Business Unit–Centric Data Storage: Many organizations are structured like holding companies, made up of many business units that maintain their own computer operations but that share some overall application platforms, such as e-mail. A single organization may also have different operating divisions that it treats as business units. Custodians working in one business unit within a larger organization may spend most of their time working on the business unit's computer system, but at least part of their time on platforms owned and managed by the parent organization. From the custodians' viewpoint, they are working on a single system. Behind the scenes, however, many different operating and data storage environments may be involved. While a custodian may create the content associated with a given data file and name it, in some business-unit environments the custodian may have little or no choice as to where the data file is saved. This is especially true when enterprise applications are used.

In terms of discovery, both the custodian and organizational computer services staff need to be considered as sources of information about the underlying computer system being used and the location(s) of related data stores.

d. Enterprise–Centric Data Storage: Virtually every organization utilizes enterprise applications in its business model. E-mail is the best example of an enterprise application. One of the key characteristics of an enterprise application is that the data file(s) associated with the application are stored and managed at a central location within the organization, typically by professional computer services staff. Custodians using the enterprise application may have desktop applications that belong to and/or interact with the enterprise application, or they may simply "log on" to the enterprise application and use it directly at its central location. While the custodian may create new data using the enterprise application and/or modify existing information, the custodian typically has no say in how the data file is named, where it is stored, or how it is managed.

In terms of discovery, both the custodian and organizational computer services staff are considered sources of information about the enterprise applications being used and the location(s) of related data stores.

e. Third Party–Centric Data Storage: With the increased use of outsourced computer operations and the use of Internet-based applications, more and more organizational data is being stored and managed by third-parties. Outsourcing means that a third-party manages the hardware and software infrastructure for an organization for a fee. In effect, the third-party is serving as the computer services department for the organization. An Internet-based application is one in which a user using the Internet goes to a third-party site and logs onto an application program provided by the third-party. The user then uses the application as if it resided on her desktop or on the enterprise computers. In both situations, the data created by the user remains with the third-party provider. In terms of discovery, the custodian, the organizational computer services staff, and the third-party's computer staff are considered sources of information about the applications being used and the location(s) of related data stores.

6. Fundamental Computer Forensic Issues

a. Forensic Disk Images

When used in conjunction with discovery, the term forensics relates to the use of specialized techniques for the recovery, authentication, and analysis of specific ESI. Forensic examinations are typically used when a matter involves issues that require the reconstruction of computer usage patterns; the examination of residual data left after deletion; technical analysis of computer usage patterns; and/or other testing of the data that may de destructive in nature. In order to conduct a forensic examination, the ESI, and the storage device on which the ESI resides, must be collected in a manner that requires specialized expertise.

The most common form of forensic collection is to make an image of the storage media on which the targeted ESI resides. This image, sometimes called a bit image, is an exact copy of the storage device—such as a hard drive, a CD, or any other disk format—including all areas that contain data and all areas that appear to be empty (but which may actually contain remnants of data). The image is a single file containing the complete contents and structure of the storage device. A disk image file is created by making a sector-by-sector copy of the source media, thereby completely copying the entire structure and contents of the storage media.

Forensic images are acquired with the use of specialized software tools. When used properly, these images contain a copy of everything that is on the target media, including live and deleted data. Forensic images are also sometimes referred to as a bitstream image, a bit image, or a cloned image. This image can be used to re-create an exact copy of the storage device on which a forensic examination can be conducted. The forensic examination can then be conducted on the re-created drive in exactly the same way in which it could have been done on the original device. Because forensic examinations often involve destructive testing, and because they require the ability to replicate their findings, this ability to work on re-created drives is critical.

The primary question when considering a forensic collection is whether or not the facts surrounding the matter at hand suggest that a forensic examination is needed. Was unique, important data deleted? Is it likely that deleted data can be recovered? Is it important to show usage activity and usage patterns? Is it important to authenticate a particular file in order to show that the represented data and/or time of creation is accurate? Do you need to confirm that all of the text in a document is original or that a critical e-mail was really sent when it appears to have been?

Because imaging software is commonly available, and because the vast majority of training programs in the field of electronic discovery revolve around forensics, there is a growing tendency to want to "image everything." But unless an argument can be made that the matter at hand will benefit from a forensic collection and additional examination, there is no reason to do a forensic collection just because the technology exists to do it.

If the matter allows a non-forensic acquisition and analysis of ESI, then a data collection is what is required. A data collection, as opposed to a forensic collection, collects files at the file level, not at the disk level, basically by copying the desired information and processing it into a review system. Data collection is faster and cheaper than a forensic collection and is the type of collection that is warranted if a forensic collection is not required.

b. File Deletion

A computer's file system determines how the computer stores and manages files on its attached storage media. There are several file systems in use today, and all offer some form of file recovery once a file is deleted. Consider the File Allocation Table (FAT) file system, one of the most commonly used file systems today, as an example. When a file is deleted on a FAT file system, its directory entry[5] in the FAT remains stored on the disk, although the file name is altered in a way that lets the system know that the storage space occupied by the (now deleted) file is again available for use by a new file or by an expanded version of an existing file. The majority of the deleted file's information, such as its name, time stamp, file length and location on the disk, remain unchanged in its directory entry in the FAT. The deleted file's content will remain on the storage media until it is overwritten by another file. The more file activity there is on a particular computer system, the more unlikely it is that a file can be recovered, as the likelihood that the storage areas where the file had resided will be overwritten is greater.

Specialized software tools, some provided with, or built into, the operating system, allow for the recovery of a deleted file provided that a new file or data set has not overwritten the areas of the storage device

---

5. A file's directory entry is much like a person's listing in a telephone book. It holds the file's name and its storage location on a piece of storage media, such as a hard drive, a CD, or a DVD. The directory entry tells the computer where to find the data file.

holding the deleted file in question. At the simplest level, these tools allow the modified file name of the deleted file to be changed back into a name format that does not indicate a deleted file. The file then becomes a "live" file again, and available for use by an application program. In some cases a greater level of reconstruction is required to retrieve some or all of a deleted file. If the directory entry for the deleted file has been overwritten, or if some of the data storage areas for the deleted file have been overwritten, it will be more difficult to recover the file.

Some computer operating systems provide a layered approach to data deletion. Microsoft's Windows platform, for example, does not really delete a file when a deletion request is made. The file is placed in a "recycle bin" where it awaits final deletion. Until the file is removed from the recycle bin, it can be easily recovered as it had not really been deleted in a technical sense. When the file is "dumped" from the recycle bin for deletion, it can often still be recovered if the space has not been reutilized.

As with forensic collection, the key question in discovery regarding the recovery of deleted data is whether or not the facts surrounding the matter at hand suggest that data recovery is needed. Was unique, important data deleted? Is it likely that deleted data can be recovered? Was the file located on a system where file activity was such that recovery is likely? Is the matter at hand one where file deletion is suspected or traditionally part of the pattern of activity for such matters, such as in trade secret theft? If the matter is one where deleted data recovery may be important, then attempts should be made to identify and recover appropriate files. If not, then deleted data recovery is not warranted and is ultimately a waste of time and resources.

As with imaging, data recovery software is commonly available, and because many of the training programs in the field of electronic discovery revolve around forensics (which is often targeted towards data recovery), there is a bias to target deleted data. But unless an argument can be made that the matter at hand will benefit from the recovery of deleted data, there is no reason to attempt such recovery just because the technology exists to do it.

II

PRESERVATION OF ELECTRONIC INFORMATION

■ ■ ■

A. RECORDS RETENTION POLICIES

ARTHUR ANDERSEN LLP v. UNITED STATES

544 U.S. 696 (2005)

CHIEF JUSTICE REHNQUIST delivered the opinion of the Court

As Enron Corporation's financial difficulties became public in 2001, petitioner Arthur Andersen LLP, Enron's auditor, instructed its employees to destroy documents pursuant to its document retention policy. A jury found that this action made petitioner guilty of violating 18 U.S.C. §§ 1512(b)(2)(A) and (B). These sections make it a crime to "knowingly use intimidation or physical force, threaten, or corruptly persuade another person ... with intent to ... cause" that person to "withhold" documents from, or "alter" documents for use in, an "official proceeding."[1] The Court of Appeals for the Fifth Circuit affirmed. We hold that the jury instructions failed to convey properly the elements of a "corrup[t] persua[sion]" conviction under § 1512(b), and therefore reverse.

Enron Corporation, during the 1990's, switched its business from operation of natural gas pipelines to an energy conglomerate, a move that was accompanied by aggressive accounting practices and rapid growth. Petitioner audited Enron's publicly filed financial statements and provided internal audit and consulting services to it. Petitioner's "engagement team" for Enron was headed by David Duncan. Beginning in 2000, Enron's financial performance began to suffer, and, as 2001 wore on, worsened. On August 14, 2001, Jeffrey Skilling, Enron's Chief Executive Officer (CEO), unexpectedly resigned. Within days, Sherron Watkins, a senior accountant at Enron, warned Kenneth Lay, Enron's newly reappointed CEO, that Enron could "implode in a wave of accounting scandals." She likewise informed Duncan and Michael Odom, one of petitioner's partners who had supervisory responsibility over Duncan, of the looming problems.

---

1. We refer to the 2000 version of the statute, which has since been amended by Congress. [See the amendment discussed below.]

On August 28, an article in the Wall Street Journal suggested improprieties at Enron, and the SEC opened an informal investigation. By early September, petitioner had formed an Enron "crisis-response" team, which included Nancy Temple, an in-house counsel.[3] On October 8, petitioner retained outside counsel to represent it in any litigation that might arise from the Enron matter. The next day, Temple discussed Enron with other in-house counsel. Her notes from that meeting reflect that "some SEC investigation" is "highly probable."

On October 10, Odom spoke at a general training meeting attended by 89 employees, including 10 from the Enron engagement team. Odom urged everyone to comply with the firm's document retention policy. He added: "If it's destroyed in the course of [the] normal policy and litigation is filed the next day, that's great.... We've followed our own policy, and whatever there was that might have been of interest to somebody is gone and irretrievable."[4] On October 12, Temple entered the Enron matter into her computer, designating the "Type of Potential Claim" as "Professional Practice—Government/Regulatory Investigation." Temple also e-mailed Odom, suggesting that he "remind the engagement team of our documentation and retention policy."

On October 16, Enron announced its third quarter results. That release disclosed a $1.01 billion charge to earnings.[5] The following day, the SEC notified Enron by letter that it had opened an investigation in August and requested certain information and documents. On October 19, Enron forwarded a copy of that letter to petitioner.

On the same day, Temple also sent an e-mail to a member of petitioner's internal team of accounting experts and attached a copy of the document policy. On October 20, the Enron crisis-response team held a conference call, during which Temple instructed everyone to "make sure to follow the [document] policy." On October 23, Enron CEO Lay declined to answer questions during a call with analysts because of "potential lawsuits, as well as the SEC inquiry." After the call, Duncan met with other Andersen partners on the Enron engagement team and told them that they should ensure team members were complying with the document policy. Another meeting for all team members followed, during which Duncan distributed the policy and told everyone to comply. These,

---

3. A key accounting problem involved Enron's use of "Raptors," which were special purpose entities used to engage in "off-balance-sheet" activities. Petitioner's engagement team had allowed Enron to "aggregate" the Raptors for accounting purposes so that they reflected a positive return. This was, in the words of petitioner's experts, a "black-and-white" violation of Generally Accepted Accounting Principles.

4. The firm's policy called for a single central engagement file, which "should contain only that information which is relevant to supporting our work." The policy stated that, "[i]n cases of threatened litigation, ... no related information will be destroyed." It also separately provided that, if petitioner is "advised of litigation or subpoenas regarding a particular engagement, the related information should not be destroyed." * * *

5. The release characterized the charge to earnings as "non-recurring." Petitioner had expressed doubts about this characterization to Enron, but Enron refused to alter the release. Temple wrote an e-mail to Duncan that "suggested deleting some language that might suggest we have concluded the release is misleading."

and other smaller meetings, were followed by substantial destruction of paper and electronic documents.

On October 26, one of petitioner's senior partners circulated a New York Times article discussing the SEC's response to Enron. His e-mail commented that "the problems are just beginning and we will be in the cross hairs. The marketplace is going to keep the pressure on this and is going to force the SEC to be tough." On October 30, the SEC opened a formal investigation and sent Enron a letter that requested accounting documents.

Throughout this time period, the document destruction continued, despite reservations by some of petitioner's managers.[6] On November 8, Enron announced that it would issue a comprehensive restatement of its earnings and assets. Also on November 8, the SEC served Enron and petitioner with subpoenas for records. On November 9, Duncan's secretary sent an e-mail that stated: "Per Dave—No more shredding.... We have been officially served for our documents." Enron filed for bankruptcy less than a month later. Duncan was fired and later pleaded guilty to witness tampering.

In March 2002, petitioner was indicted in the Southern District of Texas on one count of violating §§ 1512(b)(2)(A) and (B). The indictment alleged that, between October 10 and November 9, 2001, petitioner "did knowingly, intentionally and corruptly persuade ... other persons, to wit: [petitioner's] employees, with intent to cause" them to withhold documents from, and alter documents for use in, "official proceedings, namely: regulatory and criminal proceedings and investigations." * * * [T]he jury returned a guilty verdict. The District Court denied petitioner's motion for a judgment of acquittal.

The Court of Appeals for the Fifth Circuit affirmed. It held that the jury instructions properly conveyed the meaning of "corruptly persuades" and "official proceeding"; that the jury need not find any consciousness of wrongdoing; and that there was no reversible error. * * *

Chapter 73 of Title 18 of the United States Code provides criminal sanctions for those who obstruct justice. Sections 1512(b)(2)(A) and (B), part of the witness tampering provisions, provide in relevant part:

> "Whoever knowingly uses intimidation or physical force, threatens, or corruptly persuades another person, or attempts to do so, or engages in misleading conduct toward another person, with intent to ... cause or induce any person to ... withhold testimony, or withhold a record, document, or other object, from an official proceeding [or] alter, destroy, mutilate, or conceal an object with intent to impair the

---

6. For example, on October 26, John Riley, another partner with petitioner, saw Duncan shredding documents and told him "this wouldn't be the best time in the world for you guys to be shredding a bunch of stuff." On October 31, David Stulb, a forensics investigator for petitioner, met with Duncan. During the meeting, Duncan picked up a document with the words "smoking gun" written on it and began to destroy it, adding "we don't need this." Stulb cautioned Duncan on the need to maintain documents and later informed Temple that Duncan needed advice on the document retention policy.

object's integrity or availability for use in an official proceeding . . . shall be fined under this title or imprisoned not more than ten years, or both.''

In this case, our attention is focused on what it means to "knowingly . . . corruptly persuade" another person "with intent to . . . cause" that person to "withhold" documents from, or "alter" documents for use in, an "official proceeding."

We have traditionally exercised restraint in assessing the reach of a federal criminal statute, both out of deference to the prerogatives of Congress, * * * and out of concern that a fair warning should be given to the world in language that the common world will understand, of what the law intends to do if a certain line is passed * * *.

Such restraint is particularly appropriate here, where the act underlying the conviction—"persuasion"—is by itself innocuous. Indeed, "persuading" a person "with intent to . . . cause" that person to "withhold" testimony or documents from a Government proceeding or Government official is not inherently malign. Consider, for instance, a mother who suggests to her son that he invoke his right against compelled self-incrimination, or a wife who persuades her husband not to disclose marital confidences.

Nor is it necessarily corrupt for an attorney to "persuade" a client "with intent to . . . cause" that client to "withhold" documents from the Government. In *Upjohn Co.* v. *United States*, 449 U.S. 383 (1981), for example, we held that Upjohn was justified in withholding documents that were covered by the attorney-client privilege from the Internal Revenue Service (IRS). No one would suggest that an attorney who "persuaded" Upjohn to take that step acted wrongfully, even though he surely intended that his client keep those documents out of the IRS' hands.

"Document retention policies," which are created in part to keep certain information from getting into the hands of others, including the Government, are common in business. * * * It is, of course, not wrongful for a manager to instruct his employees to comply with a valid document retention policy under ordinary circumstances.

Acknowledging this point, the parties have largely focused their attention on the word "corruptly" as the key to what may or may not lawfully be done in the situation presented here. Section 1512(b) punishes not just "corruptly persuading" another, but "*knowingly* . . . corruptly persuading" another. The Government suggests that "knowingly" does not modify "corruptly persuades," but that is not how the statute most naturally reads. It provides the *mens rea*—"knowingly"—and then a list of acts—"uses intimidation or physical force, threatens, or corruptly persuades." * * *

The parties have not pointed us to another interpretation of "knowingly . . . corruptly" to guide us here. In any event, the natural meaning of these terms provides a clear answer. * * * Only persons conscious of wrongdoing can be said to "knowingly ... corruptly persuade." * * *

The outer limits of this element need not be explored here because the jury instructions at issue simply failed to convey the requisite consciousness of wrongdoing. Indeed, it is striking how little culpability the instructions required. For example, the jury was told that, "even if [petitioner] honestly and sincerely believed that its conduct was lawful, you may find [petitioner] guilty." The instructions also diluted the meaning of "corruptly" so that it covered innocent conduct.

* * * The District Court based its instruction on the definition of that term found in the Fifth Circuit Pattern Jury Instruction for § 1503. This pattern instruction defined "corruptly" as "knowingly and dishonestly, with the specific intent to subvert or undermine the integrity" of a proceeding. The Government, however, insisted on excluding "dishonestly" and adding the term "impede" to the phrase "subvert or undermine." The District Court agreed over petitioner's objections, and the jury was told to convict if it found petitioner intended to "subvert, undermine, or impede" governmental factfinding by suggesting to its employees that they enforce the document retention policy.

These changes were significant. No longer was any type of "dishonest[y]" necessary to a finding of guilt, and it was enough for petitioner to have simply "impede[d]" the Government's factfinding ability. * * * By definition, anyone who innocently persuades another to withhold information from the Government "get[s] in the way of the progress of" the Government. With regard to such innocent conduct, the "corruptly" instructions did no limiting work whatsoever.

The instructions also were infirm for another reason. They led the jury to believe that it did not have to find *any* nexus between the "persuasion" to destroy documents and any particular proceeding. In resisting any type of nexus element, the Government relies heavily on § 1512(e)(1), which states that an official proceeding "need not be pending or about to be instituted at the time of the offense." It is, however, one thing to say that a proceeding "need not be pending or about to be instituted at the time of the offense," and quite another to say a proceeding need not even be foreseen. A "knowingly ... corrupt persuader" cannot be someone who persuades others to shred documents under a document retention policy when he does not have in contemplation any particular official proceeding in which those documents might be material.

* * *

For these reasons, the jury instructions here were flawed in important respects. The judgment of the Court of Appeals is reversed, and the case is remanded for further proceedings consistent with this opinion.

Editor's Note:

The statutes covering destruction of records have been broadened to cover destruction in circumstances like *Arthur Andersen*.

The Sarbanes–Oxley Act amended 18 U.S.C. § 1512 to provide as follows:

(c) Whoever corruptly—

(1) alters, destroys, mutilates, or conceals a record, document, or other object, or attempts to do so, with the intent to impair the object's integrity or availability for use in an official proceeding; or

(2) otherwise obstructs, influences, or impedes any official proceeding, or attempts to do so,

shall be fined under this title or imprisoned not more than 20 years, or both.

Does this amendment cover the activity at issue in *Arthur Andersen?*

COMMENTARY

A "records retention policy" is generally understood to mean a set of official guidelines or rules governing storage and destruction of documents or ESI. Such policies typically define different types of records, how they are to be treated generally under the policies for retention purposes, and often provide retention schedules defining specific time periods for retention of certain records. Depending on the nature of the entity promulgating the policy, the retention periods applied to specific categories of records may be driven by regulatory or other legal requirements, practical business, or technical needs.

As the Supreme Court notes in the *Arthur Andersen* opinion, there is nothing wrong with having a policy that requires the destruction of documents—as long as this destruction does not occur at a time when a legal preservation duty has already arisen with respect to the documents to be destroyed under the policy. This is consistent with prior case law, which to some degree is codified in Rule 37(e) of the Federal Rules of Civil Procedure, providing that certain sanctions will not apply under ordinary circumstances where information is lost as a result of routine destruction before a preservation duty has arisen.

Moreover, there are significant legal benefits to actively managing records retention. Consistent adherence to records retention policies enables an enterprise to explain why certain records are available for production in discovery and why others are not. The availability of the "safe harbor" of Rule 37(e) is predicated, *inter alia*, on the ability to show some "routine" in the retention and destruction of records. Avoiding the cost of searching and reviewing millions of e-mails that have outlived their business utility and were under no regulatory or other legal retention requirement is another potential major benefit.

Dealing with records retention issues became more complicated with the explosion in volume and variety of ESI. As the retention of greater volumes of ESI becomes easier and less expensive due to advances in storage technology, the difficulty of selectively identifying what should be retained and what should be destroyed in compliance with records retention policies can increase. Suspending systems put in place to implement such policies, such as regular purges of e-mail from servers or recycling of backup media, in order to comply with preservation obligations, can raise significant challenges for legal and IT personnel. Not surprisingly, the issue of when and how records retention policies need to be suspended in the face of the duty to preserve has been the focus of much recent case law.

The *Arthur Andersen* case shows that the decision to comply with a retention policy by destroying records in the face of a legal preservation duty is a bad one. For a records retention policy to act as a shield against spoliation allegations, it must be shown to have been implemented consistently. Where exhortations to comply with a policy's destruction requirements come at the time a legal duty to preserve has already been triggered, compliance with the policy not only fails as a shield, but provides the very basis for a spoliation claim.

Most of the case law examining the issue of whether records were destroyed legitimately pursuant to routine records retention policies addresses situations where the defendant's actions are in question. Accordingly, it is easy to forget that plaintiffs also have a duty (as seen in *Rambus*) to suspend regular destruction under records retention policies when they reasonably anticipate litigation. Generally, plaintiffs are the parties with the earliest opportunity to anticipate litigation given that they are the ones planning it and therefore controlling the timing of its initiation.

Since the Federal Rules of Civil Procedure were amended in 2006, including the addition of Rule 37(e), courts have continued to punish failures to suspend routine document destruction pursuant to records retention policies in the face of a preservation duty. It is important to note that, in the spirit of the *Arthur Andersen* case, these cases do not fault the policies themselves—but merely the failure to suspend such policies when faced with the need to apply a litigation hold. Examination of these cases shows the variety of types of retention policies applied to electronic information and demonstrates the fundamental truth that there is no one-size-fits-all records retention policy; instead, in the language of the Advisory Committee Note to Rule 37(e), these policies should be designed to meet the "business and technical" needs of the party in question.

PROBLEMS

1. Can destruction of records under a records retention policy before those records can be reasonably anticipated to be relevant to a particular future litigation constitute spoliation? Under what circumstances?

2. Should a very short retention period for e-mail give rise to a presumption of spoliation? Why? What steps can a party with such a short retention period take to defend its policy?

B. IMPLEMENTING THE DUTY TO PRESERVE

ZUBULAKE v. UBS WARBURG LLC *"ZUBULAKE V"*

229 F.R.D. 422 (S.D.N.Y. 2004)

SCHEINDLIN, DISTRICT JUDGE

I. INTRODUCTION

This is the fifth written opinion in this case, a relatively routine employment discrimination dispute in which discovery has now lasted over two years. Laura Zubulake is once again moving to sanction UBS for its failure to produce relevant information and for its tardy production of such material. In order to decide whether sanctions are warranted, the following question must be answered: Did UBS fail to preserve and timely produce relevant information and, if so, did it act negligently, recklessly, or willfully?

This decision addresses counsel's obligation to ensure that relevant information is preserved by giving clear instructions to the client to preserve such information and, perhaps more importantly, a client's obligation to heed those instructions. Early on in this litigation, UBS's counsel—both in-house and outside—instructed UBS personnel to retain relevant electronic information. Notwithstanding these instructions, certain UBS employees deleted relevant emails. Other employees never produced relevant information to counsel. As a result, many discoverable e-mails were not produced to Zubulake until recently, even though they were responsive to a document request propounded on June 3, 2002. In addition, a number of e-mails responsive to that document request were deleted and have been lost altogether.

Counsel, in turn, failed to request retained information from one key employee and to give the litigation hold instructions to another. They also failed to adequately communicate with another employee about how she maintained her computer files. Counsel also failed to safeguard backup tapes that might have contained some of the deleted e-mails, and which would have mitigated the damage done by UBS's destruction of those e-mails.

The conduct of both counsel and client thus calls to mind the now-famous words of the prison captain in *Cool Hand Luke*: "What we've got here is a failure to communicate." Because of this failure by *both* UBS and its counsel, Zubulake has been prejudiced. As a result, sanctions are warranted.

II. FACTS

The allegations at the heart of this lawsuit and the history of the parties' discovery disputes have been well-documented in the Court's prior decisions[5] * * *. In short, Zubulake is an equities trader specializing in Asian securities who is suing her former employer for gender discrimination, failure to promote, and retaliation under federal, state, and city law.

A. Background

Zubulake filed an initial charge of gender discrimination with the EEOC on August 16, 2001. Well before that, however—as early as April 2001—UBS employees were on notice of Zubulake's impending court action. After she received a right-to-sue letter from the EEOC, Zubulake filed this lawsuit on February 15, 2002.

Fully aware of their common law duty to preserve relevant evidence, UBS's in-house attorneys gave oral instructions in August 2001—immediately after Zubulake filed her EEOC charge—instructing employees not to destroy or delete material potentially relevant to Zubulake's claims, and in fact to segregate such material into separate files for the lawyers' eventual review. This warning pertained to both electronic and hard-copy files, but did *not* specifically pertain to so-called "backup tapes," maintained by UBS's information technology personnel. In particular, UBS's in-house counsel, Robert L. Salzberg, "advised relevant UBS employees to preserve and turn over to counsel all files, records or other written memoranda or documents concerning the allegations raised in the [EEOC] charge or any aspect of [Zubulake's] employment." Subsequently—but still in August 2001—UBS's outside counsel met with a number of the key players in the litigation and reiterated Mr. Salzberg's instructions, reminding them to preserve relevant documents, "including e-mails." Salzberg reduced these instructions to writing in e-mails dated February 22, 2002—immediately after Zubulake filed her complaint—and September 25, 2002. Finally, in August 2002, after Zubulake propounded a document request that specifically called for e-mails stored on backup tapes, UBS's outside counsel instructed UBS information technology personnel to stop recycling backup tapes. *Every* UBS employee mentioned in this Opinion (with the exception of Mike Davies) either personally spoke to UBS's outside counsel about the duty to preserve e-mails, or was a recipient of one of Salzberg's e-mails.

B. Procedural History

In *Zubulake I,* I addressed Zubulake's claim that relevant e-mails had been deleted from UBS's active servers and existed only on "inaccessible" archival media (*i.e.,* backup tapes). Arguing that e-mail correspondence that she needed to prove her case existed only on those backup tapes, Zubulake called for their production. UBS moved for a protective order

---

5. *See Zubulake I,* 217 F.R.D. 309 (addressing the legal standard for determining the cost allocation for producing e-mails contained on backup tapes); *Zubulake v. UBS Warburg LLC,* 2003 WL 21087136 (S.D.N.Y. May 13, 2003) ("*Zubulake II*") (addressing Zubulake's reporting obligations); *Zubulake v. UBS Warburg LLC,* 216 F.R.D. 280 (S.D.N.Y. 2003) ("*Zubulake III*") (allocating backup tape restoration costs between Zubulake and UBS); *Zubulake v. UBS Warburg LLC,* 220 F.R.D. 212 (S.D.N.Y. 2003) ("*Zubulake IV*") (ordering sanctions against UBS for violating its duty to preserve evidence).

shielding it from discovery altogether or, in the alternative, shifting the cost of backup tape restoration onto Zubulake. Because the evidentiary record was sparse, I ordered UBS to bear the costs of restoring a sample of the backup tapes.

After the sample tapes were restored, UBS continued to press for cost shifting with respect to any further restoration of backup tapes. In *Zubulake III,* I ordered UBS to bear the lion's share of restoring certain backup tapes because Zubulake was able to demonstrate that those tapes were likely to contain relevant information. Specifically, Zubulake had demonstrated that UBS had failed to maintain all relevant information (principally e-mails) in its active files. After *Zubulake III,* Zubulake chose to restore sixteen backup tapes. In the restoration effort, the parties discovered that certain backup tapes were missing. They also discovered a number of e-mails on the backup tapes that were missing from UBS's active files, confirming Zubulake's suspicion that relevant e-mails were being deleted or otherwise lost.

Zubulake III begat *Zubulake IV,* where Zubulake moved for sanctions as a result of UBS's failure to preserve all relevant backup tapes, and UBS's deletion of relevant e-mails. Finding fault in UBS's document preservation strategy but lacking evidence that the lost tapes and deleted e-mails were particularly favorable to Zubulake, I ordered UBS to pay for the re-deposition of several key UBS employees—Varsano, Chapin, Hardisty, Kim, and Tong—so that Zubulake could inquire about the newly-restored e-mails.

C. The Instant Dispute

The essence of the current dispute is that during the re-depositions required by *Zubulake IV,* Zubulake learned about more deleted e-mails and about the existence of e-mails preserved on UBS's active servers that were, to that point, never produced. In sum, Zubulake has now presented evidence that UBS personnel deleted relevant e-mails, some of which were subsequently recovered from backup tapes (or elsewhere) and thus produced to Zubulake long after her initial document requests, and some of which were lost altogether. Zubulake has also presented evidence that some UBS personnel did not produce responsive documents to counsel until recently, depriving Zubulake of the documents for almost two years.

1. Deleted E–Mails

Notwithstanding the clear and repeated warnings of counsel, Zubulake has proffered evidence that a number of key UBS employees—Orgill, Hardisty, Holland, Chapin, Varsano, and Amone—failed to retain e-mails germane to Zubulake's claims. Some of the deleted e-mails were restored from backup tapes (or other sources) and have been produced to Zubulake, others have been altogether lost, though there is strong evidence that they once existed. Although I have long been aware that certain e-mails were deleted, the redepositions demonstrate the scope and importance of those documents.

a.   At Least One E–Mail Has Never Been Produced

At least one e-mail has been irretrievably lost; the existence of that e-mail is known only because of oblique references to it in other correspondence. It has already been shown that Chapin—the alleged primary discriminator—deleted relevant e-mails. In addition to those e-mails, Zubulake has evidence suggesting that Chapin deleted at least one other e-mail that has been lost *entirely*. An e-mail from Chapin sent at 10:47 AM on September 21, 2001, asks Kim to send him a "document" recounting a conversation between Zubulake and a co-worker. Approximately 45 minutes later, Chapin sent an e-mail complaining about Zubulake to his boss and to the human resources employees handling Zubulake's case purporting to contain a verbatim recitation of a conversation between Zubulake and her co-worker, as overheard by Kim. This conversation allegedly took place on September 18, 2001, at 10:58 AM. There is reason to believe that immediately after that conversation, Kim sent Chapin an e-mail that contained the verbatim quotation that appears in Chapin's September 21 e-mail—the "document" that Chapin sought from Kim just prior to sending that e-mail—and that Chapin deleted it. That e-mail, however, has never been recovered and is apparently lost.

Although Zubulake has only been able to present concrete evidence that this one e-mail was irretrievably lost, there may well be others. Zubulake has presented extensive proof, detailed below, that UBS personnel were deleting relevant e-mails. Many of those e-mails were recovered from backup tapes. The UBS record retention policies called for monthly backup tapes to be retained for three years. The tapes covering the relevant time period (circa August 2001) should have been available to UBS in August 2002, when counsel instructed UBS's information technology personnel that backup tapes were also subject to the litigation hold.

Nonetheless, many backup tapes for the most relevant time periods are missing * * *. Zubulake did not even learn that four of these tapes were missing until after *Zubulake IV*. Thus, it is impossible to know just how many relevant e-mails have been lost in their entirety.[32]

b.   Many E–Mails Were Deleted and Only Later Recovered from Alternate Sources

Other e-mails were deleted in contravention of counsel's "litigation hold" instructions, but were subsequently recovered from alternative sources—such as backup tapes—and thus produced to Zubulake, albeit

---

32.   In *Zubulake IV*, I held that UBS's destruction of relevant backup tapes was negligent, rather than willful, because whether the duty to preserve extended to backup tapes was "a grey area." 220 F.R.D. at 221. I further held that "litigants are now on notice, at least in this Court, that backup tapes that can be identified as storing information created by or for 'key players' must be preserved." *Id.* at 221 n.47.

Because UBS lost the backup tapes mentioned in this opinion well before *Zubulake IV* was issued, it was not on notice of the precise contours of its duty to preserve backup tapes. Accordingly, I do not discuss UBS's destruction of relevant backup tapes as proof that UBS acted willfully, but rather to show that Zubulake can no longer prove what was deleted and when, and to demonstrate that the scope of e-mails that have been irrevocably lost is broader than initially thought.

almost two years after she propounded her initial document requests. For example, an e-mail from Hardisty to Holland (and on which Chapin was copied) reported that Zubulake said "that all she wanted is to be treated like the other 'guys' on the desk." That e-mail was recovered from Hardisty's August 2001 backup tape—and thus it was on his active server as late as August 31, 2001, when the backup was generated—but was not in his active files. That e-mail therefore *must* have been deleted subsequent to counsel's warnings.

Another e-mail, from Varsano to Hardisty dated August 31, 2001—the very day that Hardisty met with outside counsel—forwarded an earlier message from Hardisty dated June 29, 2001, that recounted a conversation in which Hardisty "warned" Chapin about his management of Zubulake, and in which Hardisty reminded Chapin that Zubulake could "be a good broker." This e-mail was absent from UBS's initial production and had to be restored from backup; apparently neither Varsano nor Hardisty had retained it. This deletion is especially surprising because Varsano retained the June 29, 2001 e-mail for over two months before he forwarded it to Hardisty. Indeed, Varsano testified in his deposition that he "definitely" "saved all of the e-mails that [he] received concerning Ms. Zubulake" in 2001, that they were saved in a separate "very specific folder," and that "all of those e-mails" were produced to counsel.

As a final example, an e-mail from Hardisty to Varsano and Orgill, dated September 1, 2001, specifically discussed Zubulake's termination. It read: "LZ—ok once lawyers have been signed off, probably one month, but most easily done in combination with the full Asiapc [downsizing] announcement. We will need to document her performance post her warning HK. Matt [Chapin] is doing that." Thus, Orgill and Hardisty had decided to terminate Zubulake as early as September 1, 2001. Indeed, two days later Orgill replied, "It's a pity we can't act on LZ earlier." Neither the authors nor any of the recipients of these e-mails retained any of them, even though these e-mails were sent within days of Hardisty's meeting with outside counsel. They were not even preserved on backup tapes, but were only recovered because Kim happened to have retained copies. Rather, all three people (Hardisty, Orgill and Varsano) deleted these e-mails from their computers by the end of September 2001. Apart from their direct relevance to Zubulake's claims, these e-mails may also serve to rebut Orgill and Hardisty's deposition testimony. Orgill testified that he played no role in the decision to terminate Zubulake. And Hardisty testified that he did not recall discussing Zubulake's termination with Orgill.

These are merely examples. The proof is clear: UBS personnel unquestionably deleted relevant e-mails from their computers after August 2001, even though they had received at least two directions from counsel not to. Some of those e-mails were recovered (Zubulake has pointed to at least 45), but some—and no one can say how many—were not. And even those e-mails that were recovered were produced to Zubulake well after she originally asked for them.

2. Retained, But Unproduced, E–Mails

Separate and apart from the deleted material are a number of e-mails that were absent from UBS's initial production even though they were not deleted. These e-mails existed in the active, on-line files of two UBS employees—Kim and Tong—but were not produced to counsel and thus not turned over to Zubulake until she learned of their existence as a result of her counsel's questions at deposition. Indeed, these e-mails were not produced until after Zubulake had conducted thirteen depositions and four re-depositions.

During her February 19, 2004, deposition, Kim testified that she was *never* asked to produce her files regarding Zubulake to counsel, nor did she ever actually produce them, although she was asked to retain them. One week after Kim's deposition, UBS produced seven new e-mails. The obvious inference to be drawn is that, subsequent to the deposition, counsel for the first time asked Kim to produce her files.

* * *

On March 29, 2004, UBS produced several new e-mails, and three new e-mail retention policies, from Tong's active files. At her deposition two weeks earlier, Tong explained (as she had at her first deposition, a year previous) that she kept a separate "archive" file on her computer with documents pertaining to Zubulake. UBS admits that until the March 2004 deposition, it misunderstood Tong's use of the word "archive" to mean backup tapes; after her March 2004 testimony, it was clear that she meant active data. Again, the inference is that UBS's counsel then, for the first time, asked her to produce her active computer files. [Judge Scheindlin notes that at least one email held by Tong provides circumstantial evidence rebutting deposition statements from a Warburg supervisor that he was not involved in Zubulake's termination.]

Zubulake now moves for sanctions as a result of UBS's purported discovery failings. In particular, she asks—as she did in *Zubulake IV*—that an adverse inference instruction be given to the jury that eventually hears this case.

III. LEGAL STANDARD

Spoliation is "the destruction or significant alteration of evidence, or the failure to preserve property for another's use as evidence in pending or reasonably foreseeable litigation." "The determination of an appropriate sanction for spoliation, if any, is confined to the sound discretion of the trial judge, and is assessed on a case-by-case basis." The authority to sanction litigants for spoliation arises jointly under the Federal Rules of Civil Procedure and the court's inherent powers.

The spoliation of evidence germane "to proof of an issue at trial can support an inference that the evidence would have been unfavorable to the party responsible for its destruction." A party seeking an adverse inference instruction (or other sanctions) based on the spoliation of evidence must establish the following three elements: (1) that the party having control over the evidence had an obligation to preserve it at the time it was destroyed; (2) that the records were destroyed with a "culpable state of mind" and (3) that the destroyed evidence was "relevant" to the party's claim or defense such that a reasonable trier of fact could find that it would support that claim or defense.

In this circuit, a "culpable state of mind" for purposes of a spoliation inference includes ordinary negligence. When evidence is destroyed in bad faith (*i.e.,* intentionally or willfully), that fact alone is sufficient to demonstrate relevance. By contrast, when the destruction is negligent, relevance must be proven by the party seeking the sanctions.

In the context of a request for an adverse inference instruction, the concept of "relevance" encompasses not only the ordinary meaning of the term, but also that the destroyed evidence would have been favorable to the movant. "This corroboration requirement is even more necessary where the destruction was merely negligent, since in those cases it cannot be inferred from the conduct of the spoliator that the evidence would even have been harmful to him." This is equally true in cases of gross negligence or recklessness; only in the case of *willful* spoliation does the degree of culpability give rise to a presumption of the relevance of the documents destroyed.

IV. DISCUSSION

In *Zubulake IV*, I held that UBS had a duty to preserve its employees' active files as early as April 2001, and certainly by August 2001, when Zubulake filed her EEOC charge. Zubulake has thus satisfied the first element of the adverse inference test. As noted, the central question implicated by this motion is whether UBS and its counsel took all necessary steps to guarantee that relevant data was both preserved and produced. If the answer is "no," then the next question is whether UBS acted wilfully when it deleted or failed to timely produce relevant information—resulting in either a complete loss or the production of responsive information close to two years after it was initially sought. If UBS acted wilfully, this satisfies the mental culpability prong of the adverse inference test and also demonstrates that the deleted material was relevant. If UBS acted negligently or even recklessly, then Zubulake must show that the missing or late-produced information was relevant.

A. Counsel's Duty to Monitor Compliance

In *Zubulake IV*, I summarized a litigant's preservation obligations:

> Once a party reasonably anticipates litigation, it must suspend its routine document retention/destruction policy and put in place a "litigation hold" to ensure the preservation of relevant documents. As a general rule, that litigation hold does not apply to inaccessible backup tapes (*e.g.,* those typically maintained solely for the purpose of disaster recovery), which may continue to be recycled on the schedule

set forth in the company's policy. On the other hand, if backup tapes are accessible (*i.e.,* actively used for information retrieval), then such tapes *would* likely be subject to the litigation hold.

A party's discovery obligations do not end with the implementation of a "litigation hold"—to the contrary, that's only the beginning. Counsel must oversee compliance with the litigation hold, monitoring the party's efforts to retain and produce the relevant documents. Proper communication between a party and her lawyer will ensure (1) that all relevant information (or at least all sources of relevant information) is discovered, (2) that relevant information is retained on a continuing basis; and (3) that relevant non-privileged material is produced to the opposing party.

1. Counsel's Duty to Locate Relevant Information

Once a "litigation hold" is in place, a party and her counsel must make certain that all sources of potentially relevant information are identified and placed "on hold," to the extent required in *Zubulake IV.* To do this, counsel must become fully familiar with her client's document retention policies, as well as the client's data retention architecture. This will invariably involve speaking with information technology personnel, who can explain system-wide backup procedures and the actual (as opposed to theoretical) implementation of the firm's recycling policy. It will also involve communicating with the "key players" in the litigation, in order to understand how they stored information. In this case, for example, some UBS employees created separate computer files pertaining to Zubulake, while others printed out relevant e-mails and retained them in hard copy only. Unless counsel interviews each employee, it is impossible to determine whether all potential sources of information have been inspected. A brief conversation with counsel, for example, might have revealed that Tong maintained "archive" copies of e-mails concerning Zubulake, and that "archive" meant a separate on-line computer file, not a backup tape. Had that conversation taken place, Zubulake might have had relevant e-mails from that file two years ago.

To the extent that it may not be feasible for counsel to speak with every key player, given the size of a company or the scope of the lawsuit, counsel must be more creative. It may be possible to run a system-wide keyword search; counsel could then preserve a copy of each "hit." Although this sounds burdensome, it need not be. Counsel does not have to review these documents, only see that they are retained. For example, counsel could create a broad list of search terms, run a search for a limited time frame, and then segregate responsive documents.[75] When the opposing party propounds its document requests, the parties could negotiate a list of search terms to be used in identifying responsive documents, and counsel would only be obliged to review documents that came up as "hits" on the second, more restrictive search. The initial broad cut merely guarantees that relevant documents are not lost.

---

75. It might be advisable to solicit a list of search terms from the opposing party for this purpose, so that it could not later complain about which terms were used.

In short, it is *not* sufficient to notify all employees of a litigation hold and expect that the party will then retain and produce all relevant information. Counsel must take affirmative steps to monitor compliance so that all sources of discoverable information are identified and searched. This is not to say that counsel will necessarily succeed in locating all such sources, or that the later discovery of new sources is evidence of a lack of effort. But counsel and client must take *some reasonable steps* to see that sources of relevant information are located.

2.   Counsel's Continuing Duty to Ensure Preservation

Once a party and her counsel have identified all of the sources of potentially relevant information, they are under a duty to retain that information (as per *Zubulake IV*) and to produce information responsive to the opposing party's requests. Rule 26 creates a "duty to supplement" those responses. Although the Rule 26 duty to supplement is nominally the party's, it really falls on counsel. * * *

The *continuing* duty to supplement disclosures strongly suggests that parties also have a duty to make sure that discoverable information is not lost. Indeed, the notion of a "duty to preserve" connotes an ongoing obligation. Obviously, if information is lost or destroyed, it has not been preserved.

The tricky question is what that continuing duty entails. What must a lawyer do to make certain that relevant information—especially electronic information—is being retained? Is it sufficient if she periodically re-sends her initial "litigation hold" instructions? What if she communicates with the party's information technology personnel? Must she make occasional on-site inspections?

Above all, the requirement must be reasonable. A lawyer cannot be obliged to monitor her client like a parent watching a child. At some point, the client must bear responsibility for a failure to preserve. At the same time, counsel is more conscious of the contours of the preservation obligation; a party cannot reasonably be trusted to receive the "litigation hold" instruction once and to fully comply with it without the active supervision of counsel.

There are thus a number of steps that counsel should take to ensure compliance with the preservation obligation. While these precautions may not be enough (or may be too much) in some cases, they are designed to promote the continued preservation of potentially relevant information in the typical case.

First, counsel must issue a "litigation hold" at the outset of litigation or whenever litigation is reasonably anticipated. The litigation hold should be periodically re-issued so that new employees are aware of it, and so that it is fresh in the minds of all employees.

Second, counsel should communicate directly with the "key players" in the litigation, *i.e.,* the people identified in a party's initial disclosure and any subsequent supplementation thereto. Because these "key players'' are the ''employees likely to have relevant information,'' it is particularly important that the preservation duty be communicated clearly to them. As with the litigation hold, the key players should be periodically reminded that the preservation duty is still in place.

Finally, counsel should instruct all employees to produce electronic copies of their relevant active files. Counsel must also make sure that all backup media which the party is required to retain is identified and stored in a safe place. In cases involving a small number of relevant backup tapes, counsel might be advised to take physical possession of backup tapes. In other cases, it might make sense for relevant backup tapes to be segregated and placed in storage. Regardless of what particular arrangement counsel chooses to employ, the point is to separate relevant backup tapes from others. One of the primary reasons that electronic data is lost is ineffective communication with information technology personnel. By taking possession of, or otherwise safeguarding, all potentially relevant backup tapes, counsel eliminates the possibility that such tapes will be inadvertently recycled.

* * *

3. What Happened at UBS After August 2001?

* * *

a. UBS's Discovery Failings

UBS's counsel—both in-house and outside—repeatedly advised UBS of its discovery obligations. In fact, counsel came very close to taking the precautions laid out above. *First,* outside counsel issued a litigation hold in August 2001. The hold order was circulated to many of the key players in this litigation, and reiterated in e-mails in February 2002, when suit was filed, and again in September 2002. Outside counsel made clear that the hold order applied to backup tapes in August 2002, as soon as backup tapes became an issue in this case. *Second,* outside counsel communicated directly with many of the key players in August 2001 and attempted to impress upon them their preservation obligations. *Third,* and finally, counsel instructed UBS employees to produce copies of their active computer files.

To be sure, counsel did not fully comply with the standards set forth above. Nonetheless, under the standards existing at the time, counsel acted reasonably to the extent that they directed UBS to implement a litigation hold. Yet notwithstanding the clear instructions of counsel, UBS personnel failed to preserve plainly relevant e-mails.

b. Counsel's Failings

On the other hand, UBS's counsel are not entirely blameless. * * * In this case, counsel failed to properly oversee UBS in a number of important ways, both in terms of its duty to locate relevant information and its duty to preserve and timely produce that information.

With respect to locating relevant information, counsel failed to adequately communicate with Tong about how she stored data. Although counsel determined that Tong kept her files on Zubulake in an "archive," they apparently made no effort to learn what that meant. A few simple questions—like the ones that Zubulake's counsel asked at Tong's redeposition—would have revealed that she kept those files in a separate *active* file on her computer.

With respect to making sure that relevant data was retained, counsel failed in a number of important respects. *First,* neither in-house nor outside counsel communicated the litigation hold instructions to Mike Davies, a senior human resources employee who was intimately involved in Zubulake's termination. *Second,* even though the litigation hold instructions were communicated to Kim, no one ever asked her to produce her files. And *third,* counsel failed to protect relevant backup tapes; had they done so, Zubulake might have been able to recover some of the e-mails that UBS employees deleted.

In addition, if Varsano's deposition testimony is to be credited, he turned over "all of the e-mails that [he] received concerning Ms. Zubulake." If Varsano turned over these e-mails, then counsel must have failed to produce some of them.

In sum, while UBS personnel deleted e-mails, copies of many of these e-mails were lost or belatedly produced as a result of counsel's failures.

c. Summary

Counsel failed to communicate the litigation hold order to all key players. They also failed to ascertain each of the key players' document management habits. By the same token, UBS employees—for unknown reasons—ignored many of the instructions that counsel gave. This case represents a failure of communication, and that failure falls on counsel and client alike.

At the end of the day, however, the duty to preserve and produce documents rests on the party. Once that duty is made clear to a party, either by court order or by instructions from counsel, that party is on notice of its obligations and acts at its own peril. Though more diligent action on the part of counsel would have mitigated some of the damage caused by UBS's deletion of emails, UBS deleted the e-mails in defiance of explicit instructions not to.

Because UBS personnel continued to delete relevant e-mails, Zubulake was denied access to e-mails to which she was entitled. Even those e-mails that were deleted but ultimately salvaged from other sources (*e.g.*, backup tapes or Tong and Kim's active files) were produced 22 months after they were initially requested. The effect of losing potentially relevant e-mails is obvious, but the effect of late production cannot be underestimated either. "As a discovery deadline ... draws near, discovery conduct that might have been considered 'merely' discourteous at an earlier point in the litigation may well breach a party's duties to its opponent and to the court." * * *

I therefore conclude that UBS acted wilfully in destroying potentially relevant information, which resulted either in the absence of such information or its tardy production (because duplicates were recovered from Kim or Tong's active files, or restored from backup tapes). Because UBS's spoliation was willful, the lost information is presumed to be relevant.

B. Remedy

Having concluded that UBS was under a duty to preserve the e-mails and that it deleted presumably relevant e-mails wilfully, I now consider the full panoply of available sanctions. In doing so, I recognize that a major consideration in choosing an appropriate sanction—along with punishing UBS and deterring future misconduct—is to restore Zubulake to the position that she would have been in had UBS faithfully discharged its discovery obligations. That being so, I find that the following sanctions are warranted.

First, the jury empanelled to hear this case will be given an adverse inference instruction with respect to e-mails deleted after August 2001, and in particular, with respect to e-mails that were irretrievably lost when UBS's backup tapes were recycled. No one can ever know precisely what was on those tapes, but the content of e-mails recovered from other sources—along with the fact that UBS employees wilfully deleted e-mails—is sufficiently favorable to Zubulake that I am convinced that the contents of the lost tapes would have been similarly, if not more, favorable.

Second, Zubulake argues that the e-mails that *were* produced, albeit late, "are brand new and very significant to Ms. Zubulake's retaliation claim and would have affected [her] examination of every witness ... in this case." Likewise, Zubulake claims, with respect to the newly produced e-mails from Kim and Tong's active files, that UBS's "failure to produce these e-mails in a timely fashion precluded [her] from questioning any witness about them." These arguments stand unrebutted and are therefore adopted in full by the Court. Accordingly, UBS is ordered to pay the costs of any depositions or re-depositions required by the late production.

Third, UBS is ordered to pay the costs of this motion.[102]

Finally, I note that UBS's belated production has resulted in a self-executing sanction. Not only was Zubulake unable to question UBS's witnesses using the newly produced e-mails, but UBS was unable to prepare those witnesses with the aid of those e-mails. Some of UBS's witnesses, not having seen these e-mails, have already given deposition testimony that seems to contradict the newly discovered evidence. * * * Zubulake is, of course, free to use this testimony at trial.

---

102. Fed. R. Civ. P. 37(b)(2).

These sanctions are designed to compensate Zubulake for the harm done to her by the loss of or extremely delayed access to potentially relevant evidence.[103] They should also stem the need for any further litigation over the backup tapes.

* * *

V. CONCLUSION

In sum, counsel has a duty to effectively communicate to her client its discovery obligations so that all relevant information is discovered, retained, and produced. In particular, once the duty to preserve attaches, counsel must identify sources of discoverable information. This will usually entail speaking directly with the key players in the litigation, as well as the client's information technology personnel. In addition, when the duty to preserve attaches, counsel must put in place a litigation hold and make that known to all relevant employees by communicating with them directly. The litigation hold instructions must be reiterated regularly[,] and compliance must be monitored. Counsel must also call for employees to produce copies of relevant electronic evidence, and must arrange for the segregation and safeguarding of any archival media (*e.g.,* backup tapes) that the party has a duty to preserve.

Once counsel takes these steps (or once a court order is in place), a party is fully on notice of its discovery obligations. If a party acts contrary to counsel's instructions or to a court's order, it acts at its own peril.

UBS failed to preserve relevant e-mails, even after receiving adequate warnings from counsel, resulting in the production of some relevant e-mails almost two years after they were initially requested, and resulting in the complete destruction of others. For that reason, Zubulake's motion is granted[,] and sanctions are warranted. UBS is ordered to:

1. Pay for the re-deposition of relevant UBS personnel, limited to the subject of the newly-discovered e-mails;

2. Restore and produce relevant documents from Varsano's August 2001 backup tape;

3. Pay for the re-deposition of Varsano and Tong, limited to the new material produced from Varsano's August 2001 backup tape; and

4. Pay all "reasonable expenses, including attorney's fees," incurred by Zubulake in connection with the making of this motion.

In addition, I will give the following instruction to the jury that hears this case:

You have heard that UBS failed to produce some of the e-mails sent or received by UBS personnel in August and September 2001.

---

103. Another possible remedy would have been to order UBS to pay for the restoration of the remaining backup tapes. Zubulake, however, has conceded that further restoration is unlikely to be fruitful.

Plaintiff has argued that this evidence was in defendants' control and would have proven facts material to the matter in controversy.

If you find that UBS could have produced this evidence, and that the evidence was within its control, and that the evidence would have been material in deciding facts in dispute in this case, you are permitted, but not required, to infer that the evidence would have been unfavorable to UBS.

In deciding whether to draw this inference, you should consider whether the evidence not produced would merely have duplicated other evidence already before you. You may also consider whether you are satisfied that UBS's failure to produce this information was reasonable. Again, any inference you decide to draw should be based on all of the facts and circumstances in this case.

* * *

VI. POSTSCRIPT

The subject of the discovery of electronically stored information is rapidly evolving. When this case began more than two years ago, there was little guidance from the judiciary, bar associations[,] or the academy as to the governing standards. Much has changed in that time. There have been a flood of recent opinions—including a number from appellate courts—and there are now several treatises on the subject. In addition, professional groups such as the American Bar Association and the Sedona Conference have provided very useful guidance on thorny issues relating to the discovery of electronically stored information. Many courts have adopted, or are considering adopting, local rules addressing the subject. Most recently, the Standing Committee on Rules and Procedures has approved for publication and public comment a proposal for revisions to the Federal Rules of Civil Procedure designed to address many of the issues raised by the discovery of electronically stored information.

Now that the key issues have been addressed and national standards are developing, parties and their counsel are fully on notice of their responsibility to preserve and produce electronically stored information. The tedious and difficult fact finding encompassed in this opinion and others like it is a great burden on a court's limited resources. The time and effort spent by counsel to litigate these issues has also been time-consuming and distracting. This Court, for one, is optimistic that with the guidance now provided it will not be necessary to spend this amount of time again. It is hoped that counsel will heed the guidance provided by these resources and will work to ensure that preservation, production[,] and spoliation issues are limited, if not eliminated.

COMMENTARY

1. Do Non–Parties Have an Obligation to Preserve?

What if a party knows a non-party holds relevant information but does not itself have direct or constructive control over that information? Does that party have any obligation to ensure its preservation? If it does, how can it fulfill that obligation?

Some courts have held that the party's preservation obligation includes the duty to inform the opposing party of the relevant evidence held by the third party and the risk of its possible destruction.[1] But what ability do litigants have to ensure the third party preserves the relevant evidence? Does the notice by a party to the third party that the information is relevant to potential litigation create a duty for the third party to preserve it? If third parties independently determine that the ESI they hold will be relevant to pending or future litigation involving others, does that knowledge create a third-party preservation duty?

Generally, the answer to both questions is "no." Preservation of evidence, particularly of ESI, can be costly. Thus, courts have recognized that the obligations of non-parties to preserve evidence are different than those imposed on the parties. Unless the duty arises from a contractual agreement to preserve information or other special relationship that may give rise to the duty, non-parties generally do not have an obligation to preserve relevant data even when they anticipate it might be relevant.

Some jurisdictions, however, recognize a common law tort for either intentional or negligent third-party spoliation of evidence where the third party had reason to know of the litigation. Even in jurisdictions where no common law preservation duty of third parties is recognized, courts may still impose the duty where the third party has a contractual or other special relationship with the party seeking preservation. An example of a relationship that might give rise to a third-party duty to preserve is that between an insurance company and a policy holder involved in litigation.[2] Where no such relationship exists, courts in jurisdictions not recognizing a common law tort of third-party spoliation may instead place the onus of third-party preservation on the party seeking it.

Although the following case involves the preservation of physical evidence rather than of ESI, it nicely illustrates the point. In *MetLife Auto & Home v. Joe Basil Chevrolet, Inc.*, the New York Court of Appeals refused to recognize a common law tort for spoliation against a third-party auto insurer who had custody of a vehicle involved in a claim by a homeowner against the auto manufacturer.[3] Even though the auto insurer had agreed verbally to preserve the evidence, the court declined to find a third-party duty to preserve because there was no relationship between the home insurer and the auto insurer. The Court noted that the home insurer could have purchased the vehicle from the auto insurer, paid for the costs of preservation, or filed suit and issued a subpoena duces tecum on the non-party auto insurer. Because Metlife was suing for the auto insurer's failure to preserve the vehicle *before* the claim in the primary suit was filed, it could not have issued a production or preservation subpoena on the auto insurance company. Thus, parties informed of the

---

1. *See, e.g., Silvestri v. General Motors Corp.*, 271 F.3d 583, 591 (4th Cir. 2001).

2. *See, e.g., Fada Indus., Inc. v. Falchi Bldg. Co.*, 730 N.Y.S.2d 827, 838 (N.Y. Sup. Ct. Queens Co. 2001) ("[T]he obligation of the insurer to defend must carry with it the obligation to preserve key evidence relied upon by its insured").

3. 1 N.Y.3d 478, 483 (2004).

existence of relevant evidence held by third parties before they have the ability to issue third-party subpoenas should consider taking other steps to ensure it is preserved. Courts, however, will not intervene in pre-litigation preservation disputes.[4]

2.   Preservation Obligations and Third–Party Subpoenas

Under Rule 45, if a third party is served with a subpoena seeking documents or other production after the action has been filed, does the subpoena create an independent duty not only to produce the information, but also to preserve relevant information? Rule 45 is silent on the effect of a subpoena on the third party's preservation obligations. If a subpoena creates both a production *and* a preservation obligation, how long should the third party be required to preserve information, and what information must it maintain?[5] After a recipient has fully complied with a subpoena, most courts hold that any preservation obligation that arose with service of the subpoena terminates.

While Rule 45 allows parties to serve subpoenas on non-parties, it does not require third parties to produce ESI if it is not reasonably accessible unless the issuing party can show good cause. Do *In re Napster* and *Warner Brothers Records*, cited above, suggest that third parties served with a subpoena for ESI that is not reasonably accessible have a duty to suspend their normal document destruction policies to preserve the information until the question of good cause is resolved, regardless of the cost of doing so?

What if parties are unable to serve document subpoenas on non-parties holding relevant ESI even *after* the case is filed? How might they ensure relevant evidence is not destroyed? Under the Private Securities Litigation Reform Act, discovery in private securities fraud actions is stayed until a motion to dismiss has been decided unless discovery is necessary to preserve evidence or prevent undue prejudice to a party. The Act provides that, during the stay, *parties* have the obligation to preserve evidence as though document requests had been issued. But non-parties holding relevant evidence have no such statutory obligation. What can be done to ensure that non-parties holding relevant ESI and other evidence preserve it until the stay is lifted? Courts may permit parties to issue "preservation subpoenas" on non-parties. But most allow them to do so only with the court's permission even where non-parties' document retention and destruction policies may result in imminent destruction of relevant ESI.[6]

---

4. *See Texas v. City of Frisco*, No. 07–383, 2008 WL 828055, at *3 (E.D. Tex. Mar. 27, 2008) (finding State's request for protective order excusing it from complying with City's letter demanding that the State preserve electronic data and for a declaratory judgment on the scope of parties' preservation obligations non-justiciable because no suit had been filed and facts regarding potential litigation "not sufficiently immediate to establish an actual controversy" (quotation omitted)).

5. *See In re Napster Copyright Litig.*, 462 F. Supp. 2d 1060, 1068 (N.D. Cal. Oct. 25, 2006) (holding subpoena issued to third party imposes preservation obligation on all information relevant to the subpoena until requested materials are produced and disputes related to the subpoena have been resolved); *Warner Bros. Records v. Does 1–14*, 555 F. Supp. 2d 1, 2008 WL 60297, at *2 (D.D.C. Jan. 4, 2008) (ordering third party to preserve evidence until resolution of motions to quash third party subpoena).

6. *See, e.g., In re Cree Inc. Sec. Litig.*, 220 F.R.D. 443, 447 (M.D.N.C. 2004) (quashing preservation subpoenas served on non-parties without leave of court despite risk that routine

3. Privacy and Preservation

Even where a party may be under a preservation obligation, federal privacy laws may prevent preservation and production of relevant ESI held by parties and non-parties. For example, the Stored Communications Act prohibits providers of electronic communications services from disclosing the content of stored customer communications to any person, except the federal government upon a court-issued warrant. The Act has no exceptions for civil actions. If such communications providers cannot produce the content of communications, can they ever have a duty to preserve it? Note that many other federal laws also limit disclosure of private information, but allow entities holding such information to disclose it in response to court-approved discovery requests.[7]

Can contractual obligations regarding the privacy of customers' personal information limit the preservation obligations of a party or non-party? Suppose a website host promises not to collect or store personal information about its users. Can that party be sanctioned for failing to preserve such information after the preservation obligation arose or be ordered to preserve such information going forward? What if the privacy policy is viewed as an integral part of the service offered by the host? In *Columbia Pictures Industries v. Bunnell*, plaintiffs sought the IP addresses of a website's users who they alleged violated copyright law when using the site's file sharing service to trade copyrighted materials.[8] The website's privacy policy prohibited the site operator from collecting personal information about users not knowingly provided by those users. As a result, the website host did not preserve server log data, including the users' IP addresses. In holding that the website owner must preserve such data, including IP addresses, the court never reached the issue of whether a party's privacy policy could trump its preservation obligations or whether preservation obligations could force a party to change its customer privacy policies. Instead, the court merely concluded that IP addresses did not constitute personal information, finding that the addresses identified computers, not users.

4. Preservation Obligations Under Federal Law

An independent obligation to preserve information may arise from federal or state statutes and regulations requiring that certain types of data be preserved, regardless of whether an entity is, or may become, a party to litigation. For example, the Sarbanes–Oxley Act of 2002, passed in the wake of high profile corporate accounting scandals, created new obligations for auditors of publicly traded companies to retain all records, including electronic

---

document destruction policy might destroy relevant data); *In re Tyco Int'l, Ltd. Sec. Litig.*, No. 00 MDL 1335, 2000 WL 33654141, at *3, 5 (D.N.H. July 27, 2000) (permitting plaintiff to serve preservation subpoenas on third parties where plaintiff sought leave of court and produced evidence that similar entities "typically overwrite and thereby destroy electronic data").

7. *See, e.g.*, 15 U.S.C. §§ 6801(a), 6802, 6802(e)(8) (requiring financial institutions to protect privacy of customers' personal information, but permitting disclosure to respond to judicial process); *id.* § 6502(b) (prohibiting operators of websites and other online services from disclosing personal information collected from children without parental consent, but providing exception for response to judicial process).

8. No. CV 06–1093, 2007 WL 2080419 (C.D. Cal. May 29, 2007). This case is found at Chapter II.E, *infra*.

records, relating to audits for five years after the audit is conducted.[9] The Securities and Exchange Act, and the SEC's regulations implementing it, impose extensive record retention requirements on stock exchanges, members of the exchanges and securities dealers.[10] The Fair Labor Standards Act and the regulations issued pursuant to it require employers to retain payroll, collective bargaining agreements and other employment contract records for three years; business volume records for three years in the form in which they were maintained in the ordinary course of business; and employment and earning records, such as time cards, for two years.[11] Health care providers that participate in the Medicare program are required by the Department of Health and Human Services to retain certain medical records for five years.

Although a party may have an independent duty to retain records under federal or state law, a violation of that obligation may not necessarily result in spoliation sanctions. In *Sarmiento v. Montclair State University*, an unsuccessful job candidate filed an employment discrimination claim against the University and sought sanctions in the form of an adverse inference against the defendant for its failure to retain the selection committee's notes that related to the decision not to hire.[12] Plaintiff alleged, *inter alia*, that sanctions were warranted because the University violated federal regulations that required universities and colleges to retain hiring and other records.

The court held that "[a]lthough a regulation may supply the duty to preserve records, a party seeking to benefit from an inference of spoliation must still make out the other usual elements" of that claim. Those elements included a requirement that the litigation be reasonably foreseeable; in this case, the court held that it was not. What do you think of this result? Should foreseeability matter when an obligation to preserve data existed independent of the risk of litigation? Should independent statutory or regulatory obligations to preserve data be enforceable by parties other than the government's enforcement entity?

C. TRIGGER DATE

ZUBULAKE v. UBS WARBURG LLC *"ZUBULAKE IV"*

220 F.R.D. 212 (S.D.N.Y. 2003)

SCHEINDLIN, DISTRICT JUDGE

* * * This opinion addresses both the scope of a litigant's duty to preserve electronic documents and the consequences of a failure to preserve documents that fall within the scope of that duty.

I. BACKGROUND

This is the fourth opinion resolving discovery disputes in this case. * * * In brief, Laura Zubulake, an equities trader who earned approxi-

---

9. *See* 18 U.S.C. § 1520(a)(1)-(2).

10. *See* 15 U.S.C. § 78q(a).

11. *See* 29 U.S.C. § 211(c); 29 C.F.R. § 516.5–6.

12. 513 F. Supp. 2d 72 (D.N.J. 2007).

mately $650,000 a year with UBS, is suing UBS for gender discrimination, failure to promote, and retaliation under federal, state, and city law. She has repeatedly maintained that the evidence she needs to prove her case exists in e-mail correspondence sent among various UBS employees and stored only on UBS's computer systems.

On July 24, 2003, I ordered the parties to share the cost of restoring certain UBS backup tapes that contained e-mails relevant to Zubulake's claims. In the restoration effort, the parties discovered that certain backup tapes are missing. In particular:

	Missing Monthly Backup Tapes
Matthew Chapin (Zubulake's immediate supervisor)	April 2001
Jeremy Hardisty (Chapin's supervisor)	June 2001
Andrew Clarke and Vinay Datta (Zubulake's coworkers)	April 2001
Rose Tong (human resources)	Part of June 2001, July 2001, August 2001, and October 2001

In addition, certain isolated e-mails—created after UBS supposedly began retaining all relevant e-mails—were deleted from UBS's system, although they appear to have been saved on the backup tapes. As I explained in *Zubulake III*, "certain e-mails sent after the initial EEOC charge—and particularly relevant to Zubulake's retaliation claim—were apparently not saved at all. For example, [an] e-mail from Chapin to Joy Kim [another of Zubulake's coworkers] instructing her on how to file a complaint against Zubulake was not saved, and it bears the subject line 'UBS client attorney priviledge [sic] only,' although no attorney is copied on the e-mail. This potentially useful e-mail was deleted and resided only on UBS's backup tapes."

Zubulake filed her EEOC charge on August 16, 2001; the instant action was filed on February 14, 2002. In August 2001, in an oral directive, UBS ordered its employees to retain all relevant documents. In August 2002, after Zubulake specifically requested e-mail stored on back-up tapes, UBS's outside counsel orally instructed UBS's information technology personnel to stop recycling backup tapes.

Zubulake now seeks sanctions against UBS for its failure to preserve the missing backup tapes and deleted e-mails. * * *

II. LEGAL STANDARD

Spoliation is "the destruction or significant alteration of evidence, or the failure to preserve property for another's use as evidence in pending or reasonably foreseeable litigation." The spoliation of evidence germane "to proof of an issue at trial can support an inference that the evidence would have been unfavorable to the party responsible for its destruction." However, "the determination of an appropriate sanction for spoliation, if any, is confined to the sound discretion of the trial judge, and is assessed on a case-by-case basis." The authority to sanction litigants for spoliation arises jointly under the Federal Rules of Civil Procedure and the court's own inherent powers.

III. DISCUSSION

It goes without saying that a party can only be sanctioned for destroying evidence if it had a duty to preserve it. If UBS had no such duty, then UBS cannot be faulted. I begin, then, by discussing the extent of a party's duty to preserve evidence.

A. Duty to Preserve

"The obligation to preserve evidence arises when the party has notice that the evidence is relevant to litigation or when a party should have known that the evidence may be relevant to future litigation." Identifying the boundaries of the duty to preserve involves two related inquiries: *when* does the duty to preserve attach, and *what* evidence must be preserved?

1. The Trigger Date

In this case, the duty to preserve evidence arose, at the latest, on August 16, 2001, when Zubulake filed her EEOC charge. At that time, UBS's in-house attorneys cautioned employees to retain all documents, including e-mails and backup tapes, that could potentially be relevant to the litigation. In meetings with Chapin, Clarke, Kim, Hardisty, John Holland (Chapin's supervisor), and Dominic Vail (Zubulake's former supervisor) held on August 29–31, 2001, UBS's outside counsel reiterated the need to preserve documents.

But the duty to preserve may have arisen even before the EEOC complaint was filed. Zubulake argues that UBS "should have known that the evidence [was] relevant to future litigation," as early as April 2001, and thus had a duty to preserve it. She offers two pieces of evidence in support of this argument. *First*, certain UBS employees titled e-mails pertaining to Zubulake "UBS Attorney Client Privilege" starting in April 2001, notwithstanding the fact that no attorney was copied on the e-mail and the substance of the e-mail was not legal in nature. *Second*, Chapin admitted in his deposition that he feared litigation from as early as April 2001 * * *.

Merely because one or two employees contemplate the possibility that a fellow employee might sue does not generally impose a firm-wide duty to preserve. But in this case, it appears that almost everyone associated with Zubulake recognized the possibility that she might sue. For example, an e-mail authored by Zubulake's co-worker Vinnay Datta, concerning Zubulake and labeled "UBS attorney client priviladge [sic]," was distributed to

Chapin (Zubulake's supervisor), Holland and Leland Tomblick (Chapin's supervisor), Vail (Zubulake's former supervisor), and Andrew Clarke (Zubulake's co-worker) in late April 2001. That e-mail, replying to one from Hardisty, essentially called for Zubulake's termination: "Our biggest strength as a firm and as a desk is our ability to share information and relationships. Any person who threatens this in any way should be firmly dealt with.... Believe me that a lot of other [similar] instances have occurred earlier."

Thus, the relevant people at UBS anticipated litigation in April 2001. The duty to preserve attached at the time that litigation was reasonably anticipated.

2. Scope

The next question is: What is the scope of the duty to preserve? Must a corporation, upon recognizing the threat of litigation, preserve every shred of paper, every e-mail or electronic document, and every backup tape? The answer is clearly, "no". Such a rule would cripple large corporations, like UBS, that are almost always involved in litigation. As a general rule, then, a party need not preserve all backup tapes even when it reasonably anticipates litigation.

At the same time, anyone who anticipates being a party or is a party to a lawsuit must not destroy unique, relevant evidence that might be useful to an adversary. "While a litigant is under no duty to keep or retain every document in its possession ... it is under a duty to preserve what it knows, or reasonably should know, is relevant in the action, is reasonably calculated to lead to the discovery of admissible evidence, is reasonably likely to be requested during discovery and/or is the subject of a pending discovery request."

i. Whose Documents Must Be Retained?

The broad contours of the duty to preserve are relatively clear. That duty should certainly extend to any documents or tangible things * * * made by individuals "likely to have discoverable information that the disclosing party may use to support its claims or defenses."[25] The duty also includes documents prepared *for* those individuals, to the extent those documents can be readily identified (*e.g.*, from the "to" field in e-mails). The duty also extends to information that is relevant to the claims or defenses of *any* party, or which is "relevant to the subject matter involved in the action."[26] Thus, the duty to preserve extends to those employees likely to have relevant information—the "key players" in the case. In this case, all of the individuals whose backup tapes were lost (Chapin, Hardisty, Tong, Datta and Clarke) fall into this category.

ii. What Must Be Retained?

A party or anticipated party must retain all relevant documents (but not multiple identical copies) in existence at the time the duty to preserve

---

25.   Fed. R. Civ. P. 26(a)(1)(A).

26.   Fed. R. Civ. P. 26(b)(1).

attaches, and any relevant documents created thereafter. In recognition of the fact that there are many ways to manage electronic data, litigants are free to choose how this task is accomplished. For example, a litigant could choose to retain all then-existing backup tapes for the relevant personnel (if such tapes store data by individual or the contents can be identified in good faith and through reasonable effort), and to catalog any later-created documents in a separate electronic file. That, along with a mirror-image of the computer system taken at the time the duty to preserve attaches (to preserve documents in the state they existed at that time), creates a complete set of relevant documents. Presumably there are a multitude of other ways to achieve the same result.

iii. Summary of Preservation Obligations

The scope of a party's preservation obligation can be described as follows: Once a party reasonably anticipates litigation, it must suspend its routine document retention/destruction policy and put in place a "litigation hold" to ensure the preservation of relevant documents. As a general rule, that litigation hold does not apply to inaccessible backup tapes (*e.g.*, those typically maintained solely for the purpose of disaster recovery), which may continue to be recycled on the schedule set forth in the company's policy. On the other hand, if backup tapes are accessible (*i.e.*, actively used for information retrieval), then such tapes *would* likely be subject to the litigation hold.

However, it does make sense to create one exception to this general rule. If a company can identify where particular employee documents are stored on backup tapes, then the tapes storing the documents of "key players" to the existing or threatened litigation should be preserved if the information contained on those tapes is not otherwise available. This exception applies to *all* backup tapes.

iv. What Happened at UBS After August 2001?

By its attorney's directive in August 2002, UBS endeavored to preserve all backup tapes that existed in August 2001 (when Zubulake filed her EEOC charge) that captured data for employees identified by Zubulake in her document request, and all such monthly backup tapes generated thereafter. These backup tapes existed in August 2002, because of UBS's document retention policy, which required retention for three years. In August 2001, UBS employees were instructed to maintain *active* electronic documents pertaining to Zubulake in separate files. Had these directives been followed, UBS would have met its preservation obligations by preserving one copy of all relevant documents that existed at, or were created after, the time when the duty to preserve attached.

In fact, UBS employees did not comply with these directives. Three backup tapes containing the e-mail files of Chapin, Hardisty, Clarke and Datta created after April 2001 were lost, despite the August 2002 directive to maintain those tapes. According to the UBS document retention policy, these three monthly backup tapes from April and June 2001 should have been retained for three years.

The two remaining lost backup tapes were for the time period *after* Zubulake filed her EEOC complaint (Rose Tong's tapes for August and October 2001). UBS has offered *no* explanation for why these tapes are missing. * * * [I]t appears that UBS did not directly order the preservation of Tong's backup tapes until August 2002, when Zubulake made her discovery request.

In sum, UBS had a duty to preserve the six-plus backup tapes (that is, six complete backup tapes and part of a seventh) at issue here.

B. Remedies

* * *

Adverse Inference Instruction

Zubulake * * * argues that UBS's spoliation warrants an adverse inference instruction. Zubulake asks that the jury in this case be instructed that it can infer from the fact that UBS destroyed certain evidence that the evidence, if available, would have been favorable to Zubulake and harmful to UBS. In practice, an adverse inference instruction often ends litigation—it is too difficult a hurdle for the spoliator to overcome. The *in terrorem* effect of an adverse inference is obvious. * * * Accordingly, the adverse inference instruction is an extreme sanction and should not be given lightly.

A party seeking an adverse inference instruction (or other sanctions) based on the spoliation of evidence must establish the following three elements: (1) that the party having control over the evidence had an obligation to preserve it at the time it was destroyed; (2) that the records were destroyed with a "culpable state of mind" and (3) that the destroyed evidence was "relevant" to the party's claim or defense such that a reasonable trier of fact could find that it would support that claim or defense. In this circuit, a "culpable state of mind" for purposes of a spoliation inference includes ordinary negligence. When evidence is destroyed in bad faith (*i.e.*, intentionally or willfully), that fact alone is sufficient to demonstrate relevance. By contrast, when the destruction is negligent, relevance must be proven by the party seeking the sanctions.

a. Duty to Preserve

For the reasons already discussed, UBS had—and breached—a duty to preserve the backup tapes at issue. Zubulake has thus established the first element.

b. Culpable State of Mind

Zubulake argues that UBS's spoliation was "intentional—or, at a minimum, grossly negligent." Yet, of dozens of relevant backup tapes, only six and part of a seventh are missing. Indeed, UBS argues that the tapes were "inadvertently recycled well before plaintiff requested them and even before she filed her complaint [in February 2002]."

But to accept UBS's argument would ignore the fact that, even though Zubulake had not yet requested the tapes or filed her complaint, UBS had a duty to preserve those tapes. Once the duty to preserve attaches, any destruction of documents is, at a minimum, negligent. (Of course, this would not apply to destruction caused by events outside of the party's control, *e.g.*, a fire in UBS's offices).

Whether a company's duty to preserve extends to backup tapes has been a grey area. As a result, it is not terribly surprising that a company would think that it did *not* have a duty to preserve all of its backup tapes, even when it reasonably anticipated the onset of litigation. Thus, UBS's failure to preserve all potentially relevant backup tapes was merely negligent, as opposed to grossly negligent or reckless.

UBS's destruction or loss of Tong's backup tapes, however, exceeds mere negligence. UBS failed to include these backup tapes in its preservation directive in this case, notwithstanding the fact that Tong was the human resources employee directly responsible for Zubulake and who engaged in continuous correspondence regarding the case. Moreover, the lost tapes covered the time period *after* Zubulake filed her EEOC charge, when UBS was *unquestionably* on notice of its duty to preserve. Indeed, Tong herself took part in much of the correspondence over Zubulake's charge of discrimination. Thus, UBS was grossly negligent, if not reckless, in not preserving those backup tapes.

Because UBS was negligent—and possibly reckless—Zubulake has satisfied her burden with respect to the second prong of the spoliation test.

c. Relevance

Finally, because UBS's spoliation was negligent and possibly reckless, but not willful, Zubulake must demonstrate that a reasonable trier of fact could find that the missing e-mails would support her claims. In order to receive an adverse inference instruction, Zubulake must demonstrate not only that UBS destroyed relevant evidence as that term is ordinarily understood, but also that the destroyed evidence would have been favorable to her. "This corroboration requirement is even more necessary where the destruction was merely negligent, since in those cases it cannot be inferred from the conduct of the spoliator that the evidence would even have been harmful to him." This is equally true in cases of gross negligence or recklessness; only in the case of *willful* spoliation is the spoliator's mental culpability itself evidence of the relevance of the documents destroyed.

On the one hand, I found in *Zubulake I* and *Zubulake III* that the e-mails contained on UBS's backup tapes were, by-and-large, relevant in the sense that they bore on the issues in the litigation. On the other hand, *Zubulake III* specifically held that "nowhere (in the sixty-eight e-mails produced to the Court) is there evidence that Chapin's dislike of Zubulake related to her gender." And those sixty-eight e-mails, it should be emphasized, were the ones selected by Zubulake as being the *most* relevant among all those produced in UBS's sample restoration. There is no reason to believe that the lost e-mails would be any more likely to support her claims.

Furthermore, the likelihood of obtaining relevant information from the six-plus lost backup tapes at issue here is even lower than for the remainder of the tapes, because the majority of the six-plus tapes cover the time prior to the filing of Zubulake's EEOC charge. The tape that is most likely to contain relevant e-mails is Tong's August 2001 tape—the tape for the very month that Zubulake filed her EEOC charges. But the majority of the e-mails on that tape are preserved on the September 2001 tape. Thus, there is no reason to believe that peculiarly unfavorable evidence resides solely on that missing tape. Accordingly, Zubulake has not sufficiently demonstrated that the lost tapes contained relevant information.

d. Summary

In sum, although UBS had a duty to preserve all of the backup tapes at issue, and destroyed them with the requisite culpability, Zubulake cannot demonstrate that the lost evidence would have supported her claims. Under the circumstances, it would be inappropriate to give an adverse inference instruction to the jury.

* * * UBS Must Pay the Costs of Additional Depositions

Even though an adverse inference instruction is not warranted, there is no question that e-mails that UBS should have produced to Zubulake were destroyed by UBS. That being so, UBS must bear Zubulake's costs for re-deposing certain witnesses for the limited purpose of inquiring into issues raised by the destruction of evidence and any newly discovered e-mails. In particular, UBS is ordered to pay the costs of re-deposing Chapin, Hardisty, Tong, and Josh Varsano (a human resources employee in charge of the Asian Equities Sales Desk and known to have been in contact with Tong during August 2001).

* * *

COMMENTARY

1. When Does the Duty to Preserve Arise?

"A preservation obligation may arise from many sources, including common law, statutes, regulations, or a court order in a case."[18] In addition, courts have held that the duty to preserve arises when a party knows, or reasonably should know, that the evidence is relevant to pending or future litigation. The point at which a party had actual knowledge or notice of pending or future litigation is relatively simple to identify. By contrast, determining when a party reasonably should have anticipated litigation—that is, when a party had constructive knowledge of future litigation—is the far

---

18.   Rule 37, 2006 Advisory Committee Note.

more difficult question, and is often a key issue in dispute during court consideration of spoliation motions. Broadly put, a party should preserve evidence when the party is on notice of a potential litigation or investigation. But what is "notice"? And at what point can it be later determined that litigation should have been "reasonably anticipated"?

2. How Should Parties Identify When the Duty to Preserve Has Been Triggered?

The determination of when the duty to preserve has been triggered is inherently fact specific. The Sedona Conference has suggested that in general, "[t]he determination of whether litigation is reasonably anticipated should be based on good faith . . . a reasonable investigation and an evaluation of the relevant facts and circumstances."[19] Where a court must evaluate whether a party's decision to preserve evidence, or not to do so, was reasonable, it should ask whether that decision was made in good faith and was reasonable given the facts available to the party at the time the decision was made.

Anticipated litigation must be something more than a mere possibility or general discontent. "The future litigation must be 'probable,' which has been held to mean 'more than a possibility.' "[20] It is very likely that the duty is triggered when a party provides unequivocal notice of its intent to file a claim, even if it has not yet filed a formal complaint.[21] In general, "[r]easonable anticipation of litigation arises when an organization is on notice of a *credible threat* it will become involved in litigation or anticipates taking action to initiate litigation."[22] But what facts and circumstances might suggest a credible threat? And how "credible" must that threat be?

In *Hynix Semiconductor Inc. v. Rambus, Inc.*,[23] the plaintiff's duty to preserve was not triggered when it contemplated litigation against copyright infringers only if negotiations failed and where the litigation depended upon other contingencies. Litigation became probable only when the plaintiff interviewed litigation counsel. When parties indicate a preference for negotiation, even though litigation is a possible outcome, the duty may not yet be triggered. For other courts, the "possibility" of litigation may be sufficient to trigger the duty. In *Zubulake,* the court found a duty triggered when nearly all employees associated with Zubulake recognized the "possibility" that she might sue. Is this a different standard than the one used in *Hynix Semiconductor*? Does widespread recognition of "possible" litigation increase its probability? What if only one employee believes litigation is likely?

---

19. Sedona Conference, *The Sedona Conference Commentary on Legal Holds: The Trigger and the Process*, 3, 10 (Public Comment Version 2007), *available at* http://www.thesedonaconference. org/content/miscFiles/Legal_holds.pdf ("Sedona Legal Holds").

20. *In re Napster, Inc. Copyright Litig.*, 462 F. Supp. 2d 1060, 1068 (N.D. Cal. 2006) (quoting *Hynix Semiconductor Inc. v. Rambus*, No. C–00–20905, 2006 WL 565893, at *21 (N.D. Cal. Jan. 5, 2006)). *Accord Treppel v. Biovail Corp.*, 233 F.R.D. 363, 371 (S.D.N.Y. 2006) ("[T]he mere existence of a dispute . . . did not mean that the parties should reasonably have anticipated litigation at that time and taken steps to preserve evidence.").

21. *See Longview Fibre Co. v. CSX Transp., Inc.*, 526 F. Supp. 2d 332, 341 (N.D.N.Y. 2007) (CSX's duty to preserve track maintenance records essential to defense of property damage claim arose "at the very latest" when CSX notified defendant of its intent to sue for damage to tracks).

22. Sedona Legal Holds, at 5 (emphasis added).

23. No. 00–20905, 2006 WL 565893, at *22 (N.D. Cal. Jan. 5, 2006).

a. Plaintiffs' Duty to Preserve

When considering *plaintiffs'* duty to preserve, courts may be more likely to find the duty triggered before litigation formally commences than for defendants, in large part because plaintiffs control the timing of litigation. In *Cyntegra, Inc. v. Idexx Laboratories, Inc.*,[24] Cyntegra, a competitor to Idexx Labs, alleged that Idexx engaged in anti-competitive agreements with its buyers that severely disadvantaged Cyntegra's ability to generate revenue and profits. In March 2006, after Cyntegra was unable to make payments to an outside service that stored nearly all of Cyntegra's data, the service deleted Cyntegra's files—including information relevant to Idexx's defense. Three months later, Cyntegra filed its claim. The court asserted that because plaintiffs control when litigation begins, they "must necessarily anticipate litigation before the complaint is filed." Because all of Cyntegra's injury resulted from conduct occurring prior to March—the point at which the data were destroyed—the court concluded the plaintiff must have anticipated litigation by that date. Although plaintiff attempted to negotiate with Idexx to mitigate or eliminate the tying arrangements prior to filing suit, the court found that "[p]laintiff should have known that negotiation breakdowns were a distinct possibility, and that legal recourse might be necessary to prevent bankruptcy." How does this result compare with the outcome in *Hynix Semiconductor*, where negotiation was also a precursor to bringing suit and where evidence suggested litigation was explicitly contemplated? Can the two cases be reconciled?

Even when plaintiff does not file a claim until long after the conduct giving rise to the event occurred, the court may find reasonable anticipation of litigation. In *Silvestri v. General Motors Corp.*,[25] the plaintiff claimed his injuries sustained in a car accident were exacerbated when the vehicle's airbag failed to deploy. After the accident, Silvestri nearly immediately retained counsel, who in turn hired experts who inspected the vehicle and the accident site within weeks of the accident. One expert concluded that the airbag should have deployed and that there was therefore a valid case against GM. The experts asserted they understood the inspection was conducted in anticipation of litigation and suggested to plaintiff's counsel the need to preserve the vehicle for GM's inspection. A few months after the accident, the owner of the vehicle sold it and the new owner repaired the damage, preventing GM from inspecting the car in its post-accident/pre-repair condition. On these facts, the court found that Silvestri anticipated litigation shortly after the accident and the duty to preserve was triggered at that time.

b. Pre–Filing Communications Between Counsel

Pre-filing communications between the litigants can also provide constructive notice that litigation is likely. Demand letters stating a claim may be sufficient to trigger an obligation to preserve. But the clarity and content of pre-filing communications can significantly impact whether a party should have reasonably anticipated litigation. While something less than a clear

---

24.   No. 06–4170, 2007 WL 5193736 (C.D. Cal. Sept. 21, 2007).

25.   271 F.3d 583 (4th Cir. 2001).

indication of intent to sue may be sufficient to trigger the duty, correspondence that merely presents a basis for the dispute may be inadequate. In *Cache La Poudre Feeds LLC v. Land O'Lakes, Inc.* (set forth in Chapter II.F, *infra*), the court held that the defendant's duty to preserve evidence was *not* triggered at the time of the pre-filing communication, which the court found "equivocal" because it did not threaten litigation, suggested initial interest in avoiding litigation, and did not demand preservation of relevant materials.[26] Under the rationale of *Cyntegra, Hynix Semiconductors, Inc.,* and *Silvestri,* would the plaintiff's duty have been triggered at that time?

When a party receives pre-filing correspondence from opposing counsel that is suggestive of potential litigation, but neither specifies the nature of, or events giving rise to, the claim, nor explicitly threatens litigation, does the duty to preserve impose any obligation on the recipient to further investigate to determine whether a litigation threat exists? In *Stallings v. Bil–Jax,* the court found that although a letter from plaintiff's counsel was vague, it "provided some notice to [defendant] that Stallings might bring a lawsuit against it.... [and defendant] had ample time to make a timely request for additional information regarding the nature of the incident referred to in the letter."[27] Thus, the court found that the defendant was at least partially responsible for the destruction of relevant evidence.

c. Pre–Filing Preservation Letters

While post-litigation discovery requests clearly put a party on notice of the relevance of data requested, what of pre-filing preservation letters? Although the common law duty of preservation does not depend on receipt of a preservation letter, "prudent counsel would be wise to ensure that a demand letter ... addresses ... preservation obligations."[28] Properly crafted pre-litigation preservation letters can impose the duty of preservation. For example, a plaintiff's preservation letter sent six days after a fatal accident seeking preservation of the tractor-trailer allegedly at fault, and another request eighteen days after the accident for preservation of driving records and on-board electronic tracking devices were specific as to evidence requested and put defendant on notice that litigation was imminent.[29]

Can broad or overly inclusive preservation letters successfully trigger a pre-litigation duty to preserve all the information requested? In *Frey v. Gainey Transportation Services, Inc.,*[30] the court declined to impose sanctions on the defendant for failing to preserve evidence demanded by plaintiff in a pre-litigation preservation letter sent fifteen days after the incident giving rise to the claim and ten days before the claim was filed. While the fact that the plaintiff retained counsel should have put defendant on notice that litigation

---

   26.   244 F.R.D. 614, 622–23 (D. Colo. 2007).

   27.   243 F.R.D. 248, 250, 252 (E.D. Va. 2007).

   28.   *Cache La Poudre Feeds, LLC v. Land O'Lakes, Inc.,* 244 F.R.D. 614, 623 (D. Colo. 2007).

   29.   *See Garrett v. Albright,* No. 06–4137, 2008 WL 681766, at *2 n.5, *3 (W.D. Mo. Mar. 6, 2008).

   30.   No. 05–1493, 2006 WL 2443787 (N.D. Ga. Aug. 22, 2006).

was at least a "possibility," the court noted that compliance with the fifteen-page demand letter would have required defendant to preserve virtually all business records and would have exceeded allowable discovery under the Federal Rules of Civil Procedure.

If the preservation request is too narrow, does the receiving party have a duty to preserve relevant evidence not mentioned in the letter by the sender? In *Healthcare Advocates, Inc. v. Harding, Earley, Follmer & Frailey*,[31] the court rejected plaintiff's assertion that defendant had notice of its duty to preserve temporary cached files containing website screen shots when the plaintiff sent a post-filing subpoena seeking production of computers and *copies* of archived screen shots, requesting that nothing be deleted or altered on the computers, and notifying defendant that its actions in accessing archived copies of plaintiff's web pages may have violated federal law. The court noted that the defendant had preserved the copies and was not under a duty to preserve the cached files since the letter said nothing about preserving the temporary cached files on the computers. Moreover, the court noted that defendant could not have reasonably understood the letter to impose such a duty when defendant had never saved the cached files to the computers' hard drives.

What if the recipient of the preservation letter, but not the sender, knows of the existence of other relevant evidence not requested by the letter? Is the duty to preserve triggered? Suppose ABC Corp. receives a pre-suit preservation letter from a putative plaintiff's counsel making clear he will bring a suit under the Age Discrimination in Employment Act, claiming the company's recent implementation of a reduction in force ("RIF") plan was designed to eliminate older and more costly employees from the workforce and replace them with younger employees. The letter specifically demands that ABC Corp. preserve data held or generated by six persons, mentioned by name: the two human resources staff who implemented and managed the RIF and who now manage the hiring process; two top executives who ordered the plan; the outside consultant who designed the plan; and plaintiff's manager who fired him. Plaintiff is unaware, however, that another ABC Corp. employee generated and now maintains a database, model, and results of a statistical analysis of the impact of the RIF by age, gender, and race.

Does the letter, which does not request preservation of that data or mention the employee by name, impose on ABC Corp. a duty to preserve data held by that employee? What if the relevance of the unrequested data was more ambiguous? What result then? Is there, or should there be, a duty to inquire as to what other data not mentioned in a preservation letter might be relevant to the claim?

d. Closely Related Proceedings

Closely related investigations or proceedings involving similar facts and claims can also provide pre-filing constructive notice of future litigation. In *Zubulake*, the court identified the trigger date as the day on which the

---

31. 497 F. Supp. 2d 627 (E.D. Pa. 2007).

plaintiff's discrimination complaint was first filed with the Equal Employment Opportunity Commission ("EEOC"). An EEOC complaint at least provides the possibility of a civil suit and clearly puts an employer on notice that either a suit by the federal government or the complainant is likely to follow.

3. Application to a Hypothetical Scenario

Assume the following hypothetical scenario: An employee shouts at the supervisor, "I can't take your abuse any longer! I'm quitting, and I will sue you and the company. You'll be hearing from my lawyer!" The disgruntled employee then marches off the company premises.

a. The Defendant Employer

Is the employer now on notice of a potential litigation? Should the employer now reasonably anticipate litigation? Is litigation pending, imminent or reasonably foreseeable? Has the duty to preserve relevant ESI been triggered? The answer to this question has very serious implications. If the company decides that the above event has in fact given rise to a preservation duty, a series of significant and costly events will occur. The legal department must put into effect a litigation hold to preserve relevant data throughout the company. To do this, the company's lawyers or management will likely meet with retained counsel and then interview the pertinent witnesses about the underlying event to determine the employee's likely claims and the company's defenses. The next step is to determine what data is relevant to the claims and defenses and the multitude of locations where that data may be stored. In short, the determination of whether a triggering event has occurred has huge consequences. A "yes" answer entails significant work and expense. A "no" answer runs the risk of being second guessed years later after data has been lost.

The easy answer would be to preserve data under almost all circumstances. However, counsel cannot play it safe by preserving data every time there is a disagreement or conflict. Almost all disagreements and conflicts are resolved far short of litigation and, from a practical perspective, the cost and effort to preserve all data for every such instance would cripple large corporations that are almost always involved in litigation.

Regarding our disgruntled employee, would the answers to these questions be important to know?

1. How long has the employee worked for the company?

2. Has the employee ever brought a claim against the company or a previous employer?

3. Has the employee walked off the job on other occasions?

4. What were the employee's performance reviews?

5. Has the supervisor had other employees walk off the job?

6. Has the company received a letter threatening litigation from an attorney representing the employee?

7. Does the employee have a colorable claim?

8. What additional questions would **you** suggest?

Add at least five more questions that you think would be helpful in reaching a decision as to whether a duty to preserve is triggered.

b. The Plaintiff Employee

At some point prior to the day the lawsuit is filed, the plaintiff had come to a decision that litigation was likely. At what point must he put a litigation hold in place? Suppose that our disgruntled employee heads home after work and proceeds to draft a message to a Facebook group describing the events at work and seeking advice as to whether he should consult an attorney. Has a duty already arisen requiring him to preserve this message and all other e-mails along with postings to wikis, blogs, and other Internet locations, even before meeting with potential counsel?

If so, what is the scope of the preservation duty? Will the disgruntled employee be seeking compensation for his emotional pain and suffering? If so, is there an immediate duty to preserve all ESI reflecting on the quality of the disgruntled employee's daily activities? Additionally, what is the reach of such a preservation duty? Must the disgruntled employee request that his friends preserve their electronic data that may be relevant to his claims?

PROBLEM

Which of the following factors gives rise to a duty to preserve ESI?

A. The company receives a letter demanding preservation of data and enclosing a copy of a draft complaint.

B. The filing of a suit where the company is alleged to be a co-conspirator.

C. The receipt of a form letter from an attorney alleging a client slipped and fell on the company's premises and threatening a class action unless the matter is quickly settled for $10,000.

D. The filing of an employment discrimination charge with the State Human Rights Commission.

E. A letter to the local Better Business Bureau by a consumer alleging poor service and refusal to accept return of a defective product.

F. A computer hacker has hacked into the medical billing department of a hospital and obtained social security, date of birth, home address and credit card information for hospital patients.

G. An accounting firm reads in the paper that one of its clients is being investigated by the SEC for improperly valuing some of its assets in its financial disclosures.

H. An anonymous post on an internet service provider's online message board defames someone.

D. WHAT RECORDS MUST BE PRE-SERVED? ACCESSIBLE AND NOT REASONABLY ACCESSIBLE ESI

ZUBULAKE v. UBS WARBURG LLC "*ZUBULAKE IV*"

220 F.R.D. 212 (S.D.N.Y. 2003)

SCHEINDLIN, DISTRICT JUDGE

Editor's Note: This case is set forth in Chapter II.C, *supra*. On the question of accessible and inaccessible data, the court provided the following analysis:

A party or anticipated party must retain all relevant documents (but not multiple identical copies) in existence at the time the duty to preserve attaches, and any relevant documents created thereafter. In recognition of the fact that there are many ways to manage electronic data, litigants are free to choose how this task is accomplished. For example, a litigant could choose to retain all then-existing backup tapes for the relevant personnel (if such tapes store data by individual or the contents can be identified in good faith and through reasonable effort), and to catalog any later-created documents in a separate electronic file. That, along with a mirror-image of the computer system taken at the time the duty to preserve attaches (to preserve documents in the state they existed at that time), creates a complete set of relevant documents. Presumably there are a multitude of other ways to achieve the same result.

* * *

The scope of a party's preservation obligation can be described as follows: Once a party reasonably anticipates litigation, it must suspend its routine document retention/destruction policy and put in place a "litigation hold" to ensure the preservation of relevant documents. As a general rule, that litigation hold does not apply to inaccessible backup tapes (*e.g.*, those typically maintained solely for the purpose of disaster recovery), which may continue to be recycled on the schedule set forth in the company's policy. On the other hand, if backup tapes are accessible (*i.e.*, actively used for information retrieval), then such tapes *would* likely be subject to the litigation hold.

However, it does make sense to create one exception to this general rule. If a company can identify where particular employee documents are stored on backup tapes, then the tapes storing the documents of "key players" to the existing or threatened litigation should be preserved if the information contained on those tapes is not otherwise available. This exception applies to *all* backup tapes.

1.   What ESI Must Be Preserved?

Zubulake IV makes clear that the duty to preserve applies to *all relevant* information, including ESI, in the possession, custody or control of a party regardless of where it is located. Given that ESI is involved in virtually every aspect of daily communications, a broad interpretation of that duty could require preservation of extensive amounts of data. One court defined the types of relevant data that may be covered by a preservation obligation:

> "Documents, data, and tangible things" shall be interpreted broadly to include writings, records, files, correspondence, reports, memoranda, calendars, diaries, minutes, electronic messages, voice mail, E-mail, telephone message records or logs, computer and network activity logs, hard drives, backup data, removable computer storage media such as tapes, discs and cards, printouts, document image files, Web pages, databases, spreadsheets, software, books, ledgers, journals, orders, invoices, bills, vouchers, check statements, worksheets, summaries, compilations, computations, charts, diagrams, graphic presentations, drawings, films, charts, digital or chemical process photographs, video, phonographic, tape or digital recordings or transcripts thereof, drafts, jottings and notes, studies or drafts of studies or other similar such material. Information that serves to identify, locate, or link such material, such as file inventories, file folders, indices, and metadata, is also included in this definition.[32]

But there are some limitations on the scope of the duty to preserve: it does not include "every shred of paper, every e-mail or electronic document, and every backup tape."[33]

The degree to which ESI is "accessible" bears on the preservation obligation. *Zubulake IV* held that ESI that is "not reasonably accessible" must be preserved only if the ESI is relevant to the litigation and is not available on a more accessible source.

Zubulake IV noted that backup tapes that are routinely used for information retrieval would be considered reasonably accessible; only those used solely for disaster recovery purposes would generally be considered "not reasonably accessible." Why might backup tapes used *only* to restore a system be considered inaccessible? In part, because "by their nature [backup tapes are] indiscriminate.... They capture all information at a given time and from a given server but do not catalogue it by subject matter."[34] Backup tape systems not designed for routine retrieval are far less "readily usable." Parties thus need not suspend their normal systems for overwriting disaster recovery tapes even when they are aware the preservation duty has been triggered unless they know, or should know, that the ESI contained on them

---

32. *In re Flash Memory Antitrust Litig.,* No. C–07–00086, 2008 WL 1831668, at *1 (N.D. Cal. Apr. 22, 2008).

33. *Zubulake IV,* 220 F.R.D. at 212.

34. *McPeek v. Ashcroft,* 202 F.R.D. 31, 33 (D.D.C. 2001).

are potentially relevant to the claim and that those data are non-duplicative of other accessible information.[35]

2. Is Mere Relevance Enough to Trigger the Duty to Preserve Not Reasonably Accessible ESI?

Under *Zubulake IV*, all *relevant* ESI, even if inaccessible, must be preserved regardless of cost, if the information is not available in another accessible form. The Federal Rules of Civil Procedure likewise suggest that the mere fact of inaccessibility does not relieve a party of its preservation obligation.[36] Other courts have taken a contrary view, finding the preservation duty does not cover inaccessible ESI regardless of its relevance to potential litigation.[37]

If mere relevance triggers the duty to preserve inaccessible ESI, how do parties determine whether the information is relevant? Evaluating preservation obligations based on relevance poses particular difficulties for parties at the pre-litigation stage before parties have had the opportunity to meet and confer on preservation issues. How should parties assess *ex ante* the potential relevance of ESI before a claim has been filed? How would an *ex ante* assessment of relevance differ from an *ex post* assessment? Pre-litigation assessment necessarily depends on what the party knew or should have known about the potential claim before it was filed.[38]

Should there be a requirement for *heightened* relevance before parties are required to preserve inaccessible ESI? Must the ESI be particularly relevant to the litigation to justify costs and burdens of preserving inaccessible ESI?[39] In *Best Buy Stores L.P. v. Developers Diversified Realty Corp.*,[40] defendants sought sanctions where the plaintiff downgraded a once accessible database into an inaccessible format. The court rejected sanctions in the absence of a

---

35. *See Zubulake IV*, 220 F.R.D. at 218.

36. *See* Fed. R. Civ. P. 26(b)(2)(B), 2006 Advisory Committee Note ("[a] party's identification of sources of electronically stored information as not reasonably accessible does not relieve the party of its common-law or statutory duties to preserve evidence"); Fed. R. Civ. P. 37(e), 2006 Advisory Committee Note (parties may not "exploit the routine operation of an information system to thwart discovery obligations by allowing that operation to continue in order to destroy specific stored information that it is required to preserve").

37. *See Oxford House, Inc. v. City of Topeka*, No. 06–4004, 2007 WL 1246200 (D. Kan. Apr. 27, 2007) (noting that even if backup tapes contained relevant e-mails that had been deleted from the server and were unavailable elsewhere, there was no duty to prevent the tapes from being overwritten because they were used only for disaster recovery purposes).

38. *See, e.g., Healthcare Advocates v. Harding, Earley, Follmer & Frailey*, 497 F. Supp. 2d 627, 640–41 (E.D. Pa. 2007) (finding no duty to preserve temporary cache files of web page screenshots when party could not have reasonably known electronic files would be relevant to future litigation and copies of screenshots had been preserved); *In re Kmart Corp.*, 371 B.R. 823, 848–49 (N.D. Ill. 2007) (declining to impose sanctions where plaintiff "failed to establish that [defendant] knew there was relevant, discoverable information among the documents being destroyed pursuant to the company's preexisting document retention/destruction policy"); *Hansen v. Dean Witter Reynolds Inc.*, 887 F.Supp. 669, 676 (S.D.N.Y. 1995) (declining to impose sanctions for failing to preserve information regarding quantity of employee's output in employment discrimination claim where employer was on notice that performance would be relevant to potential litigation but quality, not quantity, was basis for performance assessments).

39. *See* Sedona Principle 9 ("[a]bsent a showing of *special need and relevance* a responding party should not be required to *preserve*, review, or produce deleted, shadowed, fragmented, or residual" ESI).

40. 247 F.R.D. 567, 570 (D. Minn. 2007).

showing that the database was of "particular relevance to this litigation," noting that because of the breadth and nature of the information in the database, it would have been "relevant to virtually any litigation involving [the plaintiff]."

3.   Should the Costs of Preserving Not Reasonably Accessible ESI Bear on the Duty to Preserve It?

Should potential relevance be weighed against the costs of preserving inaccessible ESI? In *McPeek v. Ashcroft*, the court relied upon the concept of the "marginal utility" of the ESI when considering production obligations for relevant but inaccessible information stored on backup tapes.[41] Noting that it would be impossible to know in advance what information might be on the tapes, the court weighed the "theoretical possibility" that the backup tapes would contain information relevant to the claim against the high financial and human resource costs of restoring the tapes. In *McPeek*, the Department of Justice was the defendant; thus, the court expressed concern that the time and cost of recovery would detract from the agency's other responsibilities. For courts that consider costs relative to the possible relevance of the information, how much might the limited resources and nature of the parties affect courts' evaluation of whether there was a duty to preserve relevant, non-duplicative, inaccessible ESI? While *McPeek* involved production obligations and who should bear the costs of restoration, what does the court's approach suggest about how parties' might evaluate their preservation obligations?

An approach incorporating the costs of preservation would require parties to first identify potentially relevant ESI and the sources on which it might be located, assess the likelihood that relevant information may actually be stored on those sources, evaluate the degree to which the information is accessible, and determine whether duplicate copies exist. If accessible duplicates are not available, *Zubulake* suggests the party must preserve them even if they are stored on inaccessible sources. If relevance of inaccessible ESI, rather than cost of preservation, were the only consideration, what might be the implications for large corporations that are routinely sued for a range of claims? Would they have an ongoing duty to preserve virtually all inaccessible ESI?[42]

If cost becomes a factor in evaluating the preservation obligation for not reasonably accessible ESI, *what* costs should be considered: The costs of ongoing preservation only, or both preservation costs and recovery costs that would be incurred should the inaccessible ESI later be requested in discovery? If future restoration costs are a permissible consideration in the initial preservation decision, does a decision *not* to preserve based on future restoration costs deprive a requesting party of its ability to later discover relevant ESI even when it is willing to bear recovery costs?

Which is the preferable approach: a preservation duty for inaccessible ESI based on relevance alone or a test balancing preservation costs with the value

---

41.   202 F.R.D. 31, 34 (D.D.C. 2001).

42.   *See Concord Boat Corp. v. Brunswick Corp.*, No. C–95–781, 1997 WL 33352759, at *1 (E.D. Ark. Aug. 29, 1997) (holding that a corporation was not under a duty to preserve relevant e-mails before the complaint was filed because such a duty would require the party to preserve all e-mails on the theory that most might someday be relevant to litigation).

or relevance of the information? For defendants? For plaintiffs? Who is likely to know more about what information may be relevant before a claim is filed? Who is more likely to know where relevant information is stored?

4. What Impact, if Any, Should the Size of the Claim Have on the Scope of the Preservation Duty for Not Reasonably Accessible ESI?

Consider the following scenario: Assume that Jane sues her employer for wrongful termination, a claim to which e-mail and other ESI are relevant. Jane's salary was $20,000 per year. The cost of preserving active data stores is $500. The cost of preserving backup tapes on which relevant ESI may be stored is $15,000. Shortly after Jane was fired, the employer upgraded its database. The cost of preserving the legacy database, which likely contains information relevant to whether Jane received disparate treatment relative to other similarly situated employees, is $50,000. Considering these costs, which of these data stores must the employer preserve to meet its preservation obligations? Does the relatively small amount of damages that Jane might recover mitigate the scope of the preservation duty? If the size of the claim is taken into account, what might be the implications for a claimant who seeks monetary relief that is small in the context of corporate budgets but significant to the claimant in light of his or her income and resources?

5. Does Downgrading ESI From an Accessible to an Inaccessible Format Violate the Preservation Duty?

Nf information is reasonably accessible at the time the preservation duty was triggered, what obligation do parties have to maintain that information on the accessible storage media?

The court in *Best Buy Stores L.P. v. Developers Diversified Realty Corp.* recently considered this question.[43] Plaintiff had developed a database for use in unrelated litigation. Although at the time discovery in the pending case was underway, the database was intact and searchable, it was later downgraded by storing the original data from which the database was created on difficult-to-search backup tapes—storage media generally considered to be not reasonably accessible. The court held that the plaintiff did not have a duty to maintain the data in an accessible form because, in part, preservation costs would have exceeded $27,000 per month.

A similar question was at issue in *Quinby v. WestLB AG*.[44] There, the court declined to impose sanctions on a defendant that downgraded relevant e-mails from an accessible to inaccessible format well after it had notice of potential litigation because it found the preservation duty does not include "a duty to keep the data in an accessible format." In a later decision, however, the court required defendant to bear the recovery costs since it chose to downgrade ESI it should have known would be relevant to later litigation.[45] The court in *Treppel v. Biovail* reached a contrary conclusion.[46]

---

43. 247 F.R.D. 567, 569–71 (D. Minn. 2007).

44. No. 04 Civ. 7406, 2005 WL 3453908 (S.D.N.Y. Dec. 15, 2005).

45. *See Quinby v. WestLB AG*, 245 F.R.D. 94, 111 (S.D.N.Y. 2006).

46. 233 F.R.D. 363, 372 n.4 (S.D.N.Y. 2006) (finding that "permitting the downgrading of data to a less accessible form—which systematically hinders future discovery by making the recovery of the information more costly and burdensome—is a violation of the preservation obligation").

Are there other factors that should be considered when determining whether downgrading of accessible, relevant information is a violation of the preservation duty? Should it matter if such downgrading was, or was not, a routine business practice?

6. Does the Duty to Preserve Include Metadata Embedded in ESI?

Metadata is information about a particular data set which describes "how, when and by whom it was collected, created, accessed, modified and how it was formatted."[47] Converting a file from its original, or "native," format—the form in which the file was created—into an image file, such as Adobe Portable Document Format ("PDF") or Tagged Image File Format ("TIFF"), strips the metadata, providing only a static image of the document. In addition, "stripping" technology exists to scrub documents of their metadata without converting them into another format. Some ESI, such as databases and spreadsheets created using formulae and linked data sources, cannot be stripped of metadata without losing substantial information.

Does the duty to preserve relevant ESI include preservation of documents in their native format? Metadata in the production context may provide valuable information. Rule 34 requires that documents be produced "as they are kept in the usual course of business" and, unless otherwise specified by the requesting party, in the "form . . . in which [they are] ordinarily maintained or in a reasonably usable form."[48] The 2006 Advisory Committee Note to Rule 34 illustrates the Rule's intent:

> [T]he option to produce in a reasonably usable form does not mean that a responding party is free to convert [ESI] from the form in which it is ordinarily maintained to a different form that makes it more difficult or burdensome for the requesting party to use the information efficiently in the litigation. If the responding party ordinarily maintains the information it is producing in a way that makes it searchable by electronic means, the information should not be produced in a form that removes or significantly degrades this feature.

This commentary suggests that metadata may not be stripped if it makes the documents less useful or less searchable. But the Sedona Principles provide a different interpretation:

> The form in which [ESI] is "ordinarily maintained" is not necessarily synonymous with the form in which it was created. There are occasions when business considerations involve the migration or transfer of [ESI] to other applications or systems. . . . Absent an attempt to deliberately downgrade capabilities or characteristics for the purposes of avoiding obligations during specific litigation, migration to alternative forms for business purposes is not considered inconsistent with preservation obligations.

Do you agree that Rule 34's wording suggests there is no preservation obligation to *maintain* ESI in the form in which it was originally *created*?

---

47. *The Sedona Conference® Glossary: E–Discovery & Digital Information Management* 33 (2d ed. 2007).

48. Fed. R. Civ. P. 34(b)(2)(E)(i).

Does Rule 34 suggest that metadata can be stripped from the original document format if doing so was consistent with normal preservation practices, even if the metadata were particularly relevant? Should stripping metadata be impermissible only if the purpose of doing so is to avoid discovery obligations? And if Rule 34 *does* imply an obligation to *produce* files in their native format, what does it suggest about the duty to *preserve* files in that format?

Metadata can be valuable because it provides information directly relevant to the claim, may help authenticate a document, and may aid in document management. For example, metadata may be directly relevant to a copyright infringement claim because it can demonstrate who copied, accessed or modified a file. However, one court asserted that "[m]ost metadata is of limited evidentiary value, and reviewing it can waste litigation resources."[49] What if the *only* value of the metadata is its ability to aid in document management during the litigation—that is, it provides no *substantive* information, but the embedded data allow very large quantities of ESI to be easily grouped and searched? Can preserving and producing otherwise irrelevant metadata conserve litigation resources?

In *In re Payment Card Interchange Fee & Merchant Discount Antitrust Litigation*, defendants objected to plaintiffs' production of relevant e-mails in TIFF format because it degraded their searchability, even though, if subject to optical character recognition, the TIFFs would be searchable. The court required plaintiffs, going forward, to produce e-mails in their native format, finding that the conversion to TIFF ran "afoul of the Advisory Committee's proviso that data ordinarily kept in electronically searchable form should not be produced in a form that removes or significantly degrades this feature."[50] Should metadata that is itself irrelevant to the claim but which aids in document management be preserved? If metadata can be used by the producing party to search for documents, but need not be preserved for the requesting party, what disadvantages might the requesting party face? Given that metadata may have inherent value to searchability and document authenticity, should there be a rebuttable presumption that metadata are relevant even when the metadata itself provide no substantive information that directly relates to the claims or defenses?

Some courts have issued preservation orders that explicitly include metadata among the categories of ESI that parties must preserve, or have required preservation of electronic documents in their native format.[51] In *Hagenbuch v. 3B6 Sistemi Elettronici Industriali S.R.L.*, the court rejected defendant's argument that TIFF documents provided all the relevant information plaintiff needed, holding the metadata will "allow [plaintiff] to piece together the chronology of events and figure out, among other things, who received what

---

49. *Wyeth v. Impax Labs., Inc.*, 248 F.R.D. 169, 171 (D. Del. 2006) (citing *Shirley Williams v. Sprint/United Mgmt. Co.*, 230 F.R.D. 640, 646 (D. Kan. 2005)). This case is found at Chapter V.D, *infra*.

50. No. 05–1720, 2007 WL 121426, at *4 (E.D.N.Y. Jan. 12, 2007).

51. *See In re Flash Memory Antitrust Litig.*, No. C–07–00086, 2008 WL 1831668, at *1 (N.D. Cal. Apr. 22, 2008) (reminding parties of obligation to preserve relevant documents, including "information that serves to identify, locate, or link such material ... such as metadata").

information and when."[52] By contrast, the court in *Wyeth v. Impax Laboratories, Inc.* held that since the requesting party did not specifically ask for metadata to be produced, the producing party could properly produce only static image files.[53]

Do these production decisions and the discovery obligations created under Rule 34 create an inference that the scope of the preservation duty includes preservation of documents in their native format with metadata intact, independent of any court preservation order? If parties have an obligation to produce documents in their native format, do they have an obligation to preserve them in that format?

E.   DOES ESI INCLUDE EPHEMERAL DATA?[54]

Commentary

1.   Does the Scope of the Duty to Preserve Include Relevant But Ephemeral Data?

Transitory or ephemeral data pose particular difficulties for parties considering the scope of their preservation obligation. Ephemeral data has been defined as "data not to be stored for any length of time beyond their operational use and . . . susceptible to being overwritten at any point during the routine operation of the information system."[55] Temporary cache files of web pages visited present the classic example of ephemeral data: users surf the web, web pages are temporarily cached on their computers to allow the web page to load quickly when it is next accessed, and then overwritten as the cache storage fills up. Many other forms of transitory data exist.

How should parties treat ephemeral data when their preservation duty arises? The Sedona Principles suggest that courts should not require extraordinary efforts to preserve "particularly transitory" electronically stored information.

To date courts have not sanctioned parties for failing to preserve ephemeral data. A key question for courts considering the issue may be whether ephemeral data is actually "stored" in any meaningful sense. Most courts have generally not found a duty to preserve ephemeral data. For example, in *Healthcare Advocates, Inc. v. Harding, Earley, Follmer & Frailey*, the court rejected sanctions on the defendant law firm for failure to preserve temporary cache files of archived web pages accessed through a third-party, public website. Defendant accessed the archived pages in an effort to gather evidence to defend its clients in an unrelated case brought by plaintiffs and preserved

---

52. No. 04 C 3109, 2006 WL 665005, at *3 (N.D. Ill. Mar. 8, 2006).

53. 248 F.R.D. 169, 171 (D. Del. 2006). This case is found at Chapter V.D, *infra*.

54. For a thorough and thoughtful discussion of the need to preserve ephemeral data stored in random access memory (RAM) see *Columbia Pictures Indus. v. Bunnell.*, No. CV 06–1093, 2007 WL 2080419 (C.D. Cal. May 29, 2007), *aff'd*, 245 F.R.D. 443 (C.D. Cal. May 29, 2007) (ordering preservation of server log data in copyright infringement case).

55. Kenneth J. Withers, *"Ephemeral Data" and the Duty to Preserve Discoverable Electronically Stored Information*, 37 U. Balt. L. Rev. 349, 366 (2008).

copies of the pages accessed relevant to that case. The court noted that cache files were not apparently relevant to the pending claim, were deleted automatically, and may have "been lost the second another website was visited."[56]

In *Convolve, Inc. v. Compaq Computer Corp.*,[57] the court rejected sanctions sought for the defendant's failure to preserve data readings on an electronic device used to "tune" computer hard drives, where the data collected from the device were routinely written-over when the next measurement was taken with the device. The court noted that in contrast to e-mail, "the data at issue here [were] ephemeral" and the defendants had no business reason to maintain them as "[t]hey exist[ed] only until the tuning engineer [made] the next adjustment, and then the document change[d]."[58]

One commentator has suggested that courts should consider four factors in deciding whether ephemeral data should be preserved: (1) whether the data are uniquely relevant to the litigation; (2) how the data are ordinarily treated by the party "in the ordinary course of business;" (3) whether preservation imposes excessive costs or burdens relative to the value of the data; and (4) whether technologies exist to preserve the data.[59] Just as ESI's accessibility may depend on evolving technologies that make formerly cost-prohibitive restoration economically viable, any obligation to preserve ephemeral data may depend, in part, on whether technologies exist to preserve it in a non-transitory state, and the costs associated with implementing those technologies.

2.   How Ephemeral Can ESI Be?

Notwithstanding the Magistrate Judge's remark in a footnote in *Columbia Pictures v. Bunnell* that the ruling "should not be read to require litigants in all cases to preserve and produce electronically stored information that is temporarily stored only in RAM,"[60] the decision in *Bunnell* has been criticized as representing a possible judicial expansion of the concept of what constitutes ESI for purposes of triggering legal preservation obligations under the Federal Rules. A number of other courts have also addressed the question of what constitutes ESI.[61]

As of late 2008, the *Columbia Pictures* case remains virtually the only case to require the preservation of ephemeral data in the form of RAM. Interestingly, in a later decision in the case, the court granted plaintiffs'

---

56.   497 F. Supp. 2d 627, 642 (E.D. Pa. 2007).

57.   *See* 223 F.R.D. 162, 177 (S.D.N.Y. 2004). *See also Malletier v. Dooney & Bourke, Inc.*, No. 04 Civ. 5316, 2006 WL 3851151 (S.D.N.Y. Dec. 22, 2006) (rejecting sanctions for failure to preserve purportedly relevant chat room conversations with customers on its website where the defendant did not have a means to preserve the transitory online discussions and it was unlikely the conversations would have provided relevant evidence).

58.   *Convolve, Inc.*, 223 F.R.D. at 177.

59.   *See* Kenneth J. Withers, *"Ephemeral Data" and the Duty to Preserve Discoverable Electronically Stored Information*, 37 U. Balt. L. Rev. 349, 374–77 (2008).

60.   *Columbia Pictures Indus. v. Bunnell*, No. CV 06–1093, 2007 WL 2080419, at *13, n.31 (C.D. Cal. May 29, 2007).

61.   *See, e.g., Healthcare Advocates, Inc. v. Harding, Earley, Follmer & Frailey*, 497 F. Supp. 2d 627 (E.D. Pa. 2007) (Internet cache); *Malletier v. Dooney & Bourke, Inc.*, No. 04 Civ. 5316, 2006 WL 3851151 (S.D.N.Y. Dec. 22, 2006) (chat room conversation); *Convolve Inc.*, 223 F.R.D. at 177 (oscilloscope readings).

motion for terminating sanctions due to defendants' "widespread and systematic efforts to destroy evidence."[62]

F. LITIGATION HOLDS/MONITORING

CACHE LA POUDRE FEEDS, LLC
v. LAND O'LAKES, INC.

244 F.R.D. 614 (D. Colo. 2007)

SHAFFER, MAGISTRATE JUDGE

This Matter comes before the court on Plaintiff Cache La Poudre Feed[s], LLC's Motion for Relief from Discovery Violations * * * committed by Defendants Land O'Lakes, Inc. and Land O'Lakes Farmland Feed LLC (collectively "Defendants" or "Land O'Lakes"). * * *

BACKGROUND

Plaintiff Cache La Poudre Feeds, LLC manufactures and sells animal feed in Colorado. Cache La Poudre claims that since March 1991, it has used its PROFILE trademark and sold PROFILE products in several states. * * * Plaintiff contends that in 2001, more than ten years after Cache La Poudre established rights in its PROFILE mark, Defendants Land O'Lakes, Inc. and Land O'Lakes Farmland Feeds, LLC began using the same trademark to re-brand over 400 of their products and to consolidate 36 brands of animal feed products into one brand, PROFILE. * * *

* * *

The instant case has spawned numerous discovery disputes and hearings.[3] * * * Cache La Poudre contends that relief is warranted based upon Defendants' failure to satisfy their discovery obligations * * *.

ANALYSIS

* * * Courts now face the challenge of overseeing discovery at a time when potential access to electronically stored information is virtually limitless, and when the costs and burdens associated with full discovery could be more outcome-determinative, as a practical matter, than the facts and substantive law. * * * Commentators have proposed practices and standards for discovery that reflect the explosion in electronic documents and data. See, e.g., *The Sedona Principles: Best Practices, Recommendations & Principles for Addressing Electronic Document Production* (Sedona Conference Working Group Series July 2005) [hereinafter The Sedona

---

62. *Columbia Pictures, Inc. v. Bunnell*, No. CV06–1093, 2007 WL 4877701, at *8 (C.D. Cal. Dec. 13, 2007).

3. Both sides have engaged in discovery conduct that unnecessarily protracted the litigation and increased its attendant costs for all parties. The unnecessarily rancorous tone of counsels' rhetoric, both in writing and during court hearings, has only exacerbated the situation and hindered the parties' ability to find a reasonable solution to their discovery disputes.

Principles]. The instant motion requires the court to grapple with many of these same issues.

I. Land O'Lakes' Alleged Destruction of Relevant Documents

Plaintiff's motion accuses Defendants of spoliation, based on Land O'Lakes' failure to discontinue its practice after April 2002 of routinely eliminating e-mail and overwriting backup electronic media. Cache La Poudre insists that by allowing these practices to continue, Land O'Lakes destroyed relevant and otherwise discoverable e-mails and other electronic information, thereby insuring that this material would not be available through discovery.

To ensure that the expansive discovery permitted by Rule 26(b)(1) does not become a futile exercise, putative litigants have a duty to preserve documents that may be relevant to pending or imminent litigation. See *Zubulake v. UBS Warburg, LLC*, 220 F.R.D. 212, 216 (S.D.N.Y. 2003) ("the obligation to preserve evidence arises when the party has notice that the evidence is relevant to litigation or when a party should have known that the evidence may be relevant to future litigation"). "Spoliation" has been defined as "the destruction or significant alteration of evidence, or the failure to preserve property for another's use as evidence in pending or reasonably foreseeable litigation."

* * *

In determining whether sanctions are appropriate, the court must first determine whether the missing documents or materials would be relevant to an issue at trial. If not, then the court's analysis stops there. If the missing documents would be relevant, the court must then decide whether Land O'Lakes was under an obligation to preserve the records at issue. Finally, if such a duty existed, the court must consider what sanction, if any, is appropriate given the non-moving party's degree of culpability, the degree of any prejudice to the moving party, and the purposes to be served by exercising the court's power to sanction.

Land O'Lakes began shipping its PROFILE products nationwide by at least January 2002. It is also undisputed that Land O'Lakes adopted an automatic e-mail destruction program in May 2002. Pursuant to this program, any e-mails older than 90 days would be automatically deleted, even if the e-mail was created before the elimination program was established. The relevance of e-mails and electronically stored information created after 2001 that address the development and implementation of Land O'Lakes' PROFILE brand should be self-evident.

The second prong of the court's analysis, that is Land O'Lakes' duty to preserve, poses greater problems for Cache La Poudre. In most cases, the duty to preserve evidence is triggered by the filing of a lawsuit. However, the obligation to preserve evidence may arise even earlier if a party has notice that future litigation is likely. While a party should not be permitted to destroy potential evidence after receiving unequivocal notice of impending litigation, the duty to preserve relevant documents should require more than a mere possibility of litigation. Ultimately, the court's decision must be guided by the facts of each case.

Here, Plaintiff argues that Defendants "should have and did anticipate legal engagement with Cache La Poudre as early as April 4, 2002." Having carefully reviewed all the exhibits proffered by the parties, I conclude that the record does not persuasively support Plaintiff's position.

It is undisputed that counsel for Cache La Poudre contacted Land O'Lakes' General Counsel, Peter Janzen, by telephone on April 4, 2002. During that conversation, Mr. Janzen apparently was told that an individual in Colorado had been using the phrase "Profile Showcase" as a trademark for animal feeds since 1990. Mr. Janzen was also aware in April 2002 that this same "individual filed an intent to use application in 2000 that was abandoned in 2001 for failure to respond."

On June 5, 2002, Cache La Poudre's outside counsel, Cheryl Anderson–Siler, wrote to Mr. Janzen to follow-up on her April telephone call. In her June 5th letter, Ms. Anderson–Siler stated that Cache La Poudre had been using its PROFILE trademark for at least 10 years and expressed her client's concern over the possibility of confusion for "our respective customers." Ms. Anderson–Siler warned that Land O'Lakes' "very active marketing campaign . . . may present a situation that may become a very serious problem." In closing, Ms. Anderson–Siler explained that the primary purpose of her letter

> is to clearly put [Land O'Lakes] on notice of our client's trademark rights and clearly establish the opportunities we have given Land O'Lakes to avoid exposure. The second purpose of this letter is to determine whether this situation can be resolved without litigation and media exposure . . . We think you will agree that the company's interests are best served by trying to resolve this unfortunate and difficult situation.

Rather than threatening impending litigation, Ms. Anderson–Siler's June 5th letter implied that her client preferred and was willing to explore a negotiated resolution. *Compare Washington Alder LLC v. Weyerhaeuser Co.*, 2004 WL 4076674 (D.Or.2004) (finding that a letter from Washington Alder threatening to sue for antitrust violations put Weyerhaeuser on notice of possible litigation and triggered a duty to preserve documents).

In the wake of these developments, in June 2003, the parties again raised the possibility of a non-litigious resolution. On June 3, 2003, Land O'Lakes' outside counsel contacted Ms. Anderson–Siler to "explore the possibility of obtaining a consent from your client to register" the LAND O'LAKES PROFILE mark for agricultural animal feed. Counsel closed his letter by saying he would "appreciate a call to discuss this possibility and terms." Ms. Anderson–Siler responded by letter on June 17, 2003. Her letter again expressed Cache La Poudre's concern "that Land O'Lakes is continuing to pursue registration of [its] mark as any use of such a mark in the feed industry would be likely to infringe our client's longstanding PROFILE trademark." However, rather than threatening litigation, Ms.

Anderson–Siler indicated her client "would be willing to listen to what Land O'Lakes might propose."

Cache La Poudre initiated legal action against Land O'Lakes on February 24, 2004 with the filing of its initial Complaint. As of that date, Defendants clearly had an obligation to preserve relevant evidence. On March 5, 2004, for the first time, counsel for Cache La Poudre sent a letter to Peter Janzen which specifically put Land O'Lakes on notice to "prevent spoliation, destruction, alteration, modification, concealment, loss, secretion, or removal of evidence by any of the defendants." Plaintiff's letter also notified Defendants that they had an affirmative obligation to maintain and preserve evidence.

This court recognizes that under different circumstances, a demand letter alone may be sufficient to trigger an obligation to preserve evidence and support a subsequent motion for spoliation sanctions. However, such a letter must be more explicit and less equivocal than Cache La Poudre's 2002 and 2003 correspondence with Land O'Lakes. In this case, Land O'Lakes had been selling under its PROFILE brand for several months before Ms. Anderson–Siler sent her first letter to Mr. Janzen. Although Ms. Anderson–Siler noted the potential for customer confusion and alluded to Land O'Lakes' possible "exposure," her letter did not threaten litigation and did not demand that Land O'Lakes preserve potentially relevant materials. Rather, Cache La Poudre hinted at the possibility of a non-litigious resolution. Ms. Anderson–Siler's correspondence with Land O'Lakes' outside counsel in June 2003 was no more emphatic or explicit in raising the prospect of litigation. Ms. Anderson–Siler's correspondence in 2003 also did not include a demand for preservation of evidence. Given the dynamic nature of electronically stored information, prudent counsel would be wise to ensure that a demand letter sent to a putative party also addresses any contemporaneous preservation obligations.

In fact, Cache La Poudre waited nearly two years after Anderson–Siler's April 4, 2002 telephone conference with Peter Janzen to bring the instant lawsuit. That delay, coupled with the less-than adamant tone of Cache La Poudre's letters belies Plaintiff's contention that Land O'Lakes should have anticipated litigation as early as April 4, 2002, and therefore had a duty to preserve evidence as of that date. I acknowledge that the common-law obligation to preserve relevant material is not necessarily dependent upon the tender of a "preservation letter." However, a party's duty to preserve evidence in advance of litigation must be predicated on something more than an equivocal statement of discontent, particularly when that discontent does not crystalize into litigation for nearly two years. Any other conclusion would confront a putative litigant with an intractable dilemma: either preserve voluminous records for a indefinite period at potentially great expense, or continue routine document management practices and risk a spoliation claim at some point in the future.

Plaintiff has described Land O'Lakes as a "$6 Billion dollar conglomerated entity," with no less than 40 local file servers at its main business office, and additional file servers at other business locations. According to Land O'Lakes' current Director of Technology Services, since 2002 Land O'Lakes has managed over 400 servers, each of which is backed up on a daily basis, weekly for five weeks, monthly for a year, and annually forever. Recently enacted amendments to the Federal Rules of Civil Procedure recognize that suspending or interrupting automatic features of electronic information systems can be prohibitively expensive and burdensome.

> [I]t is unrealistic to expect parties to stop such routine operation of their computer systems as soon as they anticipate litigation. It is also undesirable; the result would be even greater accumulation of duplicative and irrelevant data that must be reviewed, making discovery more expensive and time consuming.

See May 27, 2006 Report of the Advisory Committee on the Federal Rules of Civil Procedure, at 71. Under the particular facts of this case, this court finds that Defendants' duty to preserve evidence was triggered by the filing of Plaintiff's Complaint on February 24, 2004. Accordingly, Cache La Poudre's request for spoliation sanctions predicated on actions or omissions that occurred before that date is denied.

II.   Land O'Lakes' Alleged Post–Filing Discovery Misconduct

After February 24, 2004, Defendants unquestionably had an obligation to preserve and produce non-privileged materials responsive to properly framed discovery requests. Land O'Lakes insists that it fully complied with this obligation, by conducting a reasonable inquiry to find responsive documents based upon its understanding of where such documents and information could be located. In response to Cache La Poudre's discovery requests, Defendants claim to have produced over 50,000 pages of documents, including 415 e-mails related to PROFILE, and compact disks containing relevant data regarding PROFILE products.

Land O'Lakes claims to have imposed a litigation hold within a matter of days after Plaintiff filed the instant lawsuit. Defendants insist that this litigation hold prevented the destruction of any electronic documents in existence as of that date, as well as any subsequently produced electronic documents. Land O'Lakes employees "understood that they were to save any document that currently existed on their system, as well as in their files." Land O'Lakes looked for electronic documents in the possession of current employees, and printed versions of electronic documents generated by employees who left the company after February 2004. No attempt was made to find electronic versions of documents prepared by departed employees because attorneys involved in the discovery process were under the impression that those materials no longer existed in electronic form since information systems personnel routinely cleaned an employee's computer hard drive after they left the company.

* * * [W]hen Land O'Lakes received a request for production in this case * * * [current] employees who were involved in creating and marketing the PROFILE brand were asked to check for responsive materials, including paper documents, e-mails and compact disks. These materials were then turned over to outside counsel to be reviewed for relevancy. As additional requests came in, Land O'Lakes expanded its inquiry to include individuals who might have materials responsive to those particular requests. Janzen [General Counsel for the defendant] claims that he confirmed that Land O'Lakes employees understood that they were to produce all materials relating to the PROFILE litigation, and then reconfirmed that employees had produced all the required materials. However, Janzen acknowledged that he relied on the employees' ability to locate responsive documents and gave each employee the discretion to identify documents that "related to the litigation." Mr. Janzen and outside counsel simply accepted whatever materials employees provided.

Land O'Lakes concedes that it never reviewed information contained on backup tapes in identifying and producing responsive materials. * * * Land O'Lakes has approximately 400 backup tapes for the years 2001–2005. When he was deposed, Mr. Janzen testified that he understood that "backup tape is kept for ten days and then written over" and that Land O'Lakes does not have backup tapes for the computer hard drives used by former employees. Apparently, Mr. Janzen was not aware that Land O'Lakes also has monthly and annual backup tapes. Mr. Janzen concluded that it was unnecessary to review backup tapes because he believed that any documents on the backup tapes relevant to this litigation could also be found in another more readily accessible location. However, Janzen concedes that Land O'Lakes made no attempt to verify his assumption.

Mr. Janzen testified on June 15, 2006, that no efforts were made to contact former Land O'Lakes employees in the course of identifying and collecting responsive materials. Land O'Lakes apparently never contacted former employees to determine how or where they might have backed up information while they were with the company. To the extent that relevant documents had not been lost when hard drives were wiped clean, Janzen simply assumed that they [were] located on hard drives that were shared with current employees and, as such, would be found through the discovery production process.

Against this backdrop, Plaintiff argues that Land O'Lakes failed to properly discharge its obligation to locate, preserve and produce all relevant, non-privileged materials after February 24, 2004. More particularly, Cache La Poudre insists that after February 24, 2004, Defendants and their counsel failed to make certain that all sources of potentially relevant information were identified and placed "on hold." [The court discusses the factors set forth by Judge Scheindlin concerning the duty to preserve information, in *Zubulake V, supra*]

* * *

Plaintiff * * * argues that Land O'Lakes failed to properly monitor compliance with its discovery obligations by not conducting "systemwide keyword searches." Indeed, Plaintiff contends that Defendants had an "obligation" to undertake such keyword searches. I am not convinced that Judge Scheindlin's opinion in *Zubulake V* should be interpreted so inflexibly. Certainly, "once a 'litigation hold' is in place, a party and her counsel must make certain that all sources of potentially relevant information are identified and placed 'on hold.'" *Zubulake v. UBS Warburg LLC*, 229 F.R.D. at 432. In discharging that responsibility, Judge Scheindlin conceded that it might not be possible for counsel to speak with every key player, and suggested as an alternative that it "[may be] possible to run a systemwide keyword search" to identify responsive materials. I do not interpret Judge Scheindlin's suggestion as establishing an immutable "obligation." To the contrary, in the typical case, "[r]esponding parties are best situated to evaluate the procedures, methodologies, and technologies appropriate for preserving and producing their own electronic data and documents." *See The Sedona Principles*, at 31. To the extent that Plaintiff seeks sanctions based on a perceived "obligation" to conduct keyword searches, I will deny that request.

Plaintiff argues that Defendants failed to become familiar with their own computer system and their document retention policies and architecture. As a result of this shortcoming, Plaintiff believes that Land O'Lakes did not know where to look for relevant information. According to Cache La Poudre, Land O'Lakes or its litigation counsel also "had a duty to take possession or otherwise safeguard backup tapes to eliminate the possibility of inadvertent recycling." It appears that Mr. Janzen did not have a full understanding of his company's computer systems or the process for creating computer back-up tapes. However, Plaintiff's request for relief based on these shortcomings sweeps too broadly.

As noted, counsel for Land O'Lakes was required to undertake a reasonable investigation to identify and preserve relevant materials in the course of responding to Plaintiff's discovery requests. Such an investigation would not automatically include information maintained on computer back-up tapes.[12] "As a general rule, [a] litigation hold does not apply to inaccessible back-up tapes ... which may continue to be recycled on the schedule set forth in the company's policy." *Zubulake v. UBS Warburg LLC*, 229 F.R.D. at 431. As of December 2006, a party responding to discovery requests must identify but need not produce electronically stored information that is not reasonably accessible because of undue burden or cost. See Fed.R.Civ.P. 26(b)(2)(B). One such source of information might be backup tapes containing archived data. Land O'Lakes' Director of Technology Services indicates that Land O'Lakes has approximately 400 back-up tapes for the years 2001 through 2005.

In order to recover a document or file from the backup tapes that contains a specific word, such as "PROFILE," each tape would first have to be restored and then the search conducted. The restoration of each tape

---

12. *Quinby v. WestLB AG*, 2005 WL 3453908, at *7 (S.D.N.Y. 2005) (describing backup computer tapes as "'snapshots' taken at a particular point in time," and suggesting, for example, that "e-mails that are sent or received and then deleted between snapshots will not be captured on back-up tapes").

would take approximately 8 hours per tape, in serial fashion, since there are a limited number of restoration servers. It would therefore take over 3200 man hours just to restore the approximately 400 backup tapes from the last four years. Defendants claim that it would take an additional 800 man hours to search through all restored tapes.

Plaintiff claims that several Land O'Lakes employees involved in the PROFILE project left the company after the lawsuit commenced. * * * According to Plaintiff, Defendants made no attempt to preserve or place a litigation hold on the computer hard drives used by these employees. Mr. Janzen acknowledged that Land O'Lakes continued its practice of expunging the hard drives of former employees even after this litigation commenced. I find that such a procedure, if applied after February 24, 2004 with respect to employees who played a significant or decision-making role in the development and implementation of the PROFILE brand, violated Defendants' obligation to preserve evidence in this case. Cache La Poudre has not established that Defendants intentionally destroyed electronically stored information to deprive Plaintiff of discoverable information. However, the record does demonstrate that Defendants were less than thorough in discharging their duty to implement adequate steps to insure that discoverable information would be preserved.

* * * As Judge Scheindlin acknowledged, "it may not be feasible for counsel to speak with every key player" and unrealistic to presume that counsel will necessarily succeed in identifying and searching all sources of discoverable information. *Zubulake v. UBS Warburg LLC*, 229 F.R.D. at 432. However, counsel cannot turn a blind eye to a procedure that he or she should realize will adversely impact that search. Land O'Lakes directed employees to produce all relevant information, and then relied upon those same employees to exercise their discretion in determining what specific information to save. As Mr. Janzen said repeatedly, he and outside counsel simply accepted whatever documents or information might be produced by Land O'Lakes employees. Yet here, counsel was aware that an accessible source of information (i.e., computer hard drives used by departed employees) was being eliminated as a routine practice, thereby further distancing counsel from the discovery process and his monitoring obligations. By wiping clean the computer hard drives of former employees who worked on the PROFILE project, Land O'Lakes effectively eliminated a readily accessible source of potentially relevant information. This procedure is all the more questionable given Mr. Janzen's understanding that Land O'Lakes did not keep backup tapes for computer hard drives for more than ten days. Once a "litigation hold" has been established, a party cannot continue a routine procedure that effectively ensures that potentially relevant and readily available information is no longer "reasonably accessible" under Rule 26(b)(2)(B).

Finally, Plaintiff insists that Land O'Lakes failed to take affirmative steps to monitor compliance to ensure that all sources of discoverable information were identified and searched. * * *

In this case, Land O'Lakes's General Counsel and retained counsel failed in many respects to discharge their obligations to coordinate and oversee discovery. Admittedly, in-house counsel established a litigation hold shortly after the lawsuit commenced and communicated that fact to Land O'Lakes employees who were believed to possess relevant materials. However, by his own admission, Land O'Lakes' General Counsel took no independent action to verify the completeness of the employees' document production. As Mr. Janzen explained, he simply assumed that the materials he received were complete and the product of a thorough search. While Mr. Janzen presumed that e-mails generated by former employees would be located on shared computer drives utilized by current employees, he made no effort to verify that assumption. Without validating the accuracy and completeness of its discovery production, Land O'Lakes continued its routine practice of wiping clean the computer hard drives for former employees. Under the circumstances and without some showing of a reasonable inquiry, it is difficult to understand how Defendants' retained counsel could legitimately claim on July 7, 2005 [in a letter to the plaintiff] that Land O'Lakes had "made every effort to produce all documentation and provide all relevant information."

While instituting a "litigation hold" may be an important first step in the discovery process, the obligation to conduct a reasonable search for responsive documents continues throughout the litigation. A "litigation hold," without more, will not suffice to satisfy the "reasonable inquiry" requirement in Rule 26(g)(2). Counsel retains an on-going responsibility to take appropriate measures to ensure that the client has provided all available information and documents which are responsive to discovery requests. As the Advisory Committee Notes make clear, "Rule 26(g) imposed an affirmative duty to engage in pretrial discovery in a responsible manner that is consistent with the spirit and purposes of Rules 26 through 37." In this case, I find that Defendants failed to meet this standard.

* * *

IV. Sanctions

* * *

I do not find that Cache La Poudre's ability to litigate its claims has been substantially prejudiced by Defendants' failure to implement and monitor an adequate record preservation program. However, Defendants' failure to preserve potentially relevant and responsive information by wiping clean computer hard drives and counsels' failure to properly monitor the discovery process has interfered with the judicial process. Moreover, Land O'Lakes' failure to fully comply with their discovery obligations has forced Plaintiff to incur additional litigation expenses.

* * *

* * * I conclude that a monetary sanction is appropriate in this case. Cache La Poudre incurred legal expenses in connection with the pending motion that would not have been required had Land O'Lakes and it counsel undertaken a reasonable investigation to identify and preserve relevant materials, and then taken affirmative and effective steps to monitor compliance with discovery obligations. * * * I will require Defendant Land O'Lakes to pay Cache La Poudre the sum of $5,000 to reimburse some of the legal fees and expenses incurred in taking Mr. Janzen's deposition in Minneapolis, Minnesota and preparing the instant Motion for Relief from Discovery Violations. While Plaintiff almost certainly incurred fees and costs of more than $5,000 in having counsel travel to and from Minnesota, attend the Janzen deposition, and prepare a 40–page motion, the court finds that the fees and costs awarded in this Memorandum Order are appropriate under the circumstances of this case and consistent with the objectives under Rule 26(g) and Rule 34. I will also require Defendants to reimburse Plaintiff for court reporter fees and transcript costs associated with the June 15, 2006 deposition of Mark Janzen.

COMMENTARY

ESI presents unique preservation problems because it is a series of electronic impulses that are potentially voluminous and scattered into many storage locations. It is also fragile and easily prone to change and alteration without prompt affirmative preservation. The process to properly preserve this delicate and irreplaceable type of information involves three steps: (1) determining when the duty to preserve arises, (2) determining what data must be preserved, and (3) determining how to assure preservation.

1. What Should an Organization Do After the Duty to Preserve Arises?

The first step after an event triggering preservation is to convene a "claims and defenses" meeting of the company officials and the legal team to determine the case issues. Why address the issues first? Why not go directly to preservation? Not all data can or should be preserved. Even a significant dispute between a company and an important long-standing customer will likely constitute a small fraction of the data and information maintained by a company. The angry employee may be one of thousands of employees. All the data of an on-going business cannot be maintained based on the needs of a single lawsuit.

The claims and defenses assessment meeting will typically include counsel for the company ("in-house counsel"), retained counsel ("outside counsel") and the company management involved in the dispute. The goal of the assessment meeting is to determine the potential plaintiff's claims and the company defenses. Each claim is then assessed with respect to each element that will be at issue if the claim is litigated. The same process should be followed for the company's defenses.

Once the issues are identified, the assessment team (or "e-discovery team") must determine where information related to the issues resides. Most often, this is best accomplished by first determining which employees (or "custodians") generate, receive or otherwise access potentially relevant information. Each custodian will have numerous potential data locations that must be preserved. This is when representatives of the company's IT Department and Records Management Department must join the e-discovery team. Armed with knowledge of the issues and the potential custodians, counsel, company management, records manager, and IT representatives with knowledge of the company's network can begin the process of locating and securing locations that may contain relevant ESI. In some instances, referring to the company's document retention policy will also assist the team in determining where certain kinds of information are located, or whether those sources of information are no longer available.

Next, the e-discovery team must identify those employees with knowledge of the complainant's performance. For example, the e-mail of a co-worker should be preserved if there is reason to believe the e-mails may reflect the work performance of the work group.

2.   How to Preserve Relevant Data?

Counsel must issue a litigation hold notice once a duty to preserve has been determined. This notice is addressed to those persons within the company who are custodians of data locations where relevant data might lie. Here is an example of a litigation hold notice in a case involving the alleged failure to consummate the purchase of goods.

LITIGATION HOLD NOTICE
DIRECTIVE TO CEASE DESTRUCTION OF PAPER
RECORDS AND ELECTRONIC DATA

TO: Distribution List

FROM: General Counsel

DATE:

Defendants have recently been sued in a dispute involving purchase orders and product sold by Plaintiff. We intend to vigorously defend this lawsuit.

The law requires us to take immediate steps to preserve all **paper records** and **electronic data** that is relevant to the litigation. Paper records and electronic data (**including duplicates**) must be preserved at all storage locations including your office computer, home computers, and other portable electronic media such as discs and thumb drives. Failure to preserve all paper records and electronic data may result in legal sanctions.

Please immediately review the following list of **preservation categories** of documents (paper and electronic data) which must be preserved. All electronic data and paper documents including drafts, e-mail negotiations and communications related to or about any of these categories must be preserved.

1.   All documents related to any contract, negotiation, or communication with Plaintiff.

2.   All documents related to contracts and agreements with Plaintiff, including guarantees.

3.   All paper rebates submitted and processed by Defendants related to consumer purchases of Plaintiff's products. All rebate processing data and information stored in any database pertaining to Plaintiff's products.

4.   All financial and accounting records pertaining to Plaintiff.

5.   All notes, memoranda, and spreadsheets related to Plaintiff.

6.   All advertisements and promotions of Plaintiff's products.

7.   All documents and data about customer service pertaining to Plaintiff's products.

8.   All documents and data regarding the receipt of Plaintiff's products.

9.   All shipping and receiving documents and data regarding Plaintiff's products.

10. All returns of Plaintiff's products and all consumer complaints about Plaintiff's products or the quality of Plaintiff's products.

11. All information about the flat screen television market and market pricing of flat screen televisions during 2006 and 2007.

12. All consumer inquiries and complaints about Plaintiff-related rebates.

13. All documents and data about any audit or accounting with respect to Plaintiff rebates.

14. All documents and data about the advertising and promotion of Plaintiff's products.

Please determine immediately whether you have in your possession, custody or control **any paper or electronic data about, concerning, or related to** any of the above preservation categories. Such paper documents or electronic data are called responsive paper documents or electronic data.

Please determine whether any responsive data is located on your laptop or office computer, home computer, Blackberry, PDA, discs, CDs, DVD's, memory sticks, or thumb drives, or any other electronic storage location. Please immediately suspend the deletion (manual or automatic) of relevant electronic data from any location where you believe responsive data may be found.

With respect to paper documents, please check all your office files and home files. Please immediately suspend the destruction of any responsive paper documents.

> If you have any doubts about what paper or electronic data to preserve, please contact me. If you have any responsive paper documents please immediately advise your supervisor. If you have any responsive electronic data held or stored at any location or on any media **other than your office desktop computer or company laptop**, please immediately advise your supervisor.
>
> * * *

* * * The structure of a litigation hold notice is to (1) identify the litigation, (2) specify the parties to the litigation, (3) specifically identify the documents to be preserved, (4) provide a contact point within the Company to answer questions, and (5) provide for a formal verification. Most companies prefer the litigation hold notice to come from the Legal Department.

PROBLEM

You are General Counsel for Quick Feet Athletic Shoes and Clothing Company ("Quick Feet"). Complaining Consumer ("CC") has retained an attorney who has brought a class action complaint against Quick Feet. Quick Feet sells athletic products through its website and at thirty retail locations in malls around the state. Its warehouse is located in Chicago, Illinois. All consumer purchases through its website are shipped to the consumer from the Chicago warehouse by commercial ground service. The Chicago warehouse also supplies all thirty Quick Feet retail locations around the state. You have conducted your claims and defenses assessment with the management team and IT Department. You have learned from your investigation that Quick Feet contracted with three United States-based manufacturing companies to make athletic shoes using an experimental technique utilizing one-half the stitching customarily used in the industry. Using this experimental method allows the athletic shoes to be produced much more quickly than using standard methods. However, your investigation has also shown that athletic shoes manufactured under the one-half stitching method become tattered and unusable within two to three months. You have also learned from your claims and defenses assessment that Quick Feet markets its athletic equipment under the slogans "Your Gear for a Lifetime" and "Wear Me Forever." CC seeks to represent a class of national consumers who have been allegedly victimized by this deceptive and unfair marketing practice of selling inferior products in connection with false advertising claims.

Your team has informed you (1) that Quick Feet utilizes athletic shoe manufacturers that have certified that each uses production methods that meet industry standards, (2) that Quick Feet attaches to each garment a tag containing a warning that the athletic shoes are not defect free, and (3) that Quick Feet sells its athletic shoes at dramatically reduced prices compared to other branded athletic shoes.

Quick Feet maintains its own e-mail, accounting, customer service, and Internet web servers in Philadelphia, Pennsylvania and communicates with its manufacturers by e-mailing its purchase orders. First Florida pays its manufacturers by direct deposit to The USA Bank.

All sales employees at the thirty retail locations are provided laptops. Quick Feet has a data backup rotation where the oldest backup tape is one month old. Quick Feet limits the storage of e-mail inboxes and outboxes to one gigabyte of data per user. Regardless of the volume of e-mails in the inboxes and outboxes, all e-mails are automatically deleted after thirty days.

Prepare a litigation hold notice and separate directions to the IT Department regarding the preservation of data.

Once you have issued the litigation hold notice, your work to preserve relevant data is not over because a litigation hold without more will not satisfy the "reasonable inquiry" requirement in Rule 26(g)(2). As a part of the obligation to preserve relevant documents, legal counsel has the continuing duty to ensure that discoverable information is not lost. Counsel might consider taking the following steps:

- suspending the routine document retention/destruction policy;

- becoming fully aware of the client's document retention policies and data retention architecture;

- communicating with the "key players" in the litigation to understand how they stored information;

- taking reasonable steps to monitor compliance with the litigation hold so that all sources of discoverable information are identified and searched; and

- having identified all sources of potentially relevant information, retaining that information and producing information responsive to the opposing party's requests.

Compliance with a litigation hold is not a simple matter. The purpose of the litigation hold is to notify the recipients of the obligation to preserve data. But a litigation hold notice distributed throughout a company is of little value if it is not followed or implemented.

First, how does counsel assure that the litigation notice has been received and will be implemented by the company employees? Some counsel require a signed certification by the employee that the litigation hold notice has been received, understood and implemented. Here is an example of such a certification or acknowledgment.

Acknowledgment
(Please provide to your immediate supervisor)

I acknowledge I have read the above attached Litigation Hold memorandum. I will forthwith conduct a reasonable search for responsive paper documents and electronic data. I will preserve any such electronic data and paper documents. I will not delete any data from any locations that I believe may contain responsive electronic data. I understand that this preservation request is on-going and requires the continuing preservation of data, including data created or received both before and after receipt of this Notice.

_____

(sign and date)

Is this adequate to assure compliance? What is the Company's exposure if the employee fails to implement the litigation hold directive or does so in a shabby and sloppy manner? How can counsel conduct a reasonable investigation to assure the litigation hold is being implemented? No attorney has yet been faulted or sanctioned by the courts for conducting client document interviews and becoming too knowledgeable of the sources of a client's relevant data, but there are many who have been sanctioned for not doing so.[63]

Other problems associated with compliance and implementation of a litigation hold arise when there is negligence or malfeasance. For example, would it be foreseeable that an employee who has received a litigation hold notice instructing her not to destroy any ESI associated with a particular company deletes e-mail in one folder because she knows the e-mail is retained in a second folder in her inbox or because she understands that the sender of the e-mail has created a special folder that contains the e-mail? The notion that duplicative e-mails and near duplicates of e-mail must be retained is something counsel may grasp but is easily misunderstood by employees. What if the employee prints all the relevant e-mails and then deletes the electronic files? The employee might reasonably think all e-mail has been retained, when, in fact, the deletion constitutes spoliation.

With these concerns in mind, after the delivery and receipt of confirmation of the litigation hold notice, an interview should be scheduled with each custodian to review what data the custodian holds and how it must be preserved. Even if the company's IT representative has already given counsel a detailed description of what sources of company data an employee may use that are relevant to the litigation, the IT representative may have no way of knowing that a particular custodian also maintains company data relevant to the case on a personal computer at home or a portable personal USB drive. With the advent of free and unlimited e-mail storage on internet service providers like Yahoo or AOL, employees may frequently send work e-mails to their personal accounts to get around storage limits imposed on their corporate e-mail accounts. Document collection interviews with key custodians also give counsel the opportunity to confirm that the custodian has understood what is expected, and more importantly, that counsel knows the custodian has taken the time to comply with the litigation hold.

3.   Lifting Litigation Holds

Much time and money is spent on properly implementing and maintaining a legal hold, but little attention is given to lifting a legal hold. A legal hold may be lifted once the litigation is finally resolved, assuming that preserved data is not relevant to any other existing or anticipated litigation. This can be a difficult challenge if a company is simultaneously involved in multiple lawsuits, or is a large company that is constantly engaged in litigation. For example, what if an employee transfers to a different department and now her documents are relevant to more than one lawsuit—when can you lift the litigation hold on her data? What if a company settles a securities class action lawsuit, but the Securities and Exchange Commission is still investigating the company over the same disclosures that were the subject of the class action?

---

63.   *See, e.g.*, *Metropolitan Opera Assoc. v. Local 100*, 212 F.R.D. 178, 221–24 (S.D.N.Y. 2003).

With regard to a litigation hold implemented in anticipation of litigation that never materializes, how long before the hold can be lifted? The decision to lift a litigation hold must be made only after conducting due diligence to ensure that the preserved data set is not relevant to any claims or defenses for other litigation matters, including audits or investigations.

G. PRESERVATION ORDERS

CAPRICORN POWER CO., INC. v. SIEMENS WESTINGHOUSE POWER CORP.

220 F.R.D. 429 (W.D. Pa. 2004)

GIBSON, DISTRICT JUDGE

Synopsis

Both the Defendant and the Plaintiffs have filed motions requesting orders of court that direct the preservation of documents and things. The current case law does not provide a definitive test to apply when deciding such motions. Upon review of the circumstances, and being guided by present law, a three part test is developed and applied by the Court. Under such a test, both motions for an order of preservation are denied.

* * *

Factual/Procedural History

* * *

This matter came to trial before a jury on January 12, 2004 and ended in a mistrial on January 15, 2004. [The case involved a dispute over a purchased generator.] The mistrial was declared because an expert report dated June 23, 2000 was not produced by Plaintiff until January 15, 2004. The expert report was referred to by a witness on January 14, 2004 in the course of a *Daubert* hearing concerning [admissibility of] the expert opinions of Dr. Bagnall and was turned over to counsel for Defendant before the resumption of trial testimony on the morning of January 15, 2004. Prior to beginning testimony on January 15, 2004 the Court heard oral argument from both parties on the Defendant's Motion for Mistrial and subsequently granted the motion, finding that the late production prejudiced the Defendant's case as to the preparation of its expert witnesses, the cross-examination of the Plaintiffs' witnesses, as well as the fact that the expert report "may have a significant impact upon the entire posture and strategy of Defendant's case."

Subsequently, the Defendant moved for the preservation of documents in a motion filed on February 18, 2004 requesting a court order be issued to preserve all relevant material set forth in the subpoena attached to the Defendant's Motion. Based upon the testimony of Dr. Bagnall, the Defendant believes other potential materials exist that would be relevant to its case. Defendant requests an order to "fully secure all of the information gathered by Mr. Bagnall and CTC," and to "properly prepare for filing of dispositive Motions based upon this new evidence." * * *

The Plaintiffs filed their response and a counter-motion on March 9, 2004. Plaintiffs do not object to the Defendant's motion, except to the extent that they believe an order for preservation of material should be issued as to both parties.

* * *

Analysis

The Court notes that orders directing parties to preserve materials or documents are common in circumstances in which evidence is subject to being destroyed or lost in routine and sometimes not-so-routine deletion or destruction of information in various mediums. However, the reported case law concerning standards for deciding such motions is scant.

* * *

Federal Rule of Civil Procedure 34 addresses the production of documents and things and the entry onto land for discovery purposes. Absent from Rule 34 is a procedure to preserve documents, things or land from damage or destruction that could compromise the integrity or the very existence of the evidence requested. Rule 34 does refer the reader to Rule 37, the rule governing the compelling of individuals or entities to produce discovery and accompanying sanctions, when an objection to a request or a failure to respond or permit inspection occurs. Nonetheless, Rule 37 also does not address the situation where potential evidence may be compromised or destroyed.

* * *

While remaining consistent with the Federal Rules of Civil Procedure, but still addressing the need to perform the judicial duty to oversee and decide discovery disputes, this Court believes that a balancing test which considers the following three factors should be used when deciding a motion to preserve documents, things and land: 1) the level of concern the court has for the continuing existence and maintenance of the integrity of the evidence in question in the absence of an order directing preservation of the evidence; 2) any irreparable harm likely to result to the party seeking the preservation of evidence absent an order directing preservation; and 3) the capability of an individual, entity, or party to maintain the evidence sought to be preserved, not only as to the evidence's original form, condition or contents, but also the physical, spacial and financial burdens created by ordering evidence preservation.[2]

---

2. * * * It must * * * be noted that many of the * * * cases reviewed by the Court that concern the granting of an order of preservation have cited to the *Manual for Complex Litigation,* in its second, third, and fourth editions. In the fourth edition, § 11.442 entitled "Preservation" speaks to the need for preservation orders in complex litigation. Sample Order 40.25 in the *Manual* sets forth a model for a preservation order. These sections of the *Manual* do not contradict our analysis and findings. The Court recognizes that it has become routine to order the preservation of evidence prior to the beginning of the discovery period at the initial case

At the outset, in implementing this balancing test it is important to stress that the type of evidence will change from case to case and clearly the attendant circumstances of each case will dictate the necessity of the preservation order requested. The issues raised by a request for a preservation order require the trial court to exercise its discretion, and the factors set forth in the balancing test are only intended to assist the court by focusing on important areas which will arise in all such cases. Finally, it is important to note that the Court believes that a motion for a preservation order can be granted with regard to all items of evidence which are *discoverable* in accordance with Federal Rule of Civil Procedure 26(b)(1), without the necessity of establishing that the evidence will necessarily be relevant and admissible at trial.

1. Level of Concern for the Continuing Existence and Integrity of the Evidence

The first prong of the balancing test, namely the court's level of concern for the continuing existence and maintenance of the integrity of the evidence, is clearly a necessary component in the determination whether to grant or deny a preservation order. This is so because in the absence of any significant past, present or future threat to the continuing integrity or existence of the evidence, such an order is superfluous.

At times evidence may be outside of the possession of all parties and this may create a concern for the continuing existence of the evidence at question. Other circumstances may provide a basis for concern that a party is intentionally damaging or destroying the evidence, or is planning such an action, in order to compromise the case of its opponent. Still other circumstances may arise where the parties disagree as to the correct manner of the handling of the evidence. The reviewing court, as well as the parties, should be focused upon maintaining the integrity of the evidence in a form as close to, if not identical to, the original condition of the evidence. In the presence of a significant threat, if an order of court can prevent the loss, deterioration or destruction of evidence, while also considering all other relevant circumstances, then such an order may be an appropriate remedy. However, if the evidence, no matter where its location, how it is maintained, or who maintains it, will be lost, deteriorated or destroyed an order of preservation may not be necessary if the parties take immediate action to obtain or reproduce from the evidence the information needed; however, if the parties are not cooperative in this situation, then an order directing the preservation of the evidence in question in a manner that will preserve the whole of the evidence for the benefit of all parties may be necessary.

---

management conference and sometimes even before such a conference in complex litigation. *Manual for Complex Litigation, Fourth* § 11.442. The circumstances of the three motions before the Court do not concern "complex" litigation nor are we at the initial stages of discovery with all of the attendant circumstances which are normally present in cases for which the *Manual for Complex Litigation* is intended to provide guidance. *Id.* at §§ 10.1, 11.442. Therefore, the Court does not invoke any of the recommendations of that manual for the present analysis.

2. Possibility of Irreparable Harm to the Party Seeking Preservation in the Absence of a Preservation Order

Second, the degree of the harm likely to result to the party seeking the preservation order must also be weighed. At times, evidence may be a "one-of-a-kind", an irreplaceable item such as where a key item of evidence is tested through "non-destructive" means. The loss or destruction of certain evidence can result in significant prejudice to the party seeking to use it in proving the party's claims. In appropriate cases it becomes a judicial duty to protect a party from likely harm by acting to prevent the loss or destruction of evidence, thereby ensuring that the party may prosecute or defend its case in a court of law.

Additionally, certain evidence may be so integral and essential to a party's case that an order of preservation or some other manner of preventative maintenance of the evidence may be required, even in the absence of a threat of imminent, significant harm to the integrity or existence of the evidence. While such circumstances may be rare, they may require a preservation order from a court, thus allowing this second factor to overcome the absence of a significant level of concern as required under the first prong of the balancing test.

Clearly, however, a more compelling argument for a preservation order will be made where both factors are present. Considering that the loss of any evidence may damage a claim to some degree, a party could conceivably argue that the loss of any item of evidence intended to be offered at trial will cause harm sufficient to justify an order of preservation. Accordingly, while it could be argued that a court should always enter an order preserving evidence when a question arises as to its continued existence or integrity, such a reflexive, invariable judicial action in response to each motion for preservation of evidence would be impracticable and would trivialize the need for preservation orders in truly justifiable circumstances.

Therefore, where the need expressed by the moving party for a preservation order is based upon an indefinite or unspecified possibility of the loss or destruction of evidence, rather than a specific, significant, imminent threat of loss, a preservation order usually will not be justified. Also, where an imminent, specific threat to the evidence is demonstrated, but the level of harm which will result is not significant, then an order of preservation usually will not be justified. In most cases, the presence of both factor one and factor two to a significant degree will be required in order for a preservation order to be justified. However, it must be remembered that in a balancing test one factor may be so crucial that the presence of just that one factor may provide a sufficient justification for an order of preservation.

3. Ability to Maintain and Preserve the Evidence

Third, the capability to maintain the evidence sought to be preserved must also be weighed with the other two factors. Evidence can take many

forms in the world today. Considerations such as storage space, maintenance and storage fees, and physical deterioration of the evidence are just
a few of the considerations to be evaluated when considering this final
factor of the three-part balancing test. Certain circumstances may impose
burdens upon those parties and non-parties possessing evidence which
may be unfair or oppressive to the point that a judicially imposed allocation of the burdens between the parties to the civil action may be
required. Preservation of evidence may be particularly burdensome for
non-parties, considering that their interest in the pending civil action is
minuscule while the restrictions that can be imposed in a motion for
preservation may be expensive and voluminous. In such instances, the
party seeking preservation, and possibly the opposing party, may be
required to ensure the preservation of the evidence, rather than placing
that burden upon uninvolved third party possessors of the evidence.

The problems involved in the maintenance of evidence will vary
considerably depending upon the medium in which the evidence is contained. If the evidence is stored upon a computer floppy disk or hard drive,
finding physical space to store the evidence will not be as much of an issue
as it will be in the situation involving an accumulation of paper documentation over a period of many years where a preservation order may have to
encompass substantial copying and warehousing. On the other hand,
informational evidence stored within a computer hard drive may present a
difficulty in that it may be compromised or degraded as new information
is added and pieces of old information are "deleted" and subsequently
written over by the computer. As a result, the timing of the preservation
order may be of the essence, especially if the person possessing the
computer is without knowledge that the information contained on the
computer hard drive is evidence which needs to be preserved. Such a
situation may require immediate action by the court to preserve such
electronic evidence at least temporarily in order that the parties may have
an opportunity to confirm that such evidence is relevant to the claims
before the court. This computer information example is only one hypothetical scenario; the circumstances and considerations to be evaluated in
determining the need for a preservation order can be limitless since
evidence to be used at trial can be in a myriad of forms and mediums.

Applying this three part balancing test to the circumstances and
considerations present in the case *sub judice,* the Court finds no need or
justification to enter an order preserving evidence as requested by the
Defendant and Plaintiffs.

Defendant requests a preservation order for those materials cited in
its subpoena dated January 23, 2004 served upon Concurrent Technologies Corporation (hereinafter "CTC") in Johnstown. Among the materials
requested were hard and electronic copies of documents and correspondence sent to and from Dr. Bagnall; all records, written or electronic,

photographic or videographic, in CTC's possession obtained from the Colver Power Facility as well as physical pieces (the end box and shroud) from the generator at issue in the case and copies of testing results completed with regard to those pieces in addition to other written and electronic records. The Defendant asserts that a preservation order is required for the following reasons: that Dr. Bagnall during the *Daubert* hearing related the fact that other documents and materials may exist which may be relevant to the case; the need to "fully secure" this information and file "dispositive Motions based upon this new evidence"; the responsibility of a party to preserve evidence under F.R.C.P. 34; and the fact that the "Plaintiffs will not be harmed by such an Order" but that the Defendant would be "further substantially and irreparably harmed by the denial of the request to maintain the critical evidence intact from CTC." Defendant also states that it extended the time for responding to the subpoena by ten business days before filing this motion after CTC failed to comply with the extended deadline.

Under these circumstances there is no demonstration by the Defendant that evidence will be lost or destroyed. The attendant circumstances and reasons for the failure to produce the subject report, in which Dr. Bagnall participated, until the fourth day of trial, which event resulted in a mistrial, are not explained within the motion. The failure to produce that report may have resulted from a sheer oversight, rather than from any intent on the part of the Plaintiffs. The facts currently before the Court do not lead the Court to conclude that the circumstances that lead to the mistrial warrant the granting of a preservation order; indeed the report was produced following Dr. Bagnall's reliance upon it in his testimony. The report was not destroyed by the Plaintiffs but was retained as a litigation related document which was originally considered to be privileged as a consultant's report rather than a report of an expert expected to testify.

* * *

Had there been evidence of attempted damage or destruction of the report or the data compilations used to produce it, the Court's level of concern for protection of the integrity and existence of the evidence would be different. The Plaintiffs indicate in their response that they have continued to preserve the materials referenced in the Defendant's Motion. Without proof of destruction or degradation of the evidence, the Court finds that the circumstances surrounding the non-production of the report are an insufficient basis upon which to conclude that the integrity or existence of the evidence is threatened in the absence of a preservation order.

In consideration of the irreparable harm which allegedly will occur absent a preservation order, an allegation * * * which the Court understands [is] based upon the possible importance of the information which the Defendant believes may be contained in the items for which an order of preservation is requested, at this time a preservation order is found to be insufficiently justified under the second prong of [the] balancing test. The information sought could provide a valid basis for the Defendant to posit an alternative theory of circumstances that resulted in the damage of the generator. The evidence sought includes some pieces of the generator that are suspected will lead the Defendant's experts to formulate this alternative theory. As a result, this factor, namely the importance of the evidence, if more fully developed by the Defendant and supported by the facts, could have favored the granting of the preservation order. However, on the basis of the record before the Court this factor does [not] provide a sufficient basis for a preservation order.

Finally, the information available to the Court does not adequately address the issue of maintenance of the evidence with regard to such relevant considerations as: storage of the physical evidence and whether the evidence can be maintained in a state close to its "original" character which it possessed when first removed from the generator; the maintenance of electronic information, recordings and email existing within the medium of hard drives, floppy disks, or other digital storage formats; and the traditional concerns of ensuring the maintenance of paper documentation which include locating, cataloging and storing such documents for purposes of litigation. These considerations are not meant to be exhaustive, but illustrative of the concerns that need to be addressed when evaluating the burden of maintaining evidence that is ordered to be preserved by a court.

Such maintenance of the evidence considerations were not examined by either party in the case *sub judice*. However, the Court notes that most of the evidence is comprised of physical documentation and electronic documentation, in addition to physical evidence. The Plaintiffs make no claim of inconvenience or inability to maintain the evidence requested from their consultant, CTC. Therefore, the Court finds that the factor regarding the actual continuing physical maintenance and possession of the materials requested does not favor the granting of the preservation order.

In weighing all three of these factors, the Court concludes that a preservation order as requested by the Defendant is not justified or necessary under the present circumstances. While loss of the subpoenaed materials would prejudice the Defendant, the Court's level of concern for the loss or degradation of the evidence in question is not sufficiently elevated based upon the lack of the presence of a specific, imminent threat supported by the record. In addition, the other two factors do not favor the granting of a preservation order. Accordingly, the Defendant's Motion for Order of Court Directing Preservation of Documents, Software and Things is denied.

The Plaintiffs in responding to the Defendant's motion presented their own Motion for Order of Court Directing Preservation of Documents, Software and Things. The Plaintiffs initially state in their motion that they do not object to the granting of the Defendant's motion if the order encompasses information sought to be preserved by both parties and not just the Defendant. The Plaintiff then proceeds to discuss the circumstances of the Defendant filing its motion as well as Defendant's alleged failure to comply fully with requested discovery prior to the January 2004 trial. In noting various documents and things that have not been produced by the Defendant in discovery, the Plaintiffs state:

> Because of Defendant's past failures to produce documents and materials during the course of discovery in this matter and because of Defendant's apparent intent to now change the nature of its defense in this action, it is necessary for Plaintiffs to set forth herein the types of documents and materials within the possession, custody or control of Defendant that require preservation and production.

However, the Plaintiffs' motion reads more like a motion to compel documents and things not previously produced than a motion for a preservation order. There is no indication that those materials sought are in danger of being lost or destroyed. In addition, the absence of these materials apparently has not hampered or delayed the Plaintiffs' prosecution of their case in that in January 2004 this case went to trial. * * *

* * *

Motions for the preservation of evidence should be restricted to those circumstances which raise significant concern that discovery lawfully sought by a party will be lost indefinitely without immediate court action in the form of an order of preservation. The Plaintiffs' Counter–Motion for Order of Court Directing Preservation of Documents, Software and Things is denied.

* * *

COMMENTARY

Aside from providing that parties should "discuss any issues about preserving discoverable information" early in the proceedings,[64] the Federal Rules do not specify how relevant information should be preserved or how one litigant can ensure that the other will not destroy relevant information before it is produced in the course of litigation. In some cases, one or both parties may ask the court to enter a preservation order that will instruct a party to preserve certain types of information and dictate how it is to be preserved. It is important to remember, however, that a party's obligation to preserve relevant information exists even in the absence of such an order.

1. Seeking a Preservation Order

A litigant requests a preservation order because it anticipates that its opponent may fail to comply with its preservation obligations. For example, a preservation order may be entered against a party who has a history of discovery misconduct or spoliation violations or whose routine operating procedures or document retention practices will likely result in destruction.[65]

---

64. Fed. R. Civ. P. 26(f) *et seq.*

65. *See, e.g., Del Campo v. Kennedy,* No. C–01–21151, 2006 WL 2586633 (N.D. Cal. Sept. 8, 2006).

The inherently temporary or fleeting nature of certain types of information may also lead a party to seek a preservation order. In *Columbia Pictures Industries v. Bunnell*, the plaintiffs claimed that discovery of the defendants' server's RAM was necessary in order to show how often users were downloading copyrighted movies.[66] Because the RAM was overwritten every six hours, the plaintiffs sought a preservation order. After an extensive analysis, the court issued an order directing the defendants to maintain the server logs, which preserved the RAM.[67]

Sometimes, the preserving party may itself have reasons to seek a preservation order. A court order that clearly defines and delimits a litigant's obligations could benefit the preserving party by potentially reducing its administrative and financial burdens. Additionally, if the preserving party faithfully complies with the court's order, the litigant may shield itself from future spoliation claims.

If discoverable information in the hands of a non-party custodian is at risk of being destroyed before production, a preservation notice and subpoena may be issued to the third party. *In re Pacific Gateway Exchange, Inc. Securities Litigation* involved a defendant that had filed for Chapter 11 and was in bankruptcy proceedings. During this process, most of the defendant's employees had left, and there were few personnel remaining to be responsible for preservation and production. Additionally, the court noted that there may be relevant data on former employees' personal computers. Finding a "significant risk that relevant documents, both paper and electronic, could be irretrievably lost, which could result in prejudice to plaintiffs[,]" the court permitted the parties to serve a subpoena and notice to preserve documents to third parties.[68]

Similarly, *In re Tyco International, Ltd. Securities Litigation* was a multidistrict securities fraud case, in which the court agreed with plaintiffs that various third-parties, such as accountants, auditors, and consultants, may possess discoverable information about the transactions at issue. The court acknowledged that, unlike the defendants, these non-parties had not necessarily received notice of the lawsuit. Moreover, plaintiffs had produced evidence showing that because these third parties were large corporations, they would likely "overwrite and thereby destroy electronic data in the course of performing routine backup procedures."[69] Accordingly, the court held that it would permit plaintiffs to serve preservation notices and subpoenas on these non-parties, provided that plaintiffs submitted revised, "appropriately tailored" subpoenas that particularized the types of evidence to be preserved.

---

66. No. CV 06–1093, 2007 WL 2080419 (C.D. Cal. May 29, 2007).

67. *See Columbia Pictures, Inc. v. Bunnell*, 245 F.R.D. 443 (C.D. Cal. 2007) (affirming the magistrate judge's order requiring defendants to preserve and produce server logs).

68. No. C 00 1211, 2001 WL 1334747, at *1–2 (N.D. Cal. Oct. 17, 2001).

69. No. 00–MD–1335, 2000 WL 33654141, at *3 (D.N.H. Jul. 27, 2000).

2.   Issuing a Preservation Order

Some courts have taken the approach of issuing a preservation order only where the standard for injunctive relief has been met.[70] Courts applying the injunctive relief standard to a request for a preservation order generally require the requesting party to demonstrate "potential irreparable injury" and also show that there is a "real danger that the acts to be enjoined will occur, that there is no other remedy available, and that, under these circumstances, the court should exercise its discretion to afford the unusual relief provided by its injunction."[71]

Other courts have taken a different approach, recognizing a trial court's inherent power "to control the discovery process and overall case management" as a separate source of authority for issuing preservation orders.[72] In *Pueblo of Laguna v. United States*, the Court of Federal Claims held that "a document preservation order is no more an injunction than an order requiring a party to identify witnesses or to produce documents in discovery."[73] Drawing on its inherent power to manage the litigation before it, the court held that a preservation order should issue if the requesting party demonstrates "that it is necessary and not unduly burdensome."

In *Capricorn Power*, the court devised a third test that does not strictly adhere to the injunctive relief standard, but yet requires a more in-depth analysis than the *Pueblo* court. The *Capricorn Power* balancing test was intended to give particular consideration to the policies and goals of discovery by weighing the following factors: (1) the court's level of concern for the continuing existence of the evidence absent a preservation order; (2) any irreparable harm likely to result to the requesting party absent a preservation order; and (3) the capability of the other party to preserve the evidence, which takes into account "the physical, spatial and financial burdens created by ordering evidence preservation."[74]

In yet another variation, some courts, especially in complex cases, employ a standard, "first day" order at the start of the litigation that contains form language regarding the parties' preservation obligations.[75] For example, in some multidistrict litigation, the first order the court issues may automatically require all parties to "preserve all documents and other records containing information potentially relevant to the subject matter of this litigation."[76]

---

70.   *See, e.g., Madden v. Wyeth*, No. 3–03–CV–0167, 2003 WL 21443404 (N.D. Tex. Apr. 16, 2003).

71.   *Humble Oil & Refining Co. v. Harang*, 262 F.Supp. 39, 43 (E.D. La. 1966). *Accord In re Potash Antitrust Litig.*, No. 3–93–197, 1994 WL 1108312 (D. Minn. Dec. 5, 1994) (declining to issue preservation order where there was no showing that the requesting party would be irreparably harmed without it).

72.   *Capricorn Power*, 220 F.R.D. at 433.

73.   *Pueblo of Laguna v. United States*, 60 Fed. Cl. 133, 138 n.8 (2004).

74.   220 F.R.D. at 434.

75.   *See Manual for Complex Litigation* § 11.442 (4th ed. 2004) ("Before discovery starts, and perhaps before the initial conference, the court should consider whether to enter an order requiring the parties to preserve and retain documents, files, data, and records that may be relevant to the litigation.").

76.   *In re Prudential Ins. Co. of Am. Sales Practices Litig.*, 169 F.R.D. 598 (D.N.J. 1997).

State courts have also begun to address preservation of ESI. In 2006, the Conference of Chief Justices released "Guidelines for State Trial Courts Regarding Discovery of Electronically–Stored Information." The Guidelines state that a trial court should only issue a preservation order upon "a threshold showing that the continuing existence and integrity of the information is threatened." Following a threshold showing, the Guidelines instruct trial courts to consider four factors—similar to those used in *Capricorn Power*—in fashioning an order: (1) the nature of the threat to the ESI; (2) the potential for irreparable harm without an order; (3) the responding party's ability to maintain the information sought; and (4) the physical, technological, and financial burdens in preserving the information.

3. Content and Scope of Preservation Orders

A preservation order should be narrowly tailored to the specific risks and needs of the case to avoid imposing unduly burdensome requirements on the parties. Because the litigants know best what information is needed, where it is kept, and how it can most efficiently be preserved, a court may institute a general, temporary preservation order and instruct the litigants to meet and confer to develop a more detailed, customized preservation agreement. Such an order may also be useful if one party refuses to discuss in detail the issue of preservation.[77] When ordered to meet and confer to develop a preservation plan, litigants should evaluate the following considerations:[78]

(a) the extent of the preservation obligation, identifying the types of material to be preserved, the subject matter, time frame, the authors and addressees, and key words to be used in identifying responsive materials;

(b) the identification of persons responsible for carrying out preservation obligations on behalf of each party;

(c) the form and method of providing notice of the duty to preserve to persons identified as custodians of documents, data, and tangible things;

(d) mechanisms for monitoring, certifying, or auditing custodian compliance with preservation obligations;

(e) whether preservation will require suspending or modifying any routine business processes or procedures, with special attention to document management programs and the recycling of computer data storage media;

(f) the methods to preserve any volatile but potentially discoverable material, such as voicemail, active data in databases, or electronic messages;

(g) the anticipated costs of preservation and ways to reduce or share these costs; and

---

77. *See, e.g., Del Campo v. Kennedy*, No. C–01–21151, 2006 WL 2586633 (N.D. Cal. Sept. 8, 2006) (ordering the parties to meet and confer to develop a preservation plan and issuing an interim preservation order). *See also Manual for Complex Litigation* § 40.25 (4th ed. 2004) (sample interim order and direction to meet and confer).

78. These meet and confer "Subjects for Consideration" are taken from the sample preservation order in the *Manual for Complex Litigation* § 40.25 (4th ed. 2004).

(h) a mechanism to review and modify the preservation obligation as discovery proceeds, eliminating or adding particular categories of documents, data, and tangible things.

PROBLEMS

1. An American Indian tribe has sued the United States seeking an accounting and to recover for monetary loss and damages relating to the Government's alleged mismanagement of the tribe's trust funds and other properties.

A similar case is pending in another jurisdiction. In that case, Government agencies have mishandled Indian records. Documents, including electronic records, containing Indian-related information relevant to the matter have been destroyed. There has been unsatisfactory oversight of administrative procedures, and management has been unable to respond effectively when made aware of violations. Many facilities in which Indian records have been stored are in general disrepair, and there are insufficient systems and methods for ensuring preservation. Regulations regarding Indian-record retention have not been effectively implemented, and on numerous occasions, there have been improper attempts to transfer Indian records.

The plaintiff tribe in the instant case has requested that the court issue an order directing various Government agencies to take steps to ensure the preservation and availability of documents, in various media, potentially relating to its claims against the Government.

Should the court issue the requested order? Would you come to a different conclusion depending on the test used?

2. The plaintiff tribe has made specific proposals with regard to the terms of the requested preservation order. Plaintiff has asked the court to prohibit generally the destruction of records relevant to the case absent plaintiff's prior written concurrence or further order from the court. Plaintiff also requests that the court impose restrictions on the inter-and intra-agency transfer of records, requiring that no transfer of records can occur without plaintiff's concurrence or a court order. In the alternative, plaintiff requests an opportunity to examine such records prior to their movement.

Consider points (a) through (h) listed above. As counsel for plaintiff, what would you add to the proposal? As counsel for the Government, what would you challenge about the proposal? Are there important issues not addressed by plaintiff's proposal?

H. POSSESSION, CUSTODY, OR CONTROL

IN RE NTL, INC. SECURITIES LITIGATION

244 F.R.D. 179 (S.D.N.Y. 2007)

PECK, MAGISTRATE JUDGE

Plaintiffs * * * have moved for discovery sanctions against defendant NTL Europe, Inc. and "nominal non-party NTL, Inc.," claiming that they hindered and delayed document discovery in this case and allowed numerous documents and electronically stored information ("ESI"), including the e-mails of approximately forty-four of NTL's "key players," to be destroyed. * * *

FACTS

The Securities Lawsuits and NTL's Bankruptcy

The * * * plaintiffs filed suit on April 18, 2002 against a company then known as NTL, Inc. ("Old NTL"), alleging federal securities laws violations. Old NTL and several of its subsidiaries entered into Chapter 11 bankruptcy, emerging on September 5, 2002 with a "Second Amended Joint Reorganization Plan of NTL Incorporated and Certain Subsidiaries" (the "Bankruptcy Plan"). Two main companies emerged out of the bankruptcy: NTL Europe, Inc. ("NTL Europe"), the successor company to Old NTL, and NTL, Inc. ("New NTL"), formerly known as NTL Communications Corp. ([e].g., Bankruptcy Plan at 31–32.) NTL Europe was primarily responsible for selling off Old NTL's unprofitable assets, and New NTL became the surviving operational company with control of the company's European telecommunications assets. The Bankruptcy Plan specifically allowed the * * * securities lawsuits to go forward after the bankruptcy, against the individual defendants and NTL Europe (as successor to Old NTL) * * *.

Document Sharing Clauses in The Demerger Agreement and Transitional Services Agreement

Pursuant to the Bankruptcy Plan, defendant NTL Europe and non-party New NTL entered into a "Demerger Agreement" dated January 10, 2003, which specifies that:

4. ACCESS TO INFORMATION

For a period of ten years from the date of this Agreement, each party shall ... allow the other party and its personnel to have access to (during normal business hours and following not less than 48 hours' notice) and (at the expense of the party requesting the information) take copies of all documents, records or other materials containing any information which that party or any of its Group Companies or affiliated joint ventures might reasonably require to be able to comply with their respective legal, regulatory, accounting or filing obligations, or to resist, appeal, dispute, avoid or compromise any tax assessment, provided that nothing in this clause shall permit either party to copy any document, record or other material which is subject to legal privilege. Furthermore, each party shall ... allow reasonable access to such of its duly authorised personnel, at all reasonable times during business hours upon prior written notice, as are required to permit the availability, access or, subject to the above restriction, copying of such information.

* * *

Old NTL's 2002 Document Hold Memoranda

On March 13, 2002, a document "hold" memo was circulated to approximately seventeen employees of Old NTL:

> Although, under usual circumstances, destruction of documents/files, in the ordinary course is permitted, under certain circumstances, a company is under a duty to preserve documents that could be relevant to disputes with third parties. Basically, what this means is that you can have a policy that dictates which and when documents can be destroyed in the ordinary course, but once you are on notice that there may be litigation you are required to retain documents that would reasonably constitute evidence even if under your retention policy you would destroy such documents in the ordinary course.

> Accordingly, given the obvious possibility that we may encounter a heightened risk of litigious activity in the ongoing restructuring process, it is imperative that all documents that even possibly could be evidence in any such a matter be retained.

> Thank you.

On March 14, 2002, the same memorandum was forwarded to approximately twenty-eight more employees at Old NTL with the following instruction: "Please read and note carefully Lauren Blair's (Assistant General Counsel in New York) memorandum on the retention of documents. Please forward to your reports as you consider appropriate. Many thanks."

On or about June 6, 2002, while Old NTL was in bankruptcy, another document hold memorandum about the [securities actions] was circulated to employees. The memo stated in part:

> NTL Incorporated and certain of its officers have been named as defendants in a number of purported securities class action lawsuits. The complaints in those cases generally allege that NTL failed to accurately disclose its financial condition, finances and future prospects in press releases and other communications with investors prior to filing for reorganization in federal bankruptcy court.

> We presently do not know of any facts that would support these allegations, and we intend to defend the lawsuits vigorously.

> In connection with such lawsuits, NTL and its affiliates may be required to produce documents relevant to plaintiffs' claims. Therefore, as we have previously informed you, we are required to take reasonable steps to preserve all potentially relevant material that may exist (whether in paper or electronic format). Relevant materials may include sales data, minutes or notes of meetings or conversations, financial statements, credit facilities and other loan documents, press releases, PowerPoint presentations and any other documents (including drafts) relating to the business, assets, properties, condition (financial or otherwise), and results of operations of NTL or its affiliates at any time after April 1, 1999.

Please ensure that these types of documents are preserved until further notice. When in doubt about possible relevance, you should err on the side of retaining the material.

A Brief History of Discovery in this Case Relevant to this Motion

On May 2, 2005, the * * * plaintiffs served their initial document requests upon defendant NTL Europe and the individual defendants. On June 1, 2005, defendant NTL Europe and the individual defendants filed their objections and responses. Defendant NTL Europe's response to the document requests stated that "NTL will produce documents, if any, responsive to [the] request." Defendant NTL Europe, however, did not produce any responsive documents or e-mails. Defendant NTL Europe's counsel informed plaintiffs' counsel that all corporate records relating to the 1999–2002 pre-bankruptcy period were in non-party New NTL's possession and that defendant NTL Europe did not possess any of these records.

* * *

On August 16, 2005, plaintiffs served a subpoena upon non-party New NTL requesting production of essentially the same documents as plaintiffs had requested from defendant NTL Europe. Approximately two months later, non-party New NTL made seventy boxes of documents available to plaintiffs' counsel for inspection and copying.

On November 21, 2005, plaintiffs' counsel sent a letter to New NTL's counsel noting that New NTL had not produced several requested categories of documents, including financial analyses, subscriber integration and billing issues, and e-mail. On November 30, 2005, New NTL's counsel responded that New NTL does "not believe responsive documents that fall into the categories of documents which you reference in your letter as missing exist and/or can be produced," and concluded that in light of its "limited role" in the litigation, New NTL's production was "full and complete." New NTL's counsel also orally told plaintiffs' counsel that "responsive e-mails did not exist because the company's [computer] servers had been 'upgraded' after the reorganization."

* * *

On December 20, 2005, plaintiffs' counsel took a Rule 30(b)(6) deposition of Jeffrey Brodsky, defendant NTL Europe's CEO. Brodsky testified that NTL Europe does not have physical possession of Old NTL's books and records. Because non-party New NTL retained the operating telecommunications assets after the bankruptcy, New NTL had physical possession of the books and records. This was the reason that defendant NTL Europe did not produce any documents in response to plaintiffs' May 2, 2005 subpoena. * * *

In a letter dated January 24, 2006, New NTL's counsel disclosed to plaintiffs' counsel that New NTL had performed selected, targeted searches of 23,000 boxes of files in storage in four locations in the United

Kingdom and had located no additional responsive documents, and further asserted that reviewing every box in storage to locate documents responsive to plaintiffs' document requests would be "overly burdensome, unreasonable, unrealistic and extraordinarily costly for [non-party] NTL." * * *

At [a] January 25, 2006 New NTL Rule 30(b)(6) deposition, David Bond, a New NTL in-house lawyer testified that New NTL's IT system was outsourced to IBM in late 2002 or early 2003. Bond did not know what the e-mail retention policy was at the time of the outsourcing to IBM; IBM's current e-mail retention policy with respect to a former employee's e-mail account is that New NTL's IT department has access to the account for three months after an employee leaves the company, then it goes to a back-up tape for nine months, after which it may be overwritten. Bond testified that the policy with regard to the e-mail accounts of current New NTL employees is that employees are free to retain e-mails or discard them "to suit their needs." In order to retain an e-mail, an employee must move the e-mail from their inbox to a separate folder, otherwise the e-mails in the inbox will start to be deleted after approximately three months. Bond stated that employees received new computers at the time of the outsourcing to IBM, and he did not know whether e-mails written on the old computers were placed on back-up tapes as part of the outsourcing. Bond was not aware of any communications within New NTL at the time of the outsourcing to IBM regarding retention of e-mail or documents pertinent to ongoing litigation.

* * *

On February 8, 2006, plaintiffs took the deposition of George Bernet, the information technology manager at Old NTL's executive offices in New York starting in 2001. Bernet testified that no one ever asked him to save or preserve information because of threatened or pending litigation. Bernet stated that NTL's New York server was decommissioned in 2004, with all electronic files transferred to the company's UK servers. After that, the old computers from the New York office were donated to charity. Bernet testified that full back-up tapes for the New York office were moved to the company's new Manhattan offices and also to a bank vault.

On March 1, 2006, New NTL produced CD's containing the e-mail files of ten present or former NTL employees, three of which had already been provided to plaintiffs two weeks before. Therefore, as of March 1, 2006, plaintiffs had received e-mail files for only twelve of the fifty-eight employees requested. On March 13, 2006, New NTL produced the New York office back-up tapes to plaintiffs' counsel. At plaintiff[s'] expense, the back-up tapes were restored and converted to readable, searchable files. Plaintiffs' counsel's review of the back-up tapes revealed that they contained e-mails from senior executives who worked in NTL's executive offices in New York, but that the tapes did not contain any e-mail from 2001, the main year in which plaintiffs allege that defendant NTL Europe and its executives committed securities violations.

On March 17, 2006, IBM's attorney advised plaintiffs' counsel that IBM completed the searches of the New NTL electronic files in its possession, and out of a list of fifty-seven current and former NTL employees, IBM found files for thirteen employees, most of whose files New NTL's counsel previously had produced to plaintiffs. In e-mail correspondence between New NTL's counsel and plaintiffs' counsel, New NTL confirmed that it had searched several times for e-mails relating to the remaining current and former employees on the list and did not find anything at all, even though some produced documents indicate that at least three of those employees had e-mail accounts during the time period pertinent to the document request.

* * *

On June 27, 2006, plaintiffs' counsel updated the Court on the progress of discovery. As of that date, the majority of the e-mails from the files of forty-four of the current and former employees on plaintiffs' list of "key players" were still missing from New NTL's document production * * *. Additionally, very few pieces of external correspondence and personal meeting notes were provided, and no NTL communications with securities analysts or investment firms were produced. * * *

On August 14, 2006, the * * * plaintiffs provided their final update to the Court regarding discovery. The * * * plaintiffs confirmed that they had completed the depositions of the individual defendants, that they questioned the individual defendants about specific categories of missing documents and e-mails, and were told that many of the documents and e-mails from those categories previously existed but never were produced, presumably because they were discarded. * * *

ANALYSIS

* * *

II. PLAINTIFF'S MOTION FOR AN ADVERSE INFERENCE IS GRANTED

A. Legal Standard Governing Adverse Inference Instructions

"The spoliation of evidence germane to proof of an issue at trial can support an inference that the evidence would have been unfavorable to the party responsible for its destruction." *Zubulake v. UBS Warburg LLC*, 220 F.R.D. 212, 216 (S.D.N.Y. 2003). * * *

"A party that seeks an adverse inference instruction for destruction or late production of evidence must show that: (i) the party having control over the evidence had an obligation to preserve or timely produce it; (ii) the party that destroyed or failed to timely produce evidence had a 'culpable state of mind'; and (iii) the missing or tardily produced evidence is relevant to the party's claim or defense 'such that a reasonable trier of fact could find that it would support that claim or defense.' "

1. Duty to Preserve Evidence

* * *

c. Defendant NTL Europe Had "Control" Over the Relevant Documents

Defendant NTL Europe contends that, although it was the party designated after bankruptcy to continue as the defendant in this case, it nevertheless did not have "control" over any documents or ESI relevant to plaintiffs' document requests because they were in non-party New NTL's possession; therefore defendant NTL Europe contends that it was not responsible for any spoliation which may have happened since this case was filed.

* * *

Under Rule 34, "control does not require that the party have legal ownership or actual physical possession of the documents at issue; rather, documents are considered to be under a party's control when that party has the right, authority, or practical ability to obtain the documents from a non-party to the action." *Bank of New York v. Meridien BIAO Bank Tanzania Ltd.*, 171 F.R.D. 135, 146–47 (S.D.N.Y.1997); *see also, e.g., Golden Trade, S.r.L. v. Lee Apparel Co.*, 143 F.R.D. 514, 525 (S.D.N.Y. 1992) (The courts have "interpreted Rule 34 to require production if the party has the practical ability to obtain the documents from another, irrespective of his legal entitlement to the documents.").

Here, defendant NTL Europe had both the legal "right" and certainly the "practical ability" to obtain the relevant documents from New NTL, and therefore had the necessary "control" of those documents to be able to preserve and produce them in this litigation, for three separate reasons:

First, the document sharing clause in the Demerger Agreement makes it clear that New NTL was to make available to defendant NTL Europe any documents that it needed to be able to comply with its legal obligations, such as this lawsuit. Moreover, defendant NTL Europe's CEO demonstrated that NTL Europe had the simple "practical ability" to obtain the relevant documents from New NTL; he testified that "[w]henever there was a document that we needed [from New NTL] . . ., we would call [New NTL] and ask if they had it, and if they had it, they'd send it." Based on these agreements and testimony, * * * defendant NTL Europe had the legal and/or practical ability to obtain documents (including e-mail) from New NTL. * * * Accordingly, the Court holds that defendant NTL Europe had "control" over documents and ESI at New NTL for the purpose of this litigation.

Second, even if defendant NTL Europe and non-party New NTL had not been parties to the Demerger Agreement * * * this Court finds that defendant NTL Europe still should be held to have "control" over the relevant documents and ESI possessed by New NTL for the purposes of document production in this case, under the reasoning of the decision in

Bank of New York v. Meridien BIAO Bank Tanzania Ltd., 171 F.R.D. at 146–49. There, one of the original defendants went through a bankruptcy reorganization and assigned its interests to a new party. The Court in *Bank of New York* found that * * * the "[t]reatment of both assignor and assignee as parties for discovery . . . is proper when to do otherwise would frustrate discovery, regardless of whether this frustration is intentional or not . . . Otherwise a litigant by contracting with a third party could nullify and evade the rules of procedure." The Court ultimately held that "[i]t would be patently unfair if [the assignee party] were able to continue to discover relevant information from [plaintiff] while relegating [plaintiff] to seek information from [the assignor] as a non-party," and thus the Court ordered the assignee party to "produce all documents relevant to the issues in this action" that were in the assignor's possession. In so holding, the Court also noted that the assignee party had demonstrated an ability to retrieve critical documents from the assignor when needed, suggesting that the assignee party defendant had the requisite "practical ability" to obtain documents that satisfies the requirements of Rule 34.

This Court finds the situation in this case analogous to that in *Bank of New York*. Plaintiffs here filed their case against Old NTL prior to its entry into bankruptcy. Upon emergence from bankruptcy, defendant NTL Europe was assigned to be the entity to replace Old NTL in the lawsuit. Defendant NTL Europe's CEO testified that NTL Europe had the practical ability to obtain any documents it needed from New NTL. Therefore, under *Bank of New York*, * * * defendant NTL Europe had "control" over "Old NTL's" documents possessed by New NTL that were relevant to this lawsuit, and in any case, it would be patently unfair for defendant NTL Europe to benefit from the artificial separation of entities that was created after the bankruptcy. * * *

There is, however, a third reason why NTL Europe can be sanctioned for failing to produce relevant documents and electronically stored information, even if (as it claims), it had no legal or practical ability to obtain the documents and ESI from New NTL. Once the duty to preserve material for litigation arises—as it did here * * * before NTL emerged from bankruptcy—the party has a duty to initiate a "litigation hold" and preserve potentially responsive documents and ESI. *See, e.g., Zubulake v. UBS Warburg LLC*, 229 F.R.D. 422, 433–34 (S.D.N.Y. 2004). NTL initiated such a hold (or at least sent some hold memos to that effect). If defendant NTL Europe thereafter turned relevant "held" documents and ESI over to New NTL without itself preserving (or insuring that New NTL would preserve) such information for possible production in this litigation, it failed in its obligation to preserve relevant material, and thus spoliated evidence (assuming the other requirements for spoliation are met). Thus, either the Demerger Agreement gave defendant NTL Europe the ability to obtain relevant documents and ESI from New NTL, in which case it had sufficient "control" to be responsible to produce the material in discovery, or if the Demerger Agreement did not give defendant NTL Europe that right, then defendant NTL Europe failed to have a sufficient litigation hold in place and therefore engaged in spoliation when it transferred documents to New NTL. Counsel for defendant NTL Europe conceded that NTL Europe did not take any action to ensure that New NTL would preserve the documents and ESI that it received from NTL Europe after the bankruptcy.

For the reasons set forth above, defendant NTL Europe had "control" and thus a duty * * * to preserve documents and ESI relevant to this litigation, even though most of those documents and ESI ended up in the physical possession of non-party New NTL.

2. Culpable State of Mind

* * *

Defendant NTL Europe's conduct demonstrates a sufficiently culpable state of mind to warrant spoliation sanctions. While Old NTL circulated two document hold memoranda to certain employees, many NTL employees never received the memoranda. Moreover, there is no evidence that either of the two NTLs ever reminded employees (especially at New NTL) of the need to continue to preserve relevant documents and ESI. The evidence, in fact, is that no adequate litigation hold existed at the NTLs. In late 2002 or early 2003, NTL's IT system was outsourced to IBM, which apparently did not have any document hold in place at all. New NTL employees also received new computers at the time of the outsourcing to IBM, and New NTL does not know whether any e-mails written on the old computers were saved or not. Additionally, New NTL did not convey any litigation hold instructions to IBM at the time of the outsourcing. More generally, defendant NTL Europe's counsel conceded that NTL Europe took no steps after bankruptcy to ensure that New NTL personnel continued the litigation hold.

As a result, NTL Europe (through New NTL) was only able to produce e-mail files for thirteen out of fifty-seven requested current and former NTL employees who are the "key players" involved in plaintiffs' allegations. * * * Consequently, the Court finds that NTL Europe's utter failure to preserve documents and ESI relevant to plaintiffs' allegations in this case * * * to be at least grossly negligent. * * * The second requirement for imposition of an adverse inference instruction therefore is met.

3. Relevance

* * *

"Where a party destroys evidence in bad faith, that bad faith alone is sufficient circumstantial evidence from which a reasonable fact finder could conclude that the missing evidence was unfavorable to that party. Similarly, a showing of gross negligence in the destruction or untimely production of evidence will in some circumstances suffice, standing alone, to support a finding that the evidence was unfavorable to the grossly negligent party." * * *

As discussed above, the * * * plaintiffs have demonstrated that defendant NTL Europe's failure to preserve documents and ESI relevant to plaintiffs' allegations was at a minimum grossly negligent. * * * Thus, no extrinsic proof of relevance is necessary, and the * * * plaintiffs are entitled to an adverse inference spoliation instruction.

* * *

Because the * * * plaintiffs have shown that NTL Europe had the duty to preserve documents and ESI relevant to this litigation * * *, that NTL Europe was at a minimum grossly negligent in allowing documents and ESI including the e-mails of approximately forty-four key players to be destroyed, and that those e-mails were relevant to the * * * plaintiffs' claims, the * * * plaintiffs have demonstrated that an adverse inference instruction spoliation sanction against defendant NTL Europe is warranted in this case.

HATFILL v. THE NEW YORK TIMES COMPANY

242 F.R.D. 353 (E.D. Va. 2006)

O'GRADY, MAGISTRATE JUDGE

* * * Plaintiff has brought this defamation action against Defendant, after Defendant published a series of columns, written by Nicholas Kristof, alleging that Plaintiff was involved in the anthrax attacks which killed five people in 2001. * * * Plaintiff served a request for Production of Documents, under Fed. Rule Civ. P. 34, on Defendant, asking for documents related to published and unpublished reporting on the anthrax attacks involving a number of Defendant's reporters and researchers. However, this motion to compel concerns only the potentially responsive documents in the physical possession of William Broad, a science reporter for Defendant, specifically 6,000 words of interview notes stored on Mr. Broad's personal flash memory drive.[2]

I. Background

On September 15, 2006, Plaintiff deposed Mr. Broad, pursuant to a Rule 45 subpoena. During the deposition, Mr. Broad stated that he stored his unpublished materials, including the 6,000 words of interview notes related to his investigation of the anthrax attacks, on his flash drive. Mr. Broad stated that the notes memorialized approximately thirty interviews with different sources and that the sources provided the information in reliance on Mr. Broad's promise to keep the sources' identities in confidence or to keep the information confidential and use [it only] for Mr.

---

2. A flash drive is re-writable storage device integrated with a USB interface. The drive is small and lightweight such that it can [be] attached to key chain or lanyard. To access the data stored on a flash drive, the flash drive must be attached to a computer for power, but the computer can read the files off the flash drive without saving them to the computer's hard drive.

Broad's background knowledge. Mr. Broad does not recall showing the contents of the notes to anyone, including his editors at Defendant's newspaper. The flash drive, containing the notes, is always in the personal possession of Mr. Broad, although he regularly attaches the drive to computers owned by Defendant as part of his work duties.

Plaintiff argues that Defendant has failed to fully respond to its request for production because Defendant has not produced Mr. Broad's 6,000 word notes related to the anthrax investigation. Plaintiff contends that these notes are within Defendant's "possession, custody and control" regardless of whether the employee keeps the notes at home or at work and thus must be produced in response to a production request, pursuant to Rule 34(a). Plaintiff further argues that the notes are discoverable material, pursuant to Rule 26(b)(1), based on depositions of both Mr. Kristof and Mr. Broad as well as e-mail communications between the two reporters. Defendant argues that the notes are in the sole personal possession, custody, and control of Mr. Broad and thus Defendant is not required to produce the notes under Rule 34. * * *

II. Possession, Custody or Control under Rule 34(a)

Under Rule 34, the party responding to a production request must provide responsive documents which are in the possession, custody or control of the party. See Fed.R.Civ.P. 34(a)(1). The U.S. Court of Appeals for the Fourth Circuit has not interpreted the phrase "possession, custody or control." However, a number of district courts within the Fourth Circuit have considered this issue [and hold that] control is defined as actual possession of a document or "the legal right to obtain the document on demand." This two-prong definition comports with the findings of other circuits.

In this case, Defendant does not have physical possession of the flash drive containing Mr. Broad's notes. While Mr. Broad may have used computers owned by Defendant in order to access the flash drive, according to Mr. Broad, the notes themselves have not been stored on Defendant's computers. The only question remaining is whether Defendant has a legal right to obtain the notes from Mr. Broad. Defendant argues that it ceded to its reporters any right to possess or control dissemination of notes and unpublished materials. In relinquishing these rights, Defendant sought to remove uncertainty for reporters regarding dissemination of unpublished material that the reporter generates or obtains. This policy is embodied in both the collective bargaining agreement with its reporters' union requiring Defendant to provide legal representation to reporters who elect not to comply with subpoenas for their confidential work product as well as Defendant's Records Retention Policy. Finally, Defendant allows reporters to take such notes and unpublished materials with them if they leave Defendant's employment * * *. The Court finds that these actions show that Defendant has ceded any legal rights to Mr. Broad's notes, and that its policy also has a clear substantive purpose and is not an artificial wall created for the purpose of avoiding discovery requests.

The Court, therefore, finds that Defendant does not have possession, custody or control under the two-prong definition of control under Rule 34(a); thus, this Court will not compel Defendant to produce Mr. Broad's notes.

* * *

COMMENTARY

1. What Is Control?

It is important to recognize that Rules 26, 34, and 45 all have "possession, custody, or control" requirements. The requirement in Rule 26 is particularly important because it may create a trap. Under Rule 26, a party discloses documents in its "possession, custody, or control" on which it intends to affirmatively rely. Thus, a Rule 26 disclosure could be viewed as an admission that a party has "possession, custody, or control" over certain records, which may affect its responses to Rule 34 discovery demands.

a. The Factual Record

In re NTL, Inc. Securities Litigation highlights the importance of the factual record to a discovery dispute. Even more damaging than the Demerger Agreement itself may have been the testimony about access to information. NTL Europe's CEO testified that "[w]henever there was a document that we needed [from New NTL] . . ., we would call [New NTL] and ask if they had it, and if they had it, they'd send it." The court held that the CEO's testimony "demonstrated that NTL Europe had the simple 'practical ability' to obtain the relevant documents from New NTL."

b. Practical Ability

The *In re NTL* court relied, in part, on NTL Europe's "practical ability" to obtain the documents in question. Whether a party's "practical ability" to obtain discovery materials means that a party has "control" over those materials has been the subject of some debate. In *Prokosch v. Catalina Lighting, Inc.*, the court wrote: "[t]herefore, 'under Rule 34, 'control' does not require that the party have legal ownership or actual physical possession of the documents at issue; rather, documents are considered to be under a party's control when that party has the right, authority, or practical ability, to obtain the documents from a non-party to the action.' "[79] The court ordered the defendant to produce certain documents that it "may not physically possess, but which it is capable of obtaining upon demand."

The Seventh Circuit rejected the "practical ability" test in *Chaveriat v. Williams Pipe Line Co.*, in overturning a trial court's decision to exclude certain evidence because the plaintiffs failed to turn over chromatograms to the defendant for more than two years. The chromatograms were in the

---

79. 193 F.R.D. 633, 636 (D. Minn. 2000) (quoting *Bank of N.Y. v. Meridien BIAO Bank Tanzania, Ltd.*, 171 F.R.D. 135, 146 (S.D.N.Y. 1997)).

possession of NET, a third party, and the plaintiffs ultimately asked for and received them from NET. After stating the "possession, custody, or control" requirement, the court wrote:

> The plaintiffs could no doubt have asked NET to give it the chromatograms; judging from what happened later, NET would have complied; and maybe if it had balked, the plaintiffs could have bought the chromatograms from it. But the fact that a party could obtain a document if it tried hard enough and maybe if it didn't try hard at all does not mean that the document is in its possession, custody, or control; in fact it means the opposite.[80]

Similarly, in *Bleecker v. Standard Fire Insurance Co.*, the court also rejected the "practical ability test." The issue involved documents in the possession of a third-party insurance adjuster. Plaintiff asserted that the defendant had the ability to "command" the documents. The court wrote:

> Plaintiff's and Defendant's definitions of control differ greatly. Plaintiff asserts that even if a party does not have the right to require a non-party to produce documents, the party's practical *ability* to produce the documents determines whether the defendant has "control" of the document. On the other hand, defendant contends that "control" encompasses the legal *right* to obtain the requested document.[81]

The court agreed with the defendant: "In order for the material to be discoverable, defendant must have some type of legal right to the material plaintiff seeks to discover."

c.   Parties and Third–Party Data Stores

Obviously, the parties to litigation have an obligation to preserve relevant evidence, including ESI, as soon as the duty to preserve arises. Even before being formally named in a complaint, a person or entity that reasonably anticipates *becoming a party* to future litigation has the duty to preserve.

But what are the obligations of parties to preserve relevant information they know is held by third parties? This question is particularly important in the context of ESI. Today, many businesses outsource their information technology needs, both maintaining day-to-day electronic data on servers owned and operated by third-party hosts and storing long-term inactive data, such as disaster recovery backup tapes and other archival data with vendors providing off-site storage.

In addition to evidence over which a party has direct care, custody or control, the duty to preserve may extend to evidence over which a party has indirect control. In *Cyntegra, Inc. v. Idexx Laboratories*, for example, the plaintiff filed an antitrust complaint against a competitor, alleging that it engaged in an unlawful tying scheme that harmed plaintiff's business. Plaintiff stored most of its electronic data on third-party servers run by a vendor, Net Nation. Because plaintiff was delinquent on payments to NetNation, the vendor deleted plaintiff's data from its servers. In sanctioning the plaintiff for NetNation's destruction of the evidence, the court held that:

---

80.   11 F.3d 1420, 1426–27 (7th Cir. 1993).

81.   130 F. Supp. 2d 726, 739 (E.D.N.C. 2000).

Plaintiff had sufficient control and legal right over the deleted files to constitute fault. Plaintiff contracted to store business documents on NetNation's computer servers. At least until . . . payment was discontinued, Plaintiff could direct the flow of information to and from NetNation's servers. Because [Plaintiff's duty to preserve had already arisen at time payment was discontinued], it had an affirmative duty to make payments and preserve the evidence. Plaintiff cannot bypass this duty by abandoning its documents to a third-party and claiming lack of control. Plaintiff could have saved or printed the information after determining it could no longer make payments. . . . A contractual relationship with a third-party entity provides, at a minimum, an obligation to make reasonable inquiry of the third-party entity for the data at issue. . . . Plaintiff had sufficient, albeit indirect, control to preserve evidence, and by failing to do so, violated an affirmative duty.[82]

Similarly, one of the reasons that the NTL court faulted NTL Europe was that it gave documents it controlled and that should have been preserved to New NTL without any requirement that New NTL preserve the documents. Thus, the court was guarding against a litigant evading its preservation obligations by arguing that it no longer controlled the information.

d. Parent, Subsidiary, and Affiliate Corporations

Courts generally hold that a parent corporation has a sufficient degree of ownership and control over a wholly-owned subsidiary such that the parent is deemed to have control over the subsidiary's documents.[83] This principle has been applied even when the subsidiary is not owned directly but, rather, is owned by an intermediate corporation that is itself a wholly-owned subsidiary of the parent corporation.[84]

In *Alcan International Limited v. S.A. Day Manufacturing Co.*, the court ordered a U.S. corporate defendant to produce documents in the possession of its foreign affiliate. The court stated that the U.S. and foreign companies "are corporate members of a unified worldwide business entity," issue consolidated financial statements, use the same corporate logo, and have regular contact regarding the issues in the case.[85] The court wrote: "It is 'inconceivable' that [the defendant] would not have access to this information and the ability to obtain it, not only for the purpose of proving its claims in this lawsuit but also for the purpose of conducting its business. . . ."

The court reached a different result in *Goh v. Baldor Electric Co.* In that case, a dispute that involved activities in Asia, the plaintiffs sought to compel

---

82. No. 06–4170, 2007 WL 5193736, at *5 (C.D. Cal. Sept. 21, 2007).

83. *See, e.g., United States v. International Union of Petroleum & Indus. Workers*, 870 F.2d 1450, 1452 (9th Cir. 1989) ("A corporation must produce documents possessed by a subsidiary that the parent corporation owns or wholly controls."); *Camden Iron & Metal, Inc. v. Marubeni Am. Corp.*, 138 F.R.D. 438, 441 (D.N.J. 1991) (parent corporation has control over documents in physical control of wholly-owned or wholly-controlled subsidiary); *In re Uranium Antitrust Litig.*, 480 F.Supp. 1138, 1152 (N.D. Ill. 1979) (corporate parent must produce documents of wholly-owned subsidiary but not documents of 43.8%-owned subsidiary that conducted its corporate affairs separately).

84. *See Lethbridge v. British Aerospace PLC*, No. 89 Civ. 1407, 1990 WL 194915, at *1 (S.D.N.Y. Nov. 28, 1990).

85. 176 F.R.D. 75, 79 (W.D.N.Y. 1996).

Ernst & Young LLP to produce documents from Ernst & Young Singapore and Ernst & Young Thailand. The court found that plaintiffs failed to meet their burden of showing control because the three companies, while part of a common association, operated separately. Ernst & Young Singapore and Ernst & Young Thailand "refused to turn over documents to Ernst & Young LLP in Dallas because it has a policy against voluntarily providing documents to be used in litigation."[86] The court ruled: "[W]here Ernst & Young's foreign entities have refused to voluntarily provide the documents in question, it necessarily follows that Ernst & Young LLP in Dallas does not have control over the documents."

e.   Control Imposed by Law

Control may be imposed by law. *Tomlinson v. El Paso Corp.* involved claims that the employer's actions relating to a pension plan violated ERISA. Plaintiffs sought discovery of certain data from a third-party benefits administrator, and the employer claimed that it neither possessed nor controlled the data and, therefore, could not produce it. The court rejected the employer's argument. U.S. Department of Labor regulations applying to ERISA plans required that the employer maintain the data that plaintiffs sought. The court wrote:

> ERISA imposes upon the Defendants the duty to ensure that the "record-keeping system has reasonable controls" such that its employee benefits records are "accessible . . . in such a manner as they may be readily inspected or examined." . . . Defendants cannot delegate their duties to a third party under ERISA. . . . Consequently, Defendants are in possession, custody or control over the requested data . . . such that they have, or should have, the authority and ability to obtain the requested data.[87]

f.   Control Based on Agency

Corporations may have a legal right to obtain documents from their agents. In *City of Seattle v. Professional Basketball Club, LLC*, plaintiff sought the production of documents, including e-mails, from members of the limited liability corporation. The court stated:

> Here, the question is whether the City has met its burden in establishing that PBC has a legal right to obtain documents from its members. That question turns on whether a principal-agent relationship exists between PBC and its members. . . .[88]

Applying Oklahoma law, the court examined the operating agreement applicable to PBC and determined that each member was a "manager" under Oklahoma law. The court concluded: "Because a manager is an agent . . . the requisite principal-agent relationship exists to establish that PBC has the legal right to obtain documents upon demand from its members."

g.   Outside Directors

Most major U.S. corporations have outside directors as part of their boards. These directors may have material responsive to production requests.

---

86.   No. 3:98–064–T, 1999 WL 20943, at *3 (N.D. Tex. Jan. 13, 1999).

87.   245 F.R.D. 474, 477 (D. Colo. 2007).

88.   No. C07–1620, 2008 WL 539809, at *2 (W.D. Wash. Feb. 25, 2008).

Do corporations have an obligation to preserve documents in the hands of outside directors, who are deliberately separate from the corporation? In *In re Triton Energy Limited Securities Litigation*, Triton did not inform its outside directors to preserve documents. Triton argued that it only had control over its employees and the documents within the employees' possession, and the outside directors were not employees. The court never answered the question of control, but instead stated: "The Court is of the opinion that it would have been prudent and within the spirit of the law for Triton to instruct its officers and directors to preserve and produce any documents in their possession, custody, or control."[89]

h. Control Over Third Party Service Providers

In *Columbia Pictures v. Bunnell*, defendants contracted with Panther, a third-party service provider, to serve as a "middleman" for people trying to access defendants' website. Plaintiffs sought server log data from defendants, and that data was in the hands of Panther. The Magistrate Judge concluded that defendants controlled the server log data:

> The record reflects that defendants have the ability to manipulate at will how the Server Log Data is routed. Consequently, the court concludes that even though the Server Log Data is now routed to Panther and is temporarily stored in Panther's RAM, the data remains in defendants' possession, custody or control.[90]

On appeal, the district court agreed with the Magistrate Judge's conclusion that defendants controlled the server log data: "As the record reflects that Defendants have the ability to reroute the Server Log Data through their own servers . . . , the Court finds that the Magistrate Judge's finding that the Defendants' [sic] control the Server Log Data was not clearly erroneous."[91]

In *Keir v. Unumprovident Corp.*, the defendant failed to take the necessary steps to preserve back-up tapes in the possession of a third-party vendor. The plaintiffs sought the production of e-mails, which required the defendant to preserve certain back-up tapes maintained by IBM, a third-party vendor. Various errors and missteps resulted in the loss of certain potentially-relevant e-mails. While the court ultimately ruled that the mistakes were the "fault of no one," the court found that the defendant failed to consult with IBM to ensure that the relevant back-up tapes were preserved.[92]

i. Practice Note: Attorneys as Equals Before the Courts

At a hearing before the Magistrate Judge, counsel for NTL Europe consented to NTL Europe reviewing and producing documents held by New NTL. NTL Europe moved for reconsideration, alleging that the attorney was "too junior to knowingly consent." The Magistrate Judge rejected the argument: "Second-guessing a more junior attorney's representation to the Court is not a basis for a firm to seek reconsideration. It certainly is not a basis for the Court to grant it."

---

89. No. 5:98CV256, 2002 WL 32114464, at *6 (E.D. Tex. Mar. 7, 2002).

90. No. CV 06–1093, 2007 WL 2080419 (C.D. Cal. May 29, 2007).

91. *Columbia Pictures, Inc. v. Bunnell*, 245 F.R.D. 443, 453 (C.D. Cal. 2007).

92. No. 02 Civ. 8781, 2003 WL 21997747, at *13 (S.D.N.Y. Aug. 22, 2003).

PROBLEMS

1.   Plaintiff sues defendant, a former employee, for violating a non-compete agreement and the Trade Secrets Act. Plaintiff alleges that prior to resigning, and in an effort to obtain employment, defendant repeatedly sent e-mails to one of plaintiff's competitors containing sensitive information. Plaintiff moved to compel defendant to produce the e-mails that he sent to the competitor, who is now defendant's employer. Does defendant control the documents that he sent to his new employer?

2.   Plaintiff sues defendant for employment discrimination. Defendant is a U.S. corporation and its parent corporation is a foreign corporation. Plaintiff seeks to compel the defendant to produce documents in the possession of the defendant's foreign parent corporation. Should defendant be compelled to produce documents in the possession of its foreign parent? What factors should be considered in deciding whether a subsidiary corporation should be compelled to produce documents in the possession of its parent corporation?

2.   What Is Possession?

PHILLIPS v. NETBLUE, INC.

No. C 05–4401, 2007 WL 174459 (N.D. Cal. Jan. 22, 2007)

CONTI, DISTRICT JUDGE

I.   Introduction

Plaintiff Ritchie Phillips, dba R & D Computers, ("Plaintiff") brings this suit against Netblue, Inc., formerly known as YFdirect, et al. ("Defendants") alleging violations of the Controlling the Assault of Non–Solicited Pornographic and Marketing ("CAN–SPAM") Act of 2003, 15 U.S.C. §§ 7701 et seq. and California Business and Professions Code §§ 17529 et seq. Presently before the Court is Defendants' Motion to Dismiss the Complaint for Plaintiff's Failure to Preserve Evidence.

II.   Background

* * *

All or most of the emails which form the basis of this action are not traditional text-based messages. Rather, they consist, in significant part, of hyperlinks. When the recipient opens the email, the recipient's email program reads some of these hyperlinks and displays images which reside on a remote web-server; the images themselves are not contained in the email, rather the email contains instructions which tells the recipient's email program to display the images contained on the server.

Other hyperlinks contained in the email, when clicked by the recipient, direct the recipient's web browser to an advertisement. However, frequently the recipient's web browser is not directly taken to an advertisement, but is first taken to an intermediary website, namely that of the advertiser's "affiliate" which sent the email. This site then automatically redirects the recipient's web browser to [the] advertisement located on the advertiser's server.

Defendants do not claim that Plaintiff destroyed any of the emails containing these hyperlinks. Rather, Defendants fault Plaintiff, first, for not preserving the images which these hyperlinks should display when the email is open, and claim that the hyperlinks contained on these emails can no longer be used to gather these images because "[m]any of the image files no longer exist on the remote web-servers." Defendants do not allege that Plaintiff has ever had possession or control of these remote web-servers.

Defendants also fault Plaintiff for not preserving the URLs from the series of websites to which a recipient's web browser would be directed upon clicking an advertisement link in the email. Defendants state that the advertisement links contained in the emails are no longer active, but make no claim that Plaintiff had any role in their deactivation.

III. Legal Standard

* * *

Upon finding that a party has spoiled or destroyed evidence, a court may sanction it in one of three ways: by giving an adverse inference instruction to the jury; by excluding certain testimony which is based on the spoiled or destroyed evidence; or, in extreme or "outrageous" cases, dismissing the claim of the responsible party.

Fundamentally, a court's decision whether to sanction a party for allegedly spoiling or destroying evidence depends on a finding that the party had a duty to preserve the evidence in question, which it breached. Only after answering this question in the affirmative, need the court determine what, if any, sanctions are appropriate.

IV. Discussion

Determining whether a party breached its duty of preservation requires a court to determine: 1) the scope of the accused party's duty of preservation, 2) whether the evidence in question falls within this scope, and 3) whether the actions taken by the accused party violated this duty.

As noted above, Defendants have not alleged that Plaintiff destroyed or spoiled the actual emails which they received, i.e. the email messages containing a combination of text and hyperlinks. Rather, Defendants argue that Plaintiff had the obligation to memorialize the emails as they would have appeared if opened in an email program soon after their receipt, i.e. with the images which the email program would have displayed upon automatically accessing the remote web-server where those images resided. Defendants further argue that Plaintiff had the affirmative obligation "to record the series of URLs ... to get to the final website," to which a recipient would be directed upon clicking the advertisement hyperlink in the email.

In other words, Defendants maintain that Plaintiff should have: 1) opened the emails they received; 2) then captured or recorded the images which Plaintiff's email program would have displayed upon opening the email and automatically following the hyperlinks it contained; 3) clicked on any advertisement hyperlink contained in the email; and 4) recorded the URLs of the websites to which Plaintiff's web browser would have been directed upon clicking the advertising link, including the URLs of websites which did not display any information to Plaintiff, but rather just directed Plaintiff's web browser to another website.

The absurdity of this argument is patent. * * * The fundamental factor is that the document, or other potential objects of evidence, must be in the party's possession, custody, or control for any duty to preserve to attach. * * * One cannot keep what one does not have.

Defendants do not complain that Plaintiff failed to keep safe from harm or destruction what Plaintiff had; they admit that Plaintiff retained the e-mails as they were sent to him. See Motion and Reply. Rather, they complain that Plaintiff did not memorialize other evidence to which the e-mails could have [led] Plaintiff. This is not a complaint regarding Plaintiff's alleged failure to preserve evidence, but rather Plaintiff's alleged failure to gather evidence. The law imposes no obligation upon a party to gather evidence other than the requirement that a party have sufficient evidence to support their claim. The question whether either party in this action has met that requirement is one which will be decided by the jury.

V. Conclusion

For the foregoing reasons, Defendants' Motion to Dismiss the Complaint for Plaintiff's Failure to Preserve Evidence is DENIED. * * *

COMMENTARY

a. Opportunity to Possess/Functional Control

In *In re WRT Energy Securities Litigation*, the court held that a party had a duty to preserve documents which it had been given an opportunity to possess but declined. In that case, as a result of a bankruptcy, Gulfport, a third party, acquired 1,100 boxes of documents that were being preserved as part of ongoing litigation. After the parties in the securities fraud case had reviewed the documents, Gulfport's general counsel notified the parties that it intended to destroy the documents because it would be leasing the warehouse in which they were being stored. None of the parties objected to Gulfport disposing of the documents.

After the documents had been destroyed, plaintiffs disclosed, for the first time, that their expert would be opining on additional topics, and the defendants objected because it no longer had access to the documents to refute plaintiffs' expert's new opinions. The court held that plaintiffs had an obligation to preserve the documents that were relevant to previously undisclosed expert topics despite the fact that plaintiffs neither had custody of the documents nor destroyed them. The court wrote:

In the instant case, the plaintiffs ... had functional control of the Gulfport documents since they were advised that the documents would be destroyed and were given the opportunity to take custody of them. Therefore, the preservation obligation attached.[93]

As a result of plaintiffs' failure to preserve the documents, the court ruled that plaintiffs could not contest key issues at trial, that defendants would receive an adverse inference instruction, and that plaintiffs must pay for defendants' attorneys' fees associated with the motion as well as for new analyses that defendants' expert had to perform.

b.   Access Alone Does Not Equal Possession

In *In re Kuntz*, the Texas Supreme Court ruled, in a divorce proceeding, that access alone does not equal possession. In an effort to enforce a settlement agreement, the wife sought discovery about royalty payments to which the husband was entitled.[94] The documents belonged to MOXY (an oil company) and were in the possession of CLK, a consulting firm in which the husband was a manager and minority owner. Additionally, the documents contained trade secrets and the consulting agreement between MOXY and CLK obligated CLK to maintain the confidentiality of the documents.

The husband asserted that "in his individual capacity, he does not have physical possession of the requested documents and has no legal right to obtain the documents from either CLK or MOXY." The wife argued the opposite, stating that the "testimony in this case was unequivocal that the [documents] were in the [husband's] offices and he could get them anytime he wants." The Texas Supreme Court agreed with the husband:

> [Husband], an employee of CLK, lacks both physical possession of MOXY's trade secret [documents] or any "right to possess" MOXY's trade secret [documents]. At best, all [husband] has is access to MOXY's trade secret [documents] and that access is strictly limited to use of the [documents] in furtherance of his employer's services performed for MOXY. Like a bank teller with access to cash in the vault, [husband] has neither possession nor any right to possess MOXY's trade secret [documents].

c.   Possession Does Not Require Ownership

It is actual possession, not ownership, that determines whether a party must produce documents. In *In re Bankers Trust Co.*, a bank claimed that it could not produce documents in its possession because the Federal Reserve had provided the documents to the bank and maintained ownership over the documents. The court rejected the argument, stating that the bank was in "actual possession" of the documents and that "legal ownership ... is not determinative."[95]

The bank also claimed that it could not produce the documents because a federal regulation forbade the bank from doing so. The court also rejected this argument. While recognizing that "federal regulations should be adhered to

---

93.   *In re WRT Energy Sec. Litig.*, 246 F.R.D. 185, 195 (S.D.N.Y. 2007).

94.   *In re Kuntz*, 124 S.W.3d 179, 183 (Tex. 2003).

95.   *In re Bankers Trust Co.*, 61 F.3d 465, 469 (6th Cir. 1995).

and given full force ... whenever possible," the court found that the Federal Reserve, which promulgated the regulation in question, did not have "the power to promulgate federal regulations in direct contravention of the Federal Rules of Civil Procedure." The court concluded, "Congress did not empower the Federal Reserve to prescribe regulations that direct a party to deliberately disobey a court order, subpoena, or other judicial mechanism requiring the production of information."

Similarly, in *United States v. National Broadcasting Co.*, a dispute arose over former President Nixon's documents. The court wrote: "It must be noted that any determinations made by this Court regarding the motions before it does not involve the question of 'ownership' of former President Nixon's documents. What is involved here is the 'possession, custody and control' of these documents."[96]

PROBLEM

1.   Would the result have been different in *In re Kuntz* had the husband been sued in his capacity as a manager and owner of the consulting firm? Why?

---

96.   65 F.R.D. 415, 419–20 (C.D. Cal. 1974).

III

Meet and Confer (Rule 26(f)) and Initial Scheduling Conference (Rule 16)

■ ■ ■

IN RE SEROQUEL PRODUCTS LIABILITY LITIGATION
244 F.R.D. 650 (M.D. Fla. 2007)

BAKER, MAGISTRATE JUDGE

In this multidistrict litigation, Plaintiffs have sued Defendants for claims arising for alleged injuries from ingesting AstraZeneca's Seroquel, an atypical anti-psychotic medication that allegedly can cause diabetes and related disorders.

Plaintiffs have moved for sanctions based on AstraZeneca's "failure to timely comply with numerous discovery obligations since the inception of this litigation" based on four categories of conduct. Plaintiffs base their Motion for Sanctions, first, on AZ's failure to produce, in a readable format, key elements of the IND/NDA [Investigational New Drug/New Drug Applications prepared for the FDA] in November 2006 as ordered, [and] not producing a key element until June 2007. Second, Plaintiffs contend that AZ failed to produce organizational charts by January 2006 as ordered and withheld the vast majority of them until May 14, 2007. Third, Plaintiffs argue AZ failed to identify all relevant databases which it was obligated to identify in January 2007, instead identifying only a fraction; to date, Plaintiffs have now identified fifty-nine relevant databases. Fourth, Plaintiffs' strongest contention is that, although AZ was to produce electronic discovery from its self-chosen "custodians"—those employees most knowledgeable about Seroquel and its development—AZ waited until mid-May to begin production of the overwhelming majority of the documents and the documents actually produced have significant errors of omission and were not readable or searchable.

* * *

I. Background

This multidistrict litigation was transferred to the Middle District of Florida by the Judicial Panel on Multidistrict Litigation on July 10, 2006.

Doc. No. 1. On August 15, 2006, Judge Conway entered an order setting the first pretrial status and discovery conference for September 7, 2006. At that hearing there was a substantial discussion as to expectations for the progress of discovery. It was the Court's expectation that the indisputably relevant material would be produced quickly and without difficulty, despite its volume. Counsel for AZ requested 60 days to complete electronic formatting of the NDA and IND. This extra time was deemed necessary to eliminate the possibility of being unable to meet the Court's deadlines. The Court's reliance on experienced counsels' ability to accomplish routine matters routinely and timely was in vain.

During the status conference held on November 20, 2006, the Court requested that the parties meet and confer "to submit either agreed proposals to cover document preservation, production protocol and resolution of this issue about formatting of things already produced by December 5, 2006." However, instead of submitting an agreed proposal for production protocol and formatting, the parties submitted competing proposals apparently without a good faith conference * * *. Three days before the December 8, 2006 status conference, the parties finally began discussions about electronic documents being produced with searchable load files, bates-stamped TIFF's[1] and various metadata fields. Following the status conferences before the Court on December 11—which the Court had to adjourn and carry over to December 12, 2006 because the parties had been unable to agree ahead of time—the parties proposed a Joint Motion to adopt two case management orders [hereafter CMO 2].

The Joint Motion stated, "It is the stated policy of AZ counsel, and its client, ... commensurate with the goals of these MDL cases[,] ... get to Plaintiffs' counsel *in a timely manner* and in *a format usable* the necessary production documents that the opposing side will need to help them develop, evaluate, and understand their cases for purposes of ultimate prosecution and/or dismissal of cases." * * * On its face, the proposal did that. Unfortunately, AZ has not lived up to producing discovery in a timely manner or useable format.

The proposed CMO 2 submitted by the parties set forth deadlines for AstraZeneca's production of organizational charts for its corporate structure, the Seroquel team, and the drug safety team for the past ten years; listings of 80 (eighty) custodians from whom it is collecting documents; listing of databases concerning document production and preservation; timing for interviews of knowledgeable AstraZeneca IT persons, and the parties' agreed format of the production of custodial files. As the Court commented at the time, "The failure of the Defendant to investigate and understand its own records and documents and to prepare them for production has not met the expectations of the Court as discussed at the

---

1. TIFF (Tagged Image File Format) is one of the most widely used and supported graphic file formats for storing bit-mapped images, with many different compression formats and resolutions. A TIFF file is characterized by its "tif" file name extension. The Sedona Conference Glossary for E–Discovery and Digital Information Management (The Sedona Conference Working Group Series, May 2005 Version), available at http://www.thesedonaconference.org; cited in *Williams v. Sprint/United Management Co.* 230 F.R.D. 640. 643 (D. Kan. 2005).

September 2006 Conference." The Court also commented on its misgivings as to the "proposed CMO 2 regarding production and preservation of Defendant's documents, [which] still seems unduly cumbersome. Nonetheless, if the parties are confident that their agreement will allow them to present issues to the Court for appropriate consideration and disposition without delays engendered by claims of non production of information, the proposal can be approved."

On January 26, 2007, Judge Conway entered CMO 2, portions of which were adopted verbatim from the parties' proposed CMO 2. That order set forth specific undertakings and obligations regarding provision of discovery without the need for separate requests under the rules of procedure. Matters included a schedule for production of organizational charts; identification of AZ's first round of eight chosen witnesses, all of whose documents would be produced earliest; AZ's identification of relevant databases (including informal interviews with AZ's IT staff); the required format for electronic documents (including required metadata fields); and deduplication of documents.

On April 26, 2007, Plaintiffs filed their Motion to Compel Defendants to Provide Complete Certified Production of the First Eight Custodial Files and All Other Custodial Files Produced to Date; * * * The Court denied the Motion to Compel without prejudice to allow the parties time to confer "in good faith and *in extenso*" on the issues described in the Motion to Compel; the Court also set an evidentiary hearing on the matters raised in the Motion for June 13, 2007, alerting the parties:

ANY PARTY WHOSE CONDUCT NECESSITATES THE EVIDENTIARY HEARING SHOULD EXPECT THE IMPOSITION OF SANCTIONS FOR ANY UNREASONABLE OR INAPPROPRIATE CONDUCT OR POSITION TAKEN WITH RESPECT TO THESE MATTERS.

On June 8, 2007, the evidentiary hearing was canceled based on the parties' Joint Statement of Resolved Issues and Notice that a Hearing is Not Required filed on June 7, 2007. At that time, Plaintiffs accepted the representations made by AZ that corrections would be made to the problems Plaintiffs identified in the Motion to Compel, *e.g.,* load files, metadata, bates numbering, page breaks, excel spreadsheets, and blank documents; the CANDA [Computer Assisted New Drug Application, filed with the FDA] would also be produced; and the parties would continue to confer on the database production.

However, less than one month later, on July 3, 2007, Plaintiffs filed their Motion for Sanctions, one business day before the July 5, 2007 Status Conference. * * *

II. Legal Framework
Standards for Electronic Discovery in Complex Litigation

As businesses increasingly rely on electronic record keeping, the number of potential discoverable documents has skyrocketed and so also has the potential for discovery abuse. Of even more consequence in this complex litigation is the fact that it involves development of a drug that spent many years in development by an international corporation and has been distributed worldwide, with the number of Plaintiffs in this multi-district litigation exceeding 6,500. The Manual for Complex Litigation (Fourth Edition) provides the following guidance for dealing with such vast amounts of data:

> Computerized data have become commonplace in litigation. The sheer volume of such data, when compared with conventional paper documentation, can be staggering. . . . One gigabyte is the equivalent of 500,000 type-written pages. Large corporate computer networks create backup data measured in terabytes, or 1,000,000 megabytes; each terabyte represents the equivalent of 500 billion [sic] typewritten pages of plain text.

> Digital or electronic information can be stored in any of the following: mainframe computers, network servers, personal computers, hand-held devices, automobiles, or household appliances; or it can be accessible via the Internet, from private networks, or from third parties. Any discovery plan must address issues relating to such information, including the search for it and its location, retrieval, form of production, inspection, preservation, and use at trial.

* * *

> The judge should encourage the parties to discuss the scope of proposed computer-based discovery early in the case, particularly any discovery of data beyond that available to the responding parties in the ordinary course of business. The requesting parties should identify the information they require as narrowly and precisely as possible, and the responding parties should be forthcoming and explicit in identifying what data are available from what sources, to allow formulation of a realistic computer-based discovery plan. Rule 26(b)(2)(C)(iii) allows the court to limit or modify the extent of otherwise allowable discovery if the burdens outweigh the likely benefit—the rule should be used to discourage costly, speculative, duplicative, or unduly burdensome discovery of computer data and systems. . . .

* * *

MANUAL FOR COMPLEX LITIGATION § 11.446, *Discovery of Computerized Data* (Fourth Ed. 2004).

Against the backdrop of the heightened demands for usability and searchability of the electronic discovery produced in a multi-district case, is the need for the parties to confer on the format of the production, keeping in mind that the responding party is best situated to evaluate the procedures, and the need to produce the information in a reasonably usable form to enable the receiving party to have the same ability to access, search, and display the information.

Particularly in complex litigation, there is a heightened need for the parties to confer about the format of the electronic discovery being produced. Pursuant to Federal Rule of Civil Procedure 26, the parties are expected to confer, not only on the nature and basis of their claims and defenses, but also to discuss "any issues relating to disclosure or discovery or electronically stored information, including the form or forms in which it should be produced." FED. R. CIV. P. 26(f)(3). Rule 26(f) was amended on December 1, 2006 to direct the parties to discuss discovery of electronically stored information during their discovery-planning conference. FED. R. CIV. P. 26(f) advisory committee notes. * * * According to Rule 26:

> It may be important for the parties to discuss their systems, and accordingly important for counsel to become familiar with those systems before the conference. With that information, the parties can develop a discovery plan that takes into account the capabilities of their computer systems. In appropriate cases identification of, and early discovery from, individuals with special knowledge of a party's computer systems may be helpful.
>
> * * * For example, the parties may specify the topics for such discovery and the time period for which discovery will be sought. They may identify the various sources of such information within a party's control that should be searched for electronically stored information. They may discuss whether the information is reasonably accessible to the party that has it, including the burden or cost of retrieving and reviewing the information. Rule 26(f)(3) explicitly directs the parties to discuss the form or forms in which electronically stored information might be produced. *The parties may be able to reach agreement on the forms of production, making discovery more efficient.* * * *

FED. R. CIV. P. 26(f)(3), advisory committee notes (emphasis added).

A leading resource on dealing with electronic discovery is the Second Edition of the Sedona Principles, on which AZ relied at the July 26, 2007 hearing on the Motion for Sanctions. Principle 3 states, "Parties should confer early in discovery regarding the preservation and production of electronically stored information when these matters are at issue in the litigation and seek to agree on the scope of each party's rights and responsibilities." *The Sedona Principles, Second Edition: Best Practices, Recommendations & Principles for Addressing Electronic Document Discovery* (The Sedona Conference Working Group Series, 2007).[2]

* * *

III. Contentions and Analysis

* * *

---

2. The Sedona Conference is a nonprofit legal policy research and educational organization which sponsors Working Groups on cutting-edge issues of law. The Working Group on Electronic Document Production is comprised of judges, attorneys, and technologists experienced in electronic discovery and document management matters.

Particular Issues

1. IND/NDA—Plaintiffs contend that AZ failed to produce a key element of the IND/NDA in November 2006 as ordered, not producing it until June 2007, and the materials produced were not in usable form. At the September 7, 2006 hearing, AZ stated that the electronic formatting of the IND/DNA had begun. The Court allowed AZ until November 7, 2006 to produce it even though, as the Court pointed out, much of the material had been produced to the FDA in electronic format and should have been prepared for production earlier. Plaintiffs contend they had to spend "nearly two months of work" to make it suitable for substantive review and the production omitted the CANDA safety database—which was not produced until June 8, 2007.

Plaintiff[s'] expert and fact witness, Jonathan Jaffe, testified that on November 15, 2007, Plaintiffs realized the IND/NDA production was not searchable for several reasons: no metadata was retrieved; there were multi-page TIFF images, some of which consisted of more than 20,000 pages; there was nothing showing bates numbering; 8% of the entire production was in one lengthy document which could only be opened with a very powerful work station; and there were no load files; thus the production was not in a usable or searchable format. At that point, on November 17, 2006, Mr. Jaffe sent to AZ's counsel an email suggesting fixes to the IND/NDA. As of nine months later, or the date of the July 26, 2007 hearing, AZ had not fixed problems according to Mr. Jaffe, whose team attempted to fix problems themselves by splitting apart the documents and redoing the bates numbering. AZ had offered to do it for $26,000 over 6 weeks; it took Mr. Jaffe's team more than a month with a few dedicated team members.

Mr. Jaffe further testified that in November to December 2006, Plaintiffs asked for electronic documents in native or near native format, with metadata, and extracted text and image files, that had page breaks in it. Mr. Jaffe * * * described extensive efforts to resolve technical issues. Mr. Jaffe made multiple requests to speak to technical people, but he was told there was no IT person with whom he could confer regarding the IT issues.[4] * * *

* * *

3. Database Production—Plaintiffs argue AZ failed to identify all relevant databases by January 5, 2007, which it was obligated to do pursuant to CMO 2; instead AZ identified only 15 databases. However, to date, Plaintiffs have identified fifty-nine relevant databases through additional interviews, depositions, and meetings. Plaintiffs contend that AZ has produced no information whatsoever from any of these databases, and they are resisting producing databases without Requests for Production. Plaintiffs requested basic information about each database in order to

---

4. AZ's refusal to allow contact between individuals with appropriate technical backgrounds as part of the effort to resolve technical issues is an inexplicable departure from the requirements of Rule 26, the Sedona Principles and this Court's expressed expectations.

assist with prioritization, formatting and production—information which, by its own admission, AZ refused to provide until July 2, 2007.

AZ responds that it should not be sanctioned because Plaintiffs have "not even served AZ with any discovery requests for wholesale production of the databases," AZ has not violated an order to produce, and it only identified a small number of databases initially because they only had to identify those that correlated to the 14 discrete categories identified by Plaintiffs. In addition, AZ has produced IT witnesses for informal interviews and four days of 30(b)(6) depositions about AZ databases.

CMO 2 required that, by January 5, 2007, AstraZeneca provide Plaintiffs with a list of databases of the following type: 1) adverse event database; 2) sales call tracking database; 3) IMS database; 4) clinical communications database; 5) regulatory database; 6) regulatory contact databases; 7) clinical trial database; 8) medical literature database; 9) research report database; 10) documentum or similar databases (document management systems used by many pharmacy companies); 11) visitor speakers bureau and/or thought leader databases; 12) clinical payments database; 13) field force rosters; and 14) instant message, voicemail, discussion forum and prior website page databases, transcripts and recovery.

By January 25, 2007, AstraZeneca was required to allow Plaintiffs to conduct informal interviews, in person or by telephone, of a knowledgeable AstraZeneca-employed IT person or persons who can adequately address plaintiffs' questions about said databases and how information can potentially be produced or extracted from them. "If, after any such interview, Plaintiffs determine that the individual cannot adequately answer their questions or does not have the requisite knowledge about the database in question, plaintiffs shall identify the issues for which they seek additional information, and AstraZeneca shall promptly identify an IT employee with knowledge of such issues and present that person for interview." AZ's identification of the databases would not be construed as an agreement to produce them; the parties were to confer regarding the discoverability and feasibility of any request for production of a database, including the form and scope of any such production.

Testimony from the only two witnesses presented[6] who had any involvement in the discovery process (as well as the exhibits) establishes that, with respect to identification and production of relevant portions of databases, "what we have here is failure to communicate." Worse, the posturing and petulance displayed by both sides on this issue shows a disturbing departure from the expected professionalism necessary to get this case ready for appropriate disposition. Identifying relevant records and working out technical methods for their production is a cooperative

---

6. AZ's decision to offer only the testimony of a junior level attorney, only somewhat versed in technical issues and one who came late to the process is puzzling. AZ provided essentially no information as to how it organized its search for relevant material, what steps it took to assure reasonable completeness and quality control. Its efforts at finding solutions to technical problems are likewise unilluminated.

undertaking, not part of the adversarial give and take. This is not to say that the parties cannot have reasonable disputes regarding the scope of discovery. But such disputes should not entail endless wrangling about simply identifying what records exist and determining their format. This case includes a myriad of significant legal issues and complexities engendered by the number of plaintiffs. Dealing as effective advocates representing adverse interests on those matters is challenge enough. It is not appropriate to seek an advantage in the litigation by failing to cooperate in the identification of basic evidence. The parties' mode of proceeding here has prevented the presentation of any genuine issues as to the proper scope of production of material from databases. Both parties must bear some of the responsibility for the breakdown, but it is primarily AZ, as the creator and owner of the information, which has failed to make a sincere effort to facilitate an understanding of what records are kept and what their availability might be.

The Court finds sanctions are warranted for AZ's violation of the Court's explicit order in CMO 2 that the Plaintiffs were to interview AZ's IT employees and[,] if [] they still had questions after the interview, would identify the issues for which they still needed information, and AstraZeneca was to identify an IT employee with the relevant knowledge. In addition, the parties were to confer regarding the discoverability and feasibility of any request for production of a database. Based on the testimony of Mr. Jaffe, Plaintiffs' interviews of the AZ IT employees left questions about the databases unanswered because they were not clear or specific. Plaintiffs' attempt to get further clarification through the chart was within the bounds of conferring further under CMO 2.

* * * AZ stopped participating in the process to confer on the databases despite its explicit agreement to produce them and to cooperate in providing personnel familiar for Plaintiffs to interview to determine which ones to seek production of. [AZ's representative testified that] AZ never intended to produce databases, it would only produce some subset of information; yet he emailed Plaintiffs' counsel that AZ would work cooperatively with Plaintiffs on production of databases. AZ's failure to cooperate in identification leading to appropriate production of its relevant databases is conduct sanctionable under Rule 37. The relief to be awarded will be dealt with separately.

4. Custodial Production—AZ's biggest failure has been what can properly be characterized as "purposeful sluggishness" in the production from its self-chosen "custodians"—those employees most knowledgeable about Seroquel and its development. Plaintiffs contend AZ waited until mid-May 2007 to begin production of the overwhelming majority of the documents from these "custodians" and the documents produced have significant errors of omission and are not readable or searchable. Plaintiffs contend that the custodial production has a great deal of missing data, *e.g.*, although AstraZeneca has a system to deliver voicemail, faxes, and video into Outlook inboxes, none has been produced; there are few emails from some custodians, and email boxes are missing from alternate email boxes. Plaintiffs also contend that many relevant emails and documents were not identified and produced because AZ performed an unreasonable key word search.[7] Plaintiffs allege that other relevant documents were omitted because the best available de-duplication method was not used; AZ missed deadlines and produced the electronic documents late; a significant portion of the production had blank pages; new load files were not searchable, in part because the date formats in the metadata were inconsistently loaded and email attachments not consistently associated or identified; authors were not identified as custodians for files; transposed metadata recipients/authors; and no page breaks were inserted in 3.75 million pages.

AZ responds that Plaintiffs have not met the standard for imposing sanctions, which is bad faith. AZ argues that Plaintiffs' discovery issues have been a moving target, and that issues raised by Plaintiffs have been resolved or "in the process of being resolved" by July 20, 2007. AZ has produced "massive" amounts of discovery—10 million pages[8]—with few mistakes and by the June 30, 2007 deadline. AZ argues that Plaintiffs were aware that it was using search terms to limit the "custodians" discovery to identify potentially responsive electronic documents, citing the Sedona Principles. AZ contends that it gave Plaintiffs a list of its 60 search terms in April 2007 and if Plaintiffs wanted AZ to use additional terms, Plaintiff could have simply asked for them. * * *

* * *

The record shows a number of specific failings in AZ's chosen efforts to meet its discovery commitments. The key word search was plainly inadequate. Attachments, including non-verbal files, were not provided. Relevant emails were omitted. AZ's deduplication method remains mysterious. Production was tardy. AZ's efforts in preventing and solving technical problems were woefully deficient. These shortcomings were adequately and persuasively described by Plaintiffs' witnesses. * * *

AZ purported to embrace the requirements of Rule 26 and the Sedona Principles. However, the reality was to the contrary. For example, while key word searching is a recognized method to winnow relevant documents from large repositories, use of this technique must be a cooperative and informed process. Rather than working with Plaintiffs from the outset to reach agreement on appropriate and comprehensive search terms and methods, AZ undertook the task in secret. Common sense dictates that sampling and other quality assurance techniques must be employed to meet requirements of completeness. If AZ took such steps, it has not identified or validated them.

---

7. Examples include omitting Seroquel's generic name, acronyms for diabetes, hyperglycaemia spelled the British way; and endocrine. The search method apparently failed to include common misspellings or the singular forms of words and failed to make allowance for spaces or dashes.

8. In argument, AZ has repeatedly relied on the sheer volume of documents produced as an accomplishment somehow justifying its shortcomings. In the context of this case, the Court is not impressed by the large number of relevant documents, especially since vast quantities were produced in a virtually unusable manner.

Many of the other technical problems * * * likely could have been resolved far sooner and less expensively had AZ cooperated by fostering consultation between the technical staffs responsible for production. Instead, AZ shielded its third party technical contractor from all contact with Plaintiffs. This approach is antithetical to the Sedona Principles and is not an indicium of good faith.

This is not to say that AZ completely ignored its responsibilities. Mr. Dupre [a lawyer representing AZ] and other representatives from his firm did participate in extended efforts to confer with Plaintiffs. However, the lateness and general ineffectuality of these efforts was demonstrated by Mr. Dupre's concessions as to the limitations of his role. Mr. Dupre admitted on cross-examination that he had nothing to do with developing the key word search in this case and had never prepared any other key word search before; he did not know who was the architect of the key word search. Despite this lack of knowledge, he was confident that he knew how the emails were collected. Mr. Dupre also had no knowledge of how the 80 "custodians" were chosen. In response to a query from the Court, Mr. Dupre could not identify with certainty who was responsible from AZ or its counsel or vendor for assuring document production had been sufficient to comply with the Local Rules and the Sedona Principles. In terms of the documentation about how the key word search was developed, Mr. Dupre testified that AZ used [a] stock interview for "custodians"; but he was not privy to any sort of written protocol. He testified that there was no document production quality control or master plan with which he was familiar. He testified that the vendor never discussed the key word list with Plaintiff, and that vendors never participated in a meet and confer, although IT experts from lawyers attended the meet and confer.

* * *

Sanctions may be imposed against AZ under Rule 37(b)(2) based on its noncompliance with a court order, notwithstanding a lack of willfulness or bad faith, although such factors "are relevant . . . to the sanction to be imposed for the failure." 8A Charles Alan Wright, Arthur R. Miller & Richard L. Marcus, FEDERAL PRACTICE & PROCEDURE § 2283, at 608 (2d ed. 1994). * * * "Sanctions proceedings can be disruptive, costly, and may create personal antagonism inimical to an atmosphere of cooperation. Moreover, a resort to sanctions may reflect a breakdown of case management. . . . On the other hand, *the stakes involved in and the pressures generated by complex litigation may lead some parties to violate the rules.* Although sanctions should not generally be a case management tool, a willingness to resort to sanctions, *sua sponte* if necessary, may ensure compliance with the management program. . . . Although sanctions should be a last resort, they are sometimes unavoidable and may be imposed for general or specific deterrence, to punish, or to remedy the consequences of misconduct." *Id.*

Based on the testimony at the hearing, the Court is troubled by nature of the parties' efforts to "meet and confer" on specific issues. One of the apparently successful efforts to collaborate on discovery, which led to cancellation of the June hearing, was, to an unacceptable degree, illusory. AZ suspects that Plaintiffs have, to some degree, attempted to manufacture issues and to raise them just prior to scheduled status conferences so as to tarnish AZ in the eyes of the Court. This mistrust undermines the efficacy of the meet and confer requirement. AZ itself, despite what must be considerable expenditures in attempting to comply with discovery, has failed to bring appropriate personnel to the table at appropriate times to resolve non adversarial issues.

In this case, AZ never discussed with Plaintiffs which search terms to use as part of the search. There was no dialogue to discuss the search terms, as required by Rules 26 and 34. AZ eventually disclosed in April 2007 that a key word search had been conducted, not in seeking collaboration on the words to use, but rather as part of the dialogue on certifying the "custodial" production. More astounding is AZ's continued failure to produce single-page TIFF documents that would be "usable" or "reasonably accessible" in accordance with the federal discovery rules and the Sedona Principles. AZ's interpretation of CMO 2, that it did not explicitly require page breaks, is absurd—Mr. Dupre could not explain any other way the documents would be guaranteed to appear as "single pages." Mr. Dupre attributed many of the severe problems with the load files and the metadata to vendor errors. According to the Sedona Principles cited by AZ several times at the hearing, a party is responsible for the errors of its vendors. [Sedona Principle 6d]. Moreover, such problems in fundamental aspects of the production, worked on by different vendors, were inevitable in a 10 million page without the requisite quality control oversight.

CONCLUSION

The Court finds that AZ has been "purposely sluggish" in making effective production to Plaintiffs. Given the Court's mandate of a tight schedule in this case, AZ's various decisions and problems that resulted in this sluggishness appears to have benefitted AZ by limiting the time available to Plaintiffs to review information and to follow up.

* * *

[A]s a discovery deadline or trial date draws near, discovery conduct that might have been considered "merely" discourteous at an earlier point in the litigation may well breach a party's duties to its opponent and to the court. . . . [When defendant] had repeatedly missed deadlines to produce the e-mails—[defendant] was under an obligation to be as co-operative as possible. Viewed in that light, [defendant's] "purposefully sluggish" acts—particularly its as-yet-unexplained refusal to answer basic technical questions about the tape until prompted to do so by the District Court—may well have constituted sanctionable misconduct in their own right.

Residential Funding Corp. v. DeGeorge Financial Corp., 306 F.3d 99, 112 (2d Cir. 2002).

Similarly, in this case, AZ has not been as cooperative as possible in resolving the custodial issues. It is undisputed that the production "completed" on June 30, 2007 had load file, metadata, page break and key word search problems, making the 10 million pages of documents unaccessible, unsearchable, and unusable as contemplated under the Rules. It was not clear at the July 26 hearing, or even as of the date of this Order, that these profound technical issues have been resolved by the re-production efforts delivered to Plaintiffs on July 20, 2007. The Court finds that sanctions are warranted for AZ's failure to produce "usable" or "reasonably accessible" documents.

However, the Court is unable to determine the appropriate nature and amount of sanctions at this time. Plaintiffs will be allowed a further opportunity to present evidence and argument as to any prejudice or damages from AZ's failure timely to produce "usable" or "reasonably accessible" documents in this litigation, including motion costs.

COMMENTARY

As demonstrated by *In re Seroquel*, the various volume, formatting, readability, and searchability issues surrounding ESI can present difficult problems for litigants, potentially creating time-consuming and expensive discovery disputes. Consequently, courts increasingly interpret Rule 26 to require the parties to cooperate and communicate to avoid these potential problems. The 2006 Amendments to Rule 26 have impliedly removed the adversarial element from the Rule 26(f) discovery conference or "meet and confer." Recent cases indicate that attorneys, who up until recently often treated discovery as just another phase in the adversarial process, have been slow to recognize that Rule 26 now encourages cooperation and transparency in electronic discovery practices.

The meet and confer(s) called for by Rule 26(f) work in conjunction with the parties' Rule 16 pretrial conference with the court. Specifically, Rule 26(f)(1) requires the parties to meet and confer to develop a proposed discovery plan prior to the Rule 16 pretrial conference, typically scheduled by the court at the outset of the litigation for the purpose of creating a scheduling order for discovery and other pretrial matters. After the Rule 26(f) meet and confer, the parties must submit a written report to the court outlining a proposed discovery plan for the litigation. At the Rule 16 pretrial conference, the parties meet with the court to discuss, among other matters, the proposed discovery schedule and any anticipated discovery disputes. After the Rule 16 conference, the court issues a scheduling order, generally based in part on the parties' report, containing deadlines that will govern the timing of discovery and, potentially, provisions relating to the retrieval and production of ESI. The Rule 26(f) discovery conference is not merely a perfunctory exercise. Rather, it is an opportunity for the parties to educate themselves and their adversaries, anticipate and resolve electronic discovery disputes before they escalate, expedite the progress of their case, and assess and manage litigation costs. As a matter of strategy, the Rule 26(f) discovery conference provides the parties an opportunity to prepare themselves for the Rule 16 pretrial conference, so that they can demonstrate to the court that they have made diligent, good faith efforts to comply with the Rules and the court's policies and that they are, therefore, deserving of its confidence.

The obligation to address electronic discovery at the Rule 26(f) meet and confer rests with the litigants. The 2006 Amendments do not *require* judges to address electronic discovery in the Rule 16 scheduling order. Perhaps due to this flexibility, the attention paid by courts to litigants' meet and confer obligations varies widely across jurisdictions and from judge to judge. This may seem surprising given the ubiquity of electronic discovery disputes, but a survey of the relevant case law yields opinions that focus on electronic discovery in widely varying degrees. Likewise, some jurisdictions have promulgated local rules containing exhaustive lists of topics to be addressed by the parties at a Rule 26(f) meet and confer, while others limit their treatment of the issue to a simple verbatim recitation of Rule 26(f). Some courts defer heavily to the "best practices" and guidelines published by organizations such as The Sedona Conference and the American Bar Association. The following notes discuss some of the issues courts and litigants are addressing with regard to Rule 26(f).

1. The importance of the Rule 26(f) meet and confer is indirectly underscored by Rule 16(f)(1)(B), which authorizes a court to impose sanctions on a party or its attorney if either "is substantially unprepared to participate—or does not participate in good faith—in the [Rule 16 pretrial] conference." Although this provision was not directly affected by the 2006 Amendments, it incorporates by reference portions of Rule 16 and Rule 26 that were revised to address electronic discovery, effectively holding litigants to a higher standard of preparedness with regard to electronic discovery matters by subjecting them to a risk of sanctions for failure to sufficiently prepare for the Rule 16 pretrial conference.

The *Seroquel* case provides one example of a party's failure to live up to a court's Rule 16 expectations. Almost a year before writing the *Seroquel* opinion, the Magistrate Judge admonished the parties for failing to resolve their discovery and scheduling issues through the meet and confer process. Significantly, the Magistrate Judge noted that he was "flabbergasted as to how unprepared the parties [were]." Though neither party was sanctioned under Rule 16(f)(1)(B), the parties' pretrial disappointments caused the court to lose confidence in them, and its frustration with their conduct weighed heavily against them at later stages in the litigation.

If your adversary does not place a sufficient level of importance on electronic discovery, how might you nonetheless sufficiently prepare for the Rule 16 pretrial conference? Should you be prepared to discuss your client's systems, even though your adversary has not requested information about them? How might you document your efforts, and your adversary's disinterest, to protect you and your client should electronic discovery problems arise in the future?

2. The practical purpose of the Rule 26(f) meet and confer requirement is to facilitate the early identification of electronic discovery issues for the

purpose of preventing expensive and time-consuming discovery disputes. Once identified, the parties must be prepared to discuss any potentially problematic electronic discovery issues at the Rule 16 pretrial conference. The Advisory Committee Note to Rule 16 discusses the interplay between the two rules:

> The amendment to Rule 16(b) is designed to alert the court to the possible need to address the handling of discovery of electronically stored information early in the litigation if such discovery is expected to occur. Rule 26(f) is amended to direct the parties to discuss discovery of electronically stored information if such discovery is contemplated in the action. * * * In many instances, the court's involvement early in the litigation will help avoid difficulties that might otherwise arise.

If parties fail to adequately address electronic discovery issues during the Rule 26(f) meet and confer, and as a result, fail to identify to the court during the Rule 16 pretrial conference any anticipated electronic discovery issues, should they be precluded from raising any later-identified electronic discovery problems as the basis for a discovery motion? Suppose the later-identified problems could have been addressed inexpensively and efficiently had the parties bothered to discuss them at the Rule 26(f) meet and confer?

3. In *O'Bar v. Lowe's Home Centers, Inc.*, the court provided the parties lengthy and detailed "guidelines" to follow during and after their Rule 26(f) meet and confer.[1] For example, the court directed the parties to meet and confer on the following issues, among others:

A. The anticipated scope of requests for, and objections to, production of ESI, as well as the form of production of ESI and, specifically, but without limitation, whether production will be of the Native File, Static Image, or other searchable or non-searchable formats.

B. Whether Meta–Data is requested for some or all ESI and, if so, the volume and costs of producing and reviewing said ESI.

C. Preservation of ESI during the pendency of the lawsuit, specifically, but without limitation, applicability of the "safe harbor" provision of Fed.R.Civ.P. 37, preservation of Meta–Data, preservation of deleted ESI, back up or archival ESI, ESI contained in dynamic systems, ESI destroyed or overwritten by the routine operation of systems, and, offsite and offline ESI (including ESI stored on home or personal computers). This discussion should include whether the parties can agree on methods of review of ESI by the responding party in a manner that does not unacceptably change Meta–Data.

* * *

E. Identification of ESI that is or is not reasonably accessible without undue burden or cost, specifically, and without limitation, the identity of such sources and the reasons for a contention that the ESI is or is not reasonably accessible without undue burden or cost, the methods of storing and retrieving that ESI, and the anticipated costs and efforts involved in retrieving that ESI. The party asserting that ESI is not reasonably accessible without undue burden or cost should

---

1. No. 04 Civ. 19, 2007 WL 1299180 (W.D.N.C. May 2, 2007).

be prepared to discuss in reasonable detail the basis for such assertion.

The guidelines were intended to be followed by the litigants whenever possible and would be "considered by the Court in resolving discovery disputes, including whether sanctions should be awarded pursuant to Fed. R. Civ. P. 37."

The *Lowe's* approach sets forth the court's expectations clearly at the outset of discovery, but does it unduly restrict litigants' ability to independently craft their own discovery plans? In contrast, does the less prescriptive *Seroquel* approach place a greater burden on litigants to anticipate the precise standards to which their meet and confer efforts will later be held?

4. **EXCERPT FROM** Judge Lee H. Rosenthal, *A Few Thoughts on Electronic Discovery After December 1, 2006*, 116 Yale L.J. Pocket Part 167, 176–77 (2006).

> [J]udges must be simultaneously demanding and patient. Judges should not relax the emerging standard for a meaningful meet-and-confer exchange on electronic discovery issues. But at the same time, judges must understand the difficulties lawyers face in trying to learn their clients' information systems as well as the other disclosure and meet-and-confer subjects early in the case.

To what extent, if at all, should judges provide guidance to parties who lack knowledge regarding issues relating to electronic discovery? Given our adversarial system of justice, is it appropriate for judges to give such parties a "leg up" in observing and implementing the new rules? In considering this issue, is it relevant that electronic discovery practices and standards are currently rapidly evolving and vary across jurisdictions?

5. In *In re Bristol–Myers Squibb Securities Litigation*, the court noted that "lawyers try cases, not judges," and placed on the attorneys' shoulders the burden of cooperatively preparing an electronic discovery plan:

> [Rule] 26(f) provides that before a Rule 16 Conference, the parties "confer ... to develop a proposed discovery plan...." In the electronic age, this meet and confer should include a discussion on whether each side possesses information in electronic form, whether they intend to produce such material, whether each other's software is compatible * * * and how to allocate costs involved with each of the foregoing. [Local Rule] 26(b)(2) addresses the requirements of [Federal Rule] 26(f) and, in addition, requires parties to discuss any "special procedure." Moreover, the standard initial scheduling order in this District contains instructions on topics to be discussed in the preparation of a Joint Discovery Plan which include "(3) a description of all discovery problems encountered to date, the efforts undertaken by the parties to remedy these problems, and the parties' suggested resolution of problems; [and] (4) a description of the parties' further discovery needs." Although there may be room for clearer direction in existing rules and orders that explicitly address cost allocation in production of paper and electronic information, counsel

should take advantage of the required Rule 26(f) meeting to discuss issues associated with electronic discovery.[2]

6. The 2006 amendments' explicit reference to the importance of discussing electronic discovery issues during the Rule 26(f) meet and confer prompted many courts to revise their local rules. For instance, the United States District Courts for the District of Maryland and the District of Kansas have implemented detailed local rules governing electronic discovery.[3]

State court judges have also devised electronic discovery guidelines. In 2006, the Conference of Chief Justices recommended that, following an initial discovery hearing or conference, a judge "should inquire whether counsel have reached agreement on [a variety of electronic discovery issues] and address any disputes."

Given the importance of complying with a court's expectations regarding the discovery of ESI, attorneys must familiarize themselves with the electronic discovery local rules in force in each jurisdiction in which the attorney practices? If you were litigating a case in Maryland or Kansas, might you consider associating with a local counsel possessing superior knowledge of the local rules? If you found yourself practicing in a jurisdiction with a dearth of local rules governing electronic discovery, what authorities might you consult to determine what topics you should address during your meet and confer? What are the pros and cons of litigating in a jurisdiction with very specific and prescriptive local rules governing electronic discovery? Do such rules impose an unduly stringent standard on attorneys? Do they create a risk of inconsistent standards across jurisdictions? Do they hinder the natural evolution of the standards by which attorneys engage in electronic discovery?

7. Because electronic discovery consultants are often hired to assist attorneys in retrieving, preserving, and producing electronic information, is the participation of such consultants in the Rule 26(f) meet and confer necessary for the parties to have meaningful discussions about their electronic discovery activities? Recall that in *Seroquel*, the court, among other things, criticized the defendant for shielding its electronic discovery consultant from contact with the plaintiffs. Significantly, the court argued that this failure to include knowledgeable electronic discovery consultants in the meet and confer is "antithetical to the Sedona Principles and is not an indicium of good faith."

8. In determining that sanctions were warranted for discovery abuse in *Seroquel*, the court analyzed the whole of the discovery process leading up to the parties' dispute. The parties' efforts to meet and confer made up a very important part of this larger examination. Should attorneys engage in meet and confers and other electronic discovery activities with an expectation that the court may eventually scrutinize these activities? If so, how does this expectation of judicial scrutiny affect the meet and confer process? To what extent should a litigant memorialize the meet and confer process, and in what form?

---

2. 205 F.R.D. 437, 443–44 (D.N.J. 2002).

3. *See* United States District for the District of Maryland, *Suggested Protocol for Discovery of Electronically Stored Information*, available at http://www.mdd.uscourts.gov/news/news/ESIProtocol.pdf.; United States District Court for the District of Kansas, *Guidelines for Discovery of Electronically Stored Information (ESI)*, available at http://www.ksd.uscourts.gov/guidelines/electronicdiscoveryguidelines.pdf.

IV

Production Issues

■ ■ ■

A. RULE 34: FORM OF PRODUCTION (PAPER, ELECTRONIC, NATIVE, OR OTHER FORMS)

D'ONOFRIO v. SFX SPORTS GROUP, INC.

247 F.R.D. 43 (D.D.C. 2008)

Facciola, Magistrate Judge

* * *

I. Background

This lawsuit involves claims by plaintiff, Audrey (Shebby) D'Onofrio, that she received disparate treatment from her employer, SFX Sports Group, Inc. ("SFX"), based upon her gender. Plaintiff also alleges that she was subjected to a hostile work environment and was terminated in retaliation for her protected activities. She brings this lawsuit under the District of Columbia Human Rights Act ("DCHRA"), the Equal Pay Act, and the District of Columbia Family Medical Leave Act.

* * *

III. Electronically Stored Information

Many of the discovery disputes at issue in the Motion relate to electronically stored information. In particular, plaintiff * * * asks the court to compel the production of the Business Plan in its original electronic format, with accompanying metadata * * *.

A. Business Plan

* * *

Plaintiff argues that Rule 34 permits the production of documents outside of their original format only "if necessary," and, in this case, no such necessity exists. Defendants respond that: (a) plaintiff did not request that the Business Plan or any other documents be produced in a specific format; (b) production in original electronic format with metadata

145

is not required by the Federal Rules of Civil Procedure or in the absence of a clear agreement or court order, neither of which are present here; and (c) plaintiff has not made any attempt to demonstrate the relevance of the metadata.[4]

1. Rule 34—"If Necessary"

As an initial matter, plaintiff argues that Rule 34 of the Federal Rules of Civil Procedure permits the production of documents other than in their original format only "if necessary." Rule 34(a) states, in relevant part:

(a) In General. A party may serve on any other party a request . . . :

(1) to produce and permit the requesting party or its representative to inspect, copy, test, or sample the following items in the responding party's possession, custody, or control:

(A) any designated documents or electronically stored information-including writings, drawings, graphs, charts, photographs, sound recordings, images, and other data or data compilations-stored in any medium from which information can be obtained either directly or, if necessary, after translation by the responding party into a reasonably usable form[.]

Rule 34(a) does not set forth constraints on the manner of production, but instead establishes the permissible scope of a request. ("A party may serve on any other party a request . . ."). Consequently, the "if necessary" clause seized upon by plaintiff is actually a constraint on the requesting party rather than the responding party. In other words, electronic data is subject to discovery if it is stored in a directly obtainable medium. If, however, it is not stored in a directly obtainable medium, a request may be made of the responding party to translate the electronic data into a "reasonably usable form." Because the step of translating this type of electronic data adds an extra burden on the responding party, the request may only seek for it to be done "if [the translation is] necessary." It is not the case that this clause requires the responding party to produce data in its original form unless "necessary" to do otherwise.

2. Request for Specific Form of Production

This does not end the analysis of whether a responding party might be required to produce electronic data in its original form with metadata. To the contrary, Rule 34(b) states that a discovery request "may specify the form or forms in which electronically stored information is to be produced." Fed. R. Civ. P. 34(b)(1)(C). In this case, plaintiff argues that she so specified in Instruction No. 4 of Plaintiff's Requests for the Production of Documents (the "Instruction"):

---

4. Metadata has been defined as "information about a particular data set which describes how, when, and by whom it was collected, created, accessed, or modified and how it is formatted." *Williams v. Sprint/United Management Co.*, 230 F.R.D. 640, 646 (D. Kan. 2005) (quoting *The Sedona Guidelines: Best Practice Guidelines and Commentary for Managing Information & Records in the Electronic Age* App. F).

> [F]or any documents that are stored or maintained in files in the normal course of business, such documents shall be produced in such files, or in such a manner as to preserve and identify the file from which such documents were taken.

It is apparent that this language, when first written, was not meant to encompass electronic data. Instead it addresses a common concern of paper discovery: the identification of a document's custodian and origination. It is for this reason that the Instruction applies to documents "stored or maintained in files" and why it seeks to "preserve and identify" the identity of that file. Indeed, the Instruction makes perfect sense when one presumes "file" to refer to a physical file cabinet or folder.

Of course, "file" can also mean electronic data stored on an electronic medium. Using this definition, the Instruction can be strained to provide the responding party with two options for producing electronic documents: (a) produce the electronic file containing the document (i.e. a .PDF or .XLS file), or (b) produce the document in such a manner as to "preserve and identify the file from which" it was taken. The inclusion of the word "preserve" makes it very difficult to understand how the Instruction could apply to electronic documents; after all, how can the production of a document without the electronic file encompass the "preserv[ation]" of that electronic file? A more credible reading of the second option is that a document need not be produced as an electronic file if the alternate production "preserve[s the] identi[ty of] the file from which" it was taken. In practice this would likely refer to a "trailer" at the bottom of a printed electronic document containing its location on electronic storage media (*i.e.* an electronic spreadsheet could be printed on a piece of paper with the trailer "c: accounting harry FY07 charts.xls"). I do not know if defendants provided such a trailer because plaintiff did not attach the Business Plan to its Motion or provide any other detail concerning its format, other than to state that it was not in its original form with accompanying metadata. Nevertheless, it is clear that the Instruction, if applicable to electronic files, permits production of the Business Plan in a non-native form without accompanying metadata.

Ultimately, then, it does not matter whether the Instruction referred to paper or electronic files—a plain reading leads to the conclusion that plaintiff did not make a request that the Business Plan be produced solely in its original format with accompanying metadata. A motion to compel is appropriate only where an appropriate request is made of the responding party. *See* Fed. R. Civ. P. 37(a)(1)(B). Because no such request has been made concerning the Business Plan, the Court will not compel the defendant to produce it in its original form with accompanying metadata.[9] *See, e.g., Wyeth v. Impax Labs., Inc.*, No. Civ.A. 06–222, 2006 WL 3091331, at *1–2 (D. Del. Oct. 26, 2006) ("Since the parties have never agreed that

---

9. Where the requesting party "does not specify a form for producing electronically stored information, a [responding] party must produce it in a form or forms in which it is ordinarily maintained or in a reasonably usable form or forms." Fed. R. Civ. P. 34(b)(2)(e)(ii).

electronic documents would be produced in any particular format, [Plaintiff] complied with its discovery obligation by producing image files.'').

* * *

COMMENTARY AND PROBLEMS

Notwithstanding the clarity of the 2006 Amendments to Rule 34, the form of production of electronic records is fertile ground for dispute, often resulting from the parties' failure to adequately communicate and reach agreement on this issue. This failure is generally the result of (1) one or more parties' failure to specify a form of production as allowed by Rule 34; or (2) one or more parties' lack of knowledge of the technological complexities attendant to electronic discovery. As demonstrated by *D'Onofrio* and the cases discussed below, both of these pitfalls can result in costly and time-consuming motion practice, and potentially a court order requiring duplicative productions in multiple formats.

1. In *D'Onofrio*, the plaintiff's failure to specify the form in which the defendant should produce the business plan prevented the plaintiff from obtaining it in native format with the corresponding metadata, which arguably would have given her the ability to access and analyze the Business Plan both substantively and contextually, on par with her adversary. In denying the plaintiff's motion to compel, the court noted that the plaintiff failed to demonstrate that native production was necessary and warranted. Taking into account the various points made by the court, how might the plaintiff have demonstrated her need for production of the Business Plan in native format? Might the plaintiff have protected herself if, in her requests for production, she requested all documents in hard copy format but reserved her right to later request specific documents again in native format? Could the plaintiff have reasonably been expected to know, prior to reviewing the Business Plan in hard copy, that a native production was preferable? What steps, if any, might the plaintiff have taken to discern information that would have helped her to realize this preference? Would the plaintiff have benefitted from engaging in a meet and confer with the defendant in which she could ask detailed questions about the categories of information for which she intended to seek production, including questions about how that information was created, stored, and/or transmitted? Is it reasonable to expect a requesting party, who has no familiarity with the responding party's information or systems, to know which questions to ask? Had the plaintiff engaged in a meet and confer and *not* received helpful information, would this factor, if disclosed to the court, have been relevant to the court's analysis? If so, how?

2. Suppose a party requests the production of certain e-mails and their corresponding attachments, but the responding party produces the attachments separated from the e-mails, such that the requesting party has no indication of what e-mails and attachments correspond to one another. To what extent does the producing party have an obligation to ensure that attachments are produced with their corresponding parent e-mails? Does producing the e-mails divorced from their attachments comply with Rule 34(b)(2)(E)(i)'s requirement that a party produce ESI as it is ''kept in the

usual course of business''? Should a requesting party be obligated to expressly request that attachments be produced with their corresponding e-mails? Or should this be assumed?

The issue of e-mail attachment linkage was addressed in *PSEG Power New York, Inc. v. Alberici Constructors, Inc.*, where, due to a vendor software problem, the plaintiff produced three thousand e-mails divorced from their attachments.[1] Although all e-mails and attachments were produced, the requesting party was unable to determine which e-mails and attachments corresponded to one another. In considering the defendant's motion to compel a reproduction of the e-mails ''in a reasonably usable form,'' the court considered the following three factors: (1) the relevance of the requested information; (2) whether or not it was reasonably accessible; and (3) if reproduction would be unduly burdensome or costly. After consideration of these factors, the court ordered the plaintiff to reproduce the e-mails together with their attachments. Specifically, the court noted that production of e-mails divorced from their attachments did not comply with Rule 34's requirement that electronic information be produced as it is kept in the usual course of business or in a reasonably usable format.

In *PSEG*, the court noted that the discovery dispute was the result of a vendor software problem. Should the plaintiff request that the vendor reprocess the documents at no charge and reimburse the plaintiff for the costs of defending the motion to compel? Given the uncertainties and unknown expenses inherent in electronic discovery, what contractual protections might be beneficial to a party who seeks to hire an electronic discovery vendor to process and assist with the production of electronic information?

Should a requesting party that complies with Rule 34 and expressly specifies the requested form(s) of production have a reasonable expectation that the responding party will perfectly comply? To what extent should a court have such an expectation? Also consider whether a producing party should be obligated to produce information in a form that is the same as the form in which it intends to use the information in preparing and litigating the case.

3. In *Lawson v. Sun Microsystems, Inc.*, the plaintiff sent a letter to the defendant requesting production of all ESI in native format yet failed to specify the form of production in the formal discovery requests later served upon the defendant. In response to the plaintiff's formal discovery requests, the defendant produced paper copies of the responsive documents. The plaintiff moved to compel production of the documents in native format. Defendant objected, arguing that the plaintiff failed to specify the requested form of production in the document requests and noting that Rule 34(b) does not require duplicative productions in multiple formats. The court granted the plaintiff's motion to compel, holding that although the plaintiff's letter was not a formal request, it ''should nonetheless have provided Defendant sufficient notice of the form desired by Plaintiff.''[2]

---

1. *See* No. 05–0657, 2007 WL 2687670 (N.D.N.Y. Sept. 7, 2007).
2. No. 07–0196, 2007 WL 2572170, at *5 (S.D. Ind. Sept. 4, 2007).

Should the defendant's counsel have sought clarification from the plaintiff's counsel regarding the potentially conflicting instructions relating to the specified form of production? Could this problem have been avoided had the parties negotiated a stipulation regarding the form of production to ensure that there were no time-consuming and costly "miscommunications"?

4. In contrast to *Lawson*, the court in *Autotech Technologies Ltd. Partnership v. Automationdirect.com, Inc.* addressed a defendant's motion to compel production of documents in native format even though the defendant never specified this format in its requests for production and the plaintiff had already produced the same documents in hard copy. The court denied the defendant's motion to compel, explaining that defendant "was the master of its production requests; it must be satisfied with what it asked for."[3] In addition, the court stated that the defendant failed to demonstrate that the hard copy production was not "reasonably usable" within the meaning of Rule 34(b).

Based on the decisions in *Lawson* and *Autotech*, in adjudicating a motion to compel a "re-production" of documents or electronic information in a format alternative to that already produced, are the courts applying a cost-benefit analysis rather than examining whether the parties complied with the black letter law of Rule 34? In other words, is a court more likely to be persuaded by: (1) an argument that the alternative/duplicative form of production is truly necessary to prepare the case for trial; or (2) an argument that the requesting party failed to expressly state the requested form of production in accordance with Rule 34? Would an emphasis on (2) disproportionately weigh form over substance?

5. Rule 34 does not define what constitutes a "reasonably usable form" of production. Rather, the terminology is broad, allowing the Rule to evolve as technology evolves. Considering how quickly technology continues to evolve, is it reasonable to rely on older cases for guidance on what forms of production are "reasonably usable"?

6. In *3M Company v. Kanbar*, the defendant moved to compel the plaintiff to "organize" the electronic information it produced in response to the defendant's overly broad requests for production.[4] In an attempt to address the defendant's concerns, the plaintiff disclosed the custodian of each electronic document in its production. Nonetheless, the court ordered the plaintiff to reproduce the requested information in a "reasonably usable" electronic format and required both parties to meet and agree on what is "reasonably usable." Although the court granted the defendant's motion to compel, the court noted that the discovery dispute was, in part, of the defendant's "own making" as a result of the defendant's broad discovery requests.

Did the court do the parties a disservice by directing them to meet and confer rather than ruling on what constitutes a reasonably usable electronic format? Or rather, did the court simply require the parties to cooperate in solving a problem "of their own making"? Suppose you can demonstrate to

---

3.   248 F.R.D. 556, 560 (N.D. Ill. 2008).

4.   No. 06–01225, 2007 WL 1725448, at *1 (N.D. Cal. June 14, 2007).

the court that your client is a disorganized record keeper. Should this allow you to produce the documents or electronic information as kept in the usual course of "disorganized" business? If you are the requesting party, how might you narrowly tailor your discovery requests to avoid a "data dump," given the large potential volume of ESI and the time and costs associated with reviewing it? Is it feasible to do so during the initial stages of discovery when you do not yet have any familiarity with your adversary's documents, electronic systems, or record keeping practices?

7.   In contrast to *3M*, in *MGP Ingredients, Inc. v. Mars, Inc.*, the court considered similar arguments but ruled differently. In *MGP*, the defendant produced 48,000 pages of documents and ESI as they were kept in the ordinary course of business. The plaintiff moved for an order directing the defendant to specify by Bates range which documents and ESI corresponded to each of the plaintiff's discovery requests. The defendant objected to the plaintiff's motion, arguing that Rule 34 only requires that "a party who produces documents for inspection shall produce them as they are kept in the usual course of business *or* shall organize and label them to correspond with the categories in the request." The court agreed with the defendant and in denying the plaintiff's motion explained that "[t]he Rule is phrased in the disjunctive, and the producing party may choose either of the two methods for producing the documents. If the producing party produces documents in the order in which they are kept in the usual course of business, the Rule imposes no duty to organize and label the documents, provide an index of the documents produced, or correlate the documents to the particular request to which they are responsive."[5]

Under what circumstances might it be preferable to produce documents or ESI to correspond to the discovery requests rather than as kept in the ordinary course of business? Do you think the discovery disputes in *3M* and *MGP* could have been avoided if the parties had conducted a meet and confer regarding the form of production? The *MGP* court thought so.

> While the Court recognizes that Plaintiff now faces the formidable task of having to determine which documents are responsive to each particular request, Plaintiff was the party who formulated the requests in the manner it did and Plaintiff must take responsibility for undertaking the task of determining which documents relate to each set of its twenty-some requests. Plaintiff might have avoided this task by relying on a provision of Rule 34(b) which allows the parties, prior to production, to "otherwise agree" as to the manner in which the documents will be produced. In other words, the parties may, by agreement, deviate from the rule requiring the responding party [to] produce the documents (and any [ESI]) as kept in the usual course of business or to organize and label them to correspond to the requests. Here, however, there apparently was no attempt to reach such an agreement prior to the production.

8.   Processing and producing ESI can, in some instances, be significantly more costly than producing hard copy documents. As such, the expense of producing ESI may provide an incentive for litigants to request such information for the improper purpose of obtaining leverage in the litigation by

---

5.   No. 06–2318, 2007 WL 3010343 at *3 (D. Kan. Oct. 15, 2007).

increasing the adversary's litigation costs. If your adversary requests that you produce ESI, how might you demonstrate that producing the documents in electronic form would not provide significantly more information than producing the documents in hard copy form? How would you demonstrate that producing the documents in electronic form is unduly burdensome and costly?

B. SEARCH METHODS

VICTOR STANLEY, INC. v. CREATIVE PIPE, INC.

250 F.R.D. 251 (D. Md. 2008)

GRIMM, MAGISTRATE JUDGE

The plaintiff, Victor Stanley, Inc. ("VSI" or "Plaintiff") filed a motion seeking a ruling that five categories of electronically stored documents produced by defendants Creative Pipe, Inc. ("CPI") and Mark and Stephanie Pappas ("M. Pappas", "S. Pappas" or "The Pappasses") (collectively, "Defendants") in October, 2007, are not exempt from discovery because they are within the protection of the attorney-client privilege and work-product doctrine, as claimed by the Defendants. VSI argues that the electronic records at issue, which total 165 documents, are not privileged because their production by Defendants occurred under circumstances that waived any privilege or protected status. * * * For the reasons that follow, I find that all 165 electronic documents are beyond the scope of the attorney-client privilege and work-product protection because assuming, *arguendo*, that they qualified as privileged/protected in the first instance * * * the privilege/protection was waived by the voluntary production of the documents to VSI by Defendants.

Background Facts

* * * [T]he court ordered the parties' computer forensic experts to meet and confer in an effort to identify a joint protocol to search and retrieve relevant ESI responsive to Plaintiff's Rule 34 requests. This was done and the joint protocol prepared. The protocol contained detailed search and information retrieval instructions, including nearly five pages of keyword/phrase search terms. * * * Counsel for Defendants had previously notified the court on March 29, 2007, that individualized privilege review of the responsive documents "would delay production unnecessarily and cause undue expense." To address this concern, Defendants gave their computer forensics expert a list of keywords to be used to search and retrieve privileged and protected documents from the population of documents that were to be produced to Plaintiff. * * *

After receiving Defendants' ESI production in September, 2007, Plaintiff's counsel began their review of the materials. They soon discovered documents that potentially were privileged or work-product protected and immediately segregated this information and notified counsel for Defendants of its production, following this same procedure each time they identified potentially privileged/protected information. * * *

* * * Defendants, who bear the burden of proving that their conduct was reasonable for purposes of assessing whether they waived attorney-client privilege by producing the 165 documents to the Plaintiff, have failed to provide the court with information regarding: the keywords used; the rationale for their selection; the qualifications of M. Pappas and his attorneys to design an effective and reliable search and information retrieval method; whether the search was a simple keyword search, or a more sophisticated one, such as one employing Boolean proximity operators;[9] or whether they analyzed the results of the search to assess its reliability, appropriateness for the task, and the quality of its implementation. While keyword searches have long been recognized as appropriate and helpful for ESI search and retrieval, there are well-known limitations and risks associated with them, and proper selection and implementation obviously involves technical, if not scientific knowledge. *See, e.g., The Sedona Conference Best Practices Commentary on the Use of Search & Information Retrieval Methods in E–Discovery*, 8 Sedona Conf. J. 189, 194–95, 201–02 ("'[A]lthough basic keyword searching techniques have been widely accepted both by courts and parties as sufficient to define the scope of their obligation to perform a search for responsive documents, the experience of many litigators is that simple keyword searching alone is inadequate in at least some discovery contexts. This is because simple keyword searches end up being both over-and under-inclusive in light of the inherent malleability and ambiguity of spoken and written English (as well as all other languages).'"). To address this known deficiency, the Sedona Conference suggests as best practice points, inter alia:

Practice Point 3. The choice of a specific search and retrieval method will be highly dependent on the specific legal context in which it is to be employed.

Practice Point 4. Parties should perform due diligence in choosing a particular information retrieval product or service from a vendor.

---

9. Keyword searching may be accomplished in many ways. The simplest way is to use a series of individual keywords. Using more advanced search techniques, such as Boolean proximity operators, can enhance the effectiveness of keyword searches. Boolean proximity operators are derived from logical principles, named for mathematician George Boole, and focus on the relationships of a "set" of objects or ideas. Thus, combining a keyword with Boolean operators such as "OR," "AND," "NOT," and using parentheses, proximity limitation instructions, phrase searching instructions, or truncation and stemming instructions to require a logical order to the execution of the search can enhance the accuracy and reliability of the search. *The Sedona Conference Best Practices Commentary on the Use of Search & Information Retrieval Methods in E–Discovery,* 8 Sedona Conf. J. (2007) at 200, 202, 217–18 ("Sedona Conference Best Practices"). In addition to keyword searches, other search and information retrieval methodologies include: probabilistic search models, including "Bayesian classifiers" (which searches by creating a formula based on values assigned to particular words based on their interrelationships, proximity, and frequency to establish a relevancy ranking that is applied to each document searched); "Fuzzy Search Models" (which attempt to refine a search beyond specific words, recognizing that words can have multiple forms. By identifying the "core" for a word the fuzzy search can retrieve documents containing all forms of the target word); "Clustering" searches (searches of documents by grouping them by similarity of content, for example, the presence of a series of same or similar words that are found in multiple documents); and "Concept and Categorization Tools" (search systems that rely on a thesaurus to capture documents which use alternative ways to express the same thought). *See Sedona Conference Best Practices, supra,* at 217–23.

Practice Point 5. The use of search and information retrieval tools does not guarantee that all responsive documents will be identified in large data collections, due to characteristics of human language. Moreover, differing search methods may produce differing results, subject to a measure of statistical variation inherent in the science of information retrieval.

Practice Point 6. Parties should make a good faith attempt to collaborate on the use of particular search and information retrieval methods, tools and protocols (including as to keywords, concepts, and other types of search parameters).

Practice Point 7. Parties should expect that their choice of search methodology will need to be explained, either formally or informally, in subsequent legal contexts (including in depositions, evidentiary proceedings, and trials).

* * *

Use of search and information retrieval methodology * * * requires the utmost care in selecting methodology that is appropriate for the task because the consequence of failing to do so, as in this case, may be the disclosure of privileged/protected information to an adverse party, resulting in a determination by the court that the privilege/protection has been waived. Selection of the appropriate search and information retrieval technique requires careful advance planning by persons qualified to design effective search methodology. The implementation of the methodology selected should be tested for quality assurance; and the party selecting the methodology must be prepared to explain the rationale for the method chosen to the court, demonstrate that it is appropriate for the task, and show that it was properly implemented. In this regard, compliance with the Sedona Conference Best Practices for use of search and information retrieval will go a long way towards convincing the court that the method chosen was reasonable and reliable, which * * * may very well prevent a finding that the privilege or work-product protection was waived.

In this case, the Defendants have failed to demonstrate that the keyword search they performed on the text-searchable ESI was reasonable. Defendants neither identified the keywords selected nor the qualifications of the persons who selected them to design a proper search; they failed to demonstrate that there was quality-assurance testing; and when their production was challenged by the Plaintiff, they failed to carry their burden of explaining what they had done and why it was sufficient.

* * *

Conclusion

* * * [T]he court finds that the Defendants waived any privilege or work-product protection for the 165 documents at issue by disclosing them to the Plaintiff. Accordingly, the Plaintiff may use these documents as evidence in this case, provided they are otherwise admissible. * * *

COMMENTARY

1. Strengths and Weaknesses of Keyword Searching

Law students are well versed in using Westlaw, Lexis, and, increasingly, their favorite Internet browser and search engine, to search for case law precedent. However, the information retrieval task of searching for "the" case (or a select few cases) to support a particular legal proposition made in a brief is a very different one than the task confronting the lawyer in e-discovery, for any number of reasons. In the case of e-discovery, upon receipt of a Rule 34 document request, counsel and client are under a duty to make a reasonable search for "all" relevant, non-privileged documents and ESI within the scope of the particular request (assuming the request is well-framed). The task of finding "all" relevant documents and ESI is increasingly elusive, first because databases of all kinds are growing larger, and second, due to the inherent complexities involved in conducting searches through collections of ESI—both due to a myriad of ESI applications, as well as the broad variety of sources where ESI may be stored (e.g. servers, databases, PDAs, backup tapes). Even in the simplest case requiring a search of online e-mail, there is no guarantee that using keywords will always prove sufficient.

EXCERPT FROM *The Sedona Conference® Best Practice Commentary on the Use of Search and Information Retrieval Methods in E–Discovery* (2007), 8 Sedona Conf. J, *available at* http://www.thesedonaconference.org.

Issues with Keywords

Keyword searches work best when the legal inquiry is focused on finding particular documents and when the use of language is relatively predictable. For example, keyword searches work well to find all documents that mention a specific individual or date, regardless of context. However, although basic keyword searching techniques have been widely accepted both by courts and parties as sufficient to define the scope of their obligation to perform a search for responsive documents, the experience of many litigators is that simple keyword searching alone is inadequate in at least some discovery contexts. This is because simple keyword searches end up being both over-and under-inclusive in light of the inherent malleability and ambiguity of spoken and written English (as well as all other languages). Keyword searches identify all documents containing a specified term regardless of context, and so they can possibly capture many documents irrelevant to the user's query. For example, the term "strike" could be found in documents relating to a labor union tactic, a military action, options trading, or baseball, to name just a few (illustrating "polysemy," or *ambiguity* in the use of language). The problem of the relative percentage of "false positive" hits or noise in the data is potentially huge, amounting in some cases to huge numbers of files which must be searched to find responsive documents. On the other hand, keyword searches have the potential to miss documents that contain a word that has the same meaning as the term used in the query, but is not specified. For example, a user making queries about labor actions might miss an email referring to a "boycott" if that particular word was not included as a keyword, and a lawyer investigating tax fraud via options trading might miss an email referring to "exercise price" if that term was not specifically searched (illustrating "synonymy" or *variation* in the use of language). And of course, if authors of records are inventing words "on the fly," as they have done through history, and now are doing with increasing frequency in electronic communications, such problems are compounded. Keyword searches can also exclude common or inadvertently misspelled instances of the term (*e.g.*, "Phillip" for "Philip," or "strik" for "strike") or variations on "stems" of words (*e.g.* "striking"). So too, it is well known that even the best of optical character recognition (OCR) scanning processes introduce a certain rate of random error into document texts, potentially transforming would-be keywords into something else. Finally, using keywords alone results in a return set of potentially responsive documents that are not weighted and ranked based upon their potential importance or relevance. In other words, each document is considered to have an equal probability of being responsive upon further manual review.

More advanced keyword searches using "Boolean" operators and techniques borrowed from "fuzzy logic" may increase the number of relevant documents and decrease the number of irrelevant documents retrieved. These searches attempt to emulate the way humans use language to describe concepts. In essence, however, they simply translate ordinary words and phrases into a Boolean search argument. Thus, a natural language search for "all birds that live in Africa" is translated to something like ("bird* + liv* + Africa"). At the present time, it would appear that the majority of automated litigation support providers and software continue to rely on keyword searching. Such methods are limited by their dependence on matching a specific, sometimes arbitrary choice of language to describe the targeted topic of interest. The issue of whether there is room for improvement in the rate of "recall" (as defined in the next section) of relevant documents in a given collection is something lawyers must consider when relying on simple and traditional input of keywords alone.

Use of Alternative Search Tools and Methods

Lawyers are beginning to feel more comfortable using alternative search tools to identify potentially relevant electronically stored information. These more advanced text mining tools include "conceptual search methods" which rely on semantic relations between words, and/or which use "thesauri" to capture documents that would be missed in keyword searching.

* * *

"Concept" search and retrieval technologies attempt to locate information that relates to a desired concept, without the presence of a particular word or phrase. The classic example is the concept search that will recognize that documents about Eskimos and igloos are related to Alaska, even if they do not specifically mention the word "Alaska."

* * *

Other automated tools rely on "taxonomies" and "ontologies" to help find documents conceptually related to the topic being searched, based on commercially available data or on specifically compiled information. This information is provided by attorneys or developed for the business function or specific industry (*e.g.*, the concept of "strike" in labor law *vs.* "strike" in options trading). These tools rely on the information that linguists collect from the lawyers and witnesses about the key factual issues in the case—the people, organization, and key concepts relating to the business as well as the idiosyncratic communications that might be lurking in documents, files, and emails. For example, a linguist would want to know how union organizers or company officials might communicate plans, any special code words used in the industry, the relationships of collective bargaining units, company management structure, and other issues and concepts. Another type of search tool relies on mathematical probabilities that a certain text is associated with a particular conceptual category. These types of machine learning tools, which include "clustering" and "latent semantic indexing," are arguably helpful in addressing cultural biases of taxonomies because they do not depend on linguistic analysis, but on mathematical probabilities. They can also help to find communications in code language and neologisms. For example, if the labor lawyer were searching for evidence that management was targeting neophytes in the union, she might miss the term "n00b" (a neologism for "newbie"). This technology, used in government intelligence, is particularly apt in helping lawyers find information when they do not know exactly what to look for. For example, when a lawyer is looking for evidence that key players conspired to violate the labor union laws, she will usually not know the "code words" or expressions the players may have used to disguise their communications.

* * *

For a more in-depth discussion of alternatives to keyword searching, see the Appendix to the Sedona Search Commentary (discussing various new search technologies).

2. Should Expert Testimony Be Required to Explain to the Trier of Fact How Search Protocols Were Constructed?

UNITED STATES v. O'KEEFE

537 F.Supp.2d 14 (D.D.C. 2008)

FACCIOLA, MAGISTRATE JUDGE

The indictment charges that the defendant, Michael John O'Keefe, Sr., when employed by the Department of State in Canada, received, *quid pro quo*, gifts and other benefits from his co-defendant, Sunil Agrawal, for expediting visa requests for employees of Agrawal's company, STS Jewels.

By his Order of April 27, 2007, Judge Friedman required the government to conduct a thorough and complete search of both its hard copy and electronic files in "a good faith effort to uncover all responsive information in its possession custody or control."

The first category of "responsive information," as defined by Judge Friedman, was "requests respecting visa applications submitted by or on behalf of STS Jewels employees—including requests for expedited visa interview appointments, decisions granting or denying such interview requests, and the grant or denial of the visas themselves." This search was to be of the files of the consulates in 1) Toronto, Canada, 2) Ottawa, Canada, 3) Matamoros, Mexico, 4) Mexico City, Mexico, 5) Nogales, Mexico, and 6) Nuevo Laredo, Mexico.

The second category of "responsive information" was "all written rules, policies, procedures and guidelines regarding the treatment of expedited visa application appointments and visa application approvals at the above-mentioned posts in Canada and Mexico." The government was also required to "produce any memoranda, letters, e-mails, faxes and other correspondence prepared or received by any consular officers at these posts that reflect either policy or decisions in specific cases with respect to expediting" visa applications.

As to the latter, Judge Friedman emphasized his expected scope of the search and the necessity for it. He stated:

> [I]t now appears from discovery produced on March 21, 2007 that employees below the level of consular officers—including even consulate secretaries and non-U.S. citizen employees—may approve requests for and schedule expedited visa interview appointments. The files of any such persons and the consulates themselves therefore also must be searched. Such communications go directly to the defense of showing that the requests made by or on behalf of STS employees are similar to other requests for expedited visa interview appointments that (it is asserted) have routinely been granted without the provision of anything of value.

Defendants, who have received the government's submission in compliance with this Order, have moved to compel, protesting that the government has not fulfilled the responsibilities Judge Friedman imposed.

I. Detailed Information About the Government's Searches

First, for each location searched, defendants demand a comprehensive description of all of the sources that were searched (both paper and electronic), how each source was searched, and who conducted the search.

In its opposition, the government produced the declaration of Peggy L. Petrovich, the Visa Unit Chief at the United States Consulate General in Toronto, Canada. According to Ms. Petrovich, she, along with her five-member staff, did the following in her effort to comply with Judge Friedman's April 27, 2007, Order:

* * *

B.   Electronic Record Files

1.   Search and Yield: She searched all active servers and backup tapes (retained for two weeks) and that search yielded "responsive e-mails, the [Standard Operating Procedures] previously mentioned, and the NIV (Non–Immigrant Visa) Schedule Calendar located on Toronto's shared public drive."

2.   Parameters of the Search Conducted: "[T]he electronic search included all e-mail and stand-alone electronic documents, e.g., documents prepared on our office software applications, regarding expedited appointments located on shared drives, personal drives and hard drives for all consular officers and locally-engaged staff, i.e., secretaries and other employees, who approved or scheduled expedited non-immigrant visa interviews, or who played any role in the process."

3.   Search Terms: She used the following search terms: "early or expedite* or appointment or early & interview or expedite* & interview." She had "[t]he Information Management Staff conduct the search of personal and hard drives because they have access to all drives from the network server, not just shared drives."

4.   Review of Results: She reviewed the results of the search and "removed only those clearly about wholly unrelated matters, e.g., emails about staff members' early departures or dentist appointments." She "made sure that all emails residing in the shared email address folders that related to expedited appointments were included in the results . . . that were produced in electronic format and provided on cd-rom."

5.   Deleted Emails: "According to the Information Management staff, any emails deleted prior to [her] search" in May 2007 are gone. Electronically stored information is backed up for two weeks and then the back up tapes are reused and their previous contents obliterated. "No other back-up server for electronic documents, either on-or off-site, exists."

6.   O'Keefe Emails: "All currently existing responsive emails located during the search of Michael O'Keefe's personal drive were included in the cd-rom" that the government gave the defendants. Since the hard drives from the computers O'Keefe used were previously seized by the government, they could not be searched.

7.   SOPs: "The only other responsive materials discovered during the electronic search for stand-alone electronic documents were the SOPs [described in paragraph 4, supra] and the NIV Schedule Calendar which was provided in hard copy format."

8.   Lack of documents: There were no responsive documents from "Mike Schimmel, the previous visa unit chief; Peggy Petrovich, the current visa unit chief; Pat Haye, the visa assistant who has main responsibility for processing expedited appointment requests; and, Jane Boyd, the visa assistant who has main responsibility for scheduling appointments for diplomatic and official applicants."

II. Problems with the Government's Production

* * *

B. Electronic Production

Defendants marshal several objections and concerns about the government's search of the electronically stored information. They take the government to task for 1) not interviewing the employees as to their use of electronic means as a form of communication regarding expedited reviews, 2) not having the employees search their own electronically stored information and 3) not indicating what software it used to conduct the search or how it ascertained what search terms it would use.

Defendants caution that, if forensic searchware was not used, there is a likelihood that stored e-mail folders in .pst files were either not searched or not searched accurately. * * *

* * *

* * * Whether search terms or "keywords" will yield the information sought is a complicated question involving the interplay, at least, of the sciences of computer technology, statistics and linguistics. *See* George L. Paul & Jason R. Baron, *Information Inflation: Can the Legal System Adapt?'*, 13 Rich. J.L. & Tech. 10 (2007). Indeed, a special project team of the Working Group on Electronic Discovery of the Sedona Conference is studying that subject and their work indicates how difficult this question is. *See The Sedona Conference, Best Practices Commentary on the Use of Search and Information Retrieval*, 8 The Sedona Conf. J. 189 (2007), *available at* http://www.thesedonaconference.org/content/miscFiles/Best_Practices_Retrieval_Methods_revised_cover_and_preface.pdf. Given this complexity, for lawyers and judges to dare opine that a certain search term or terms would be more likely to produce information than the terms that were used is truly to go where angels fear to tread. This topic is clearly beyond the ken of a layman and requires that any such conclusion be based on evidence that, for example, meets the criteria of Rule 702 of the Federal Rules of Evidence [governing expert testimony]. Accordingly, if defendants are going to contend that the search terms used by the government were insufficient, they will have to specifically so contend in a motion to compel and their contention must be based on evidence that meets the requirements of Rule 702 of the Federal Rules of Evidence.

* * *

3. Can Search Protocols Be Negotiated?

EXCERPT FROM George L. Paul & Jason R. Baron, *Information Inflation: Can the Legal System Adapt?*, 13 Rich. J.L. & Tech. 10 (2007):

The parties meet and confer on the nature of each other's computer hardware and software applications. Proposals are exchanged on the scope of search obligations, in terms of databases and applications to be searched, what active and possibly legacy media are to be made subject to search, and any limitations on scope keyed to particular individuals within an institution, particular time periods, or other ways to limit the scope of the search obligation. Keywords are proposed as a basis for conducting searches, with attention paid to negotiating appropriate Boolean strings of terms, with a full range of proximity operators, wildcard, truncation and stemming terms (to the extent any or all such techniques can be utilized). Alternative concept-based search methodologies are discussed, to the extent either party has experience in using and has found to be efficacious in finding documents. A timetable is agreed upon for conducting initial searches.

BOOLEAN NEGOTIATION EXERCISE

Hypothetical Complaint: *The Estate of Virginia Vesta v. Agni Paper Co., et al.*

A Complaint has been filed for compensatory and punitive damages alleging wrongful death, negligence, and medical malpractice. Plaintiff Virginia Vesta is a resident of Halema'uma'u City in the State of Vulcan. She was employed at a pilot plant owned and operated by defendant Agni Paper Company. The Complaint alleges that on January 2, 2008, Vesta drove to the Agni Pilot Plant where she parked her car in the company parking lot, after which she proceeded to her work station where her job was to sample paper prototypes of various types of stationery that Agni produces. Agni is a company known for its fire-resistant stationery. It has developed special patents for certain types of paper with unusually high heat tolerances and also designs custom stationery for corporations located in fire-prone areas. The likelihood of whether an object will burn under certain circumstances is measured in terms of "ignition propensity." At approximately 3 p.m. on January 2, 2008, plaintiff was engaged in testing the ignition propensity of two particular grades of stationery. Vesta had recommended to the company that all debris and loose paper be removed from the surrounding areas prior to testing samples; however, no action was taken on plaintiff's requests. On that date, during a routine test, Vesta was seriously burned and injured by the explosion and fire caused by a machine jam. She later succumbed to her injuries at a local hospital.

The Complaint alleges a cause of action for wrongful death, due to Agni Paper's failure to provide written safety instructions to its employees concerning safe operation of testing equipment, failure to provide strict supervision of dangerous testing operations, failure to follow standard practices of removing debris and loose paper from the testing area prior to starting sample testing, and failure to heed plaintiff's recommendation that debris and loose paper be removed.

Plaintiff has propounded dozens of requests for production of documents and ESI under Rule 34, one of which is the following:

REQUEST FOR PRODUCTION No. 15: Produce all reports, written memoranda, correspondence, and other documents related to any complaints, inspection reports, or warnings received from any governmental agency concerning working environment or conditions, or standards violations related to safety.

(i) Exercise: devise a proposed search protocol for the purpose of launching an automated search of defendant's database.

(ii) Consider the following proposed Boolean strings as the product of back and forth negotiations between plaintiff and defendant.

Defendant's Proposed String: (complain! OR "inspection report!" OR warning!) AND [(working w/5 (environment OR condition*)) OR (standard* w/3 violation*)] AND safety

Plaintiff's Proposed String: (complaint! OR critic! OR notif! OR notice) AND (inspect! OR apprais! OR exam! OR investing! OR review!) AND (warning! OR precaution! OR caution!) AND (work! OR occupation! OR industry! OR factory OR manufactur!) AND (environment! OR atmosphere! OR surrounding! OR setting!) AND (condition! OR circumstance!) AND (safety OR security! OR assurance!) AND (violat! OR infraction! OR infring! OR breach!)

Defendant's Rejoinder to Plaintiff's Proposal: (complaint! OR notification! OR notice) AND (inspect! OR apprais! OR exam! OR investing! OR review!) AND (warning! OR precaution! OR caution!) AND (work! OR occupation! OR industry! OR factory OR manufactur!) AND (environment! OR atmosphere! OR surrounding! OR setting!) AND (condition! OR circumstance!) AND safety AND (violation! OR infraction! OR infring! OR breach!) AND ((OSHA OR NIOSH OR NFPA OR CPSC) OR ("Occupational Safety & Health Administration" OR "National Institute for Occupational Safety and Health" OR "National Fire Protection Association" OR "Consumer Product Safety Commission"))

Final Agreed upon Negotiated String: (complaint! OR notification! OR notice) AND (inspect! OR apprais! OR exam! OR investing! OR review!) AND (warning! OR precaution! OR caution!) AND (work! OR occupation! OR industry! OR factory OR manufactur!) AND (environment! OR atmosphere! OR surrounding! OR setting!) AND (condition! OR circumstance!) AND (safety) AND (violation! OR infraction! OR infring! OR breach!)

NEGOTIATION COMMENTARY

At the outset of the negotiation for this string, plaintiff agreed to strike the terms "security* " and "assurance* " from plaintiff's original proposal. Assume that it had been previously agreed that the term "safety* " was sufficient to locate documents responsive to workplace safety issues raised by the Complaint. At the request of defendant, plaintiff also agreed to remove the term "criticism* " from the string under the rationale that documents discussing government complaints or warnings would use more formal language. Although not in its original proposal, defendant proposed that certain government agencies (OSHA, NIOSH, NFPA, and the CPSC) concerned with workplace safety should be added to the string, to avoid retrieving documents that would involve ancillary issues related to other government agencies. Plaintiff conceded that while the four agencies suggested by defendant would be those most likely concerned with workplace safety, these agencies would not always be named in the actual documents discussing their warnings and related matters. Defendant asserted that any official communications to or from the parties would almost certainly name the agency on either the letterhead or address area. Plaintiff countered that the request appropriately asks for more than just official communications and memoranda and that internal e-mail or more informal documents might very well assume that the reader would know the agency at issue and not name it explicitly. Defendant reluctantly conceded that such less-formal documents would be arguably responsive to the request and agreed to a string that did not include the names of the four agencies that it had proposed.

What do you see as the strengths or weaknesses of entering into negotiations on the scope of a Boolean string? What would you have done differently than the way in which the negotiations proceeded above?

C. USE OF TECHNOLOGY FOR SEARCH AND REVIEW

1. The Use of Selection Criteria and Filtering to Manage ESI

CLEARONE COMMUNICATIONS, INC. v. CHIANG

No. 07 Civ. 37, 2008 WL 920336 (D. Utah Apr. 1, 2008)

NUFFER, MAGISTRATE JUDGE

Plaintiff ClearOne Communications, Inc. (ClearOne) makes a * * * motion for entry of a search protocol order. * * * The search protocol is to be used to search the data from computers used by the WideBand Defendants (Andrew Chiang, Jun Yang, Lonny Bowers, and WideBand Solutions, Inc.) which were imaged pursuant to two orders issued last year. The first imaging order required that a third party engaged by ClearOne create and maintain custody of images of certain of WideBand Defendants' computers, while the second order provided that a third party retained by WideBand create and maintain custody of certain images of other of WideBand Defendants' computers. Neither order gave ClearOne direct access to the images or data. However, all that information is subject to existing discovery requests.

The second imaging order sought to establish "a protocol for searching the mirror images . . . to identify relevant and responsive documents." * * * The protocol as it now stands requires key word searches by technical experts; review of search result reports by WideBand Defendants' counsel for facial claims of privilege; delivery of the reports to ClearOne counsel for preliminary assertion of responsiveness; WideBand Defendants' counsel's review for responsiveness and privilege; and delivery of documents and privilege logs.

The issue before the court is establishment of the search terms—and the issue is greatly simplified by the parties' agreement on many search terms. ClearOne has accepted, with five additions, the search terms proposed by WideBand Defendants in September 2007. The dispute arises over the conjunctive or disjunctive use of the terms.

Conjunctive or Disjunctive Search

Essentially, there are three categories of search criteria: "Name" (searching for names of specific individuals); "Tech" (searching for a particular technological reference); and "License" terms (searching for terms relating to the licensing of certain source code). WideBand Defendants say it is "reasonable to require some connectors that would narrow the search results to subjects relevant to the issues in this lawsuit." Specifically, WideBand Defendants request "that the 'Name' and 'License' search terms be combined with the 'Tech' terms."

As to the "Name" terms, conjunctive search seems necessary. Otherwise, every occurrence of the "Name" terms will result in a positive hit, meaning that virtually every document in the electronic media will be identified as potentially responsive. In a relatively small business such as WideBand, almost every document will refer to one of the key employees in the company. Requiring a hit of one "Name" term AND one "Tech" term will ensure that more responsive documents are flagged as potentially responsive.

However, as to the "License" terms, conjunctive search could be excessively narrow. Again, because WideBand is a relatively small company, licensing activity would be relatively small. By comparison, technology is the core of its business, so disjunctive use of the "Tech" terms would probably result in an excessive number of false positives.

ClearOne * * * argues for the use of additional terms which it claims come from its Honeybee code, which it claims WideBand Defendants misappropriated. WideBand Defendants claim this code is nothing more than Texas Instrument library code which is freely available and reproducible. WideBand objects that the proposed additional search terms are "extremely broad" and are not linked "to any particular discovery responses." WideBand Defendants also say that use of these terms takes an important issue from the jury.

The newly proposed search terms are not extremely broad. In fact, they are specifically identified by ClearOne as contained within or very closely related to specific code that ClearOne uses. Without deciding whether that specific code is copyrighted or a trade secret of ClearOne, it is clear that the use of these terms, in the disjunctive, will yield evidence that is potentially very significant to this case. No ultimate facts are found or established by the use of words in a protocol, in spite of ClearOne's urgings and WideBand Defendants' protests. This is a discovery order. * * * ClearOne is free to ask the jury to draw inferences, but WideBand is also free to explain to the jury what WideBand claims actually happened.

Further, the search protocol is not the "last word" on electronic discovery in this case. The use of key word protocols is one step in the process which contemplates many more steps, including review of search result reports by WideBand Defendants' counsel for facial claims of privilege; delivery of reports to ClearOne counsel for preliminary assertion of responsiveness; WideBand Defendants' counsel's review of the reports and documents for responsiveness and privilege; and delivery of documents and privilege logs.

This order is not the last word on key words, either. If documents are discovered which suggest that other documents exist which were not identified as potentially responsive, or if a surprisingly small or unreasonably large number of documents is identified as potentially responsive, refinement may be needed. Much of the argument is now speculative, since there is no actual experience with a search. This first protocol may suffice, or it may in effect be a sampling which reveals the need for more- or less-or different-key words.

* * *

2.   The Use of Technology for Review

TREPPEL v. BIOVAIL CORP.

233 F.R.D. 363 (S.D.N.Y. 2006)

FRANCIS, MAGISTRATE JUDGE

* * * The plaintiff in this action, Jerry I. Treppel, alleges that the defendants engaged in a smear campaign that destroyed his career as a securities analyst. In his initial complaint, he asserted claims of defamation, tortious interference with prospective economic advantage, prima facie tort, and civil conspiracy against the defendants, Biovail Corporation ("Biovail"); its Chairman and Chief Executive Officer, Eugene Melnyk; its General Counsel, Kenneth C. Cancellara; Sitrick and Company, Inc.; and Michael S. Sitrick. Mr. Treppel now moves pursuant to Rule 37(a) of the Federal Rules of Civil Procedure for an order compelling the defendants to * * * answer a range of questions concerning their electronic data management practices * * *.

* * *

Biovail has yet to produce any documents in response to the plaintiff's document request. When it received the request, Biovail suggested defining the scope of any review of electronic records by stipulating which files would be searched and what search terms would be utilized. The plaintiff declined, apparently believing that "the use of search terms has no application to the standard discovery process of locating and producing accessible hard copy and electronic documents." The plaintiff's assumption is flawed. Even in a case involving exclusively hard copy documents, there is no obligation on the part of a responding party to examine every scrap of paper in its potentially voluminous files in order to comply with its discovery obligations. Rather, it must conduct a diligent search, which involves developing a reasonably comprehensive search strategy. Such a strategy might, for example, include identifying key employees and reviewing any of their files that are likely to be relevant to the claims in the litigation. Defined search strategies are even more appropriate in cases involving electronic data, where the number of documents may be exponentially greater. *See* * * * *The Sedona Principles; Best Practices Recommendations & Principles for Addressing Electronic Document Production, Principle 11* (2003) ("A responding party may properly access and identify potentially responsive electronic data and documents by using reasonable selection criteria, such as search terms or samples."). Thus, the plaintiff's refusal to stipulate to a search methodology in this case was apparently based on a misconception of the scope of the responding party's obligation. At the same time, it was a missed opportunity; the plaintiff might have convinced Biovail to broaden its search in ways that would uncover more responsive documents and avoid subsequent disputes.

Yet the plaintiff's recalcitrance does not excuse Biovail's failure to produce any responsive documents whatsoever. Biovail suggested a strategy by which it would search the computer files of Mr. Melnyk, Mr. Cancellara, and Kenneth Howling, its director of investor relations, using the search terms: (i) Treppel, (ii) Jerry, (iii) Bank of America, (iv) Banc of America, (v) BAS, and (vi) BofA. (Steiner 9/1/05 Letter at 2). Absent agreement with Mr. Treppel about a search strategy, Biovail should have proceeded unilaterally, producing all responsive documents located by its search. It shall now do so promptly. In addition, Biovail shall provide the plaintiff with a detailed explanation of the search protocol it implements.

This ruling is not an endorsement of the methodology that Biovail has suggested, either in relation to the choice of files to be searched or the terms to be applied. It is, instead, an interim step that is subject to revision once Biovail has responded to the interrogatories relating to its electronic data and the plaintiff has articulated any specific concerns about the scope of the search.

Conclusion

For the reasons discussed above, the plaintiff's motion to compel is granted to the extent that Biovail and Mr. Melnyk * * * shall promptly conduct a diligent search, explain the search protocol they use, and produce the responsive documents so located * * *.

D.   METADATA

WILLIAMS v. SPRINT/UNITED MANAGEMENT CO.

230 F.R.D. 640 (D. Kan. 2005)

WAXSE, MAGISTRATE JUDGE

Plaintiff Shirley Williams filed this suit on behalf of herself and others similarly situated, asserting that her age was a determining factor in Defendant's decision to terminate her employment during a reduction-in-force (RIF). * * * The parties are presently engaged in discovery concerning the merits of Plaintiffs' pattern and practice allegations. This matter is presently before the Court on Defendant's Response to the Court's July 12, 2005 Order, which ordered Defendant to show cause why it should not produce electronic Microsoft Excel spreadsheets in the manner in which they were maintained and why it should not be sanctioned for "scrubbing" the metadata * * * prior to producing them to Plaintiffs without either the agreement of the parties or the approval of the Court.

I. Background Information

Plaintiff Williams commenced this action in April 2003, and, to date, the docket reflects that over 3300 pleadings and orders have been filed. * * * Due to the highly contentious nature of this litigation, the Magistrate Judge has conducted discovery conferences twice a month since March 2005 to resolve discovery issues identified by the parties. One of the ongoing discovery disputes has been Defendant's production of spreadsheets that relate to the RIFs at issue in this case. [After many conferences and orders of the court, the court ordered the defendant to produce the spreadsheets in the format in which they were used in the ordinary course of business. The defendant then produced the spreadsheets in Excel form.]

At the July 7, 2005 discovery conference, Plaintiffs' counsel advised the Court that Defendant, prior to producing the electronic versions of the Excel spreadsheets, had utilized software to scrub the spreadsheet files to remove the metadata. Plaintiffs claim this metadata would have contained information such as file names, dates of the file, authors of the file, recipients of the file, print-out dates, changes and modification dates, and other information. Plaintiffs' counsel stated that Defendant did not provide them with any type of log of what information was scrubbed. Plaintiffs' counsel also advised the Court that Defendant had locked certain cells and data on the Excel spreadsheets prior to producing them so that Plaintiffs could not access those cells.

Defendant admitted that it had scrubbed the metadata from and locked certain data on the spreadsheets prior to producing them. It argued that the spreadsheets' metadata is irrelevant and contains privileged information. Defendant further argued that Plaintiffs never requested the metadata be included in the electronic Excel spreadsheets it produced and that metadata was never discussed at any of the discovery conferences.

After hearing the respective arguments of counsel, the Court ordered Defendant to show cause why it should not be sanctioned for not complying with "what at least I understood my Order to be, which was that electronic data be produced in the manner in which it was maintained, and to me that did not allow for the scrubbing of metadata because when I talk about electronic data, that includes the metadata." * * * The Court advised Defendant that if it could show justification for scrubbing the metadata and locking the cells, the Court would certainly consider it, but cautioned that "it's going to take some clear showing or otherwise there are going to be appropriate sanctions, which at least will be the production of the information in the format it was maintained."

* * *

II. Discussion

* * *

Metadata

* * * Defendant claims that it scrubbed the metadata from the spreadsheets to preclude the possibility that Plaintiffs could "undelete" or recover privileged and protected information properly deleted from the spreadsheets and to limit the information in the spreadsheets to those pools from which it made the RIF decisions currently being litigated. In an attempt to justify its actions, Defendant contends that emerging standards of electronic discovery articulate a presumption against the production of metadata, which is not considered part of a document, unless it is both specifically requested and relevant. Defendant next argues that Plaintiffs never sought the production of metadata. Finally, Defendant argues that its removal of metadata was consistent with, if not compelled by, * * * prior orders. Defendant asserts that these reasons support a determination that it has shown cause for its removal of the metadata from the Excel spreadsheets prior to producing them to Plaintiffs.

1. Emerging standards of electronic discovery with regard to metadata

a. What is metadata?

Before addressing whether Defendant was justified in removing the metadata from the Excel spreadsheets prior to producing them to Plaintiffs, a general discussion of metadata and its implications for electronic document production in discovery is instructive.

Metadata, commonly described as "data about data," is defined as "information describing the history, tracking, or management of an electronic document." Appendix F to The Sedona Guidelines: Best Practice Guidelines & Commentary for Managing Information & Records in the Electronic Age defines metadata as "information about a particular data set which describes how, when and by whom it was collected, created, accessed, or modified and how it is formatted (including data demographics such as size, location, storage requirements and media information.)" Technical Appendix E to the Sedona Guidelines provides an extended description of metadata. It further defines metadata to include "all of the contextual, processing, and use information needed to identify and certify the scope, authenticity, and integrity of active or archival electronic information or records." Some examples of metadata for electronic documents include: a file's name, a file's location (e.g., directory structure or pathname), file format or file type, file size, file dates (e.g., creation date, date of last data modification, date of last data access, and date of last metadata modification), and file permissions (e.g., who can read the data, who can write to it, who can run it). Some metadata, such as file dates and sizes, can easily be seen by users; other metadata can be hidden or embedded and unavailable to computer users who are not technically adept.

Most metadata is generally not visible when a document is printed or when the document is converted to an image file. Metadata can be altered intentionally or inadvertently and can be extracted when native files are converted to image files. Sometimes the metadata can be inaccurate, as when a form document reflects the author as the person who created the template but who did not draft the document. In addition, metadata can come from a variety of sources; it can be created automatically by a computer, supplied by a user, or inferred through a relationship to another document.

Appendix E to The Sedona Guidelines further explains the importance of metadata:

> Certain metadata is critical in information management and for ensuring effective retrieval and accountability in record-keeping. Metadata can assist in proving the authenticity of the content of electronic documents, as well as establish the context of the content. Metadata can also identify and exploit the structural relationships that exist between and within electronic documents, such as versions and drafts. Metadata allows organizations to track the many layers of rights and reproduction information that exist for records and their multiple versions. Metadata may also document other legal or security requirements that have been imposed on records; for example, privacy concerns, privileged communications or work product, or proprietary interests.

The Microsoft Office Online website lists several examples of metadata that may be stored in Microsoft Excel spreadsheets, as well as other Microsoft applications such as Word or PowerPoint: author name or initials, company or organization name, identification of computer or network server or hard disk where document is saved, names of previous document authors, document revisions and versions, hidden text or cells, template information, other file properties and summary information, non-visible portions or embedded objects, personalized views, and comments.

It is important to note that metadata varies with different applications. As a general rule of thumb, the more interactive the application, the more important the metadata is to understanding the application's output. At one end of the spectrum is a word processing application where the metadata is usually not critical to understanding the substance of the document. The information can be conveyed without the need for the metadata. At the other end of the spectrum is a database application where the database is a completely undifferentiated mass of tables of data. The metadata is the key to showing the relationships between the data; without such metadata, the tables of data would have little meaning. A spreadsheet application lies somewhere in the middle. While metadata is not as crucial to understanding a spreadsheet as it is to a database application, a spreadsheet's metadata may be necessary to understand the spreadsheet because the cells containing formulas, which arguably are metadata themselves, often display a value rather than the formula itself. To understand the spreadsheet, the user must be able to ascertain the formula within the cell.

Due to the hidden, or not readily visible, nature of metadata, commentators note that metadata created by any software application has the potential for inadvertent disclosure of confidential or privileged information in both a litigation and non-litigation setting, which could give rise to an ethical violation. One method commonly recommended to avoid this inadvertent disclosure is to utilize software that removes metadata from electronic documents. The process of removing metadata is commonly called "scrubbing" the electronic documents. In a litigation setting, the issue arises of whether this can be done without either the agreement of the parties or the producing party providing notice through an objection or motion for protective order.

b. Whether emerging standards of electronic discovery articulate a presumption against the production of metadata

With the increasing usage of electronic document production in discovery, metadata presents unique challenges regarding the production of documents in litigation and raises many new discovery questions. The group of judges and attorneys comprising the Sedona Conference Working Group on Best Practices for Electronic Document Retention and Production (Sedona Electronic Document Working Group) identified metadata as one of the primary ways in which producing electronic documents differs from producing paper documents. The Sedona Electronic Document Working Group also recognized that understanding when metadata should be specifically preserved and produced represents one of the biggest challenges in electronic document production.

Defendant contends that emerging standards of electronic discovery articulate a presumption against the production of metadata. To determine whether Defendant's contention is accurate, the Court must first identify the emerging standards for the production of metadata. Then the Court must determine whether these emerging standards provide any guidance on the issue before the Court, i.e., whether a court order directing a party to produce electronic documents as they are maintained in the ordinary course of business requires the producing party to produce those documents with the metadata intact. A related issue is determining which party has the initial burden with regard to the disclosure of metadata. Does the requesting party have the burden to specifically request metadata and demonstrate its relevance? Or does the party ordered to produce electronic documents have an obligation to produce the metadata unless that party timely objects to production of the metadata?

The Court starts with the current version of Federal Rule of Civil Procedure 34. This rule provides that "[a]ny party may serve on any other party a request (1) to produce and permit the party making the request, or someone acting on the requestor's behalf, to inspect and copy, any designated documents (including writings, drawings, graphs, charts, photographs, phonorecords, and other data compilations from which information can be obtained, translated, if necessary, by the respondent through detection devices into reasonably usable form)." "A party who produces documents for inspection shall produce them as they are kept in the usual course of business or shall organize and label them to correspond with the categories in the request."

Federal Rule of Civil Procedure 34 includes "data compilations" in the listing of items that constitute a "document." * * * The current version of Rule 34, however, provides limited guidance with respect to when "data compilations" or other types of electronic documents have to be produced and in what form they should be produced.

In the past year, the Civil Rules Advisory Committee has proposed to the Judicial Conference several amendments to the Federal Rules of Civil Procedure addressing the discovery of electronically stored information. [These amendments ended up taking effect on December 1, 2006]. One of the proposed amendments to Rule 34(a) adds "electronically stored information" as a separate category along with "any designated documents." In addition, the proposed amendments to Rule 34(b) add the following language about the production of electronically stored information:

Unless the parties otherwise agree, or the court otherwise orders,

* * *

(ii) if a request for electronically stored information does not specify the form or forms of production, a responding party must produce the information in a form or forms in which it is ordinarily maintained, or in a form or forms that are reasonably usable.

* * *

Although the proposed amendments to Rule 34 use the phrase "in a form or forms in which it is ordinarily maintained," they provide no further guidance as to whether a party's production of electronically stored information "in the form or forms in which it is ordinarily maintained" would encompass the electronic document's metadata.

In the few cases where discovery of metadata is mentioned, it is unclear whether metadata should ordinarily be produced as a matter of course in an electronic document production. * * *

Having concluded that neither the federal rules nor case law provides sufficient guidance on the production of metadata, the Court next turns to materials issued by the Sedona Conference Working Group on Electronic Document Production. The Court finds two of the Sedona Principles for Electronic Document Production particularly helpful in determining whether Defendant was justified in scrubbing the metadata from the electronic spreadsheets. Principle 9 states that "[a]bsent a showing of special need and relevance a responding party should not be required to preserve, review, or produce deleted, shadowed, fragmented, or residual data or documents." Principle 12 provides that "[u]nless it is material to resolving the dispute, there is no obligation to preserve and produce metadata absent agreement of the parties or order of the court."

Comment 9.a. to the Sedona Principles for Electronic Document Production * * * suggests that the best approach to understanding what constitutes a "document" is to examine what information is readily available to the computer user in the ordinary course of business. If the information is in view, it should be treated as the equivalent of a paper "document." Data that can be readily compiled into viewable information, whether presented on the screen or printed on paper, is also a "document" under Rule 34. The comment, however, cautions that data hidden and never revealed to the user in the ordinary course of business should not be presumptively treated as a part of the "document," although there are circumstances in which the data may be relevant and should be preserved and produced. The comment concludes that such data may be discoverable under Rule 34, but the evaluation of the need for and relevance of such discovery should be separately analyzed on a case-by-case basis. Comment 9.a. provides the following illustration:

> A party demands that responsive documents, "whether in hard copy or electronic format," be produced. The producing party objects to producing the documents in electronic format and states that production will be made through PDF or TIF images on CD–ROMs. The producing party assembles copies of the relevant hard copy memoranda, prints out copies of relevant e-mails and electronic memoranda, and produces them in a PDF or TIF format that does not include metadata. Absent a special request for metadata (or any reasonable basis to conclude the metadata was relevant to the claims and defenses in the litigation), and a prior order of the court based on a showing of need, this production of documents complies with the ordinary meaning of Rule 34.

Metadata is specifically discussed in depth in Comment 12.a. to the Sedona Principles. The comment states that "[a]lthough there are exceptions to every rule, especially in an evolving area of the law, there should be a modest legal presumption in most cases that the producing party need not take special efforts to preserve or produce metadata." The comment further notes that it is likely to remain the exceptional situation in which metadata must be produced.

The comment lists several ways in which routine preservation and production of metadata may be beneficial. The comment balances these potential benefits against the "reality that most of the metadata has no evidentiary value, and any time (and money) spent reviewing it is a waste of resources." The comment concludes that a reasonable balance is that, unless the producing party is aware or should be reasonably aware that particular metadata is relevant, the producing party should have the option of producing all, some, or none of the metadata. The comment sets forth one important caveat to giving the option of producing metadata to the producing party: "Of course, if the producing party knows or should reasonably know that particular metadata is relevant to the dispute, it should be produced."

c. Application to this case

The narrow issue currently before the Court is whether, under emerging standards of electronic discovery, the Court's Order directing Defendant to produce electronic spreadsheets as they are kept in the ordinary course of business requires Defendant to produce those documents with the metadata intact. * * * While recognizing that the Sedona Principles and comments are only persuasive authority and are not binding, the Court finds the Sedona Principles and comments particularly instructive in how the Court should address the electronic discovery issue currently before it.

Comment 9.a. to the Sedona Principles for Electronic Document Production * * * uses viewability as the determining factor in whether something should be presumptively treated as a part of a "document." Using viewability as the standard, all metadata ordinarily visible to the user of the Excel spreadsheet application should presumptively be treated as part of the "document" and should thus be discoverable. For spreadsheet applications, the user ordinarily would be able to view the contents of the cells on the spreadsheets, and thus the contents of those cells would be discoverable.

* * * With regard to metadata in general, the Court looks to Principle 12 and Comment 12.a. to the Sedona Principles. Based upon this Principle and Comment, emerging standards of electronic discovery appear to articulate a general presumption against the production of metadata, but provide a clear caveat when the producing party is aware or should be reasonably aware that particular metadata is relevant to the dispute.

Based on these emerging standards, the Court holds that when a party is ordered to produce electronic documents as they are maintained in the ordinary course of business, the producing party should produce the electronic documents with their metadata intact, unless that party timely objects to production of metadata, the parties agree that the metadata should not be produced, or the producing party requests a protective order. The initial burden with regard to the disclosure of the metadata would therefore be placed on the party to whom the request or order to produce is directed. The burden to object to the disclosure of metadata is appropriately placed on the party ordered to produce its electronic documents as they are ordinarily maintained because that party already has access to the metadata and is in the best position to determine whether producing it is objectionable. Placing the burden on the producing party is further supported by the fact that metadata is an inherent part of an electronic document, and its removal ordinarily requires an affirmative act by the producing party that alters the electronic document.

i. Relevancy

Defendant maintains that the metadata it removed from its electronic spreadsheets has absolutely no evidentiary value and is completely irrelevant. It argues that Plaintiffs' suggestion that the metadata may identify the computers used to create or modify the spreadsheets or reveal titles of documents that may assist in efforts to piece together the facts of the RIFs at issue in this case has no relevance to Plaintiffs' claim that Defendant maintained discriminatory policies or practices used to effectuate a pattern and practice of age discrimination. Defendant likewise argues that the metadata is not necessary because the titles of documents can be gleaned from the subject spreadsheets, and these titles adequately describe the data included in such spreadsheets.

The Court agrees with Defendant that certain metadata from the spreadsheets may be irrelevant to the claims and defenses in this case. The Court, however, does not find that all of the spreadsheets' metadata is irrelevant. In light of Plaintiffs' allegations that Defendant reworked pools of employees in order to improve distribution to pass its adverse impact analysis, the Court finds that some of the metadata is relevant and likely to lead to the discovery of admissible evidence. While the Court cannot fashion an exhaustive list of the spreadsheet metadata that may be relevant, the Court does find that metadata associated with any changes to the spreadsheets, the dates of any changes, the identification of the individuals making any changes, and other metadata from which Plaintiffs could determine the final versus draft version of the spreadsheets appear relevant. Plaintiffs' allegation that Defendant reworked the pools is not a new allegation. Thus, Defendant should reasonably have known that Plaintiffs were expecting the electronic spreadsheets to contain their metadata intact. Furthermore, if Defendant believed the metadata to be irrelevant, it should have asserted a relevancy objection instead of making the unilateral decision to produce the spreadsheets with the metadata removed.

ii. Reliability

Defendant also argues that the metadata removed from the electronic spreadsheets may be inaccurate and therefore has no evidentiary value. The Court finds that this is not sufficient justification for removing the metadata absent agreement of the parties or the Court's approval. If Defendant had any concerns regarding the accuracy or reliability of the metadata, it should have communicated those concerns to the Court before it scrubbed the metadata.

iii. Privilege

Defendant also argues that production of certain metadata removed by Defendant would facilitate the revelation of information that is attorney-client privileged and/or attorney work product. Defendant claims that through the use of easily accessible technology, metadata may reveal information extracted from a document, such as * * * protected or privileged matters. It further claims that metadata may create a data trail that reveals changes to prior drafts or edits.

* * *

For any * * * metadata Defendant claims is protected by the attorney-client privilege or as attorney work product, the Court finds that Defendant should have raised this issue prior to its unilateral decision to produce the spreadsheets with the metadata removed. Fed. R. Civ. P. 26(b)(5) requires a party withholding otherwise discoverable information on the basis of privilege to make the claim expressly and to describe the nature of the documents, communications, or things not produced or disclosed in a manner that, without revealing the privileged information, will enable the other parties to assess the applicability of the privilege. Normally, this is accomplished by objecting and providing a privilege log for "documents, communications, or things" not produced.

In this case, Defendant has failed to object and has not provided a privilege log identifying the electronic documents that it claims contain privileged metadata. Defendant has not provided the Court with even a general description of the purportedly privileged metadata that was scrubbed from the spreadsheets. As Defendant has failed to provide any privilege log for the electronic documents it claims contain metadata that will reveal privileged communications or attorney work product, the Court holds that Defendant has waived any attorney-client privilege or work product protection with regard to the spreadsheets' metadata * * *.

2. Plaintiffs never requested the production of metadata

Defendant also argues that Plaintiffs never requested the metadata and that metadata was never mentioned during any of the discovery conferences. * * * Defendant is correct in asserting that Plaintiffs never expressly requested metadata and that the Court never expressly ordered Defendant to produce the electronic spreadsheets' metadata. However, taken in the context of Plaintiffs' stated reasons for requesting the Excel spreadsheets in their native electronic format and the Court's repeated statements that the spreadsheets should be produced in the electronic form in which they are maintained, the Court finds that Defendant should have reasonably understood that the Court expected and intended for Defendant to produce the spreadsheets' metadata along with the Excel spreadsheets. If Defendant did not understand the Court's ruling, it should have requested clarification of the Court's order. As the Sedona Working Group on Electronic Document Production observed: "Of course, if the producing party knows or should reasonably know that particular metadata is relevant to the dispute, it should be produced." Here, the Court finds that Defendant should have reasonably known that the metadata was relevant to the dispute and therefore should have either been produced or an appropriate objection made or motion filed.

* * *

III. Sanctions

The Court's Show Cause Order also required Defendant to show cause why it should not be sanctioned for its failure to comply with the Court's ruling directing Defendant to produce electronic spreadsheets in the manner in which they were maintained. Defendant states that it did not understand the Court's direction to produce electronic spreadsheets included the production of metadata and that its actions were not made in bad faith. It points out that it has already produced hundreds of documents in response to formal and informal requests for production, answered hundreds of interrogatories, and produced and scheduled scores of witnesses for deposition in support of its assertion that it has acted in good faith throughout this litigation.

The Court concludes that Defendant has shown cause why it should not be sanctioned for its actions in scrubbing the metadata * * *. Although the Court intended its ruling requiring Defendant to produce the electronic RIF-related spreadsheets in the manner in which they were ordinarily maintained to include the metadata, the Court recognizes that the production of metadata is a new and largely undeveloped area of the law. This lack of clear law on production of metadata, combined with the arguable ambiguity in the Court's prior rulings, compels the Court to conclude that sanctions are not appropriate here.

The Court, however, wants to clarify the law regarding the production of metadata in this case. When the Court orders a party to produce an electronic document in the form in which it is regularly maintained, i.e., in its native format or as an active file, that production must include all metadata unless that party timely objects to production of the metadata, the parties agree that the metadata should not be produced, or the producing party requests a protective order.

* * *

IT IS THEREFORE ORDERED that Defendant has failed to show cause why it should not produce the electronic spreadsheets in the manner in which they were maintained[,] * * * which includes the spreadsheets' metadata. * * *

WYETH v. IMPAX LABORATORIES, INC.

248 F.R.D. 169 (D. Del. 2006)

FARNAN, DISTRICT JUDGE

Pending before the Court is Defendant Impax's ("Impax") Motion To Compel Production Of Documents.

* * *

2. *Production Of Responsive Documents In Their Native Format*

Impax contends that Wyeth should be ordered to produce electronic documents in their native format, complete with metadata, and not in the

Tagged Image File Format ("TIFF") in which they were produced. Impax also contends that a document database created by Wyeth for purposes of the Teva Litigation is discoverable and should be produced. In response, Wyeth contends that Impax is not entitled to electronic copies in their natural state for two reasons: (1) Impax has not made a particularized showing of need for the metadata, and (2) collection of this data would be overly burdensome.

Metadata is defined as "information describing the history, tracking, or management of an electronic document." Removal of metadata from an electronic document usually requires an affirmative alteration of that document, through scrubbing or converting the file from its native format to an image file, for example. Most metadata is of limited evidentiary value, and reviewing it can waste litigation resources.

Emerging standards of electronic discovery appear to articulate a general presumption against the production of metadata. The Default Standard for Discovery of Electronic Documents utilized in this District follows this general presumption. Paragraph 6 directs parties to produce electronic documents as image files (e.g. PDF or TIFF) if they cannot agree on a different format for production. "Default Standard For Discovery of Electronic Documents ("E–Discovery")," Ad Hoc Committee for Electronic Discovery of the U.S. District Court for the District of Delaware, http://www.ded.uscourts.gov/Announce/Policies/Policy01.htm. [hereinafter "Default Standard"]. However, if the requesting party can demonstrate a particularized need for the native format of an electronic document, a court may order it produced. Therefore, the producing party must preserve the integrity of the electronic documents it produces. Failure to do so will not support a contention that production of documents in native format is overly burdensome.

Since the parties have never agreed that electronic documents would be produced in any particular format, Wyeth complied with its discovery obligation by producing image files. Further, neither party has argued that the need for accessing metadata was foreseeable or generally necessary. Finally, Impax has not demonstrated a particularized need for the metadata or database production it has requested. Therefore, this part of Impax's Motion is denied.

COMMENTARY

A large amount of ESI, unlike paper, is associated with or contains information that is not readily apparent on the screen view of the file. This additional information is usually known as "metadata." Metadata includes information about the document or file that is recorded by the computer to assist in storing and retrieving the document or file. The information may also be useful for system administration as it reflects data regarding the generation, handling, transfer, and storage of the document or file within the computer system. Much metadata is neither created by nor normally accessible to the computer user.

There are many examples of metadata. Such information includes file designation, create and edit dates, authorship, comments, and edit history. Indeed, electronic files may contain hundreds or even thousands of pieces of such information. For instance, e-mail has its own metadata elements that include, among about 1,200 or more properties, such information as the dates that mail was sent, received, replied to or forwarded, blind carbon copy information, and sender address book information. Typical word processing documents not only include prior changes and edits but also hidden codes that determine such features as paragraphing, font, and line spacing. The ability to recall inadvertently deleted information is another familiar function, as is tracking of creation and modification dates.

Similarly, electronically created spreadsheets may contain calculations that are not visible in a printed version or hidden columns that can only be viewed by accessing the spreadsheet in its "native" application—that is, the software application used to create or record the information. Internet documents contain hidden data that allow for the transmission of information between an Internet user's computer and the server on which the Internet document is located. So-called "meta-tags" allow search engines to locate websites responsive to specified search criteria. "Cookies" are text files placed on a computer (sometimes without user knowledge) that can, among other things, track usage and transmit information back to the cookie's originator. Generally, the metadata associated with files used by most people today (such as Microsoft Office documents) is known as "application metadata." This metadata is embedded in the file it describes and moves with the file when it is moved or copied. On the other hand, "system metadata" is not embedded within the file it describes but stored externally. System metadata is used by the computer's file system to track file locations and store information about each file's name, size, creation, modification, and usage.

Understanding when metadata is relevant and subject to preservation and production represents one of the biggest challenges in electronic discovery. Sometimes metadata is needed to authenticate a disputed document or to establish facts material to a dispute, such as when a file was accessed in a suit involving theft of trade secrets. In most cases, however, the metadata will have no material evidentiary value—it does not matter when a document was printed, or who typed the revisions, or what edits were made before the document was circulated. There is also the real danger that information recorded by the computer as application metadata may be inaccurate. For example, when a new employee uses a word processing program to create a memorandum by using a memorandum template created by a former employee, the metadata for the new memorandum may incorrectly identify the former employee as the author. However, the proper use of metadata in litigation may be able to provide substantial benefit by facilitating more effective and efficient searching and retrieval of ESI.

When deciding what metadata may be relevant, consider these definitions from *The Sedona Conference Glossary of E–Discovery and Digital Information Management (Second Edition)* (December 2007 Version).

* **Application Metadata:** Data created by the application specific to the ESI being addressed, embedded in the file and moved with the file when copied; copying may alter application metadata.

* **Document Metadata:** Properties about the file stored in the file, as opposed to document content. Often this data is not immediately viewable in the software application used to create/edit the document but often can be accessed via a "Properties" view. Examples include document author and company, and create and revision dates. Contrast with File System Metadata and Email Metadata.

* **E-mail Metadata:** Data stored in the e-mail about the e-mail. Often this data is not even viewable in the e-mail client application used to create the e-mail, e.g., blind copy addressees, received date. The amount of e-mail metadata available for a particular e-mail varies greatly depending on the e-mail system. Contrast with File System Metadata and Document Metadata.

* **Embedded Metadata:** Generally hidden, but an integral part of ESI, such as "track changes" or "comments" in a word processing file or "notes" in a presentation file. While some metadata is routinely extracted during processing and conversion for e-discovery, embedded data may not be. Therefore, it may only be available in the original, native file. *See also* Application Metadata and Metadata.

* **File System Metadata:** Metadata generated by the system to track the demographics (name, size, location, usage, etc.) of the ESI and, not embedded within, but stored externally from the ESI.

* **Metadata:** Data typically stored electronically that describes characteristics of ESI, found in different places in different forms. Metadata can describe how, when and by whom ESI was collected, created, accessed, modified and how it is formatted. It can be altered intentionally or inadvertently. Certain metadata can be extracted when native files are processed for litigation. Some metadata, such as file dates and sizes, can easily be seen by users; other metadata can be hidden or embedded and unavailable to computer users who are not technically adept. Metadata is generally not reproduced in full form when a document is printed to paper or electronic image.

* **Native Format:** Electronic documents have an associated file structure defined by the original creating application. This file structure is referred to as the "native format" of the document. Because viewing or searching documents in the native format may require the original application (for example, viewing a Microsoft Word document may require the Microsoft Word application), documents may be converted to a neutral format as part of the record acquisition or archive process. "Static" formats (often called "imaged formats"), such as TIFF or PDF, are designed to retain an image of the document as it would look viewed in the original creating application but do not allow metadata to be viewed or the document information to be manipulated. In the conversion to static format, the metadata can be processed, preserved and electronically associated with the static format file. However, with technology advancements, tools and applications are becoming increasingly available to allow viewing and searching of documents in their native format, while still preserving all metadata.

* **User–Added Metadata:** Data, possibly work product, created by a user while copying, reviewing or working with a file, including annotations and subjective coding information.

* **Vendor–Added Metadata:** Data created and maintained by the electronic discovery vendor as a result of processing the document. While some vendor-added metadata has direct value to customers, much of it is used for process reporting, chain of custody and data accountability.

PROBLEMS

1. What is relevant metadata? Consider this example. Lotus notes e-mail contains over fifteen thousand potential metadata fields. Assume that vendors in the industry have only ever encountered six thousand of them. Assume further that popular litigation support software only handle roughly one hundred metadata fields.

    a. How would you decide which metadata fields to produce?

    b. Would you/should you only produce those metadata fields that you consider "relevant?"

    c. What if the opposing party did not ask for metadata?

    d. What about attachments to e-mail? How might metadata from the attachments and the e-mail differ? What are your potential obligations regarding e-mail attachment metadata?

2. *Williams v. Sprint* teaches that it is important to preserve metadata and that it is easy to unintentionally alter metadata. What are the dangers of reviewing native files sent to you by a client before they are produced to the opposing party? What steps are necessary to ensure that the metadata is not altered before production to the opposing party? What steps do you consider reasonable?

E. ON–SITE INSPECTIONS—NEUTRAL EXPERTS, CONFIDENTIALITY PROTECTION, INSPECTION PROTOCOLS

FERRON v. SEARCH CACTUS, LLC

No. 2:06–CV–327, 2008 WL 1902499 (S.D. Ohio Apr. 28, 2008)

FROST, DISTRICT JUDGE

The Court held a telephone conference in this action on April 14, 2008, in which all parties were represented and this Court considered and decided the protocol for viewing and preserving information contained on Plaintiff's computer systems. This Opinion and Order memorializes that decision.

I. Background

Plaintiff is an attorney who utilizes his home and office computers for storing and working with information related to the representation of clients, the maintenance of lawsuits such as this action and other actions or potential actions similar to the subject matter of the instant action, and his personal life. Out of these three categories of information, the information related to the representation of clients in cases unrelated to email and advertising litigation has no relevance to this case and contain documents that are protected by the attorney-client privilege. The information that may be categorized as personal also has no relevance to this case and may be confidential in nature, e.g., banking and credit card information. However, the third category of information, i.e., information related to email and website advertising litigation is relevant and discoverable.

In this Court's Opinion and Order which granted in part and denied in part Defendant Search Cactus' motion for summary judgment, it held that "only the unsolicited emails Plaintiff received at jferron@ferronlaw. com after April 3, 2006 can be used to support his claim under the [Ohio Consumer Sales Practices Act] OCSPA." Thus, it is necessary for the parties to ascertain which of the emails Plaintiff received were unsolicited. As Defendants contend, Plaintiff's computer systems contain the only available documentary evidence that can show the pathways taken by Plaintiff to solicit the emails or the absence of those pathways.

II.　Defendants' Discovery Requests

Defendants have requested an inspection of Plaintiff's computer systems so as to capture specific information relevant to this case that Plaintiff has not produced and, Defendants contend[,] has not been placed on a litigation hold. Specifically, Defendant wishes to inspect Plaintiff's computer systems to ascertain whether Plaintiff's efforts with respect to receiving the emails and visiting the websites (that are at the heart of this action) constituted a consumer transaction under the OCSPA, or whether Plaintiff's opening of the emails and any attempts to obtain free merchandise were part of a business designed to profit from email litigation.

The parties agree that a forensic computer expert must be utilized to obtain the information that the Court has determined Defendants are entitled to discover.[3] This is because a distinctive feature of computer operations is the routine alteration and deletion of information that attends ordinary use of the computer. Many steps essential to computer operation may alter or destroy information, for reasons that have nothing to do with how that information might relate to litigation. As a result, the ordinary operation of computer systems creates a risk that a party may lose potentially discoverable information without culpable conduct on its part. The routine operation of computer systems includes the alteration and overwriting of information, often without the operator's specific direction or awareness, a feature with no direct counterpart in hard-copy

---

3. The Court also notes that the parties disagree about the types of information that must be analyzed on the computers in order to reconstruct internet browser history. Plaintiff's computer consultant has attested that the internet browsing history may be re-constructed through a limited examination of certain directories on the computers' hard drive. Defendant[s'] computer consultant has attested that such an analysis can only occur by analyzing a complete mirror image of the hard drives of the computers.

documents. Such features are essential to the operation of electronic information systems. On March 19, 2008, this Court held a telephone conference with the parties, directed that inspection of Plaintiff's computer systems' hard drives was appropriate, and instructed the parties to discuss and propose a protocol for the inspection.

III. Analysis

The parties were unable to agree on a protocol for inspection of Plaintiff's computer systems' hard drives and requested another conference with this Court to address the issue. At the April 14, 2008 telephone conference, this Court considered the parties' arguments related to the inspection of Plaintiff's computers. The issues of concern were how to protect Plaintiff's confidential personal information that is stored on the computers, e.g., personal banking and credit card information, and how to prevent Plaintiff from waiving the attorney-client privilege by allowing the information on the computers to be viewed by any third party.

Initially, the Court explains that the 2006 amendments to Rule 34 of the Federal Rules of Civil Procedure clarify "that discovery of electronically stored information stands on equal footing with discovery of paper documents." Fed. R. Civ. P. 34 Advisory Committee's Note on 2006 Amendments. Consequently, without a qualifying reason, Defendants are no more entitled to access to Plaintiff's electronic information storage systems than to Plaintiff's warehouses storing paper documents.

Here, the Court concludes that there are qualifying reasons sufficient to permit Defendants access to Plaintiff's computer systems: Plaintiff has apparently failed to fulfill his "duty to preserve information because of pending or reasonably anticipated litigation," Fed. R. Civ. P. 37 Advisory Committee's Note on 2006 Amendments, and Plaintiff has not otherwise produced the relevant information. Moreover, * * * Plaintiff's computers contain the only available documentary evidence of his visits to the websites in issue and such evidence has not otherwise been produced * * *.

* * *

The Court will now consider Plaintiff's concerns regarding this Court's order allowing inspection of Plaintiff's computer systems' hard drives.

A. Confidential Personal Information

The parties and this Court agree that Plaintiff's personal information is confidential in nature and is irrelevant to this lawsuit. Defendants request a current mirror image[5] of Plaintiff's computer systems' hard drives, contending that Plaintiff's removal of any information from the computer hard drives can unwittingly cause deletion of other, possibly relevant, information.

---

5. A mirror image copy represents a snapshot of the computer's records. It contains all the information in the computer, including embedded, residual, and deleted data.

This Court attempts to strike a balance between protecting Plaintiff's personal confidential information and Defendant[s'] allegation that deletion can cause a loss of data. * * * To strike a balance between these competing interests, this Court ORDERS Plaintiff's forensic computer expert to mirror image both of Plaintiff's computer systems' hard drives and for Plaintiff to store the images safely. Plaintiff's forensic computer expert shall then remove only Plaintiff's personal confidential information that could not reasonably lead to the discovery of information relevant to this litigation. Plaintiff shall provide Defendants with the protocol his expert utilized to remove the confidential information.

B. Attorney–Client Privileged Information

Plaintiff argues that if he is required to allow Defendants' forensic computer expert to review and copy Plaintiff's computer systems' hard drives, it will simultaneously cause the loss of the attorney-client privilege that has attached to the information related to Plaintiff's other clients because that information will be viewed by a third party. This Court disagrees.

First, the Court notes that it is Plaintiff himself that has caused this issue to become problematic because of his failure to place a sufficient litigation hold on his computer systems as of the date he anticipated this litigation. * * *

Second, Defendants have offered to have their forensic computer expert review with Plaintiff the findings and allow Plaintiff to identify the privileged documents that will then be removed before the information is forwarded to Defendants. * * *

Finally, the Court is not heedless of the intrusion copying Plaintiff's computer systems' hard drives will cause. In *Playboy Enters. v. Welles*, 60 F. Supp. 2d 1050, 1054 (S.D. Cal. 1999), a case upon which Defendants rely, the court stated that the mirror imaging process took approximately four to eight hours for each computer. This amount of time is certainly reasonable to remedy Plaintiff's failure of his duty to preserve the relevant computer-stored evidence in this action.

Accordingly, this Court ORDERS Plaintiff to permit Defendants' forensic computer expert to mirror image Plaintiff's computer systems' hard drives. Defendants' expert shall review his findings in confidence with Plaintiff prior to making any findings available to Defendants. Plaintiff shall identify for deletion any information that is irrelevant and create a specific privilege log of any relevant information for which he claims privilege. The expert shall remove the information claimed as privileged and provide all other information to Defendants.

C. Forensic Computer Experts

It appears to the Court that both of the forensic computer experts presented to it are qualified. In certain situations, courts appoint computer forensic experts to act as officers of the court to help ''reduce privacy intrusions and privilege waiver issues during forensic analysis." * * * Thus, the two identified computer forensic experts shall serve as officers of this Court.

With regard to the cost of the forensic examinations, at least initially, the parties will bear the costs associated with their chosen expert.

IV. Conclusion

Based on the foregoing, this Court ORDERS:

1. Within seven days of the date of this Opinion and Order, Plaintiff's forensic computer expert shall mirror image both of Plaintiff's computer systems' hard drives and Plaintiff shall preserve this mirror image.

2. Plaintiff's forensic computer expert shall then remove only Plaintiff's confidential personal information from the mirror image of Plaintiff's computer systems' hard drives. Plaintiff's expert shall provide Defendants with the protocol he utilized to remove the confidential information.

3. Plaintiff shall then provide Defendants' computer forensic expert access to his computer systems' hard drives.

4. Defendants' forensic computer expert shall mirror image Plaintiff's computer systems' hard drives in approximately four to eight hours for each system. If the expert finds that this is not enough time, Plaintiff is expected to be reasonable in allowing some additional time. Defendant is expected to be considerate with regard to scheduling times that are less intrusive to Plaintiff and his business.

5. Defendants' expert shall review his findings in confidence with Plaintiff prior to making any findings available to Defendants.

6. Plaintiff shall identify for deletion any information that is irrelevant and create a specific privilege log of any relevant information for which he claims privilege. The computer forensic expert shall remove the information claimed as privileged and provide all other information to Defendants.

7. Defendants' expert shall provide Plaintiff with the protocol he utilized to remove the privileged information.

8. Forensic computer experts C. Matthew Curtin and Scott T. Simmons shall act as officers of this Court. Defendants shall be responsible for remunerating Mr. Curtin and Plaintiff shall be responsible for remunerating Mr. Simmons.

COMMENTARY

On occasion, a court will require the mirror imaging[6] of the hard drives of any computers that contain documents responsive to an opposing party's

---

6. A "mirror image" is generally described as "a forensic duplicate, which replicates bit for bit, sector for sector, all allocated and unallocated space, including slack space, on a computer request for production. Litigants often request a court-ordered inspection of their adversary's computer hard drives where the parties cannot agree on a protocol or there is evidence that relevant ESI will be found on a computer hard drive that the adversary has failed to produce. Such court-ordered inspections are warranted where the ESI in question goes to the heart of the action.

The federal courts derive their authority to order such inspections from Rule 34(a), which allows parties to request that another party:

> produce and permit the requesting party ... to inspect, copy, test, or sample any designated documents or electronically stored information— including writings, drawings, graphs, charts, photographs, sound recordings, images, and other data or data compilations stored in any medium from which information can be obtained-translated, if necessary, by the respondent into reasonably usable form.

However, Rule 34(a) is not meant to create a routine right of direct access to the opponent's electronic information systems. Court-ordered inspections of computer hard drives usually require on-site access and can be intrusive and burdensome, causing significant inconvenience and interruption to business operations of the responding party. Furthermore, a computer hard drive is likely to contain a significant quantity of non-relevant, privileged and confidential information which raises significant privacy concerns.

Courts must therefore carefully craft inspection protocols that balance the need for discovery of relevant information against the risk of disclosure of privileged material and undue intrusiveness resulting from inspecting or testing such systems. The details of these protocols may vary depending on the unique facts and circumstances of each case, but generally comprise the following: (1) a forensic expert will obtain the images of the computer hard drives; (2) the images will be maintained by the party whose hard drives were imaged; (3) the producing party will have the opportunity to remove any non-relevant or privileged information; and (4) responsive information found on the images will be disclosed to the requesting party with a log identifying any material removed based on a claim of privilege.

1. Denying Requests for On–Site Inspections

Courts have been cautious in requiring the mirror imaging of computers where the request is extremely broad in nature and the connection between the computers and the claims in the lawsuit are vague or unsubstantiated. Mere conjecture or suspicion that an adversary has not produced discoverable information is not enough. For example, in *Hedenburg v. Aramark American Food Services*, an employment discrimination case, the defendant sought a mirror image of the plaintiff's home computer. The defendant contended that the plaintiff's personal correspondence with unnamed third parties (in the form of e-mails or Internet postings) might reveal discrepancies in her testimony about the alleged discriminatory events and the impact of certain events on her emotional state. The defendant argued that access to a plaintiff's computer was common in employment cases, and offered to have the

---

hard drive." *Balboa Threadworks, Inc. v. Stucky*, No. 05–1157, 2006 WL 763668, at *3 (D. Kan. Mar. 24, 2006).

hard drive mirror image sent to a special master in an effort to resolve the problem of disclosing privileged or other non-discoverable information. The plaintiff argued that she had already made a diligent search of her computer files. She objected to the discovery as a fishing expedition and refused to permit the defendant access to her home computer's hard drive.

The court observed that such a search is sometimes permitted where the contents of the computer go to the heart of the case. Here, the court found that the central claims in the case were wholly unrelated to the contents of plaintiff's computer, and that defendant was "hoping blindly to find something useful in its impeachment of the plaintiff."[7] In denying defendant's motion, the court stated:

> Defendant essentially seeks a search warrant to confirm that Plaintiff has not memorialized statements contrary to her testimony in this case. If the issue related instead to a lost paper diary, the court would not permit the Defendant to search the plaintiff's property to ensure that her search was complete.

Similarly, in *Williams v. Massachusetts Mutual Life Insurance Co.*, a wrongful termination case, the plaintiff sought the court's help in obtaining from defendants a particular e-mail he claimed to have seen and possessed at one point, but no longer possessed. He sought an order appointing a neutral computer forensics expert to conduct the search for the e-mail, and, in the event the e-mail was discovered, to conduct an additional, more detailed electronic investigation "to locate and retrieve all electronic communications related to his employment and termination that have not as yet been produced by defendants."[8]

In denying the request, the court reasoned that the plaintiff had presented no credible evidence that the defendants were unwilling to produce computer-generated documents, whether now or in the future, or that they had withheld relevant information. "Before permitting such an intrusion into an opposing party's information system—particularly where, as here, that party has undertaken its own search and forensic analysis and has sworn to its accuracy—the inquiring party must present at least some reliable information that the opposing party's representations are misleading or substantively inaccurate."

Even where there is some evidence that data on an adversary's computer systems is responsive, courts may deny a request for inspection by imaging where the burden on the responding party is too great. In *Ponca Tribe of Indians of Oklahoma v. Continental Carbon*, the court rejected the plaintiffs' request that they be permitted to image or download all information stored in defendant's "data historian" program.[9] The plaintiffs initially proposed imaging or mirroring the data historian as a means of easily obtaining the requested information. However, the defendant objected and argued that such imaging would necessarily require approximately one hundred days to complete and that any such imaging would violate the licensing for the operating

---

7. *See Hedenburg v. Aramark Am. Food Servs.*, No. 06 Civ. 5267, 2007 WL 162716, at *1–2 (W.D. Wash. Jan. 17, 2007).

8. *Williams v. Massachusetts Mut. Life Ins. Co.*, 226 F.R.D. 144, 145 (D. Mass. 2005).

9. No. 05 Civ. 445, 2006 WL 2927878, at *1–2 (W.D. Okla. Oct. 11, 2006).

software used by defendant. The plaintiffs further suggested that the information be downloaded into a database using defendant's software. The defendant responded that it did not own the software modules, but that such software could be purchased for approximately $5,000 and would require another $5,000 in training/programming to make the modules useable. The court concluded that production of the data historian information was unduly burdensome, and noted that the plaintiffs had failed to present a sufficient argument demonstrating that their need for the information contained within the data historian outweighed the burden of producing it.

2.   Granting Requests for On–Site Inspections

There are times, however, when a court permits an on-site inspection of an adversary's computer. In *Cenveo Corp. v. Slater*, the plaintiff sought to have its expert create a mirror image of the defendants' hard drives, which would then be searched for responsive information. Cenveo alleged that the defendants, its former employees, had used Cenveo's computers to steal its trade secrets, confidential information, and business opportunities. The court held that an on-site inspection and mirror imaging of the hard drives was warranted "[b]ecause of the close relationship between plaintiff's claims and defendants' computer equipment."[10]

Similarly, in *Ameriwood Industries v. Liberman*, another trade secrets case in which the plaintiff alleged that the defendants—its former employees—had used the plaintiff's computers and confidential files to divert its business to the defendants' new company, the court granted the plaintiff's motion to allow an independent expert to obtain and search a mirror image of the defendants' computer equipment. The court based its ruling on "the close relationship between plaintiff's claims and defendants' computer equipment, and [had] cause to question whether defendants have produced all responsive documents."[11] The court found that deleted versions of e-mails, which were not produced, might exist on the defendants' computers, along with other relevant data such as where certain files were sent and whether the defendants accessed other confidential files.

When courts permit inspection, they usually order measures to protect confidentiality, such as having an independent computer forensics expert conduct the imaging. In addition, the producing party is generally allowed to review the information for privilege and responsiveness before producing it to the requesting party. In *Ameriwood*, for example, the plaintiff's computer forensics expert was ordered to first provide responsive files retrieved from the defendants' hard drives to defendants' counsel, who could review the records for privilege and responsiveness before sending them to plaintiff's counsel.

3.   Is a "Neutral" Computer Forensics Expert Required?

In addition to facilitating disclosure of relevant evidence, a central purpose of a court-imposed inspection is to protect the responding party's privacy and privileges in the ESI being searched. To this end, courts often require

---

10.   No. 06 Civ. 2632, 2007 WL 442387, at *2 (E.D. Pa. Jan. 31, 2007).

11.   No. 06 Civ. 524, 2006 WL 3825291, at *1 (E.D. Mo. Dec. 27, 2006).

that the designated expert be made an "officer of the court" or be subject to strict confidentiality agreements or protective orders.[12]

A key issue is whether the appointed expert must be independent and neutral, or whether it is acceptable to use the forensic expert of one of the parties. While some protocols call for independent experts, often one of the litigant's experts will be appointed to the task in order to minimize costs and complexity.

For example, in *Calyon v. Mizuho Securities USA Inc.*, the plaintiff maintained that only its expert—as opposed to the defendants' expert or an independent third-party expert—would possess the requisite incentive to search exhaustively for evidence.[13] The defendants argued that granting the plaintiff's expert "unfettered access" to home computers and computer storage devices would impermissibly invade the privacy rights of the defendants and their non-party family members who also used the computers. The defendants proposed that their own expert review the mirror images by using search terms provided by the plaintiff, or, alternatively, that a search be performed by an independent expert, who would presumably be appointed by the court.

The court denied access to the plaintiff's expert to image and search the defendants' home computers and also rejected the suggestion that an independent expert be appointed to perform the work, noting that:

> [the plaintiff] does not appear to dispute that the defendants' expert has the technological capability to perform this search. Moreover, the [defendants'] counsel and expert have stated that they are willing to work cooperatively with [plaintiff]'s counsel and expert on an on-going basis to develop and refine search techniques to ensure that all responsive information is identified. In the end, other than arguing that only its expert has the proper incentives to conduct an exhaustive search, [plaintiff] provides no specific basis for why it believes the [defendants'] expert would not thoroughly search the hard drive images. [Plaintiff]'s argument about proper incentives is simply too generalized a basis for granting it *carte blanche* access to the [defendants'] personal hard drives, access that [plaintiff] itself acknowledges as "extraordinary." Finally, . . . the Court finds no need, at this time, to appoint [an independent expert], which would introduce yet another layer of expertise to a case where each side has already retained experts of their choice, and which would make the prosecution of this action more costly.

---

12.   *See, e.g., Cenveo Corp. v. George Slater,* No. 06 Civ. 2632, 2007 WL 442387 (E.D. Pa. Jan. 31, 2007) (once expert is chosen, plaintiff shall notify defendants, and the expert shall execute a confidentiality agreement agreed to by the parties and sign a copy of the protective order); *Simon Prop. Grp. L.P. v. mySimon, Inc.,* 194 F.R.D. 639 (S.D. Ind. 2000) (because the expert served as an officer of the court, disclosure of communication to the expert not deemed a waiver of the attorney-client privilege or any other privilege.).

13.   No. 07 Civ. 2241, 2007 WL 1468889, at *1 (S.D.N.Y. May 18, 2007).

F. DISCOVERY FROM MOST KNOWLEDGEABLE PERSON

HEARTLAND SURGICAL SPECIALTY HOSPITAL, LLC v. MIDWEST DIVISION, INC.

No. 05–2164, 2007 WL 1054279 (D. Kan. Apr. 9, 2007)

BOSTWICK, MAGISTRATE JUDGE

Before the Court is Defendants' Joint Motion to Compel Heartland Surgical Specialty Hospital LLC ("Heartland") to Produce a Rule 30(b)(6) Witness with Knowledge of Its Production of Documents and Data. In the motion, Defendants seek an order compelling Heartland to produce a witness who can testify regarding topics 8, 9, 10, 16, and 17 of Defendants' notice of 30(b)(6) deposition. * * *

FACTUAL BACKGROUND

Defendants' Rule 30(b)(6) deposition notice to Heartland on November 14, 2006 identified 55 separate topics for the deposition. The notice was discussed during the status conference held on November 16, 2006, and the Court granted Defendants' request to split the noticed deposition topics into two Rule 30(b)(6) depositions. Defendants were allowed 11 deposition hours over 2 days for topics 1 through 17 and 24 hours over 4 days for topics 18 through 55. Defendants commenced their first Rule 30(b)(6) deposition over topics 1 through 17 on November 28, 2006.

This motion concerns only whether Heartland has complied with the requirements of Rule 30(b)(6) with respect to its designated representative's responses to deposition questions on topics 8, 9, 10, 16, and 17. Those topics are described in the deposition notice as follows:

Topic 8: "The document retention policies applicable to any [Heartland] Financial Records, [Heartland] Patient Records, [Heartland] Financial Reports, or [Heartland] Plans and Forecasts."

Topic 9: "The destruction, alteration, or loss of any [Heartland] Financial Records, [Heartland] Patient Records, [Heartland] Financial Reports, or [Heartland] Plans and Forecasts."

Topic 10: "The capabilities of [Heartland's] AdvantX, Great Plains, and Softmed software, the data stored or used with that software, and the reports that can be generated with that software."

Topic 16: "The capabilities of the computer systems and software that [Heartland] uses or has used to create, transmit, or store e-mails and other electronic documents, and the extent to which [Heartland] can identify and produce information responsive to discovery requests in this Lawsuit that are stored in those systems."

Topic 17: "[Heartland's] search for, identification of and production of documents and information responsive to discovery requests in this Lawsuit."

DISCUSSION

* * *

Judge Rushfelt has set out the general guidelines with respect to Rule 30(b)(6) depositions:

> For a Rule 30(b)(6) deposition to operate effectively, the * * * corporation must designate and adequately prepare witnesses to address these matters. If the rule is to promote effective discovery regarding corporations the spokesperson must be informed. A notice of deposition made pursuant to Rule 30(b)(6) requires the corporation to produce one or more officers to testify with respect to matters set out in the deposition notice or subpoena. A party need only designate, with reasonable particularity, the topics for examination. The corporation then must not only produce such number of persons as will satisfy the request, but more importantly, prepare them so that they may give complete, knowledgeable and binding answers on behalf of the corporation. . . .

> Rule 30(b)(6) implicitly requires the designated representative to review all matters known or reasonably available to it in preparation for the Rule 30(b)(6) deposition. This interpretation is necessary in order to make the deposition a meaningful one and to prevent the sandbagging of an opponent by conducting a half-hearted inquiry before the deposition but a thorough and vigorous one before the trial. This would totally defeat the purpose of the discovery process. The Court understands that preparing for a Rule 30(b)(6) deposition can be burdensome. However, this is merely the result of the concomitant obligation from the privilege of being able to use the corporate (or other organizational) form in order to conduct business. A party does not fulfill its obligations at the Rule 30(b)(6) deposition by stating it has no knowledge or position with respect to a set of facts or area of inquiry within its knowledge or reasonably available. . . .

Starlight Int'l Inc. v. Herlihy, 186 F.R.D. 626, 638 (D. Kan. 1999). The initial question, then, is whether Defendants' notice described with "reasonable particularity" the matters on which examination was requested. If it did, then Defendants satisfied their burden and Heartland was required to produce a knowledgeable designee.

Courts in this district have found a notice of Rule 30(b)(6) deposition topics to be overbroad when the notice lists topics, but then indicates that the listed topics are not exclusive. Here, the Court specifically limited the parties to the noticed topics 1 through 17, so there can be no argument of overbreadth on the basis that the notice was not limited to the topics designated. Likewise, a notice is not overbroad when its plain language identifies the subject matter of the testimony sought,

The Court finds that Defendants' notice as to topics 1 through 17 described matters with reasonable particularity and satisfied Rule 30(b)(6). Topics 8 and 9 identify the "document retention policies" and "destruction, alteration, or loss" of Heartland's financial records, patient records, financial reports, and plans and forecasts, as those terms are defined in the notice. The definitions of patient records and financial reports do use the phrase "including but not limited to," but are then followed by an extensive example list of the records and reports for which information is sought by Defendants. However, it is clear both from the language used in topics 8 and 9 and from the definitions provided what specific information is being sought. Topic 10 very specifically lists the information sought by Defendants (capabilities, data, and reports from three listed software programs), as does topic 16 (computer systems and software used for Heartland's email and electronic documents). The plain language of topic 17 involves Heartland's compliance with discovery requests. It is true that Defendants sought a large amount of information, but there can be no claim that Heartland could not identify the "outer limits of the areas of inquiry." Further, these topics are relevant to the discovery and documents produced to date in this litigation. *See* FED. R. CIV. P. 26(b)(1) (stating broad allowance of discovery into "any matter, not privileged," and "reasonably calculated to lead to the discovery of admissible evidence").

Having established that the notice provided to Heartland was sufficient, Heartland had a duty to adequately prepare a knowledgeable witness with respect to the noticed topics. As previously noted, Defendants' motion concerns only topics 8, 9, 10, 16, and 17, and Defendants have identified 6 specific question areas that could not be answered by Ms. Holley [the representative designated by Heartland for the Rule 30(b)(6) deposition]:

1. What computer servers does Heartland use, and what data are stored on them?

2. What computers, disk drives, and databases were searched for responsive documents?

3. What are [Heartland's] document retention policies with respect to e-mail, and what was done to prevent deletion or destruction of responsive e-mail?

4. Who is [Heartland's] e-discovery vendor, what was the vendor instructed to do, and what did it do?

5. What was done to eliminate non-responsive documents from [Heartland's] production?

6. What are the reporting capabilities of [Heartland's] Great Plains and AdvantX software, and can [Heartland] export its Great Plains and AdvantX databases to a file for production to defendants?

* * *

With regard to question 1, when asked about specific servers previously identified within Heartland documents, and the storage and retention of data items on those servers, Ms. Holley could not identify some of the servers and did not know the storage or retention policies for some identified servers. With regard to question 2, Ms. Holley did not know which network drivers were searched for responsive discovery documents, whether individual user drives for former employees were searched for responsive discovery documents, whether physician owners' e-mails saved to Heartland servers were searched for responsive discovery documents, whether archived e-mails were searched for responsive discovery documents, whether the voice-mail server was searched for responsive discovery documents, whether the hard drives of individual computers were searched for responsive discovery documents, or whether former employees Kim Krause and Jim Morse's individual computer hard drives were searched for responsive discovery documents. With regard to question 4, Ms. Holley did not know "exactly how they [the e-discovery vendor] searched" the Heartland servers, or "what all was on" the CD database that was produced to Defendants. Because Heartland's e-discovery vendor is an agent of Heartland, Ms. Holley should have been educated on this issue as it is encompassed within topic 17. With regard to question 5, Ms. Holley did not know whether Heartland's counsel did anything to determine if produced electronic documents were responsive to discovery requests. Heartland's counsel are the agents of Heartland and Ms. Holley should have been educated on this issue as it is encompassed within topic 17. With regard to question 6, Ms. Holley did not know whether Heartland's computer systems (AdvantX and Great Plains) could export data for varying means of production. This overall showing with regard to these questions establishes that Ms. Holley was unprepared to answer questions on topics 10, 16, and 17.

With regard to the question 3 identified above, however, Defendants have not shown that Ms. Holley was either unprepared or did not have the requisite knowledge to adequately answer the question. In totality regarding question 3, Defendants cite the following portions of the transcript.

Q. I've looked through Deposition Exhibit 31 and did not see a policy about deletion or archiving of E-mail. Is there such a policy?

A. All of the policies related to document retention have been included in this packet.

Q. Okay. Does Heartland Surgical Specialty Hospital routinely delete E-mail?

A. Not to my knowledge.

Q. Are there size limitations on an individual E-mail account user's mailbox?

A. Not that I'm aware of. . . .

Q. Do individual E-mail account holders have the ability to save E-mail files outside their mailbox?

A. Yes.

Q.   Where would those E-mails be-where are the potential places those E-mails could be saved?

A.   They're instructed to save those E-mail documents or attachments into their personal drive on the server.

Q.   Are you aware of any other places that E-mail account holders have saved E-mails and attachments?

A.   I wouldn't know.

Q.   Is there any policing of the policy that E-mails and attachments are to be saved to the personal drive?

MR. McGUIRE: Object to form. Vague and ambiguous.

Q.   (By Mr. Bien) Is there anyone who checks to make sure that the policy is followed?

A.   I don't know specifically.

Q.   Who would be the person who would be responsible-or withdraw that. Who would be the person with knowledge about whether the policy that E-mails and attachments are to be saved to a personal drive is followed?

A.   Mr. Coffman would have knowledge of that.

The excerpted transcript portions show only that the policies Heart-land has have been given to Defendants, that Heartland does not routinely delete e-mail or limit individual user's e-mail account sizes, and that Ms. Holley did not have knowledge of whether a specific policy was regulated or enforced. The excerpted transcript portions do not show, as Defendants propound, that Ms. Holley did not know the document retention policies with respect to e-mail and what was done to prevent deletion or destruction of responsive e-mail. Defendants have not shown that Ms. Holley was unprepared to answer this question as encompassed by topics 8 and 9.

* * *

While the questions asked in the deposition, particularly about the capabilities of Heartland's computers and software, may have been detailed in nature, they clearly fall within the topics described in the notice. The fact that Ms. Holley had to state, in response to numerous questions, that the answer to the question would be known by either Mr. Coffman (Heartland's Director of Information Technology) or Mr. Van Horn (Heartland's Chief Financial Officer) clearly indicates that Plaintiff had available other persons who could have been used as additional Rule 30(b)(6) witnesses to respond to at least some of the first seventeen topics on behalf of the corporation. It also indicates that Plaintiff did not adequately prepare the tendered witness to answer the questions set out in the identified topics. The Court, therefore, finds that Heartland failed to produce a knowledgeable representative with respect to topics 10, 16, and 17.

Regarding the requested relief sought, *Starlight* instructs:

Corporations, partnerships, and joint ventures have a duty to make a conscientious, good-faith effort to designate knowledgeable persons for Rule 30(b)(6) depositions and to prepare them to fully and unevasively answer questions about the designated subject matter. If the designated persons do not possess personal knowledge of the matters set out in the deposition notice, the entity is obligated to prepare the designees so that they may give knowledgeable and binding answers for the organization. If it becomes obvious during the course of the deposition that the designee is deficient, the organization is obligated to provide a substitute.

Heartland did not designate a knowledgeable person with regard to topics 10, 16, and 17 of the Rule 30(b)(6) deposition. Ms. Holley did not possess personal knowledge of these topics and was not prepared to give knowledgeable answers regarding the topics on behalf of the corporation. Ms. Holley's designation as the Rule 30(b)(6) designee was deficient as to these topics and Heartland must provide a substitute Rule 30(b)(6) designee.

Plaintiff argues that Defendants will have the opportunity to take fact witness depositions of other Heartland employees, including its CFO and Director of Information Technology. This, however, is not the same as a Rule 30(b)(6) deposition which presents the testimony of the corporation itself rather than just the personal knowledge of the witness.

Defendants broadly request an additional Rule 30(b)(6) deposition with respect to topics 8, 9, 10, 16, and 17, but they make their motion based on the questions discussed above. Of course, once questions 1, 2, 4, 5, and 6 are answered (the Court finds that question 3, on topics 8 and 9, has already been adequately answered), Defendants may, and probably will, have additional follow-up questions directly related to topics 10, 16, and 17. For this reason, Defendants may conduct an additional Rule 30(b)(6) deposition of Heartland, on topics 10, 16, and 17. Defendants are limited to questions 1, 2, 4, 5, and 6 and any follow-up questions that flow naturally and directly from these questions. The deposition will be limited to six (6) hours in duration.

COMMENTARY

Depositions of the "person most knowledgeable" are nothing new. There has been a long and relatively undisturbed tradition permitting the deposition of the individual in the best position to know certain information, and whose testimony speaks for and is binding on a partnership, corporation, or other non-individual legal entity. In fact, there was no change to Rule 30(b)(6) in the 2006 Rule Amendments. However, since the advent of electronic discovery, depositions noticed under Rule 30(b)(6), or its state law equivalent, have taken on additional importance in counsel's effort to understand the creation, identification, and retention of potentially relevant ESI.

Persons testifying as Rule 30(b)(6) witnesses "shall testify as to matters known or reasonably available to the organization." A witness designated as the most knowledgeable person is not simply testifying about matters within his or her own personal knowledge. Rather, this individual is speaking on behalf of the corporation about matters to which the corporation has reasonable access. It is improper for a witness to deny knowledge of facts within the knowledge of the organization as a whole or reasonably knowable by the organization. This is to avoid the gamesmanship by which various officers or managing agents of a corporation are deposed but each disclaims knowledge of facts that must be known by someone in the company. In a further effort to address this problem, many courts have held that a party cannot present evidence on a subject after its Rule 30(b)(6) witness claimed to have no knowledge about a subject that is properly described in the deposition notice.[14] When served with a "person most knowledgeable" deposition notice, an organization or corporation must therefore designate a witness who either knows the information requested in the notice, or who can reasonably obtain that knowledge.

There is some debate over whether or not the subjects outlined in a Rule 30(b)(6) notice limit the scope of the examination. The majority rule is that in the absence of an agreement, depositions are only limited by the relevance and privilege bounds described by Rule 26(b).[15] However, some courts have held that the requirement that a party noticing the Rule 30(b)(6) deposition "describe with reasonable particularity the matters on which examination is requested" limits the scope of the deposition to the contents of that notice.[16]

The topics covered in a 30(b)(6) deposition must be relevant to the claims or defenses involved, and not be redundant.[17] The topics must also be stated with "reasonable particularity," according to the Rule and its many state equivalents.[18] In order to avoid delay and objections to an overly broad deposition notice, the party requesting a 30(b)(6) deposition should carefully craft the notice to describe the topics of examination. Rather than broadly seeking information about the computer systems in general terms, the notice should specify what particular aspect of the corporate information systems (*e.g.* e-mail message creation, storage, and deletion) are to be covered.

Companies and organizations should consider e-discovery issues when selecting a "person most knowledgeable" for Rule 30(b)(6) depositions pertaining to electronic preservation and production matters. If the witness does not understand the systems and architecture involved in the request, the result could be prolonged litigation, confusion, and disputes over the costs of finding the appropriate person. Depending on the subjects described in the deposition notice, many organizations routinely designate an IT professional or record retention manager as the appropriate witness for "person most knowledgeable" depositions. The search for the right person for a particular

---

14. *See Rainey v. American Forest & Paper Ass'n, Inc.*, 26 F. Supp. 2d 82, 94 (D.D.C. 1998); *United States v. Taylor,* 166 F.R.D. 356, 359–63 (M.D.N.C. 1996).

15. *See, e.g., Overseas Private Inv. Corp. v. Mandelbaum*, 185 F.R.D. 67 (D.D.C. 1999); *King v. Pratt & Whitney,* 161 F.R.D. 475, 476 (S.D. Fla. 1995).

16. *See, e.g., Paparelli v. Prudential Ins. Co. of Am.*, 108 F.R.D. 727, 729 (D. Mass. 1985).

17. *See Cunningham v. Standard Fire Ins. Co.*, No. 07 Civ. 2538, 2008 WL 2668301, at *5 (D. Colo. July 1, 2008) (deposition on "storage, preservation and backup of emails" not relevant to claims for breach of insurance contract or bad faith in adjusting an individual claim).

18. Rule 30(b)(6). *See also* California Code of Civil Procedure § 2025.230.

system, or an outdated legacy application, can nonetheless be tedious and time consuming.

The "person most knowledgeable" may be someone outside the litigation entirely, such as a storage vendor or third-party contractor responsible for system backups or archiving of electronic records. In fact, an organization cannot refuse to designate a witness on the ground that the potential deponents are beyond the control or direction of the company.

What types of topics should be included in a notice for the deposition of a person most knowledgeable about a company's e-mail system? Would the IT Director be an appropriate witness for a large bank to provide in response to a deposition notice concerning the creation, storage, and retention of e-mail messages? Why or why not?

Draft a sample 30(b)(6) notice seeking information about a company's IT infrastructure, storage and retention related to e-mail.

G. WHEN MUST NOT REASONABLY ACCESSIBLE DATA BE PRODUCED?

W.E. AUBUCHON CO., INC. v. BENEFIRST, LLC

245 F.R.D. 38 (D. Mass. 2007)

HILLMAN, MAGISTRATE JUDGE

INTRODUCTION

By order of this Court dated September 7, 2006, the Defendant, BeneFirst, LLC ("BeneFirst"), was ordered to produce medical claims files, including actual bills in its possession, custody, or control. On September 18, 2006, BeneFirst filed the instant Motion for Reconsideration of Court's Discovery Order Related to Medical Bills together with an accompanying memorandum and affidavit. BeneFirst claims that the documents are not reasonably accessible because the cost of their production far outweighs their value to the Plaintiffs. For the reasons set forth below, I deny the motion.

BACKGROUND

This case involves the administration of qualified benefits plans under the Employee Retirement Income Security Act of 1974 ("ERISA"). W.E. Aubuchon Co., Inc. ("Aubuchon") is the employer, sponsor and administrator of the W.E. Aubuchon Co., Inc. Employee Medical Benefit Plan ("Aubuchon Plan"). Aubuchon is the sponsor and Aubuchon Distribution, Inc. ("Aubuchon Distribution") is the employer and administrator of the W.E. Aubuchon Co., Inc. & Aubuchon Distribution, Inc. Employee Medical Benefit Plan ("Aubuchon Distribution Plan," and, together with the Aubuchon Plan, the "ERISA Plans").

BeneFirst, which is a Massachusetts limited liability company based in Marshfield, Massachusetts, entered into a contract with the Plaintiffs pursuant to which BeneFirst assumed the rights, duties and obligations to administer the ERISA Plans, as a third-party administrator. BeneFirst's obligations included "investigating and determining eligibility, payments, co-pays, coinsurance and subrogation claims," for which BeneFirst allegedly "exercised discretion and control over [its] decisions [presumably with respect to payment of claims] and was paid to execute these duties properly." The Plaintiffs charge that BeneFirst failed to perform its duties in a reasonably prudent manner, thereby breaching its fiduciary duty (Counts I and II) and that it breached the underlying contract by failing to provide services accurately and completely (Counts III and IV).

In the initial motion to compel, Plaintiffs sought, among other things, to compel BeneFirst to produce all medical claims files, including the actual medical bills in BeneFirst's custody or control. This Court ruled that BeneFirst was to provide those files and bills. It is that ruling that is the subject of this motion for reconsideration.

FACTS

BeneFirst is no longer in operation. Therefore, I will set out a historical summary of the procedures utilized by BeneFirst for processing, storing and retrieving claims at the time it administered the ERISA Plans. In order to comply with this Court's initial ruling, BeneFirst would have to hire personnel to retrieve the claims sought by the Plaintiffs in accordance with the procedures described below.

BeneFirst would typically receive requests for payment from medical providers who had provided covered medical services to Aubuchon/Aubuchon Distribution personnel. These requests for payment were on claim forms. These claims would be sorted or "batched" into client groups for processing. Once processed for payment, the claim forms were retained for a 60 day period. After 60 days, the batch of claim forms would be scanned and stored as electronic images and then destroyed. These scanned forms were stored in groups according to their processing date and the person who processed the claim.

If a claim needed to be retrieved after the 60 day period, the claim number, processor, and date of processing would be needed in order to retrieve the image. If all of this information was available, then the search would take 3–4 minutes. If all of the information was not available, it could take upwards of 7 minutes. It is particularly important to the search process to have the name of the person who processed the claim because on any given day, 3–4 claims examiners would process Plaintiffs' claims and during the relevant period, 14 different examiners were employed. Furthermore, for parts of 2001, 2002 and 2003, BeneFirst utilized an outside vendor to process claims. The outside vendor would scan the claims and return them to BeneFirst on a CD–R for further processing. The images scanned by the outside vendor would then be batched in the same way as was done during in-house processing.

The search process for retrieving claims is further complicated by the fact that there is no index of images per se. The images are stored on

BeneFirst's server first, according to year of processing, then by claims examiner, then by the month of processing, and finally by the actual processing date. Inexplicably, BeneFirst's system was not set up for the wholesale retrieval of claim images on a group by group basis.

During the 3.5 years at issue in this litigation, BeneFirst was administering up to 48 different plans and, by its estimation, processed between 550,000 and 600,000 claims. Of that number, 34,112 claims were submitted for processing under the ERISA Plans. Of that number, the Plaintiffs have narrowed their request, based upon a dollar value, to approximately 3,000 claims. BeneFirst estimates that it would cost approximately $80,000.00 and take almost 4,000 hours to retrieve all 34,112 claims. They have not provided a cost/time estimate for the retrieval of the 3,000 claims.

DISCUSSION

Our courts have repeatedly reiterated that "notice pleading standard relies on liberal discovery rules" and that "it is now beyond dispute that broad discovery is a cornerstone of the litigation process contemplated by the Federal Rules of Civil Procedure." *Zubulake v. UBS Warburg*, 217 F.R.D. 309, 311 (S.D.N.Y. 2003). While the principle is relatively straightforward, its application is not. This principle of liberal discovery is sorely tested when the object of the discovery is electronic data. As of December 1, 2006, the Federal Rules of Civil Procedure were amended to give greater guidance to courts and litigants in dealing with electronic discovery issues. There are four key areas of change to the Rules that address electronic discovery: early attention to e-discovery issues; the role of accessibility; the form of production; and sanctions under Rule 37. This case squarely presents the question of whether the information sought is reasonably accessible within the meaning of the Rule and if not, whether it still should be produced.

The Recent Amendments

On December 1, 2006, Rule 26 was amended, in relevant part, to provide the following limitation to the general rule that a party may obtain discovery of any matter, not privileged, that is relevant to such party's claim or defenses:

> A party need not provide discovery of electronically stored information from sources that the party identifies as not reasonably accessible because of undue burden or cost. On motion to compel discovery or for a protective order, the party from whom discovery is sought must show that the information is not reasonably accessible because of undue burden or cost. If that showing is made, the court may nonetheless order discovery from such sources if the requesting party shows good cause, considering the limitations of Rule 26(b)(2)(C). The court may specify conditions for the discovery.

F.R.C.P. 26(b)(2)(B).

* * *

Application of The Rule 26 Amendment

Under Rule 26, as revised, this Court must determine whether the information sought is reasonably accessible. If the information is not reasonably accessible, this Court may still order discovery if Aubuchon shows good cause for requesting the information, taking into consideration the limitations of Rule 26(b)(2)(C).

Is the requested information "reasonably accessible" within the meaning of FRCP 26(b)(2)?

BeneFirst asserts that the requested claims forms are not reasonably accessible within the meaning of FRCP 26(b)(2)(B) because of the high cost to retrieve such information (both in monetary terms and in terms of the man hours it would require to retrieve the information). BeneFirst contends that the high cost/time to retrieve such data is necessitated by the fact that it is maintained in an inaccessible format.

* * *

In this case, the records sought by the Plaintiffs are stored on a server used by BeneFirst in Pembroke Massachusetts, which is clearly an accessible format. However, because of BeneFirst's method of storage and lack of an indexing system, it will be extremely costly to retrieve the requested data. I am hard pressed to understand the rationale behind having a system that is only searchable by year of processing, then claims examiner, then the month of processing, and finally the claims date. None of these search criteria reflect the name of the individual claimant, the date that the claimant received the medical service, who the provider was, or even the company that employed the benefit holder. It would seem that such a system would only serve to discourage audits and the type of inquiries that have led to the instant litigation. Nevertheless, the retrieval of the records will be costly and for the purposes of this decision, I find that such retrieval would involve undue burden or cost. Accordingly, the images are not reasonably accessible within the meaning of Fed. R. Civ. P. 26(b)(2)(B).

Since the images are not reasonably accessible is there "good cause" to order their production?

The Plaintiffs argue that the information they have requested goes to the heart of their case and that they have established "good cause" for production of the same. In making a determination of whether the requesting party has established "good cause," this Court must consider whether: "(i) the discovery sought is unreasonably cumulative or duplicative, or is obtainable from some other source that is more convenient, less burdensome, or less expensive; (ii) the party seeking discovery has had ample opportunity by discovery in the action to obtain the information sought; or (iii) the burden or expense of the proposed discovery outweighs its likely benefit, taking into account the needs of the case, the amount in controversy, the parties' resources, the importance of the issues at stake in the litigation, and the importance of the proposed discovery in resolving the issues." Fed. R. Civ. P. 26(b)(2)(C). To the extent not covered by the aforementioned factors, the Court should also consider:

> (1) the specificity of the discovery request; (2) the quantity of information available from other and more easily accessed sources; (3) the failure to produce relevant information that seems likely to have existed but is no longer available on more easily accessed sources; (4) the likelihood of finding relevant, responsive information that cannot be obtained from other, more easily accessed sources; (5) predictions as to the importance and usefulness of the further information; (6) the importance of the issues at stake in the litigation; and (7) the parties' resources.

Fed. R. Civ. P. 26 Advisory Committee's note, to 2006 Amendment.

The specificity of the discovery request.

BeneFirst's Motion seeks reconsideration of this Court's earlier discovery order which ordered BeneFirst to produce "all claims files, including the actual bills in BeneFirst's possession or control." The parties have responded intelligently and vigorously to this Order and there is no misunderstanding or confusion about the specificity of the information sought by the Plaintiffs.

This factor favors the Plaintiffs.

The quantity of information available from other and more easily accessed sources; The failure to produce relevant information that seems likely to have existed but is no longer available from more easily accessed sources.

The gravamen of the Plaintiffs' Amended Complaint is that BeneFirst mishandled their employees' medical claims by failing to determine eligibility for payment, the availability of co-payment and co-insurance, and subrogation. The processing of the claim forms was presumably the mechanism for making these determinations. While the Amended Complaint and subsequent pleadings are silent, the relevant time period appears to be from 2001 to 2004.

According to BeneFirst, the original claim forms and medical bills were processed by hand, kept for 60 days, converted to a digital image and then destroyed. Therefore, digital images which constitute the information requested by the Plaintiffs are in the custody and control of BeneFirst and are not available through any other source.

These factors favor the Plaintiffs.

Predictions as to the importance and usefulness of the further information; the likelihood of finding relevant, responsive information that cannot be obtained from other, more easily accessed sources.

I agree with the Plaintiffs that the requested claim forms and medical bills are clearly an integral part of the litigation; the requested information goes not only to BeneFirst's culpability, but also to the amount of damages, if any, to which the Plaintiffs may be entitled. There can be no serious contention that the information is not highly relevant. In fact, it is difficult to imagine how this case could be prosecuted or defended without the claims forms and attendant bills. As previously found, they are not available from any other source (a determination which is uncontroverted).

These factors favor the Plaintiffs.

The importance of the issues at stake in the litigation.

While the importance of the claims/issues in this case are real and substantial vis a vis the parties, such claims/issues to not raise any global concerns.

This factor favors the Defendants (if it favors any party at all).

The parties' resources.

While the Defendant has understandably engaged in a lengthy discussion of the cost of production, neither party has provided the court with any information about their resources. BeneFirst does represent that they no longer have a full time staff and that in order to retrieve the images that they would have to hire temporary help. At the same time, as previously noted, the Plaintiffs have significantly narrowed the breadth of their request and therefore, the time and cost for BeneFirst to produce the requested information should be significantly reduced.

Given the lack of information available to the Court, this factor is neutral.

Other relevant considerations.

In addition to the above 7 factors, it is important to note that a provision in the Service Agreement between the parties provided that: "The Records are the property of the Plan Sponsor. The Plan Sponsor has the right of continuing access to their records...." In other words, although in the custody and control of BeneFirst, the records at issue are the property of the Plaintiffs.

The Plaintiffs Have Met Their Burden To Establish Good Cause.

On balance, I find that the Plaintiffs have clearly established good cause for requiring BeneFirst to produce the requested information. * * * [T]he Plaintiffs have significantly narrowed their original request from approximately 34,000 claims to a list of approximately 3,000. This reduction should serve to reduce the time and expense of retrieving the requested information. Under the circumstances, I find that the requested information should be produced by BeneFirst at its own expense.

ORDER

For the reasons set forth above, BeneFirst's Motion for Reconsideration of Court's Discovery Order Related to Medical Bills is denied. Bene-

First shall produce the Medical Bills and Claims Forms for the approximately 3,000 claims as specified by the Plaintiffs at their own expense.

COMMENTARY

1.   Using Sampling to Determine Accessibility

In an age where virtually every piece of data is technically accessible, a rational and defensible approach must be taken in discovery to determine what data is reasonably accessible under the undue burden or cost test. As discussed earlier, a party in litigation only needs to search for, and to produce data from, accessible sources of ESI.

The Rule gives no guidance as to how the determination of accessibility can be made using real data. A successful declaration of "non-accessibility," of course, effectively removes that particular ESI from the discovery process (absent a showing of good cause). The value associated with such a wholesale removal of data from further discovery virtually guarantees that there will be a tendency—indeed an incentive—to interpret difficulty of any kind as a sign of "non-accessibility."

Certain forms of ESI, such as backup tapes, legacy data and multi-table, enterprise databases, for example, are often quickly labeled as "not reasonably accessible" because of the inherent cost and difficulty associated with incorporating them into the discovery process. Because of the cost/benefit of removing a set of ESI from discovery, battles will be waged over how accessible a particular set of ESI is from a technical point of view rather than based on whether or not responsive data is likely to be found and whether the benefit of retrieval outweighs the cost.

a.   Everything Is Accessible—For a Price

The determination of whether or not a particular source of ESI is accessible does not primarily depend upon the type of data (format) or the type of media on which it is stored (form). There are hardware and software tools that allow the restoration of virtually any type of data from virtually any type of form—for a price. Given that ability, the primary issue is not whether the data can be restored, but whether it is worth the cost to restore.

The fundamental question is:

"Will the uniqueness and/or quality of responsive data that I get from any particular set of ESI justify the cost of the acquisition of that data?"

This critical question should be addressed at every meet-and-confer and court hearing on the issue of the accessibility of ESI.

b.   Marginal Utility

In terms of discovery, the marginal utility of ESI is the probative value from one additional unit of ESI relative to the cost necessary to identify, locate, retrieve, review and produce that unit. Thus, parties engaged in discovery should be prepared to provide a comprehensive analysis as to why a particular set of ESI may or may not be reasonably accessible from a marginal utility point of view with respect to the particular litigation.

The arguments for a particular set of ESI not being reasonably accessible include:

1.   *There is no responsive data on [the particular source of ESI].* If a particular source of ESI can be shown to have no responsive data, then any cost associated with identifying, locating, retrieving or reviewing it would be too much. Because there is no requirement to produce non-responsive data, there should be no requirement to deal with it in discovery, regardless of the cost. There is a tendency today to argue that if data is easily accessible—such as live (online) data—then it should be searched as a matter of course. This is no more legitimate than arguing that another set of data is not reasonably accessible just because it is on a backup tape. Both should be subjected to the marginal utility test.

2.   *There is responsive data on [the particular source of ESI], but the same data is available in another, more accessible, location.* If it can be shown that the same data can be retrieved from other lower-cost sources—from an online source rather than from a backup tape, for example—then the lower-cost source is preferable.

3.   *There is some responsive data on [the particular source of ESI], but the cost to obtain it is not worth the value the responsive data would provide.* This is the classic marginal utility argument. While there may be some data on the particular source of ESI that is arguably responsive, there is something about the data set—its volume, quality, or uniqueness—that makes retrieval unnecessary when compared with the cost to recover it. To be persuasive, this argument requires enough detail to justify the claims being made.

4.   *We have no idea what is on [the particular source of ESI] but we do know that it will be difficult and expensive to deal with.* This is the classic argument that is often used in an attempt to remove a set of ESI from the discovery process. It is based on a simplistic reading of the concept of accessibility, and attempts to capitalize on the "burden and cost" language of the rule without giving any consideration to the "undue" component. While it may be true that a given source of ESI will be difficult and/or expensive to deal with, such a fact alone should not be enough to remove that ESI from consideration.

The problem with arguments one, two, and three above is that in order to make them successfully, you need to have enough detailed information about the ESI in question so that you can choose which argument to make and then defend it. The problem with argument four is that it is simply inadequate.

i.   *Sampling*

At first blush, the argument about ESI, marginal utility, and accessibility can appear circular. In order to make a defensible argument about accessibility, one must have some detailed information about the data contained within the ESI. But if one can gather such information, then how can it claim that the ESI is not reasonably accessible?

While some systemic arguments can be made (*i.e.* the underlying data processing platform had no relation to the matter at hand; or, the data set is outside the time frame at issue), the most common way to defensibly prepare an "accessible/inaccessible" argument for a particular set of ESI is to use sampling.

Sampling allows one to test the questioned ESI and to extract the metrics needed to develop a marginal utility argument in a cost-effective, timely and defensible manner. While there are different sampling models that can be applied based on the underlying data set and the nature of the matter being litigated, the theory behind sampling is consistent and parties should be prepared to present a sampling argument for including or excluding ESI. The basis of all sampling is that a subset of a population will reveal something about that population as a whole with some specified degree of certainty.

ii. Sampling Hypothetical

For the purposes of our hypothetical, we will assume that we have a single backup tape from a single computer for each day of the year. Furthermore, we will assume that it costs $1,000 to restore and retrieve all of the data from a single backup tape.

The examples below illustrate how different restored subsets of tapes can yield different percentages of the total set of data. By assessing the varying amounts of data restored vis-à-vis the associated restoration cost, one can begin to evaluate the marginal utility associated with the various restoration sets and be prepared to fully evaluate the burden and cost of retrieving a particular set of ESI. Note that the actual percentages for all subsets will vary depending upon the manner in which the backup was conducted, the nature of the data being backed up, and the underlying usage patterns of the system(s) being restored.

In order to retrieve all of the data from a set of backup tapes, every daily backup tape would have to be restored for a total cost of $365,000.

* Quarterly Tapes

Because backup tapes contain multiple copies of the same data, much of what is on any given subset of tapes is duplicative. Given this characteristic, subsets of tapes can be selected and tested to determine how much unique data they contain and what it costs to obtain that data. As can be seen in the graphic above, quarterly tapes can be selected and approximately eighty percent of the entire set of data will be recovered for a cost of only $5,000.[19]

* Monthly Tapes

Selecting monthly tapes (twelve month-end tapes plus the first tape in the set as a baseline) will result in the recovery of approximately ninety percent of the entire set of data for a cost of only $13,000.

---

19. The actual percentages for all subsets will vary depending upon the manner in which the backup was conducted, the nature of the data being backed up, and the underlying usage patterns of the system(s) being restored.

* Weekly Tapes

Choosing weekly tapes (each Friday's tape plus the first tape in the set as a baseline) recovers approximately ninety-four percent of the entire set of data for a cost of $61,000.

iii. Data Analysis

Through sampling one can develop a set of metrics that show the costs related to the quantities of unique data recovered. When combined with a review process to establish the percentage of responsive data being restored, an even more detailed analysis can be created relating recovery cost to responsive item counts.

Summary

Techniques like sampling can be used to provide a more thorough and more defensible basis for arguing that a given set of ESI is reasonably accessible or not. Only by providing metrics related to cost, volume, quality and uniqueness can a proper data discovery plan be crafted. Simplistic arguments about data being easy or hard to retrieve are meaningless without a careful analysis of marginal utility.

2. When Should a Court Permit Discovery of ESI From a Not Reasonably Accessible Source?

Rule 26(b)(2)(B) explicitly limits initial discovery of ESI to information from reasonably accessible sources. The Rule establishes a procedure for the discovery of not reasonably accessible ESI:

> (B) A party need not provide discovery of electronically stored information from sources that the party identifies as not reasonably accessible because of undue burden or cost. On motion to compel discovery or for a protective order, the party from whom discovery is sought must show that the information is not reasonably accessible because of undue burden or cost. If that showing is made, the court may nonetheless order discovery from such sources if the requesting party shows good cause, considering the limitations of Rule 26(b)(2)(C). The court may specify conditions for the discovery.

If a requesting party seeks ESI from a source identified as not reasonably accessible and the parties are unable to reach agreement regarding discovery from such sources, a motion to compel discovery may be brought. This procedure is sometimes referred to as a two-tired approach, where the parties first examine information that can be provided from fully accessible sources and then determine whether it is necessary to search less-accessible sources.

The 2006 Advisory Committee Note to Rule 26(b)(2) explains the criteria to be used in determining whether to permit discovery of ESI:

> Once it is shown that a source of electronically stored information is not reasonably accessible, the requesting party may still obtain discovery by showing good cause, considering the limitations of Rule 26(b)(2)(C) that balance the costs and potential benefits of discovery. The decision whether to require a responding party to search for and produce information

that is not reasonably accessible depends not only on the burdens and costs of doing so, but also on whether those burdens and costs can be justified in the circumstances of the case. Appropriate considerations may include: (1) the specificity of the discovery request; (2) the quantity of information available from other and more easily accessed sources; (3) the failure to produce relevant information that seems likely to have existed but is no longer available on more easily accessed sources; (4) the likelihood of finding relevant, responsive information that cannot be obtained from other, more easily accessed sources; (5) predictions as to the importance and usefulness of the further information; (6) the importance of the issues at stake in the litigation; and (7) the parties' resources.

3. Is ESI From a Not Reasonably Accessible Source Presumptively Not Discoverable?

The new Rule requires that the responding party bear the burden of demonstrating that data is not reasonably accessible based on the costs and burdens of recovering the data, while the requesting party must show good cause once that showing has been made. This is a change from the general presumption of the discoverability of relevant information. One commentator has criticized this change.

EXCERPT FROM Henry S. Noyes, *Good Cause Is Bad Medicine for the New E–Discovery Rules*, 21 Harv. J.L. & Tech. 49, 83–84 (2007):

First, placing the burden on the requesting party would necessarily mean that the information is presumptively not discoverable, contrary to the stated intention of the rulemakers. Second, placing the burden on the requesting party is inconsistent with the amended [Rule's] requirement that the requesting party show "good cause, considering the limitations of Rule 26(b)(2)(C)." For all other discovery scenarios in which Rule 26(b)(2)(C) applies, the party *opposing* discovery has the burden of demonstrating that the request is unduly burdensome or overbroad. Third, [Rule 26(b)(2)(B) permits the responding party to move for a protective order, but shifts the burden to show good cause for the order from the moving party, which ordinarily bears it, to the party seeking discovery].

* * *

Under the 2006 amendments, it is unclear whether ESI that is not reasonably accessible is presumptively not discoverable. On the one hand, the plain language of the amended [Rule] contemplates a presumption of nondiscoverability. Moreover, during the period of public comment, some commentators assumed that the amended rule would alter the normal presumption of discoverability. The rulemaking history ... supports a different interpretation.... The [chair of the Advisory Committee] "emphasized that the rule is not one of presumed non-discoverability, but instead makes the existing proportionality limit more effective in a novel area in which the rules can helpfully provide better guidance."[20]

---

20. Committee on Rules of Practice & Procedure, Judicial Conference of the U.S., *Meeting of June 15–16 Minutes* 25 (statement of Judge Lee Rosenthal, Chair), *available at* http://www. uscourts.gov/rules/Minutes/ST_June_2005.pdf.

If the goal of the Committee was to retain the presumption of discoverability, did it succeed?

4. How Should Counsel Address Rule 26(b)(2)(B) "Good Cause" Issues?

The Committee Note to Rule 26(b)(2)(B) provides a roadmap of the considerations associated with good cause. But one author offers additional practical guidance:

EXCERPT FROM Theodore C. Hirt, *The Two–Tier Discovery Provision of Rule 26(b)(2)(B)—A Reasonable Measure for Controlling Electronic Discovery?*, 13 Rich. J. L. & Tech. 12, 20–21 (2007)

Counsel for both parties will need to inventory what information sources were actually searched from the first tier. A court will want specifics on the "quantity of information available from other and more easily accessed sources." Counsel for the requesting party will want to be conversant with what relevant information the first tier of discovery yielded. The quality of that information will have to be assessed as well to support the requesting party's position that other information sources must be searched.

The responding party can defend its position effectively if it has been careful and comprehensive in its previous responses to the first tier of discovery. Counsel will need to document how it has provided information from the reasonably accessible sources. The more comprehensive the showing, the more reasonable a counsel's position will be that second tier sources should not be searched. Counsel for the responding party also should determine what information sources no longer exist, what kind of information was stored on them, and whether that information has migrated to other systems. That will be important because the court will evaluate the failure to produce relevant information that seems likely to have existed but is no longer available on more easily accessed sources.

Existing case law will be of considerable assistance in resolving these disputes. Courts, if given enough information about the information sources at issue, can use Rule 26(b)(2) factors to resolve these disputes. When, for example, the issue is whether relevant information might be stored on a specific information source, the court can weigh the likelihood of such information being located and contrast the expected yield of that new relevant information against the information the party already has obtained in discovery. Courts have developed experience in evaluating the burdens imposed on a producing party to locate and retrieve information from electronic sources—where the producing party can demonstrate substantial burdens in connection with such location and retrieval, the requesting party must be able to demonstrate that there will be tangible benefits from access to that information and ... how the requested information will be important to the resolution of the issues in the case.

5. Is the Rule 26(b)(2)(B) Good Cause Standard Different From the Other Good Cause Standards in Rule 26?

There are two other good cause standards in Rule 26. Rule 26(b)(1) applies a good cause standard to court ordered discovery of information relevant to the subject matter of the action. Rule 26(c) applies a good cause standard for issuance of a protective order. Should the good cause standard differ for production of ESI? Does the presumption of non-discoverability of data that is not reasonably accessible suggest there should be a lesser good cause standard than applies elsewhere in the rules? Given that Rule 26(b)(2)(B) references good cause in the context of Rule 26(b)(2)(C)'s limitations, is the good cause standard more stringent for not reasonably accessible information?

6. Should Courts Weigh the "Marginal Utility" of Allowing Discovery of Information That Is Not Reasonably Accessible?

The court in *McPeek v. Ashcroft* described the use of the marginal utility test in considering whether to allow discovery of not reasonably accessible information. In assessing burden under Rule 26(c), the court reasoned that:

> A fairer approach borrows, by analogy, from the economic principle of "marginal utility." The more likely it is that the backup tape contains information that is relevant to a claim or defense, the fairer it is that the government agency search at its own expense. The less likely it is, the more unjust it would be to make the agency search at its own expense.[21]

In *Oxford House, Inc. v. City of Topeka*, the court applied the marginal utility test and held that although the defendant could potentially access certain deleted e-mails sought by the plaintiff from the defendant's backup tapes, production of those e-mails would be unduly burdensome. The court observed that discovery should generally be allowed unless "the hardship is unreasonable in light of the benefits to be secured from the discovery."[22] In this case, however, the likelihood of retrieving the e-mails was low because the backup tapes containing the e-mails had probably been overwritten, and the cost to retrieve the data and search for the relevant e-mails was high. On this basis the court denied the plaintiff's motion to compel production.

7. When Are Objections Waived Under the Two–Tier System?

Suppose that after discovery and production is underway, the producing party determines that some of the requested ESI is not reasonably accessible. Has the producing party waived an objection by failing to object promptly and state in its initial written responses that the ESI is not reasonably accessible?

In *Cason–Merenda v. Detroit Medical Center*, in addressing defendant's post production motion for cost-shifting, the court reasoned that the defendant could have designated the requested information as "not reasonably accessible" and refused to complete production unless ordered to do so before incurring the costs to recover the data. The court found that the defendant failed to make a timely motion for relief under Rule 26(b)(2)(B), reasoning that:

> It offends common sense ... to read the rule in a way that requires (or permits) the producing party to suffer "undue burden or cost" *before*

---

21.   202 F.R.D. 31, 34 (D.D.C. 2001).

22.   No. 06–4004, 2007 WL 1246200, at *4 (D. Kan. Apr. 27, 2007).

raising the issue with the court. Under such a reading, a court would be powerless to avoid unnecessary expense or to specify any meaningful "conditions" for the discovery other than cost sharing. Furthermore, the requesting party would be stripped of its implicit right to elect either to meet the conditions or forego the requested information. The Rule, if it is to be sensible and useful, must be read as a means of *avoiding* undue burden or cost, rather than simply distributing it.[23]

8. Is a Requesting Party Entitled to Take Discovery to Test the Assertion That the Information It Seeks Is Not Reasonably Accessible?

The Advisory Committee Note to Rule 26(b)(2)(B) explains that the requesting party may need discovery to test the assertion that certain sources are not reasonably accessible. Such discovery may include depositions, inspection of data sources, and limited data sampling, which can help refine search parameters and determine the benefits and burdens associated with a fuller search. Indeed, the concept of data sampling has been adopted by courts as a method to address accessibility issues and determine whether further discovery is appropriate. Thus, the requesting party may issue a more targeted Rule 34 request, seeking a sample of information from the sources at issue.

H. COST SHARING/COST SHIFTING

1. Accessible Data—Rule 26(b)(2)(B)

ZUBULAKE v. UBS WARBURG LLC *"ZUBULAKE I"*

217 F.R.D. 309 (S.D.N.Y. 2003)

SCHEINDLIN, DISTRICT JUDGE

The world was a far different place in 1849, when Henry David Thoreau opined (in an admittedly broader context) that "[t]he process of discovery is very simple." That hopeful maxim has given way to rapid technological advances, requiring new solutions to old problems. The issue presented here is one such problem, recast in light of current technology: To what extent is inaccessible electronic data discoverable, and who should pay for its production?

I. INTRODUCTION

The Supreme Court recently reiterated that our "simplified notice pleading standard relies on liberal discovery rules and summary judgment motions to define disputed facts and issues and to dispose of unmeritorious claims." Thus, it is now beyond dispute that "[b]road discovery is a cornerstone of the litigation process contemplated by the Federal Rules of Civil Procedure." The Rules contemplate a minimal burden to bringing a claim; that claim is then fleshed out through vigorous and expansive discovery.

---

23. No. 06–15601, 2008 WL 2714239, at *2 (E.D. Mich. July 7, 2008).

In one context, however, the reliance on broad discovery has hit a roadblock. As individuals and corporations increasingly do business electronically—using computers to create and store documents, make deals, and exchange e-mails—the universe of discoverable material has expanded exponentially.[6] The more information there is to discover, the more expensive it is to discover all the relevant information until, in the end, "discovery is not just about uncovering the truth, but also about how much of the truth the parties can afford to disinter."

This case provides a textbook example of the difficulty of balancing the competing needs of broad discovery and manageable costs. Laura Zubulake is suing UBS Warburg LLC, UBS Warburg, and UBS AG (collectively, "UBS" or the "Firm") under Federal, State and City law for gender discrimination and illegal retaliation. Zubulake's case is certainly not frivolous[8] and if she prevails, her damages may be substantial. She contends that key evidence is located in various e-mails exchanged among UBS employees that now exist only on backup tapes and perhaps other archived media. According to UBS, restoring those e-mails would cost approximately $175,000.00, exclusive of attorney time in reviewing the e-mails. Zubulake now moves for an order compelling UBS to produce those e-mails at its expense.

II. BACKGROUND

A. Zubulake's Lawsuit

UBS hired Zubulake on August 23, 1999, as a director and senior salesperson on its U.S. Asian Equities Sales Desk (the "Desk"), where she reported to Dominic Vail, the Desk's manager. At the time she was hired, Zubulake was told that she would be considered for Vail's position if and when it became vacant.

In December 2000, Vail indeed left his position to move to the Firm's London office. But Zubulake was not considered for his position, and the Firm instead hired Matthew Chapin as director of the Desk. Zubulake alleges that from the outset Chapin treated her differently than the other members of the Desk, all of whom were male. In particular, Chapin "undermined Ms. Zubulake's ability to perform her job by, inter alia: (a) ridiculing and belittling her in front of co-workers; (b) excluding her from work-related outings with male co-workers and clients; (c) making sexist remarks in her presence; and (d) isolating her from the other senior salespersons on the Desk by seating her apart from them." No such actions were taken against any of Zubulake's male co-workers.

---

6. [See] Rowe Entm't, Inc. v. William Morris Agency, Inc., 205 F.R.D. 421, 429 (S.D.N.Y.2002) (explaining that electronic data is so voluminous because, unlike paper documents, "the costs of storage are virtually nil. Information is retained not because it is expected to be used, but because there is no compelling reason to discard it"), aff'd, 2002 WL 975713 (S.D.N.Y. May 9, 2002).

8. Indeed, Zubulake has already produced a sort of "smoking gun": an e-mail suggesting that she be fired "ASAP" after her EEOC charge was filed, in part so that she would not be eligible for year-end bonuses. See 8/21/01 e-mail from Mike Davies to Rose Tong ("8/21/01 e-Mail").

Zubulake ultimately responded by filing a Charge of (gender) Discrimination with the EEOC on August 16, 2001. On October 9, 2001, Zubulake was fired with two weeks' notice. On February 15, 2002, Zubulake filed the instant action * * *. UBS timely answered on March 12, 2002, denying the allegations. UBS's argument is, in essence, that Chapin's conduct was not unlawfully discriminatory because he treated everyone equally badly. On the one hand, UBS points to evidence that Chapin's anti-social behavior was not limited to women: a former employee made allegations of national origin discrimination against Chapin, and a number of male employees on the Desk also complained about him. On the other hand, Chapin was responsible for hiring three new female employees to the Desk.

B. The Discovery Dispute

Discovery in this action commenced on or about June 3, 2002, when Zubulake served UBS with her first document request. At issue here is request number twenty-eight, for "[a]ll documents concerning any communication by or between UBS employees concerning Plaintiff." The term document in Zubulake's request "includ[es], without limitation, electronic or computerized data compilations." On July 8, 2002, UBS responded by producing approximately 350 pages of documents, including approximately 100 pages of e-mails. UBS also objected to a substantial portion of Zubulake's requests.

On September 12, 2000—after an exchange of angry letters and a conference before United States Magistrate Judge Gabriel W. Gorenstein—the parties reached an agreement (the "9/12/02 Agreement"). With respect to document request twenty-eight, the parties reached the following agreement, in relevant part:

Defendants will [ ] ask UBS about how to retrieve e-mails that are saved in the firm's computer system and will produce responsive e-mails if retrieval is possible and Plaintiff names a few individuals.

Pursuant to the 9/12/02 Agreement, UBS agreed unconditionally to produce responsive e-mails from the accounts of five individuals named by Zubulake: Matthew Chapin, Rose Tong (a human relations representation who was assigned to handle issues concerning Zubulake), Vinay Datta (a co-worker on the Desk), Andrew Clarke (another co-worker on the Desk), and Jeremy Hardisty (Chapin's supervisor and the individual to whom Zubulake originally complained about Chapin). UBS was to produce such e-mails sent between August 1999 (when Zubulake was hired) and December 2001 (one month after her termination), to the extent possible.

UBS, however, produced no additional e-mails and insisted that its initial production (the 100 pages of e-mails) was complete. As UBS's opposition to the instant motion makes clear * * * UBS never searched for responsive e-mails on any of its backup tapes. To the contrary, UBS informed Zubulake that the cost of producing e-mails on backup tapes would be prohibitive (estimated at the time at approximately $300,000.00).

Zubulake, believing that the 9/12/02 Agreement included production of e-mails from backup tapes, objected to UBS's nonproduction. In fact, Zubulake knew that there were additional responsive e-mails that UBS had failed to produce because she herself had produced approximately 450 pages of e-mail correspondence. Clearly, numerous responsive e-mails had been created and deleted[19] at UBS, and Zubulake wanted them.

On December 2, 2002, the parties again appeared before Judge Gorenstein, who ordered UBS to produce for deposition a person with knowledge of UBS's e-mail retention policies in an effort to determine whether the backup tapes contained the deleted e-mails and the burden of producing them. In response, UBS produced Christopher Behny, Manager of Global Messaging, who was deposed on January 14, 2003. Mr. Behny testified to UBS's e-mail backup protocol, and also to the cost of restoring the relevant data.

C. UBS's E–Mail Backup System

In the first instance, the parties agree that e-mail was an important means of communication at UBS during the relevant time period. Each salesperson, including the salespeople on the Desk, received approximately 200 e-mails each day. Given this volume, and because Securities and Exchange Commission regulations require it, UBS implemented extensive e-mail backup and preservation protocols. In particular, e-mails were backed up in two distinct ways: on backup tapes and on optical disks.

1. Backup Tape Storage

UBS employees used a program called HP OpenMail, manufactured by Hewlett–Packard, for all work-related e-mail communications. With limited exceptions, all e-mails sent or received by any UBS employee are stored onto backup tapes. To do so, UBS employs a program called Veritas NetBackup, which creates a "snapshot" of all e-mails that exist on a given server at the time the backup is taken. Except for scheduling the backups and physically inserting the tapes into the machines, the backup process is entirely automated.

UBS used the same backup protocol during the entire relevant time period, from 1999 through 2001. Using NetBackup, UBS backed up its e-mails at three intervals: (1) daily, at the end of each day, (2) weekly, on Friday nights, and (3) monthly, on the last business day of the month.

---

19. The term "deleted" is sticky in the context of electronic data. " 'Deleting' a file does not actually erase that data from the computer's storage devices. Rather, it simply finds the data's entry in the disk directory and changes it to a 'not used' status—thus permitting the computer to write over the 'deleted' data. Until the computer writes over the 'deleted' data, however, it may be recovered by searching the disk itself rather than the disk's directory. Accordingly, many files are recoverable long after they have been deleted—even if neither the computer user nor the computer itself is aware of their existence. Such data is referred to as 'residual data.' " Shira A. Scheindlin & Jeffrey Rabkin, *Electronic Discovery in Federal Civil Litigation: Is Rule 34 Up to the Task?*, 41 B.C. L.Rev. 327, 337 (2000). Deleted data may also exist because it was backed up before it was deleted. Thus, it may reside on backup tapes or similar media. Unless otherwise noted, I will use the term "deleted" data to mean residual data, and will refer to backed-up data as "backup tapes."

Nightly backup tapes were kept for twenty working days, weekly tapes for one year, and monthly tapes for three years. After the relevant time period elapsed, the tapes were recycled.

Once e-mails have been stored onto backup tapes, the restoration process is lengthy. Each backup tape routinely takes approximately five days to restore, although resort to an outside vendor would speed up the process (at greatly enhanced costs, of course). Because each tape represents a snapshot of one server's hard drive in a given month, each server/month must be restored separately onto a hard drive. Then, a program called Double Mail is used to extract a particular individual's e-mail file. That mail file is then exported into a Microsoft Outlook data file, which in turn can be opened in Microsoft Outlook, a common e-mail application. A user could then browse through the mail file and sort the mail by recipient, date or subject, or search for key words in the body of the e-mail.

Fortunately, NetBackup also created indexes of each backup tape. Thus, Behny was able to search through the tapes from the relevant time period and determine that the e-mail files responsive to Zubulake's requests are contained on a total of ninety-four backup tapes.

2. Optical Disk Storage

In addition to the e-mail backup tapes, UBS also stored certain e-mails on optical disks. For certain "registered traders," probably including the members of the Desk, a copy of all e-mails sent to or received from outside sources (i.e., e-mails from a "registered trader" at UBS to someone at another entity, or vice versa) was simultaneously written onto a series of optical disks. Internal e-mails, however, were not stored on this system.

UBS has retained each optical disk used since the system was put into place in mid–1998. Moreover, the optical disks are neither erasable nor rewritable. Thus, UBS has every e-mail sent or received by registered traders (except internal e-mails) during the period of Zubulake's employment, even if the e-mail was deleted instantaneously on that trader's system.

The optical disks are easily searchable using a program called Tumbleweed. Using Tumbleweed, a user can simply log into the system with the proper credentials and create a plain language search. Search criteria can include not just "header" information, such as the date or the name of the sender or recipient, but can also include terms within the text of the e-mail itself. For example, UBS personnel could easily run a search for e-mails containing the words "Laura" or "Zubulake" that were sent or received by Chapin, Datta, Clarke, or Hardisty.[28]

---

28. Rose Tong, the fifth person designated by Zubulake's document request, would probably not have been a "registered trader" as she was a human resources employee.

III. LEGAL STANDARD

* * *

[Judge Scheindlin sets forth the pre–2006 Rule 26(b)(1) and Rule 26(b)(2), referring to the latter as codifying a "proportionality test."]

Finally, "[u]nder [the discovery] rules, the presumption is that the responding party must bear the expense of complying with discovery requests, but [it] may invoke the district court's discretion under Rule 26(c) to grant orders protecting [it] from 'undue burden or expense' in doing so, including orders conditioning discovery on the requesting party's payment of the costs of discovery."

The application of these various discovery rules is particularly complicated where electronic data is sought because otherwise discoverable evidence is often only available from expensive-to-restore backup media. That being so, courts have devised creative solutions for balancing the broad scope of discovery prescribed in Rule 26(b)(1) with the cost-consciousness of Rule 26(b)(2). By and large, the solution has been to consider cost-shifting: forcing the requesting party, rather than the answering party, to bear the cost of discovery.

By far, the most influential response to the problem of cost-shifting relating to the discovery of electronic data was given by United States Magistrate Judge James C. Francis IV of this district in *Rowe Entertainment, Inc.[v. William Morris, Inc.]*. Judge Francis utilized an eight-factor test to determine whether discovery costs should be shifted. Those eight factors are:

(1) the specificity of the discovery requests; (2) the likelihood of discovering critical information; (3) the availability of such information from other sources; (4) the purposes for which the responding party maintains the requested data; (5) the relative benefits to the parties of obtaining the information; (6) the total cost associated with production; (7) the relative ability of each party to control costs and its incentive to do so; and (8) the resources available to each party.[33]

Both Zubulake and UBS agree that the eight-factor *Rowe* test should be used to determine whether cost-shifting is appropriate.

IV. DISCUSSION

A. Should Discovery of UBS's Electronic Data Be Permitted?

Under Rule 34, * * * "[e]lectronic documents are no less subject to disclosure than paper records." This is true not only of electronic documents that are currently in use, but also of documents that may have been deleted and now reside only on backup disks.

That being so, Zubulake is entitled to discovery of the requested e-mails so long as they are relevant to her claims, which they clearly are. As noted, e-mail constituted a substantial means of communication among

---

33. 205 F.R.D. at 429.

UBS employees. To that end, UBS has already produced approximately 100 pages of e-mails, the contents of which are unquestionably relevant.

Nonetheless, UBS argues that Zubulake is not entitled to any further discovery because it already produced all responsive documents, to wit, the 100 pages of e-mails. This argument is unpersuasive for two reasons. First, because of the way that UBS backs up its e-mail files, it clearly could not have searched all of its e-mails without restoring the ninety-four backup tapes (which UBS admits that it has not done). * * * Second, Zubulake herself has produced over 450 pages of relevant e-mails, including e-mails that would have been responsive to her discovery requests but were never produced by UBS. These two facts strongly suggest that there are e-mails that Zubulake has not received that reside on UBS's backup media.

B.   Should Cost–Shifting Be Considered?

Because it apparently recognizes that Zubulake is entitled to the requested discovery, UBS expends most of its efforts urging the court to shift the cost of production to "protect [it] ... from undue burden or expense." Faced with similar applications, courts generally engage in some sort of cost-shifting analysis, whether the refined eight-factor *Rowe* test or a cruder application of Rule 34's proportionality test, or something in between.

The first question, however, is whether cost-shifting must be considered in every case involving the discovery of electronic data, which—in today's world—includes virtually all cases. In light of the accepted principle, stated above, that electronic evidence is no less discoverable than paper evidence, the answer is, "No." The Supreme Court has instructed that "the presumption is that the responding party must bear the expense of complying with discovery requests...." Any principled approach to electronic evidence must respect this presumption.

Courts must remember that cost-shifting may effectively end discovery, especially when private parties are engaged in litigation with large corporations. As large companies increasingly move to entirely paper-free environments, the frequent use of cost-shifting will have the effect of crippling discovery in discrimination and retaliation cases. This will both undermine the "strong public policy favor[ing] resolving disputes on their merits," and may ultimately deter the filing of potentially meritorious claims.

Thus, cost-shifting should be considered only when electronic discovery imposes an "undue burden or expense" on the responding party.[46] The burden or expense of discovery is, in turn, "undue" when it "outweighs its likely benefit, taking into account the needs of the case, the amount in controversy, the parties' resources, the importance of the issues

---

46.   Fed. R. Civ. P. 26(c).

at stake in the litigation, and the importance of the proposed discovery in resolving the issues."[47]

Many courts have automatically assumed that an undue burden or expense may arise simply because electronic evidence is involved. This makes no sense. Electronic evidence is frequently cheaper and easier to produce than paper evidence because it can be searched automatically, key words can be run for privilege checks, and the production can be made in electronic form obviating the need for mass photocopying.

In fact, whether production of documents is unduly burdensome or expensive turns primarily on whether it is kept in an accessible or inaccessible format (a distinction that corresponds closely to the expense of production). * * * Whether electronic data is accessible or inaccessible turns largely on the media on which it is stored. Five categories of data, listed in order from most accessible to least accessible, are described in the literature on electronic data storage:

1. *Active, online data:* "On-line storage is generally provided by magnetic disk. It is used in the very active stages of an electronic record's life—when it is being created or received and processed, as well as when the access frequency is high and the required speed of access is very fast, i.e., milliseconds." Examples of online data include hard drives.

2. *Near-line data:* "This typically consists of a robotic storage device (robotic library) that houses removable media, uses robotic arms to access the media, and uses multiple read/write devices to store and retrieve records. Access speeds can range from as low as milliseconds if the media is already in a read device, up to 10–30 seconds for optical disk technology, and between 20–120 seconds for sequentially searched media, such as magnetic tape." Examples include optical disks.

3. *Offline storage/archives:* "This is removable optical disk or magnetic tape media, which can be labeled and stored in a shelf or rack. Off-line storage of electronic records is traditionally used for making disaster copies of records and also for records considered 'archival' in that their likelihood of retrieval is minimal. Accessibility to off-line media involves manual intervention and is much slower than on-line or near-line storage. Access speed may be minutes, hours, or even days, depending on the access-effectiveness of the storage facility." The principled difference between nearline data and offline data is that offline data lacks "the coordinated control of an intelligent disk subsystem," and is, in the lingo, JBOD ("Just a Bunch Of Disks").

---

47. Fed. R. Civ. P. 26(b)(2)(iii). * * * [A] court is also permitted to impose conditions on discovery when it might be duplicative, *see* Fed. R. Civ. P. 26(b)(2)(i), or when a reasonable discovery deadline has lapsed, *see id.* 26(b)(2)(ii). Neither of these concerns, however, is likely to arise solely because the discovery sought is of electronic data.

4. *Backup tapes*: "A device, like a tape recorder, that reads data from and writes it onto a tape. Tape drives have data capacities of anywhere from a few hundred kilobytes to several gigabytes. Their transfer speeds also vary considerably ... The disadvantage of tape drives is that they are sequential-access devices, which means that to read any particular block of data, you need to read all the preceding blocks." As a result, "[t]he data on a backup tape are not organized for retrieval of individual documents or files [because] ... the organization of the data mirrors the computer's structure, not the human records management structure." Backup tapes also typically employ some sort of data compression, permitting more data to be stored on each tape, but also making restoration more time-consuming and expensive, especially given the lack of uniform standard governing data compression.

5. *Erased, fragmented or damaged data*: "When a file is first created and saved, it is laid down on the [storage media] in contiguous clusters ... As files are erased, their clusters are made available again as free space. Eventually, some newly created files become larger than the remaining contiguous free space. These files are then broken up and randomly placed throughout the disk." Such broken-up files are said to be "fragmented," and along with damaged and erased data can only be accessed after significant processing.

Of these, the first three categories are typically identified as accessible, and the latter two as inaccessible. The difference between the two classes is easy to appreciate. Information deemed "accessible" is stored in a readily usable format. Although the time it takes to actually access the data ranges from milliseconds to days, the data does not need to be restored or otherwise manipulated to be usable. "Inaccessible" data, on the other hand, is not readily usable. Backup tapes must be restored using a process similar to that previously described, fragmented data must be de-fragmented, and erased data must be reconstructed, all before the data is usable. That makes such data inaccessible.

The case at bar is a perfect illustration of the range of accessibility of electronic data. As explained above, UBS maintains e-mail files in three forms: (1) active user e-mail files; (2) archived e-mails on optical disks; and (3) backup data stored on tapes. The active (HP OpenMail) data is obviously the most accessible: it is online data that resides on an active server, and can be accessed immediately. The optical disk (Tumbleweed) data is only slightly less accessible, and falls into either the second or third category. The e-mails are on optical disks that need to be located and read with the correct hardware, but the system is configured to make searching the optical disks simple and automated once they are located. For these sources of e-mails—active mail files and e-mails stored on optical disks—it would be wholly inappropriate to even consider cost-shifting. UBS maintains the data in an accessible and usable format, and can respond to Zubulake's request cheaply and quickly. Like most typical discovery requests, therefore, the producing party should bear the cost of production.

E-mails stored on backup tapes (via NetBackup), however, are an entirely different matter. Although UBS has already identified the ninety-four potentially responsive backup tapes, those tapes are not currently accessible. In order to search the tapes for responsive e-mails, UBS would have to engage in the costly and time-consuming process detailed above. It is therefore appropriate to consider cost shifting.

C. What Is the Proper Cost–Shifting Analysis?

In the year since *Rowe* was decided, its eight factor test has unquestionably become the gold standard for courts resolving electronic discovery disputes. But there is little doubt that the *Rowe* factors will generally favor cost-shifting. Indeed, of the handful of reported opinions that apply *Rowe* or some modification thereof, all of them have ordered the cost of discovery to be shifted to the requesting party.

In order to maintain the presumption that the responding party pays, the cost-shifting analysis must be neutral; close calls should be resolved in favor of the presumption. The *Rowe* factors, as applied, undercut that presumption for three reasons. First, the *Rowe* test is incomplete. Second, courts have given equal weight to all of the factors, when certain factors should predominate. Third, courts applying the *Rowe* test have not always developed a full factual record.

1. The *Rowe* Test Is Incomplete

a. A Modification of Rowe: Additional Factors

Certain factors specifically identified in the Rules are omitted from *Rowe's* eight factors. In particular, Rule 26 requires consideration of "the amount in controversy, the parties' resources, the importance of the issues at stake in the litigation, and the importance of the proposed discovery in resolving the issues." Yet *Rowe* makes no mention of either the amount in controversy or the importance of the issues at stake in the litigation. These factors should be added. Doing so would balance the *Rowe* factor that typically weighs most heavily in favor of cost-shifting, "the total cost associated with production." The cost of production is almost always an objectively large number in cases where litigating cost-shifting is worthwhile. But the cost of production when compared to "the amount in controversy" may tell a different story. A response to a discovery request costing $100,000 sounds (and is) costly, but in a case potentially worth millions of dollars, the cost of responding may not be unduly burdensome.

Rowe also contemplates "the resources available to each party." But here too—although this consideration may be implicit in the *Rowe* test— the absolute wealth of the parties is not the relevant factor. More important than comparing the relative ability of a party to pay for discovery, the focus should be on the total cost of production as compared to the resources available to each party. Thus, discovery that would be too expensive for one defendant to bear would be a drop in the bucket for another.

Last, "the importance of the issues at stake in the litigation" is a critical consideration, even if it is one that will rarely be invoked. For example, if a case has the potential for broad public impact, then public policy weighs heavily in favor of permitting extensive discovery. Cases of this ilk might include toxic tort class actions, environmental actions, so-called "impact" or social reform litigation, cases involving criminal conduct, or cases implicating important legal or constitutional questions.

b. A Modification of Rowe: Eliminating Two Factors

Two of the *Rowe* factors should be eliminated:

First, the *Rowe* test includes "the specificity of the discovery request." Specificity is surely the touchstone of any good discovery request, requiring a party to frame a request broadly enough to obtain relevant evidence, yet narrowly enough to control costs. But relevance and cost are already two of the *Rowe* factors (the second and sixth). Because the first and second factors are duplicative, they can be combined. Thus, the first factor should be: the extent to which the request is specifically tailored to discover relevant information.

Second, the fourth factor, "the purposes for which the responding party maintains the requested data" is typically unimportant. Whether the data is kept for a business purpose or for disaster recovery does not affect its accessibility, which is the practical basis for calculating the cost of production. Although a business purpose will often coincide with accessibility—data that is inaccessible is unlikely to be used or needed in the ordinary course of business—the concepts are not coterminous. In particular, a good deal of accessible data may be retained, though not in the ordinary course of business. For example, data that should rightly have been erased pursuant to a document retention/destruction policy may be inadvertently retained. If so, the fact that it should have been erased in no way shields that data from discovery. As long as the data is accessible, it must be produced.

* * *

c. A New Seven–Factor Test

Set forth below is a new seven-factor test based on the modifications to *Rowe* discussed in the preceding sections.

1. The extent to which the request is specifically tailored to discover relevant information;

2. The availability of such information from other sources;

3. The total cost of production, compared to the amount in controversy;

4. The total cost of production, compared to the resources available to each party;

5. The relative ability of each party to control costs and its incentive to do so;

6.   The importance of the issues at stake in the litigation; and

7.   The relative benefits to the parties of obtaining the information.

2.   The Seven Factors Should Not Be Weighted Equally

Whenever a court applies a multi-factor test, there is a temptation to treat the factors as a check-list, resolving the issue in favor of whichever column has the most checks. But "we do not just add up the factors." When evaluating cost-shifting, the central question must be, does the request impose an "undue burden or expense" on the responding party? Put another way, "how important is the sought-after evidence in comparison to the cost of production?" The seven-factor test articulated above provide some guidance in answering this question, but the test cannot be mechanically applied at the risk of losing sight of its purpose.

Weighting the factors in descending order of importance may solve the problem and avoid a mechanistic application of the test. The first two factors—comprising the marginal utility test—are the most important. These factors include: (1) The extent to which the request is specifically tailored to discover relevant information and (2) the availability of such information from other sources. "The more likely it is that the backup tape contains information that is relevant to a claim or defense, the fairer it is that the [responding party] search at its own expense. The less likely it is, the more unjust it would be to make the [responding party] search at its own expense. The difference is at the margin."

The second group of factors addresses cost issues: "How expensive will this production be?" and, "Who can handle that expense?" These factors include: (3) the total cost of production compared to the amount in controversy, (4) the total cost of production compared to the resources available to each party and (5) the relative ability of each party to control costs and its incentive to do so. The third "group"—(6) the importance of the litigation itself—stands alone, and as noted earlier will only rarely come into play. But where it does, this factor has the potential to predominate over the others. Collectively, the first three groups correspond to the three explicit considerations of Rule 26(b)(2)(iii). Finally, the last factor—(7) the relative benefits of production as between the requesting and producing parties—is the least important because it is fair to presume that the response to a discovery request generally benefits the requesting party. But in the unusual case where production will also provide a tangible or strategic benefit to the responding party, that fact may weigh against shifting costs.

D.   A Factual Basis Is Required to Support the Analysis

Courts applying *Rowe* have uniformly favored cost-shifting largely because of assumptions made concerning the likelihood that relevant information will be found. * * * But such proof will rarely exist in advance of obtaining the requested discovery. The suggestion that a plaintiff must not only demonstrate that probative evidence exists, but also prove that electronic discovery will yield a "gold mine," is contrary to the plain language of Rule 26(b)(1), which permits discovery of "any matter" that is "relevant to [a] claim or defense."

The best solution to this problem is * * * [to require] the responding party to restore and produce responsive documents from a small sample of backup tapes * * *. When based on an actual sample, the marginal utility test will not be an exercise in speculation—there will be tangible evidence of what the backup tapes may have to offer. There will also be tangible evidence of the time and cost required to restore the backup tapes, which in turn will inform the second group of cost-shifting factors. Thus, by requiring a sample restoration of backup tapes, the entire cost-shifting analysis can be grounded in fact rather than guesswork.[77]

IV. CONCLUSION AND ORDER

In summary, deciding disputes regarding the scope and cost of discovery of electronic data requires a three-step analysis:

First, it is necessary to thoroughly understand the responding party's computer system, both with respect to active and stored data. For data that is kept in an accessible format, the usual rules of discovery apply: the responding party should pay the costs of producing responsive data. A court should consider cost-shifting only when electronic data is relatively inaccessible, such as in backup tapes.

Second, because the cost-shifting analysis is so fact-intensive, it is necessary to determine what data may be found on the inaccessible media. Requiring the responding party to restore and produce responsive documents from a small sample of the requested backup tapes is a sensible approach in most cases.

Third, and finally, in conducting the cost-shifting analysis, the following factors should be considered, weighted more-or-less in the following order:

1. The extent to which the request is specifically tailored to discover relevant information;

2. The availability of such information from other sources;

3. The total cost of production, compared to the amount in controversy;

4. The total cost of production, compared to the resources available to each party;

5. The relative ability of each party to control costs and its incentive to do so;

6. The importance of the issues at stake in the litigation; and

7. The relative benefits to the parties of obtaining the information.

---

77. Of course, where the cost of a sample restoration is significant compared to the value of the suit, or where the suit itself is patently frivolous, even this minor effort may be inappropriate.

Accordingly, UBS is ordered to produce all responsive e-mails that exist on its optical disks or on its active servers (i.e., in HP OpenMail files) at its own expense. UBS is also ordered to produce, at its expense, responsive e-mails from any five backups tapes selected by Zubulake. UBS should then prepare an affidavit detailing the results of its search, as well as the time and money spent. After reviewing the contents of the backup tapes and UBS's certification, the Court will conduct the appropriate cost-shifting analysis.

COMMENTARY

With advances in technology, written communications now take place at lightning speed. As electronic communications supplant both traditional paper correspondence and telephonic conferences, employees now find it more convenient to e-mail or text message someone sitting in the office next to them rather than pick up the phone or walk next door. This has resulted in the creation and storage of massive amounts of electronic data, much of which is of an informal or personal nature. The costs of processing such voluminous amounts of data to find the few nuggets that are relevant to a specific litigation, compounded by attorney review time, are staggering.[24]

Litigants find themselves held hostage by their data and the costs of electronic discovery may force them to settle, despite the merits of their case. As e-discovery becomes a prominent part of litigation, litigants are seeking ways to control their e-discovery related costs and more and more often ask courts to shift the burden of these expenses to the adversary.

The landmark decisions in the *Zubulake* case went a long way in setting the stage for the adoption of the amendments to the Federal Rules of Civil Procedure in 2006 that addressed these concerns regarding electronic discovery. The *Zubulake* approach towards limiting or conditioning discovery only if it is unduly burdensome has since been embraced by the 2006 amendment to Rule 26, which provides that a party need not provide discovery of ESI that is not reasonably accessible, unless good cause is found; the Rule specifically leaves the door open to cost-sharing in appropriate circumstances.

Amended Rule 26 as Applied to Accessible Data

While the 2006 amendments to Rule 26(b)(2) explicitly apply to cost-shifting for data that is not reasonably accessible, do the amendments also apply to accessible data? While Rule 26(b)(2)(B) explicitly applies only to data that is not reasonably accessible, Rule 26(b)(2)(C) is applicable to both accessible data and data that is not reasonably accessible. Nonetheless, there remains a question as to whether cost-shifting is available for accessible data.

This question was considered by a Magistrate Judge in a series of opinions culminating in *Peskoff v. Faber.* In that case, the court held that "cost-shifting does not even become a possibility unless there is first a

---

24. *See, e.g., Toshiba Am. Elec. Components, Inc. v. Lexar Media,* 124 Cal.App.4th 762 (Dec. 3, 2004) (estimated cost to process some eight hundred back up tapes, including identification and restoration of the files, searching for responsive items and producing the data, was between $1.5 to $1.9 million).

showing of inaccessibility. Thus, it cannot be argued that a party should ever be relieved of its obligation to produce accessible data merely because it may take time and effort to find what is necessary."[25] The court also noted, however, that "the search for data, even if accessible, must be justified under the relevancy standard of Rule 26(b)(1)." The better rule is that cost-shifting is available even for accessible data based on the proportionality factors set forth in Rule 26(b)(2)(C). In short, the court always has the option to condition discovery on the requesting party's payment of costs for production.[26]

PROBLEM

The plaintiff has sued his former government employer, County, alleging that his employment position was eliminated as part of County's restructuring that unfairly targeted her because she provided information to federal investigating authorities regarding improper handling of tax refunds by County. The plaintiff's request for documents about the restructuring and reorganization of County produced approximately four terabytes of data extracted from various computers of County employees and supervisors. A terabyte of data is equivalent to 500 million typewritten pages. The defendant contends that the request to search this data is unduly burdensome. According to the defendant, it has already spent $25,000 in litigation costs related to discovery and would have to spend an additional $49,000 to complete the search requested by the plaintiff. The potential recovery of the lawsuit is less than $100,000. The defendant has asked that the search costs be shifted to the plaintiff. If you are the judge, how would you resolve this dispute? How would you argue this matter on behalf of the defendant and the plaintiff? Draft an argument applying the proportionality test for each side using the factors set forth in Rule 26(b)(2)(C)(iii).

2.   Not Reasonably Accessible Data—Rule 26(b)(2)(B)

ZUBULAKE v. UBS WARBURG LLC "*ZUBULAKE III*"

216 F.R.D. 280 (S.D.N.Y. 2003)

SCHEINDLIN, DISTRICT JUDGE

On May 13, 2003, I ordered defendants UBS Warburg LLC, UBS Warburg, and UBS AG (collectively "UBS") to restore and produce certain e-mails from a small group of backup tapes. Having reviewed the results of this sample restoration, Laura Zubulake now moves for an order compelling UBS to produce all remaining backup e-mails at its expense. UBS argues that based on the sampling, the costs should be shifted to Zubulake.

---

25.   *Peskoff v. Faber*, 244 F.R.D. 54, 62 (D.D.C. 2007).

26.   *See Grant v. Homier Distrib. Co., Inc.*, No. 3:07–CV–116, 2007 WL 2446753 (N.D. Ind. Aug. 24, 2007) (holding that a court may order discovery subject to the requesting party's payment of production costs). *See also* 2006 Advisory Committee Note to 26(b)(2)(B) ("The limitations of Rule 26(b)(2)(C) apply to all discovery of electronically stored information.").

For the reasons fully explained below, Zubulake must share in the costs of restoration, although UBS must bear the bulk of that expense. In addition, UBS must pay for any costs incurred in reviewing the restored documents for privilege.

I. BACKGROUND

* * * In brief, Zubulake, an equities trader who earned approximately $650,000 a year with UBS, is now suing UBS for gender discrimination, failure to promote, and retaliation under federal, state, and city law. To support her claim, Zubulake seeks evidence stored on UBS's backup tapes that is only accessible through costly and time-consuming data retrieval. In particular, Zubulake seeks e-mails relating to her that were sent to or from five UBS employees: Matthew Chapin (Zubulake's immediate supervisor and the alleged primary discriminator), Jeremy Hardisty (Chapin's supervisor and the individual to whom Zubulake originally complained about Chapin), Rose Tong (a human relations representative who was assigned to handle issues concerning Zubulake), Vinay Datta (a co-worker), and Andrew Clarke (another co-worker). The question presented in this dispute is which party should pay for the costs incurred in restoring and producing these backup tapes.

In order to obtain a factual basis to support the cost-shifting analysis, I ordered UBS to restore and produce e-mails from five of the ninety-four backup tapes that UBS had then identified as containing responsive documents; Zubulake was permitted to select the five tapes to be restored. UBS now reports, however, that there are only seventy-seven backup tapes that contain responsive data, including the five already restored. I further ordered UBS to "prepare an affidavit detailing the results of its search, as well as the time and money spent." UBS has complied by submitting counsel's declaration.

According to the declaration, Zubulake selected the backup tapes corresponding to Matthew Chapin's e-mails from May, June, July, August, and September 2001. That period includes the time from Zubulake's initial EEOC charge of discrimination (August 2001) until just before her termination (in the first week of October 2001).UBS hired an outside vendor, Pinkerton Consulting & Investigations, to perform the restoration.

Pinkerton was able to restore each of the backup tapes, yielding a total of 8,344 e-mails. That number is somewhat inflated, however, because it does not account for duplicates. Because each month's backup tape was a snapshot of Chapin's server for that month—and not an incremental backup reflecting only new material—an e-mail that was on the server for more than one month would appear on more than one backup tape. For example, an e-mail received in January 2001 and deleted in November 2001 would have been restored from all five backup tapes. With duplicates eliminated, the total number of unique e-mails restored was 6,203.

Pinkerton then performed a search for e-mails containing (in either the e-mail's text or its header information, such as the "subject" line) the terms "Laura", "Zubulake", or "LZ". The searches yielded 1,541 e-mails, or 1,075 if duplicates are eliminated. Of these 1,541 e-mails, UBS deemed approximately 600 to be responsive to Zubulake's document request and they were produced. UBS also produced, under the terms of the May 13 Order, fewer than twenty e-mails extracted from UBS's optical disk storage system.

Pinkerton billed UBS 31.5 hours for its restoration services at an hourly rate of $245, six hours for the development, refinement and execution of a search script at $245 an hour, and 101.5 hours of "CPU Bench Utilization" time for use of Pinkerton's computer systems at a rate of $18.50 per hour. Pinkerton also included a five percent "administrative overhead fee" of $459.38. Thus, the total cost of restoration and search was $11,524.63. In addition, UBS incurred the following costs: $4,633 in attorney time for the document review (11.3 hours at $410 per hour) and $2,845.80 in paralegal time for tasks related to document production (16.74 hours at $170 per hour). UBS also paid $432.60 in photocopying costs, which, of course, will be paid by Zubulake and is not part of this cost-shifting analysis.[24] The total cost of restoration and production from the five backup tapes was $19,003.43.

UBS now asks that the cost of any further production—estimated to be $273,649.39, based on the cost incurred in restoring five tapes and producing responsive documents from those tapes—be shifted to Zubulake. The total figure includes $165,954.67 to restore and search the tapes and $107,694.72 in attorney and paralegal review costs. These costs will be addressed separately below.

II. LEGAL STANDARD

* * *

Although "the presumption is that the responding party must bear the expense of complying with discovery requests," requests that run afoul of the Rule 26(b)(2) proportionality test may subject the requesting party to protective orders under Rule 26(c), "including orders conditioning discovery on the requesting party's payment of the costs of discovery." A court will order such a cost-shifting protective order only upon motion of the responding party to a discovery request, and "for good cause shown." Thus, the responding party has the burden of proof on a motion for cost-shifting.

III. DISCUSSION

A. Cost-shifting Generally

In *Zubulake I,* I considered plaintiff's request for information contained only on backup tapes and determined that cost-shifting might be

---

24. *See* Fed. R. Civ. P. 34(a) (permitting the requesting party to "inspect and copy" any documents it asks for); *see also In re Bristol–Myers Squibb Sec. Litig.,* 205 F.R.D. 437, 440 (D.N.J. 2002) (imposing cost of photocopying electronic documents on requesting party).

appropriate. It is worth emphasizing again that cost-shifting is potentially appropriate only when inaccessible data is sought. When a discovery request seeks accessible data–for example, active on-line or near-line data– it is typically inappropriate to consider cost-shifting.

In order to determine whether cost-shifting is appropriate for the discovery of inaccessible data, [the court applied the new 7–factor test quoted in *Zubulake I*]. * * *

B. Application of the Seven Factor Test

1. Factors One and Two

As I explained in *Zubulake I,* the first two factors together comprise the "marginal utility test" * * *:

> The more likely it is that the backup tape contains information that is relevant to a claim or defense, the fairer it is that the [responding party] search at its own expense. The less likely it is, the more unjust it would be to make the [responding party] search at its own expense. The difference is "at the margin."

These two factors should be weighted the most heavily in the cost-shifting analysis.

a. The Extent to Which the Request Is Specifically Tailored to Discover Relevant Information

The document request at issue asks for "[a]ll documents concerning any communication by or between UBS employees concerning Plaintiff," and was subsequently narrowed to pertain to only five employees (Chapin, Hardisty, Tong, Datta, and Clarke) and to the period from August 1999 to December 2001. This is a relatively limited and targeted request, a fact borne out by the e-mails UBS actually produced, both initially and as a result of the sample restoration.

At oral argument, Zubulake presented the court with sixty-eight e-mails (of the 600 she received) that she claims are "highly relevant to the issues in this case" and thus require, in her view, that UBS bear the cost of production. And indeed, a review of these e-mails reveals that they are relevant. Taken together, they tell a compelling story of the dysfunctional atmosphere surrounding UBS's U.S. Asian Equities Sales Desk (the "Desk"). Presumably, these sixty-eight e-mails are reasonably representative of the seventy-seven backup tapes.

A number of the e-mails complain of Zubulake's behavior. Zubulake was described by Clarke as engaging in "bitch sessions about the horrible men on the [Desk]," and as a "conduit for a steady stream of distortions, accusations and good ole fashioned back stabbing," and Hardisty noted that Zubulake was disrespectful to Chapin and other members of the Desk. And Chapin takes frequent snipes at Zubulake. There are also complaints about Chapin's behavior. In addition, Zubulake argues that several of the e-mails contradict testimony given by UBS employees in sworn depositions.

While all of these e-mails are [relevant] none of them provide any direct evidence of discrimination. To be sure, the e-mails reveal a hostile relationship between Chapin and Zubulake—UBS does not contest this. But nowhere (in the sixty-eight e-mails produced to the Court) is there evidence that Chapin's dislike of Zubulake related to her gender.

b.   The Availability of Such Information from Other Sources

The other half of the marginal utility test is the availability of the relevant data from other sources. Neither party seemed to know how many of the 600 e-mails produced in response to the May 13 Order had been previously produced. UBS argues that "nearly all of the restored e-mails that relate to plaintiff's allegations in this matter or to the merits of her case were already produced." This statement is perhaps too careful, because UBS goes on to observe that "the vast majority of the restored e-mails that were produced do not relate at all to plaintiff's allegations in this matter or to the merits of her case." But this determination is not for UBS to make; as the saying goes, "one man's trash is another man's treasure."

It is axiomatic that a requesting party may obtain "any matter, not privileged, that is relevant to the claim or defense of any party." The simple fact is that UBS previously produced only 100 pages of e-mails, but has now produced 853 pages (comprising the 600 responsive e-mails) from the five selected backup tapes alone. UBS itself decided that it was obliged to provide these 853 pages of e-mail pursuant to the requirements of Rule 26. Having done so, these numbers lead to the unavoidable conclusion that there are a significant number of responsive e-mails that now exist only on backup tapes.

If this were not enough, there is some evidence that Chapin was concealing and deleting especially relevant e-mails. When Zubulake first filed her EEOC charge in August 2001, all UBS employees were instructed to save documents relevant to her case. In furtherance of this policy, Chapin maintained separate files on Zubulake. However, certain e-mails sent after the initial EEOC charge—and particularly relevant to Zubulake's retaliation claim—were apparently not saved at all. For example, the e-mail from Chapin to Joy Kim instructing her on how to file a complaint against Zubulake was not saved, and it bears the subject line "UBS client attorney priviledge [sic] only," although no attorney is copied on the e-mail. This potentially useful e-mail was deleted and resided only on UBS's backup tapes.

In sum, hundreds of the e-mails produced from the five backup tapes were not previously produced, and so were only available from the tapes. The contents of these e-mails are also new. Although some of the substance is available from other sources (e.g., evidence of the sour relationship between Chapin and Zubulake), a good deal of it is only found on the backup tapes (e.g., inconsistencies with UBS's EEOC filing and Chapin's deposition testimony). Moreover, an e-mail contains the precise words used by the author. Because of that, it is a particularly powerful form of proof at trial when offered as an admission of a party opponent.

c. Weighing Factors One and Two

The sample restoration, which resulted in the production of relevant e-mail, has demonstrated that Zubulake's discovery request was narrowly tailored to discover relevant information. And while the subject matter of some of those e-mails was addressed in other documents, these particular e-mails are only available from the backup tapes. Thus, direct evidence of discrimination may only be available through restoration. As a result, the marginal utility of this additional discovery may be quite high.

While restoration may be the only means for obtaining direct evidence of discrimination, the existence of that evidence is still speculative. The best that can be said is that Zubulake has demonstrated that the marginal utility is potentially high. All-in-all, because UBS bears the burden of proving that cost-shifting is warranted, the marginal utility test tips slightly against cost-shifting.

2. Factors Three, Four and Five

"The second group of factors addresses cost issues: 'How expensive will this production be?' and, 'Who can handle that expense?'"

a. The Total Cost of Production Compared to the Amount in Controversy

UBS spent $11,524.63, or $2,304.93 per tape, to restore the five back-up tapes. Thus, the total cost of restoring the remaining seventy-two tapes extrapolates to $165,954.67.

In order to assess the amount in controversy, I posed the following question to the parties: Assuming that a jury returns a verdict in favor of plaintiff, what economic damages can the plaintiff reasonably expect to recover? Plaintiff answered that reasonable damages are between $15,271,361 and $19,227,361, depending upon how front pay is calculated. UBS answered that damages could be as high as $1,265,000.

Obviously, this is a significant disparity. At this early stage, I cannot assess the accuracy of either estimate. Plaintiff had every incentive to high-ball the figure and UBS had every incentive to low-ball it. It is clear, however, that this case has the potential for a multi-million dollar recovery. Whatever else might be said, this is not a nuisance value case, a small case or a frivolous case. Most people do not earn $650,000 a year. If Zubulake prevails, her damages award undoubtedly will be higher than that of the vast majority of Title VII plaintiffs.

In an ordinary case, a responding party should not be required to pay for the restoration of inaccessible data if the cost of that restoration is significantly disproportionate to the value of the case. Assuming this to be a multi-million dollar case, the cost of restoration is surely not "significantly disproportionate" to the projected value of this case. This factor weighs against cost-shifting.

b. The Total Cost of Production Compared to the Resources Available to Each Party

There is no question that UBS has exponentially more resources available to it than Zubulake. While Zubulake is an accomplished equities trader, she has now been unemployed for close to two years. Given the difficulties in the equities market and the fact that she is suing her former employer, she may not be particularly marketable. On the other hand, she asserts that she has a $19 million claim against UBS. So while UBS's resources clearly dwarf Zubulake's, she may have the financial wherewithal to cover at least some of the cost of restoration. In addition, it is not unheard of for plaintiff's firms to front huge expenses when multi-million dollar recoveries are in sight. Thus, while this factor weighs against cost shifting, it does not rule it out.

c. The Relative Ability of Each Party to Control Costs and Its Incentive to Do So

Restoration of backup tapes must generally be done by an outside vendor. Here, UBS had complete control over the selection of the vendor. It is entirely possible that a less-expensive vendor could have been found. However, once that vendor is selected, costs are not within the control of either party. In addition, because these backup tapes are relatively well-organized—meaning that UBS knows what e-mails can be found on each tape—there is nothing more that Zubulake can do to focus her discovery request or reduce its cost. Zubulake has already made a targeted discovery request and the restoration of the sample tapes has not enabled her to cut back on that request. Thus, this factor is neutral.

3. Factor Six: The Importance of the Issues at Stake in the Litigation

As noted in *Zubulake I*, this factor "will only rarely come into play." Although this case revolves around a weighty issue—discrimination in the workplace—it is hardly unique. Claims of discrimination are common, and while discrimination is an important problem, this litigation does not present a particularly novel issue. If I were to consider the issues in this discrimination case sufficiently important to weigh in the cost-shifting analysis, then this factor would be virtually meaningless. Accordingly, this factor is neutral.

4. Factor Seven: The Relative Benefits to the Parties of Obtaining the Information

Although Zubulake argues that there are potential benefits to UBS in undertaking the restoration of these backup tapes—in particular, the opportunity to obtain evidence that may be useful at summary judgment or trial—there can be no question that Zubulake stands to gain far more than does UBS, as will typically be the case. Certainly, absent an order, UBS would not restore any of this data of its own volition. Accordingly, this factor weighs in favor of cost-shifting.

5. Summary and Conclusion

Factors one through four tip against cost-shifting (although factor two only slightly so). Factors five and six are neutral, and factor seven favors cost-shifting. As noted in my earlier opinion in this case, however, a list of factors is not merely a matter of counting and adding; it is only a guide. Because some of the factors cut against cost shifting, but only slightly so—in particular, the possibility that the continued production will produce valuable new information—some cost-shifting is appropriate in this case, although UBS should pay the majority of the costs. There is plainly relevant evidence that is only available on UBS's backup tapes. At the same time, Zubulake has not been able to show that there is indispensable evidence on those backup tapes (although the fact that Chapin apparently deleted certain e-mails indicates that such evidence may exist).

The next question is how much of the cost should be shifted. It is beyond cavil that the precise allocation is a matter of judgment and fairness rather than a mathematical consequence of the seven factors discussed above. Nonetheless, the analysis of those factors does inform the exercise of discretion. Because the seven factor test requires that UBS pay the lion's share, the percentage assigned to Zubulake must be less than fifty percent. A share that is too costly may chill the rights of litigants to pursue meritorious claims. However, because the success of this search is somewhat speculative, any cost that fairly can be assigned to Zubulake is appropriate and ensures that UBS's expenses will not be unduly burdensome. A twenty-five percent assignment to Zubulake meets these goals.

C. Other Costs

The final question is whether this result should apply to the entire cost of the production, or only to the cost of restoring the backup tapes. The difference is not academic—the estimated cost of restoring and searching the remaining backup tapes is $165,954.67, while the estimated cost of producing them (restoration and searching costs plus attorney and paralegal costs) is $273,649.39 ($19,003.43 for the five sample tapes, or $3,800.69 per tape, times seventy-two unrestored tapes), a difference of $107,694.72.

As a general rule, where cost-shifting is appropriate, only the costs of restoration and searching should be shifted. Restoration, of course, is the act of making inaccessible material accessible. That "special purpose" or "extraordinary step" should be the subject of cost-shifting. Search costs should also be shifted because they are so intertwined with the restoration process; a vendor like Pinkerton will not only develop and refine the search script, but also necessarily execute the search as it conducts the restoration. However, the responding party should always bear the cost of reviewing and producing electronic data once it has been converted to an accessible form. This is so for two reasons.

First, the producing party has the exclusive ability to control the cost of reviewing the documents. In this case, UBS decided—as is its right—to have a senior associate at a top New York City law firm conduct the privilege review at a cost of $410 per hour. But the job could just as easily have been done (while perhaps not as well) by a first-year associate or contract attorney at a far lower rate. UBS could similarly have obtained paralegal assistance for far less than $170 per hour.

Moreover, the producing party unilaterally decides on the review protocol. When reviewing electronic data, that review may range from reading every word of every document to conducting a series of targeted key word searches. Indeed, many parties to document-intensive litigation enter into so-called "claw-back" agreements that allow the parties to forego privilege review altogether in favor of an agreement to return inadvertently produced privileged documents. The parties here can still reach such an agreement with respect to the remaining seventy-two tapes and thereby avoid any cost of reviewing these tapes for privilege.

Second, the argument that all costs related to the production of restored data should be shifted misapprehends the nature of the cost-shifting inquiry. Recalling that cost-shifting is only appropriate for inaccessible—but otherwise discoverable—data, it necessarily follows that once the data has been restored to an accessible format and responsive documents located, cost-shifting is no longer appropriate. Had it always been accessible, there is no question that UBS would have had to produce the data at its own cost. * * *

Documents stored on backup tapes can be likened to paper records locked inside a sophisticated safe to which no one has the key or combination. The cost of accessing those documents may be onerous, and in some cases the parties should split the cost of breaking into the safe. But once the safe is opened, the production of the documents found inside is the sole responsibility of the responding party. The point is simple: technology may increasingly permit litigants to reconstruct lost or inaccessible information, but once restored to an accessible form, the usual rules of discovery apply.

IV. CONCLUSION

For the reasons set forth above, the costs of restoring any backup tapes are allocated between UBS and Zubulake seventy-five percent and twenty-five percent, respectively. All other costs are to be borne exclusively by UBS. * * *

COMMENTARY

As discussed above, litigants have been seeking means to ameliorate the related costs and burdens of processing and producing copious amounts of electronic data. One way of addressing these concerns is to shift the cost of production from the producing party to the requesting party. Under the *Zubulake* decisions, the accessibility of the data sought was a major consideration in determining whether to shift costs. However, the mere fact that data is inaccessible does not require a court to shift costs to the requesting party.

The court must also analyze the utility of the data and other circumstances, such as whether the data can be found in other more accessible locations.

Ultimately the *Zubulake* court came to the conclusion that the plaintiff should pay twenty-five percent of the restoration costs. In *Zubulake III*, however, the court specifically limited the cost to be shared to search and retrieval costs—the costs associated with making inaccessible data accessible. But the court explicitly declined to shift the cost of attorney review time. However, restoration of data is only one step in the electronic discovery process that begins with data management and ends in the courtroom or hearings. As noted in *Zubulake III,* the costs to restore and search the backup tapes represented less than two-thirds of the total costs for the production of the backup tape data.[27]

Often the most significant cost driver associated with e-discovery is the human review and analysis of the culled data. The Sedona Conference estimates that the cost to review one gigabyte of text on average is $25,000. Thus, the front end work to reduce the amount of data pays significant dividends in reducing reviewing costs.

PROBLEMS

1.   Would the application of *Rowe's* eight factors to the *Zubulake* case have changed the result? You be the judge. Write the *Zubulake* opinion using the eight factors of *Rowe*. Is the result the same? Did you shift some or all of the costs to the plaintiff Laura Zubulake?

Questions under *Zubulake's* cost-shifting analysis

Zubulake's analytical framework leaves a number of questions, including the following:

a.   Does *Zubulake III* encourage "e-discovery blackmail" where plaintiffs with small claims will propound e-discovery requests for relevant data that far exceeds the amount in controversy, essentially requiring the Defendant to settle before incurring the cost of electronic discovery?

b.   Does *Zubulake III* encourage companies to maintain data in inaccessible locations in order to shift costs to the opponent and thus deter litigation?

c.   Why should a party that invests in modern accessible data systems be at a cost disadvantage when litigating against a party that is an information era "dinosaur"?

2.   How would you as a judge apply the *Zubulake* seven factor test to a company that intentionally keeps information on inaccessible backup media? Is there a *Zubulake* factor that addresses this situation?

The 2006 Federal Rules Amendment

The 2006 Advisory Committee Note to Rule 26(b)(2)(B) provides that the decision as to whether a party must search sources that are not reasonably accessible depends on whether the burden can be justified under the circumstances of the case. A court may permit discovery of such sources on a

---

27.   *See Zubulake*, 216 F.R.D. at 289–90.

showing of "good cause." The Advisory Committee then listed a number of factors that might be considered under the "good cause" test:

> Appropriate considerations may include: (1) the specificity of the discovery request; (2) the quantity of information available from other and more easily accessed sources; (3) the failure to produce relevant information that seems likely to have existed but is no longer available on a more easily accessed sources; (4) the likelihood of finding relevant, responsive information that cannot be obtained from other, more easily accessed sources; (5) predictions as to the importance and usefulness of the further information; (6) the importance of the issues at stake in the litigation; and (7) the parties' resources.

3. Compare the 2006 Advisory Committee Note to the *Zubulake* seven factor test. Is there a meaningful difference?

With respect to data from sources that are not reasonably accessible, how do the seven factors in the Advisory Committee Note compare to the factors articulated in Rule 26(b)(2)(C)(iii)? *Zubulake I* and *III* were written under the authority of the old Rule 26(B)(2)(b) which became Rule 26(b)(2)(C)(iii). Did the Advisory Committee merely recast *Zubulake's* seven factors into its Note? If so, does Rule 26(b)(2)(C)(iii) add anything to the mix? Must a court consider the good cause factors and then the 26(b)(2)(C) factors? Would such an effort be duplicative?

In *Quinby v. WestLB AG*, the Magistrate Judge considered a request for cost-shifting in another employment discrimination case.[28] The court addressed a request to shift costs for data which had been moved to backup tapes pursuant to a company policy of moving active data to a backup media when an employee is no longer employed by the company. Such practices are called "data-downgrading" and some courts have frowned on this practice.[29] *Quinby* determined that the cost of retrieving data for six departed employees would not be shifted to the requesting plaintiff if the defendant was on reasonable notice at the time of the data transfer that the data would potentially be relevant to resolving Quinby's claims.

> I submit, however, that if a party creates its own burden or expense by converting into an inaccessible format data that it should have reasonably foreseen would be discoverable material at a time when it should have anticipated litigation, then it should not be entitled to shift the costs of restoring and searching the data.[30]

The court found this to be the case with some of the terminated employees.

> Because I find that, with the exception of Barron's e-mails, defendant should have reasonably anticipated having to produce all the Former Employees' e-mails, I consider the *Zubulake* cost-shifting factors with respect to the costs of restoring and searching only Barron's e-mails.

The court then applied the *Zubulake* seven factor test. Ultimately the court determined that thirty percent of the cost should be shifted. Again, the court

---

28.   245 F.R.D. 94 (S.D.N.Y. 2006).

29.   *See, e.g., Treppel v. Biovail Corp.*, 233 F.R.D. 363, 372 n.4 (S.D.N.Y. 2006).

30.   *Quinby*, 245 F.R.D. at 104.

was not impressed with the marginal utility of the e-mails that were recovered from the backup tapes by using many broad search terms.

> Even though these e-mails may be relevant, and I appreciate that discrimination is frequently subtle and often proven by circumstantial evidence, I find that merely 71 pages of relevant documents from that period of time is quite low when compared to the volume of documents produced, particularly considering that much of the alleged wrongdoing took place in 2003. . . . In light of the low number of relevant e-mails, and in spite of the fact that the e-mails are only on backup tapes, the marginal utility test is low and leans in favor of cost shifting.

In short the court determined that the marginal relevance of Barron's e-mails was low because they lay on the fringe of relevance.

Two other factors in support of cost-shifting were advanced by the defendant. First, the defendant claimed that the additional costs (twenty-five percent) of expediting the production of backup tapes should be shifted to the plaintiff. The court denied the request. Interestingly the court did not rule out consideration of the demand for expedited discovery as a factor, but merely stated that the defendant had not met its burden.

Next, the defendant asked for the costs of complying with the plaintiff's request to produce the documents in a second format. The court denied the request as untimely. Should the costs be shifted if the requesting party seeks production in a non-native format or a second format?[31]

PROBLEM

What facts would justify a shift of the costs of expedited production? Construct a factual scenario where you believe such cost-shifting would be justified. Would this be covered by the factor as to which party is best able to control costs?

I. PRODUCTION FROM NON–PARTIES PURSUANT TO RULE 45

IN RE SUBPOENA DUCES TECUM TO AOL, LLC

550 F. Supp. 2d 606 (E.D. Va. 2008)

LEE, DISTRICT JUDGE

THIS MATTER is before the Court on State Farm Fire and Casualty Co.'s Objections to Magistrate Judge Poretz's Order, entered on November 30, 2007, quashing State Farm's subpoena to AOL, LLC. This case concerns Cori and Kerri Rigsby's claims that State Farm's subpoena issued to AOL violated the Electronic Communications Privacy Act ("Privacy Act"), codified as 18 U.S.C. §§ 2701–03 (2000), [and] imposed an undue burden on the Rigsbys * * *. The issue before the Court is whether

---

31. *See* Fed. R. Civ. P. 34(b)(2)(E)(iii) ("A party need not produce the same electronically stored information in more than one form.").

Magistrate Judge Poretz clearly erred by granting the Rigsbys' Motion to Quash, where State Farm's civil discovery subpoena requested: (1) production of the Rigsbys' e-mails from AOL; [and] (2) all of Cori Rigsby's e-mails from a six-week period * * *. The Court upholds Magistrate Judge Poretz's decision quashing State Farm's subpoena, and holds that it was not clearly erroneous for the following reasons: (1) the Privacy Act prohibits AOL from producing the Rigsbys' e-mails in response to State Farm's subpoena because a civil discovery subpoena is not a disclosure exception under the Act; [and] (2) State Farm's subpoena imposes an undue burden on the Rigsbys because the subpoena is overbroad and the documents requested are not limited to subject matter relevant to the claims or defenses in McIntosh. Thus, Magistrate Judge Poretz's Order is affirmed.

I. BACKGROUND

Cori and Kerri Rigsby are non-party witnesses in McIntosh v. State Farm Fire & Casualty Co., an action pending in the Southern District of Mississippi. The Rigsbys were employed as insurance adjusters by E.A. Renfroe and Co. ("E.A. Renfroe") and discovered what they believed to be fraud with respect to State Farm's treatment of Thomas and Pamela McIntosh's Hurricane Katrina damage claim. The Rigsbys provided supporting documents to state and federal law enforcement authorities and filed a qui tam action, United States ex rel. Rigsby v. State Farm Insurance Co., in the Southern District of Mississippi, alleging that State Farm defrauded the United States Government by improperly shifting costs from State Farm's wind damage coverage to the federal flood insurance program.

In the course of discovery litigation related to McIntosh, State Farm issued a subpoena through this Court to AOL, requesting production of documents from the Rigsbys' e-mail accounts pertaining to Thomas or Pamela McIntosh, State Farm Fire & Casualty Co.'s claims handling practices for Hurricane Katrina, Forensic Analysis & Engineering Corporation's documents for Hurricane Katrina, and E.A. Renfroe & Co.'s claims handling practices for Hurricane Katrina over a ten-month period.[2] State Farm's subpoena also requested any and all documents, including electronically stored information, related to Cori Rigsby's e-mail account or address from September 1, 2007, to October 12, 2007, a six-week period where Cori Rigsby and her attorneys allegedly concealed from State Farm that her computer had crashed. * * * The Rigsbys * * * moved to quash State Farm's subpoena, claiming that the subpoena violated the Privacy

---

2. State Farm alleges that the Rigsbys admitted to: (1) stealing approximately 15,000 confidential documents from a State Farm laptop computer provided to the Rigsbys when they worked for E.A. Renfroe; (2) forwarding the stolen information via e-mail to the Rigsbys' personal AOL accounts; and (3) providing the stolen information to attorney Dickie Scruggs, who used the stolen information to file hundreds of lawsuits against State Farm, including McIntosh. In McIntosh, Magistrate Judge Walker ruled that "State Farm is entitled to know the basis for the Rigsbys' charges of wrongdoing," and ordered the Rigsbys "to produce the requested documents within their actual or constructive possession" to State Farm.

Act, [and] was overbroad and unduly burdensome * * *. [The magistrate judge granted the motion to quash the subpoena.]

* * *

II. DISCUSSION

* * *

B. Analysis

1. The Privacy Act

The Court upholds Magistrate Judge Poretz's Order, quashing State Farm's subpoena, because the plain language of the Privacy Act prohibits AOL from producing the Rigsbys' e-mails, and the issuance of a civil discovery subpoena is not an exception to the provisions of the Privacy Act that would allow an internet service provider to disclose the communications at issue here. * * *

The statutory language of the Privacy Act must be regarded as conclusive because it contains plain and unambiguous language and a coherent and consistent statutory scheme. Section 2701 clearly establishes a punishable offense for intentionally accessing without or exceeding authorization and obtaining electronic communications stored at an electronic communication service facility. 18 U.S.C. § 2701 (2000). Section 2702 plainly prohibits an electronic communication or remote computing service to the public from knowingly divulging to any person or entity the contents of customers' electronic communications or records pertaining to subscribing customers. Additionally, § 2702 lists unambiguous exceptions that allow an electronic communication or remote computing service to disclose the contents of an electronic communication or subscriber information. Section 2703 provides instances related to ongoing criminal investigations where a governmental entity may require an electronic communication or remote computing service to disclose the contents of customers' electronic communications or subscriber information. Protecting privacy interests in personal information stored in computerized systems, while also protecting the Government's legitimate law enforcement needs, the Privacy Act creates a zone of privacy to protect internet subscribers from having their personal information wrongfully used and publicly disclosed by "unauthorized private parties," S.Rep. No. 99–541, at 3 (1986).

In * * * *Federal Trade Commission v. Netscape Communications Corp.*, the court denied the Federal Trade Commission's ("FTC") motion to compel, where an internet service provider, a non-party in the underlying action, refused to turn over documents containing subscriber identity information to the FTC. 196 F.R.D. 559 (N.D.Cal.2000). The FTC filed a civil lawsuit against the subscribers for violating the FTC unfair competition statute. During pre-trial discovery, the FTC issued a subpoena to the internet service provider pursuant to Federal Rule of Civil Procedure 45.

The court distinguished discovery subpoenas from trial subpoenas based on differences in scope and operation and concluded that Congress would have specifically included discovery subpoenas in the Privacy Act if Congress meant to include this as an exception requiring an internet service provider to disclose subscriber information to a governmental entity. The court held that the statutory phrase "trial subpoena" does not apply to discovery subpoenas in civil cases and declined to allow the FTC to use Rule 45 to circumvent the protections built into the Privacy Act that protect subscriber privacy from governmental entities.

In *O'Grady v. Superior Court*, the Court of Appeal of the State of California * * * held that enforcement of a civil subpoena issued to an e-mail service provider is inconsistent with the plain terms of the Privacy Act. 139 Cal.App.4th 1423, 44 Cal.Rptr.3d 72, 76–77 (2006). Apple brought a civil action against several unknown defendants for wrongfully publishing on the World Wide Web Apple's secret plans to release a new product. To identify the unknown defendants, Apple issued civil discovery subpoenas to non-party internet service providers, requesting copies of any e-mails that contained certain keywords from the published secret plans. * * * The court * * * found that any disclosure by an internet service provider of stored e-mail violates the Privacy Act unless it falls within an enumerated exception to the general prohibition. Emphasizing the substantial burden and expense that would be imposed on internet service providers if they were required to respond to every civil discovery subpoena issued in a civil lawsuit and how such a policy may discourage users from using new media, the court refused to create an exception for civil discovery and found the subpoenas unenforceable under the Privacy Act.

* * * AOL, a corporation that provides electronic communication services to the public, may not divulge the contents of the Rigsbys' electronic communications to State Farm because the statutory language of the Privacy Act does not include an exception for the disclosure of electronic communications pursuant to civil discovery subpoenas.* * * Because State Farm is a private party and this is a civil lawsuit, none of the exceptions for governmental entities under § 2703 apply. Furthermore, agreeing with the reasoning in *Netscape*, the Court holds that "unauthorized private parties" and governmental entities are prohibited from using Rule 45 civil discovery subpoenas to circumvent the Privacy Act's protections.

* * * [T]he Court finds that the Privacy Act protects the Rigsbys' stored e-mails because the Rigsbys have a legitimate interest in the confidentiality of their personal e-mails being stored electronically by AOL. Agreeing with the reasoning in *O'Grady*, this Court holds that State Farm's subpoena may not be enforced consistent with the plain language of the Privacy Act because the exceptions enumerated in § 2702(b) do not include civil discovery subpoenas. Furthermore, § 2702(b) does not make any references to civil litigation or the civil discovery process. For the foregoing reasons, Magistrate Judge Poretz did not clearly err when he found that the Privacy Act prohibits AOL from producing the Rigsbys' e-

mails in response to State Farm's subpoena because the Privacy Act's enumerated exceptions do not authorize disclosure pursuant to a civil discovery subpoena.

2. Undue Burden

The Court upholds Magistrate Judge Poretz's Order, quashing State Farm's subpoena, because the subpoena is overbroad to the extent that it does not limit the documents requested to subject matter relevant to the claims or defenses in McIntosh and imposes an undue burden on the Rigsbys. "A party or attorney responsible for issuing and serving a subpoena must take reasonable steps to avoid imposing undue burden or expense on a person subject to the subpoena." Fed.R.Civ.P. 45(c)(1). A court must quash or modify a subpoena that subjects a person to an undue burden. Fed. R. Civ. P. 45(c)(3)(A)(iv). When a non-party claims that a subpoena is burdensome and oppressive, the non-party must support its claim by showing how production would be burdensome. A subpoena imposes an undue burden on a party when a subpoena is overbroad.

* * *

* * * State Farm's subpoena must be quashed because it imposes an undue burden on the Rigsbys by being overbroad and requesting "all" of Cori Rigsby's e-mails for a six-week period. * * * State Farm's subpoena is overbroad because it does not limit the e-mails requested to those containing subject matter relevant to the underlying action or sent to or from employees connected to the litigation, other than Cori Rigsby. Although State Farm limited the e-mails requested to an allegedly relevant six-week period, * * * State Farm's subpoena remains overbroad because the e-mails produced over a six-week period would likely include privileged and personal information unrelated to the McIntosh litigation, imposing an undue burden on Cori Rigsby. Thus, Magistrate Judge Poretz did not clearly err when he found that State Farm's subpoena was overbroad and imposed an undue burden on Cori Rigsby because State Farm's subpoena did not limit the documents requested to subject matter relevant to *McIntosh*.

* * *

COMMENTARY

1. How Can ESI Be Obtained From Nonparties?

ESI may be obtained from nonparties by service of a subpoena. Rule 45 contains a number of provisions similar to those found in Rules 26(b) and 34(b)(2).

2. Does a Third Party Have an Obligation to Preserve Evidence Relevant to Other Litigation?

EXCERPT FROM *The Sedona Conference Commentary on Non–Party Production & Rule 45 Subpoenas 3* (2008):

Third parties may have obligations to preserve evidence relevant to others' litigation imposed by contract or other special relationship once they have notice of the existence of the dispute. Some courts place a burden on the party to have the non-party preserve the evidence. And at least one court has ruled that the issuance of a subpoena to a third party imposes a legal obligation on the third party to preserve information relevant to the subpoena including ESI, at least through the period of time it takes to comply with the subpoena and resolve any issues before the court.[32]

Case law does not require a non-party to continue to preserve materials after [it has] taken reasonable measures to produce responsive information. In some circumstances, however, the receipt of a subpoena may serve to notify a non-party that it may become a party in the litigation or in a future litigation. In that case the non-party should take affirmative steps to preserve documents responsive to the subpoena and the potential broader scope of the proceeding. However, service of and compliance with a nonparty subpoena is not, in and of itself, sufficient to serve as a notice of future litigation.

3. Is Some Information Protected From Disclosure by Federal Law?

A number of federal laws limit disclosure of information. The Health Insurance Portability and Accountability Act ("HIPAA") was enacted in 1996 to address various issues related to health insurance and medical care. One of the purposes of HIPAA is to provide uniform privacy protection for health care records. Title II of HIPAA provides extensive rules regarding the secure storage and exchange of electronic data transactions and requirements promoting the confidentiality and privacy of individually identifiable health information.

The Federal Wiretap Act prohibits the unauthorized interception and disclosure of wire, oral or electronic communications. "Electronic communication" includes e-mail, voice mail, cellular telephones, and satellite communications. Online communications are covered by the Act. Federal courts have consistently held that, in order to be intercepted, electronic communications must be acquired contemporaneously with transmission and that electronic communications are not intercepted within the meaning of the Act if they are retrieved from storage.[33]

The Electronic Communications Privacy Act ("ECPA"), discussed in *AOL*, *supra*, extensively amended the Federal Wiretap Act. The ECPA prohibits the interception of wire, oral, or electronic communications, or the use of electronic means to intercept oral communications or to disclose or use any communications that were illegally intercepted. ECPA restrictions regarding

---

32. *See In re Napster Copyright Litig.*, 462 F.Supp.2d 1060, 1068 (N.D. Cal. Oct. 25, 2006) (organization had legal obligation to preserve documents based on third-party subpoena).

33. *See, e.g. Theofel v. Farey–Jones*, 359 F.3d 1066, 1077 (9th Cir. 2004) (no "interception" occurred in violation of Wiretap Act when defendant allegedly gained unauthorized access to plaintiff's e-mails that were already delivered to recipients and stored electronically by plaintiff's Internet service provider).

disclosure of stored e-mail information facially apply only to public systems and e-mails stored within such systems.[34]

The Stored Communications and Transactional Records Act, created as part of the ECPA, prohibits certain access to electronic communications service facilities, as well as disclosure by such services of information contained on those facilities. It provides a private right of action against those who knowingly or intentionally violate the Act. The Act is sometimes useful for protecting the privacy of e-mail and other Internet communications when discovery is sought from a third-party provider.

The Act prohibits service providers from knowingly disclosing the contents of a communication to any person or entity while in electronic storage by that service. It also prohibits the service provider from knowingly disclosing to any governmental agency any record or other information pertaining to a subscriber of the service. Accordingly, most service providers will not disclose such information without a subpoena.[35]

In *Jessup–Morgan v. America Online, Inc.*, a subscriber sued AOL, alleging a violation of the Act, invasion of privacy, and other claims arising out of the provider's disclosure of her identity pursuant to a subpoena.[36] The plaintiff had posted messages inviting users to see sexual liaisons with her paramour's wife. The court held that disclosure of the subscriber's identity did not violate the Act because the Act specifically authorizes the disclosure of subscriber information to private parties.

The Computer Fraud and Abuse Act makes it illegal to access a "protected" computer under certain circumstances, including computers operated by or on behalf of financial institutions.[37] The Act also makes it a crime to intentionally access a computer without authorization or to exceed authorized access, and obtain information from any "protected computer" if the conduct involved an interstate or foreign communication. A "protected computer" is a computer: (1) used exclusively by a financial institution; or (2) used by or for a financial institution, and the conduct constituting the offense affects that use by or for the financial institution; or (3) used in interstate or foreign commerce or communication.[38]

PROBLEM

Draft a motion to quash a subpoena using the facts in *In re Subpoena Duces Tecum to AOL*.

---

34. *See, e.g., Andersen Consulting LLP v. UOP*, 991 F.Supp. 1041 (N.D. Ill. 1998) (holding proprietary system operated by employer was not public system, although accounting firm was permitted to use system during project).

35. *See Theofel v. Farey–Jones,* 359 F.3d 1066, 1073 (9th Cir. 2004) (disclosure by Internet service provider of customer's e-mail messages pursuant to an invalid and overly broad civil subpoena did not constitute "authorized" disclosure by the provider, as would allow the defendant to avoid liability under the Act).

36. 20 F. Supp. 2d 1105 (E.D. Mich. 1998).

37. 18 U.S.C. § 1030 *et seq.*

38. *See, e.g., International Airport Ctrs., LLC v. Citrin*, 440 F.3d 418 (7th Cir. 2006) (former employee's installation and use of secure-erasure program to delete files on employer-issued laptop prior to leaving that job was sufficient for employer to state a claim under Computer Fraud and Abuse Act).

J. CROSS–BORDER PRODUCTION ISSUES

BACKGROUND

Societe Nationale Industrielle Aerospatiale v. United States District Court for the Southern District of Iowa[39]

The plaintiffs in *Aerospatiale* were U.S. citizens who filed claims for negligence and breach of warranty against a French airplane manufacturer. Initial discovery was conducted pursuant to the Federal Rules of Civil Procedure without objection. However, upon plaintiffs' second request for the production of documents and admissions, the defendants filed a motion for a protective order. Defendants alleged that the Hague Convention, which prescribes certain procedures by which a judicial authority in one contracting state may request evidence located in another contracting state, dictated the exclusive procedures that must be followed for pretrial discovery. In addition, defendants argued that under French penal law, they could not respond to discovery requests that did not comply with the Hague Convention. A Magistrate Judge denied the motion, and the Court of Appeals denied defendants' mandamus petition, holding, *inter alia*, that when a district court has jurisdiction over a foreign litigant, the Hague Convention does not apply even though the information sought may be physically located within the territory of a foreign signatory to the Convention.

On appeal, the Supreme Court held that the Hague Convention does not provide exclusive or mandatory procedures for obtaining documents and information located in a foreign signatory's territory. Rather, the plain language of the Convention, as well as the history of its proposal and ratification by the U.S., "unambiguously supports the conclusion that it was intended to establish optional procedures that would facilitate the taking of evidence abroad." Accordingly, the Convention does not deprive district courts of their jurisdiction to order a foreign national party to produce evidence physically located within a signatory nation. Any contrary holding, the Court reasoned, would

> effectively subject every American court hearing a case involving a national of a contracting state to the internal laws of that state. Interrogatories and document requests are staples of international commercial litigation, no less than of other suits, yet a rule of exclusivity would subordinate the court's supervision of even the most routine of these pretrial proceedings to the actions or, equally, to the inactions of foreign judicial authorities.

The Court further noted that a rule of exclusivity would create three "unacceptable asymmetries." *First*, within any lawsuit between a national of the U.S. and a national of another contracting party, the foreign party could obtain discovery under the Federal Rules of Civil Procedure, while

---

39. 482 U.S. 522 (1987).

the domestic party would be required to resort first to the procedures of the Hague Convention. This imbalance would run counter to the fundamental maxim of discovery that "[m]utual knowledge of all the relevant facts gathered by both parties is essential to proper litigation." *Second*, a rule of exclusivity would enable a company that is a citizen of another contracting state to compete with a domestic company on uneven terms, since the foreign company would be subject to less extensive discovery procedures in the event that both companies were sued in an American court. The Court noted that the French airplane manufacturer "made a voluntary decision to market their products in the United States," and that as a result, "[t]hey are entitled to compete on equal terms with other companies operating in this market." Correspondingly, the French manufacturer was subject to the same discovery burdens associated with American judicial procedures as its American competitors. The Court reasoned that "[a] general rule according foreign nationals a preferred position in pretrial proceedings in our courts would conflict with the principle of equal opportunity that governs the market they elected to enter." *Third*, the Court noted that

> since a rule of first use of the Hague Convention would apply to cases in which a foreign party is a national of a contracting state, but not to cases in which a foreign party is a national of any other foreign state, the rule would confer an unwarranted advantage on some domestic litigants over others similarly situated.

The Court rejected the French manufacturer's argument that a rule of first resort to the Hague Convention procedures was necessary to accord respect to the sovereignty of states in which evidence was located. Even though the Court conceded that in civil law jurisdictions such as France, the process of obtaining evidence is normally conducted by a judicial officer rather than by private attorneys, if primacy or exclusivity were required it would have been described in the text of the treaty. The Court further reasoned that, in this context, the concept of international comity requires a particularized analysis of the respective interests of the foreign and requesting nations. Such analysis must include consideration of the particular facts of each case, the sovereign interests at issue, and the likelihood that resorting to the procedures of the Hague Convention would prove effective.

In a footnote, the Court explained that the

> French "blocking statute" . . . does not alter our conclusion. It is well settled that such statutes do not deprive an American court of the power to order a party subject to its jurisdiction to produce evidence even though the act of production may violate that statute. *See Societe Internationale Pour Participations Industrielles et Commerciales, S.A. v. Rogers*, 357 U.S. 197, 204–206 (1958). Nor can the enactment of such a statute by a foreign nation require American courts to engraft a rule of first resort onto the Hague Convention, or

otherwise to provide the nationals of such a country with a preferred status in our courts.

Justice Blackmun acknowledged in his concurring and dissenting opinion that "[s]ome might well regard the Court's decision in this case as an affront to the nations that have joined the United States in ratifying the Hague Convention on the Taking of Evidence." The dissent observed a risk in "relegating it to an 'optional' status, without acknowledging the significant achievement in accommodating divergent interests that the Convention represents." Justice Blackmun concluded as follows:

> I can only hope that courts faced with discovery requests for materials in foreign countries will avoid the parochial views that too often have characterized the decisions to date. Many of the considerations that lead me to the conclusion that there should be a general presumption favoring use of the Convention should also carry force when courts analyze particular cases. The majority fails to offer guidance in this endeavor, and thus it has missed its opportunity to provide predictable and effective procedures for international litigants in United States courts.

STRAUSS v. CREDIT LYONNAIS, S.A.

242 F.R.D. 199 (E.D.N.Y. 2007)

MATSUMOTO, MAGISTRATE JUDGE

* * * [P]laintiffs, United States citizens, and several estates, survivors and heirs of United States citizens, who are victims of terrorist attacks in Israel allegedly perpetrated by the Islamic Resistance Movement ("HAMAS"), allege that defendant Credit Lyonnais, S.A. ("Credit Lyonnais") is civilly liable for damages pursuant to 18 U.S.C. § 2333(a) for: (1) aiding and abetting the murder, attempted murder, and serious bodily injury of American nationals located outside the United States in violation of 18 U.S.C. § 2332; (2) knowingly providing material support or resources to a foreign terrorist organization in violation of 18 U.S.C. § 2339B; and (3) financing acts of terrorism, in violation of 18 U.S.C. § 2339C. On October 5, 2006, Judge Sifton granted defendant's motion to dismiss the first claim, but denied its motion as to the second and third claims.

* * *

BACKGROUND

Plaintiffs are individuals and estates, survivors and heirs of individuals who were injured or killed in thirteen separate terrorist attacks, allegedly perpetrated by HAMAS in Israel between March 28, 2002 and August 19, 2003. * * * Credit Lyonnais is a financial institution incorporated and headquartered in France * * * [and] conducts business in the United States and maintains an office at 601 Brickell Key Drive, Miami, Florida, 33131. Plaintiffs further allege that Credit Lyonnais maintains bank accounts in France for Le Comite de Bienfaisance et de Secours aux

Palestinians ("CBSP"), and that although CBSP describes itself as a charitable organization, it is part of HAMAS's fundraising infrastructure and a member of the Union of Good. The Union of Good, plaintiffs maintain, is an organization established by the Muslim Brotherhood and comprised of more than fifty Islamic charitable organizations worldwide, and is a "principal fundraising mechanism for HAMAS."

* * *

Plaintiffs allege that for more than thirteen years, defendant Credit Lyonnais "maintained an account for CBSP in Paris and provided HAMAS with material support in the form of financial services." Plaintiffs further allege that, through CBSP, Credit Lyonnais "has knowingly transferred significant sums of money to HAMAS-controlled entities" and "knowingly provided material support . . . to a designated FTO [Foreign Terrorist Organization], and has provided substantial assistance to HAMAS in the commission of acts of international terrorism in Israel, including the terrorist attacks that injured the plaintiffs." Accordingly, plaintiffs contend that Credit Lyonnais is civilly liable to them for damages pursuant to 18 U.S.C. § 2333(a), for providing "material support and resources" to a Specially Designated Global Terrorist ("SDGT") (in violation of § 2339B) and providing or collecting funds "with the knowledge that such funds are to be used" to support terrorism (in violation of § 2339C).

PLAINTIFFS' MOTION TO COMPEL

A. Plaintiffs' Discovery Requests.

On June 30, 2006, plaintiffs served Credit Lyonnais with their First Request for the Production of Documents. At issue are Document Requests Nos. 1–3, 11–13 and 15, in which plaintiffs request:

● No. 1: All account records maintained by, or in the custody and control of Defendant that concern CBSP, including account opening records, bank statements, wire transactions, deposit slips and all correspondence between Defendant and CBSP.

● No. 2: All documents and communications by or to Defendant concerning CBSP, including all internal reports and the contents of any internal investigations undertaken by Defendant that reference CBSP.

● No. 3: All non-privileged documents and communications by or to the Defendant from or to banking regulatory authorities in the United States, the Republic of France, or the European Union . . . concerning CBSP and or accounts maintained by the Defendant on CBSP's behalf.

● No. 11: All documents concerning Defendant's decision in January 2002 to close CBSP's accounts maintained by Credit Lyonnais including any documents that were the catalyst or basis of any decision to close or freeze said accounts.

● No. 12: All documents concerning Defendant's actual closure in January 2002 of CBSP's accounts maintained by Credit Lyonnais including any documents that were the catalyst or basis of any decision to close or freeze said accounts.

• No. 13: All documents concerning Credit Lyonnais's anti-money laundering efforts, "Know Your Customer" procedures, or other measures Credit Lyonnais used to prevent the rendering of financial services to Terrorists and Terrorist Organizations.

• No. 15: Copies of all internal Credit Lyonnais documents related to the following subjects and/or departments: [enumerating departments and procedures for account opening, security, customer accounts, compliance, internal audits, bank secrecy and terror financing designations or warnings].

* * *

In response, Credit Lyonnais objected to * * * plaintiffs' Document Requests * * * on the grounds that, inter alia, the requests,

> seek the disclosure of commercial and financial information in violation of Article 1 bis of French law No. 68–678 ("Article 1 bis"), which prohibits such disclosure in connection with a foreign judicial proceeding, except pursuant to an enforceable international treaty or agreement. Under Article 1 bis, [Credit Lyonnais] would be exposed to liability under French law unless disclosure proceeds in accordance with the Convention of 18 March 1970 on the Taking of Evidence Abroad in Civil or Commercial Matters (the "Hague Convention"), 23 U.S.T. 2555, TIAS 7444, 847 UNTS 231, to which France and the United States are parties. Such liability would be avoided by following Hague Convention procedures, which should therefore be followed here.

In addition, Credit Lyonnais also objected to all discovery requests, to the extent they seek the disclosure of information and/or production of documents in violation of applicable French laws prohibiting the disclosure of information relating to a criminal investigation. The knowing disclosure of the existence and/or substance of a criminal investigation with the objective of adversely affecting criminal proceedings constitutes a criminal offense under French law and is sanctionable by imprisonment and substantial monetary penalties under Article L 434–7–2 of the French Criminal Code.

As discussed herein, Articles 11 and L 434–7–2 of the French Criminal Code prohibit disclosure of information relating to a criminal investigation to persons "likely to be involved as perpetrators, co-perpetrators, accomplices or receivers in the commission of these infractions ... for the purpose of interfering with the progress of the investigations or the search for the truth...."

Credit Lyonnais also objected to plaintiffs' discovery requests on the grounds that they "seek the disclosure of information in violation of applicable French bank customer secrecy obligations" and "applicable French anti-money laundering laws." Credit Lyonnais further noted that failure to comply with the above regulations "constitutes a criminal offense under French law and is sanctionable by imprisonment and a substantial monetary penalty under Article 226–13 of the French Criminal Code."

In order to avoid civil and criminal liability under these statutes, Credit Lyonnais twice "requested [CBSP] to release [Credit Lyonnais] from its secrecy obligations in order to permit disclosure of information in [Credit Lyonnais's] possession related to CBSP." On July 20 and September 14, 2006, the bank's French counsel sent letters to CBSP's counsel, and has yet to receive any substantive response. Instead, CBSP's counsel simply objected to disclosing correspondence between counsel for CBSP and counsel for Credit Lyonnais. Credit Lyonnais has also sought the French government's guidance regarding plaintiffs' discovery demands by sending two letters and leaving one follow-up phone message with the French Ministry of Justice, but similarly has received no response.

* * *

C.   The [Relevant Factors] * * *.

In determining whether to compel production of documents located abroad from foreign parties, courts in the Second Circuit consider the following * * * factors elucidated by the Supreme Court in *Aerospatiale* and set forth in Restatement of Foreign Relations Law of the United States § 442(1)(c):

- the importance to the ... litigation of the documents or other information requested;

- the degree of specificity of the request;

- whether the information originated in the United States;

- the availability of alternative means of securing the information;
  * * *

- the extent to which noncompliance with the request would undermine important interests of the United States, or compliance with the request would undermine the important interests of the state where the information is located;

- the competing interests of the nations whose laws are in conflict;

- the hardship of compliance on the party or witness from whom discovery is sought.

* * *

Having already considered the third factor—noting that the information sought by plaintiffs' discovery requests did not originate in the United States—the court will consider the remaining six factors, beginning with the first.

1. The requested information is crucial to the litigation.

* * *

* * * Given plaintiffs' allegations regarding Credit Lyonnais's provision of financial services to CBSP for more than thirteen years, including accepting deposits from and/or distributing funds to alleged terrorist organizations on behalf of CBSP the court finds that the discovery sought is both relevant and crucial to the litigation of plaintiffs' claims. Because the documents and information sought by plaintiffs are highly relevant and important to the claims and defenses in this action, the court finds that this second factor weighs heavily in plaintiffs' favor.

2. The discovery requests are narrowly tailored.

Rst. § 442(1)(c) also provides, "[A] court or agency in the United States should take into account ... the degree of specificity of the request...." * * * Here, the court finds that the requested discovery is relevant, vital and narrowly tailored to the litigation. * * * Plaintiffs' discovery requests are sufficiently focused on the vital issues in this case: whether and to what extent Credit Lyonnais knowingly provided "material support and resources" to Specially Designated Terrorist Organizations, and/or "financial services" to a terrorist organization. Plaintiffs' discovery requests seek, inter alia, documentation of the relationship between defendant and CBSP, the nature and extent of the services that defendant provided to CBSP, the collection or distribution of funds by Credit Lyonnais that may have been used by CBSP and/or its associates to support terrorism, and Credit Lyonnais's knowledge of CBSP's alleged terrorist connections. * * * Plaintiffs have established that their discovery demands are specifically tailored to their claims.

3. Availability of alternative methods: plaintiffs are not required to seek discovery initially or exclusively through the Hague Convention.

Section § 442(1)(c) of the Restatement also requires the court to consider the "availability of alternate means of securing the information...." The court notes that plaintiffs do not have direct or ready access to Credit Lyonnais's records through means other than discovery demands. Only Credit Lyonnais can provide plaintiffs with responses to their requested discovery.

Credit Lyonnais argues that plaintiffs "may be able to obtain the discovery they seek through letters of request pursuant to the Hague Convention...." Both France and the United States are signatories to the Hague Convention, which provides internationally agreed-upon means for conducting discovery in foreign states and which defendant here urges plaintiffs to use. As a signatory to the Hague Convention, France generally has agreed to produce documents sought by foreign courts by responding to letters rogatory from the requesting party.

The United States Supreme Court, in *Aerospatiale,* determined that parties seeking discovery need not resort to the Hague Convention as their first and exclusive means for securing foreign discovery, explaining:

> An interpretation of the Hague Convention as the exclusive means for obtaining evidence located abroad would effectively subject every American court hearing a case involving a national of a [signatory] state to the internal laws of that state. Interrogatories and document requests are staples of international ... litigation, no less than of other suits, yet a rule of exclusivity would subordinate the court's supervision of even the most routine of these pretrial proceedings to the actions or, equally, to the inactions of foreign judicial authorities.

* * *

Addressing the applicability of French blocking statutes, the Court continued,

> It is clear that American courts are not required to adhere blindly to the directives of [a foreign blocking statute]. Indeed, the language of the statute, if taken literally, would appear to represent an extraordinary exercise of legislative jurisdiction by the Republic of France over a United States district judge, forbidding him or her to order any discovery from a party of French nationality, even simple requests for admissions or interrogatories that the party could respond to on the basis of personal knowledge.... Extraterritorial assertions of jurisdiction are not one-sided.

Therefore, plaintiffs in this case need not seek discovery initially or exclusively through the Hague Convention, but, instead, may appropriately seek from this court an order compelling discovery. The court notes, however, that although plaintiffs are not required to resort to the Hague Convention, they are not discouraged from doing so.

4. The mutual interests of the United States and France in combating terrorism outweigh the French interest, if any, regarding the disputed discovery.

The comity factor-requiring analysis of the competing interests of the United States and France "is of the greatest importance in determining whether to defer to the foreign jurisdiction." The court finds that this factor weighs strongly in favor of plaintiffs. The interests of the United States and France in combating terrorist financing, as evidenced by the legislative history of the ATA, * * * Presidential Executive Orders, and both countries' participation in international treaties and task forces aimed at disrupting terrorist financing, outweigh the French interest, if any, in precluding Credit Lyonnais from responding to plaintiffs' discovery requests. Indeed, France's interest in having Credit Lyonnais respond to plaintiffs' discovery requests is evident from France's execution of international treaties facilitating international cooperation to combat terrorism, and its requirement that banks monitor and report customer ties to terrorists.

* * *

France, like the United States, also has expressed and demonstrated a profound and compelling interest in eliminating terrorist financing. That France has an interest in eradicating the financing of terrorism by imposing monitoring and reporting obligations on its banks regarding customers who finance, or may be suspected of financing, terrorist acts around the world, is established by the fact that France has signed international treaties that mandate such monitoring and disclosure and explicitly direct the member countries to cooperate in legal proceedings against suspected terrorist financing groups. Along with the United States, France is a signatory to the United Nation[s] International Convention for the Suppression of the Financing of Terrorism. Article 12 of the Convention provides,

> 1.   States Parties shall afford one another the greatest measure of assistance in connection with criminal investigations or criminal or extradition proceedings in respect of the offenses set forth in article 2, including assistance in obtaining evidence in their possession necessary for the proceedings.

> 2.   States Parties may not refuse a request for mutual legal assistance on the ground of bank secrecy.

Although Article 12 prescribes assistance and cooperation among signatory nations in connection with criminal investigations and extradition proceedings, plaintiffs' action seeking compensation for victims of international terrorist attacks and discovery from a bank alleged to be providing material support to terrorists, is not inconsistent with the French and American interests in international cooperation to detect and fight global terror.

* * *

Accordingly, ordering Credit Lyonnais to provide plaintiffs with discovery would not "undermine the important interests of the state where the information is located," but rather, enforce them.

* * *

5.   Credit Lyonnais will not face substantial hardship by complying with plaintiffs' requests.

* * *

Credit Lyonnais argues that, because the "French laws prohibiting [Credit Lyonnais's] production of the discovery sought by plaintiffs are valid and enforceable," it would face substantial hardship by complying with plaintiffs' requests. The bank "and its personnel would incur substantial civil, administrative and criminal liability—including fines, imprisonment and the prospect of lawsuits—if they were to violate those laws. . . ." Credit Lyonnais also asserts that it would "suffer enormous professional and reputational hardship if it betrayed its customer's confidence by disclosing the customer's protected information in violation of French bank secrecy laws." Glaringly absent from the submission by Credit Lyonnais is any indication that civil or criminal prosecutions by the French government or civil suits by CBSP are likely, rather than mere possibilities. * * * [C]ourts have already considered and found unpersuasive the potential imposition of the same penalties Credit Lyonnais cites here. The Supreme Court examined Articles 1–3 of French Penal Code Law No. 80–538, the French blocking statute, and ordered discovery notwithstanding the penalties that could be imposed, stating, "It is clear that American courts are not required to adhere blindly to the directives of such a statute." *Aerospatiale*, 482 U.S. at 544. [The court cites other cases reviewing the French blocking statutes at issue in this case; those cases conclude that the blocking statutes would not prevent disclosure in cases similar to this one.]

Although Credit Lyonnais has demonstrated that French bank secrecy laws have been enforced, the bank has failed to demonstrate that either CBSP or the French government would likely seek to sanction the bank for complying with a United States court order compelling disclosure of documents and information regarding CBSP's accounts. CBSP has shown no interest in protecting, much less asserting, its privacy right, as established by [the fact that] the French government has failed to submit any objections to producing the requested information, in response to three inquiries by Credit Lyonnais.* * * Despite Credit Lyonnais's assertions that the "professional and reputational consequences" would be severe if it "betrayed its customer's confidence," * * * France * * * has warned financial institutions that they could be exposed "to significant reputational, operational and legal risk" if they engage in business relationships with "high risk" customers such as charities collecting funds related to terrorist activities.

Furthermore, on March 10, 2006, the court entered a confidentiality order in this case, which further lessens Credit Lyonnais's potential hardship.

Credit Lyonnais has not demonstrated any likelihood that it will be pursued civilly or criminally if it responds to plaintiffs' discovery requests, particularly where the French interest in preventing terrorist financing through monitoring and reporting is so clearly demonstrated, and neither France nor CBSP have indicated that it objects to the bank responding to plaintiffs' discovery. Thus, "the goals of the plaintiffs in this case clearly are consistent with the objectives of the French Government, as evidenced by that government's" domestic laws incorporating international recommendations to combat terrorist financing.

6. Credit Lyonnais has acted in good faith.

The last factor courts in this Circuit consider in determining whether to order production is "the good faith shown by the party resisting discovery." * * * In this case, Credit Lyonnais has made at least two efforts to contact CBSP for its consent for Credit Lyonnais to respond to plaintiffs' discovery requests, and at least three efforts to contact the French Ministry of Justice for guidance. By sending two letters each to CBSP and the French government, and leaving one telephone message with the French Ministry, the defendant has made "good faith, diligent efforts" to secure discovery.

However, "notwithstanding [a litigant's] good faith, [the court is] not precluded from issuing a production order." The court notes that the bank's second attempts to contact CBSP and the French Ministry were made following court orders to do so. Therefore, "[w]hile evincing a measure of good faith, the Court is not convinced that defendant's efforts, are sufficient to tilt the balance in its favor," and against disclosure.

CONCLUSION

* * * [T]he mutual interests of the United States and France in thwarting terrorist financing outweighs the French interest in preserving bank customer secrecy–especially where France has not expressed an interest in precluding discovery responses pursuant to its bank secrecy or other statutes, and has demonstrated its national interest in cooperating in international efforts to detect, monitor and report customer links to terrorist organizations, and freeze funds used for terrorist financing. Notably, Credit Lyonnais has shown a specific interest in CBSP, having investigated CBSP's connections to terrorism and/or money laundering, reported CBSP's activities * * * and, presumably detecting a connection with terrorism and/or money laundering, closed CBSP's accounts. In addition, the requested discovery originated outside of the United States, is crucial to this litigation and is specifically tailored to the issues in this case. Plaintiffs do not have viable alternative means of securing the discovery, as the Hague Convention can be costly, uncertain and time-consuming, and only Credit Lyonnais or CBSP have access to the requested records. Moreover, although Credit Lyonnais has made good faith efforts to provide the requested discovery, Credit Lyonnais has not demonstrated that it is likely to face substantial hardship by complying with plaintiffs' discovery requests. * * *

Accordingly, by June 25, 2007, Credit Lyonnais shall produce all documents responsive to plaintiffs' Document Requests * * *.

COMMENTARY

Cross-border electronic discovery poses a "Catch–22" situation in which the need to gather relevant information from foreign jurisdictions may squarely conflict with blocking statutes and data privacy regulations that prohibit or restrict such discovery—often upon threat of severe civil and criminal sanctions. Cross-border discovery has become a major source of international legal conflict,[40] and at the heart of this conflict are vastly differing notions of discovery and data privacy and protection.[41]

Federal courts in the U.S. are often skeptical of efforts to preclude the discovery of relevant information from a foreign parent or affiliate. And the frequency and intensity of these conflicts are heightened by an expanding global marketplace and the proliferation of ESI. The conviction in 2007 of a French attorney for seeking information relating to U.S.-based litigation may cause courts in the U.S. to revisit their consistent rulings, described below, that compel cross-border discovery notwithstanding foreign blocking statutes or data protection and privacy regulations.[42]

A number of cases have addressed the conflict between the interest of a party to a U.S. litigation in obtaining discovery of foreign electronic information and the foreign entity's interest in privacy.

1. *Columbia Pictures, Inc. v. Bunnell*[43]

In *Columbia Pictures, Inc. v. Bunnell*, discussed at length in Chapter II, *supra*, the defendants had engaged a third-party web hosting service in the Netherlands just a month prior to the Magistrate Judge's evidentiary hearing on the issue of whether RAM data had to be preserved and produced. The defendants argued that they could not provide the requested discovery because to do so would violate a Dutch blocking statute, and thus subject them to civil and criminal penalties. The defendants additionally cited an opinion of the Amsterdam District Court, which held that

> [a] service provider may, in certain circumstances, be obliged to provide rights holders (or their representatives) with the information asked for. For this, the Court must first of all be satisfied that there have been (unlawful) infringement activities by the subscribers concerned and, secondly, that it is beyond reasonable doubt that those whose identifying information is made available are also actually those who have been guilty of the relevant activities.[44]

Relying upon the Supreme Court's holding in *Aerospatiale, supra*, the *Columbia Pictures* court emphasized that " '[foreign] statutes do not deprive an American court of the power to order a party subject to its jurisdiction to produce evidence even though the act of production may violate that statute.' "Even assuming that Netherlands law prohibited the discovery at issue, the court concluded that the Magistrate Judge's decision ordering discovery was based on the proper legal standard and the applicable balancing test.

---

40. *See Restatement (Third) of Foreign Relations* § 442 Reporters' Note, n.1 (1987).

41. *See* EU Data Protection Directive 95/46/EC restricting the processing and transfer of "personal data," which is defined as any data that identifies, or can result in the identification of a person.

42. *See In re Advocat "Christopher X,"* Cour de Cassation, French Supreme Court, Dec. 12, 2007, Appeal no. 07–83228.

43. 245 F.R.D. 443 (C.D. Cal. 2007).

44. *Id.* at 453 (citing *BREIN Foundation v. UPC Nederland B.V.*, Fabrizio Decl. Ex. 28).

2. *Lyondell–Citgo Refining, LP v. Petroleos De Venezuela, S.A.*[45]

In response to a discovery dispute between the plaintiff, a Texas-based owner of an oil refinery, and the defendant, the Venezuelan national oil company, the Magistrate Judge ordered the defendant to produce the requested Board of Director minutes and other documents. Because the defendant responded to the plaintiff's discovery requests, which had been pending for months, "on the 11th hour, if not the 13th hour," the court reasoned that the defendant could not be trusted to review the disputed material. Accordingly, the Magistrate Judge gave the plaintiff the "unusual opportunity" to search the Board minutes directly for relevant and responsive documents. The defendant objected to the discovery order, claiming that the documents contained classified information relating to national security, and that disclosure of this material would subject the defendant to criminal penalties under Venezuelan law. The district court affirmed the discovery order, but the defendant persisted in its objection based on Venezuelan law and sought reconsideration.

In again denying the defendant's request to set aside the Magistrate Judge's order, the district court explained that the defendant did not provide any additional information that might compel a different finding. The district court had previously applied a balancing test to determine the reasonableness of ordering discovery from the foreign defendant, and concluded that the possibility of criminal penalties was not sufficiently strong to impede discovery. Holding otherwise based on defendant's objection, which contained only generalized statements about the need to protect national security, would grant any government or government-related party an "unfair advantage over its adversary." Because the defendant neither provided precise reasons for asserting confidentiality, nor confined the assertion of privilege to a narrow set of documents, and given the highly deferential standard of review applicable to a Magistrate's non-dispositive discovery rulings, the district court found that the Magistrate Judge was not clearly erroneous in ordering the production of the disputed documents.

---

45. No. 02 Civ. 0795, 2005 WL 356808 (S.D.N.Y. Feb. 15, 2005).

V

SPOLIATION AND SANCTIONS

■ ■ ■

A. WHAT CONSTITUTES SPOLIATION?

1. Definition and Standard

CONNOR v. SUN TRUST BANK

546 F. Supp. 2d 1360 (N.D. Ga. 2008)

VINING, DISTRICT JUDGE

This action is brought under the Family and Medical Leave Act of 1993 ("FMLA"), 29 U.S.C. §§ 2601–19 (2000). The plaintiff alleges that her former employer, Sun Trust, violated the FMLA by interfering with her substantive rights and retaliating against her for engaging in protected activity. After conducting discovery, the plaintiff has filed a Motion for Sanctions for Destruction of Evidence * * *. For the following reasons, the motion for sanctions is granted * * *.

I. FACTUAL BACKGROUND

The plaintiff is a former vice president level employee of Sun Trust who began her employment in 2004. Throughout her employment, the plaintiff worked in Sun Trust's Business Performance Group ("BPG"), a division of the Enterprise Information Services ("EIS") department, and she reported to BPG Manager Leslie Weigel. Toward the end of her employment, the plaintiff's duties included managing internal communications for EIS and serving as communications manager for Sun Trust's Project 2010, a joint project between Sun Trust and IBM to improve the delivery of technology projects to Sun Trust; she also managed Sun Trust's Enterprise Publication Services ("EPS") group, which handled internal communications to Sun Trust employees about bank operating procedures and policies. As part of her responsibilities with the EIS communications team, Project 2010, and the EPS group, the plaintiff was given responsibility in June 2006 to manage eight employees assigned to these various groups.

* * *

254

In November 2006, the plaintiff adopted a child and took two months of FMLA leave starting on November 8, 2006, and ending on January 2, 2007. * * * While the plaintiff was on FMLA leave, her responsibilities for the EPS group were taken away. In December 2006, one of the EPS group employees, Mr. Swanson, unexpectedly resigned. The three EPS group employees were located in Orlando (the plaintiff was located in Atlanta) and Mr. Swanson served as the on-site supervisor for the other two EPS group employees. After Mr. Swanson resigned, Ms. Weigel, the plaintiff's supervisor and business manager of BPG, approached Ms. Bitzis, the senior manager of the Banking Services department, which was another department of EIS that had a large team co-located in the same Orlando building. They discussed transferring the EPS group and its two remaining junior-level members to the Banking Services department.

The resignation of the on-site supervisor for the EPS group in Orlando created a "supervision gap" that the plaintiff contends would have been filled by her had she not been on FMLA leave. Sun Trust disputes this point and asserts that even if the plaintiff had not been on leave, Sun Trust still would have faced the "supervision gap" because the plaintiff could not have provided direct supervision over the two Orlando-based employees from her office in Atlanta. In any event, Sun Trust maintains that having Banking Services absorb the EPS group was in the best long-term interests of EPS and that it would have happened even if the plaintiff had not been on FMLA leave at the time. * * * [I]t is her loss of three out of six employees as a result of the transfer of the EPS group while she was out on leave that the plaintiff asserts substantially diminished her management position and converted it into something less than full time.

On January 2, 2007, the plaintiff returned to work. About eleven days after the plaintiff had returned, her supervisor, Ms. Weigel, decided to fire the plaintiff, and informed her of the decision two weeks later. Approximately two weeks after notifying the plaintiff, Ms. Weigel sent an email to the senior management team of EIS on February 12, 2007, informing them that the plaintiff's job had been eliminated.

The plaintiff asserts that the reason her supervisor fired her was because of the removal of all but three of the plaintiff's direct reports. According to the plaintiff, the removal of her direct reports and changes in job responsibilities substantially diminished her job and thus violated her rights under the FMLA. She further contends that this reason is confirmed in an email sent by Ms. Weigel on February 12, 2007 ("February 12 email"), in which Ms. Weigel states that the reason the plaintiff's position was eliminated was based on the changes to the plaintiff's teams and the reduction from eight to three people being managed by her. Sun Trust disputes the reasoning for the plaintiff's termination and suggests that the reduction in direct reports is only part of the justification. Another reason was, for example, that the changes in the make-up of the plaintiff's teams supported a determination that the plaintiff's functions could be absorbed by other members of BPG and no longer justified keeping the plaintiff's position. Nevertheless, Sun Trust does not dispute that Ms. Weigel told the BPG team that the reason she fired the plaintiff was because she could not justify the plaintiff's position with only three remaining direct reports. Irrespective of how Ms. Weigel justified her decision, Sun Trust asserts that the facts show plaintiff was terminated for reasons wholly unrelated to her FMLA leave and thus do not violate her rights under the FMLA.

B. Motion for Sanctions

With respect to the February 12 email, the plaintiff has put that document into the record as evidence of illegal interference with her substantive rights under the FMLA. The email from Ms. Weigel informs her team about her decision to eliminate the plaintiff's position and states.

> All,
>
> I wanted to let you know that all of my team has received the information about my decision to eliminate the [plaintiff's] Comms manager position as of the end of March. Maria has talked with her team as well. You are free to discuss it with your team as you see fit.
>
> A couple of talking points—
>
> 1. My decision was based on the changes to the make-up of the team that resulted in a reduction from 8 to 3 people being managed, by this position[.]
>
> 2. The remaining 3 people ... will begin reporting directly to me.
>
> Let me know if you have other questions. Thanks, Leslie

Notably, Sun Trust did not produce this email during discovery; the plaintiff procured it through other means. It is undisputed that had the plaintiff not happened to otherwise come by the February 12 email she would not have known of its existence despite its obvious relevance to her claims and Sun Trust's duty to produce it. Sun Trust's failure to produce this relevant document is the basis for the plaintiff's motion for sanctions.

On or about February 21, 2007, approximately nine days after the February 12 email, Sun Trust received a letter from the plaintiff's attorney advising Sun Trust of her FMLA claims and the likelihood of litigation. The plaintiff's attorney also cautioned Sun Trust to identify and preserve all relevant documents relating to the plaintiff's termination. In view of the plaintiff's claims and aware of Sun Trust's obligation to take affirmative steps to preserve all relevant documents, Sun Trust's Senior Vice President and Deputy General Counsel for Regulatory Affairs, Brian Edwards, initiated an internal investigation. Within days he identified employees likely to possess relevant information and issued preservation instructions to Ms. Weigel (the plaintiff's supervisor), Ms. Drury (human resources representative to BPG), and Sue Johnson (head of human resources and Ms. Drury's supervisor), among others. Mr. Edwards' preservation instructions included express guidance to identify and preserve all documents in their possession, including email communications, that related to the plaintiff's termination.

The preservation instructions were issued and received on or about February 22, 2007, approximately ten days after the February 12 email was sent. It is undisputed that at least two employees, Ms. Weigel (the February 12 email sender) and Ms. Johnson (one of the February 12 email recipients), would have been in possession of the February 12 email at the time they received the preservation instructions absent some affirmative action on their part to delete the message prior to receiving the instructions.

The timing of the email and the preservation instructions is important because Sun Trust's email system automatically deletes all emails from the company's server that are more than thirty days old. To preserve an email and prevent it from being automatically deleted, employees must take steps to archive their messages outside of the email system. While Sun Trust does back up its email servers on a daily basis for disaster recovery purposes, the backup tapes are retained for only seven to ten days before being overwritten. Consequently, an email deleted immediately after being sent or received by an employee will survive on the server only seven to ten days; meanwhile, an email not archived and retained on an employee's server account for the maximum thirty days will survive on the server for up to thirty-seven to forty days. Thus, any inquiry into whether an employee had access to a relevant email for purposes of preservation requires determining the amount of time between when the email was first on the email server and when preservation should have commenced. It is also necessary to inquire into what, if any, steps were taken to delete a message before preservation instructions were given.

With respect to Ms. Weigel's actions concerning preservation of related documents and in particular emails, it is her failure to preserve and produce her February 12 email that is primarily the basis for the plaintiff's motion. It is undisputed that Ms. Weigel failed to preserve the February 12 email after she had been instructed to do so on or about February 22. This of course assumes that the February 12 email was still on Ms. Weigel's server account or had been archived at least ten days after it was sent. Sun Trust has stated that although she does not archive every email, Ms. Weigel does employ a general practice of archiving her email messages from her inbox and her sent mail folders weekly.

After Ms. Weigel was instructed on about February 22 to identify and preserve all documents relevant to the plaintiff's claims, including emails, she searched her email archives and provided relevant emails to Sun Trust's counsel. However, she did not provide the February 12 email. On or about September 10, 2007, when the plaintiff produced a copy of the February 12 email, Ms. Weigel again searched her email archive to determine if she had overlooked that particular message when gathering relevant documents. At that point, Ms. Weigel apparently realized that she had a gap in her sent email archive for the period of January 1, 2007, through February 18, 2007, thus indicating that she had indeed not archived the February 12 email or any others during that period.

The obvious effect of the gap in archived sent emails was that by mid-March (long before the plaintiff advised Sun Trust of the existence of the February 12 email) those emails would have been deleted for having been on the Sun Trust's email server over thirty days. Consequently, when Ms. Weigel went to redo the search of her email messages, she naturally could not locate the February 12 email if it had not been archived. * * * Sun Trust asserts that the reason for the gap in Ms. Weigel's archived sent items is because Ms. Weigel apparently did not follow her usual practice of archiving all of her sent email for the relevant time period. This apparently happens when Ms. Weigel is very busy and falls behind in her archiving routine.

With respect to Ms. Johnson, she similarly undertook a search for all relevant documents in her possession, including emails, sometime between February 22 (when she was given the preservation instruction) and March 5 (the date Sun Trust's counsel met with Ms. Weigel and Ms. Drury, and the date by which counsel had already received Ms. Johnson's documents). However, Ms. Johnson also did not produce the February 12 email though Sun Trust admits she received the message. It is apparently Ms. Johnson's usual practice to delete all incoming messages that do not require her follow-up. Based on this, Sun Trust asserts that Ms. Johnson likely deleted the email as soon as she received it because the February 12 email required no action from Ms. Johnson and because she was already aware of Ms. Weigel's decision to terminate the plaintiff. Assuming that she did delete the message soon after receipt, it would have been unavailable for her or Sun Trust to preserve. Consequently, the February 12 email allegedly no longer existed on Ms. Johnson's email profile on the server when she was given the preservation instructions and, therefore, it could not have been produced by her.

II. ANALYSIS

* * *

The plaintiff * * * moves this court for spoliation sanctions against Sun Trust for destroying the February 12 email. A court may sanction a party for spoliation of evidence by (1) dismissing the case, (2) excluding expert testimony, or (3) issuing jury instructions that raise a presumption against the spoliator. *Flury v. Daimler Chrysler Corp.*, 427 F.3d 939, 945 (11th Cir. 2005). To determine whether spoliation has occurred, a court must address five factors: (1) prejudice to the non-spoiling party as a result of the destruction of evidence, (2) whether the prejudice can be cured, (3) practical importance of the evidence, (4) whether the spoiling party acted in good or bad faith, and (5) the potential for abuse of expert testimony about evidence not excluded. *Id.*

With respect to the first factor, this court concludes that the plaintiff has been prejudiced by Sun Trust's failure to produce the February 12 email during discovery. Although it is true that the plaintiff obtained the February 12 email through other means, that fact does not alleviate the damage done to the plaintiff's case when very relevant evidence, such as the February 12 email, is not produced during discovery and is subsequently destroyed by operation of Sun Trust's automatic deletion of emails that are more than thirty days old and not archived. If relevant evidence is not produced, for whatever reason, and then is destroyed before either party learns of the existence of that evidence, then the absence of the relevant evidence prejudices the party that would have relied on it to prove its case.

Here, the prejudice to the plaintiff is more attenuated than the prejudice present in *Flury*. In that case, the plaintiff brought a product liability claim against a vehicle manufacturer for injury caused by the failure of a vehicle's airbag to deploy during a collision. However, the plaintiff allowed the vehicle to be destroyed and, consequently, the defendant was prejudiced because it could not examine the vehicle's condition or airbag control unit. In this case, the prejudice resulting from Sun Trust's failure to produce an undisputedly relevant email raises a concern that * * * there were other relevant emails in existence at that time but which were also not produced, and there is no satisfactory answer because all emails not archived by the email users had since been automatically deleted from the server.

With respect to the second and third factors, this court concludes that the prejudice to the plaintiff can be cured and that the evidence is important to her case because such evidence, like the February 12 email, goes directly to Sun Trust's reasons for terminating her employment.

With respect to the fourth factor, this court concludes that Sun Trust acted in bad faith. This determination requires weighing Sun Trust's culpability against the resulting prejudice to the plaintiff, but it does not require a finding of malice. Here, the conduct of Ms. Weigel is particularly important because she sent the February 12 email and, as the plaintiff's direct supervisor, made the decision to terminate the plaintiff. However, approximately ten days after sending the February 12 email, Ms. Weigel failed to produce it in response to Sun Trust counsel's preservation instructions. Assuming, as Sun Trusts argues, that Ms. Weigel did not employ her general practice of weekly archiving her sent items, that nevertheless does not explain why she failed to preserve the document. The February 12 email still would have been in Ms. Weigel's account on Sun Trust's email server for approximately another twenty days until the system automatically deleted the email for being over thirty days old. The only way Ms. Weigel could not have preserved the February 12 email when she conducted her search of relevant emails, again assuming that she inadvertently failed to archive the message, was if she had affirmatively deleted the February 12 email from her sent items before the thirty day limit had expired. Moreover, it is doubtful that Ms. Weigel was not aware of the direct relevance of her February 12 email a mere ten days after she had sent it. In view of these facts, Ms. Weigel and, therefore, Sun Trust was at least minimally culpable for the failure to disclose the February 12 email. As discussed above, the failure to disclose the February 12 email prejudiced the plaintiff and, therefore, Sun Trust acted in bad faith.

With respect to the fifth factor, this court concludes that there is a potential for abuse. Although the leading cases on spoliation sanctions * * * involve the potential for abuse by experts, the analysis under this fifth spoliation factor is focused on whether the non-spoliating party, despite its ability to present evidence in support of its claims, has had a full opportunity to discover the most relevant and most reliable evidence. Here, the plaintiff has not had such an opportunity because Sun Trust's failure to produce what is arguably the most relevant email raises doubts about its assertions that there were never any others in existence. The absence of any other relevant emails, other than the February 12 email which Sun Trust did not produce, raises the potential for abuse by Sun Trust, albeit slight, because even the mere non-existence of emails relating to Sun Trust's reasons for terminating the plaintiff can support Sun Trust's defense that it did not interfere with the plaintiff's FMLA rights or terminate her in retaliation for exercising those rights.

Therefore, this court concludes spoliation of evidence has occurred and that sanctions are warranted against Sun Trust. This spoliation, however, can be cured by a sanction less severe than outright dismissal. In view of the minimal culpability of Sun Trust and the slight potential for abuse, the court will instruct the jury as to the appropriate inference to draw from the absence of evidence.

2. Culpability—Intentional, Bad Faith, Grossly Negligent, or Negligent Conduct

RESIDENTIAL FUNDING CORP. v. DeGEORGE FINANCIAL CORP.

306 F.3d 99 (2d Cir. 2002)

CABRANES, CIRCUIT JUDGE

We consider here the standard district courts should employ in determining whether a party's failure to comply with discovery requests warrants the imposition of sanctions.

DeGeorge Financial Corp., DeGeorge Home Alliance, Inc., and De-George Capital Corp. (collectively, "DeGeorge") appeal from a final judgment in favor of Residential Funding Corporation ("RFC") entered by the United States District Court * * * after a jury trial on cross-claims for breach of contract. On appeal, DeGeorge challenges only the District Court's denial of its motion for sanctions—in the form of an adverse inference instruction—for RFC's failure to produce certain e-mails in time for trial. The District Court denied the motion based on its finding that the delay in producing the e-mails was not caused by an action of RFC that was taken in bad faith or with gross negligence and its finding that

DeGeorge had not shown that the missing e-mails would be favorable to its case.

We hold that (1) where, as here, the nature of the alleged breach of a discovery obligation is the non-production of evidence, a District Court has broad discretion in fashioning an appropriate sanction, including the discretion to delay the start of a trial (at the expense of the party that breached its obligation), to declare a mistrial if trial has already commenced, or to proceed with a trial with an adverse inference instruction; (2) discovery sanctions, including an adverse inference instruction, may be imposed where a party has breached a discovery obligation not only through bad faith or gross negligence, but also through ordinary negligence; (3) a judge's finding that a party acted with gross negligence or in bad faith with respect to discovery obligations is ordinarily sufficient to support a finding that the missing or destroyed evidence would have been harmful to that party, even if the destruction or unavailability of the evidence was not caused by the acts constituting bad faith or gross negligence; and (4) in the instant case, the District Court applied the wrong standard in deciding DeGeorge's motion for sanctions.

Accordingly, we vacate the order of the District Court denying DeGeorge's motion for sanctions and remand with instructions for a renewed hearing on discovery sanctions.

I. Background

This litigation involved cross-claims for, inter alia, breach of contract, with the parties' dispute centered principally on events in the latter part of 1998. RFC initiated the case by filing suit on January 15, 1999 * * *.

* * *

On January 4, 2001, the parties held a discovery planning conference * * *. At that meeting, the parties agreed that discovery would commence "immediately" and be completed by August 1, 2001, and that the case would be ready for trial by September 1, 2001. On January 19, 2001, the District Court entered a scheduling order reflecting the parties' agreed-upon discovery schedule.

On April 12, 2001, DeGeorge served its document discovery requests, which included a request for all documents, including electronic mail, relating to DeGeorge. RFC responded to DeGeorge's document requests on May 22, 2001, and asserted no objection to the request for e-mail.

During the first week of June 2001, the parties agreed that they would "work diligently to obtain hard copies of emails that were in computer form so that [they] could have a mutual production of emails." On June 8, 2001, RFC told DeGeorge that it was "in the process of retrieving e-mails from the back-up tapes" and that "[it] would let [DeGeorge] know when it had an estimate on a production date for the e-mails that are being retrieved off of the storage tapes."

In mid-June 2001, after RFC's in-house lawyer responsible for technology issues determined that "RFC did not have the internal resources necessary to retrieve [the e-mails from the back-up tapes] in the permitted time frame," RFC retained Electronic Evidence Discovery, Inc. ("EED") to assist RFC in the e-mail retrieval project.

In early July 2001, RFC informed DeGeorge that it had been unable to retrieve any emails from its back-up tapes. DeGeorge requested copies of the back-up tapes so that it could have its technical experts attempt to retrieve e-mails from them, and indicated its willingness to enter into any requested confidentiality agreement. RFC refused to produce the back-up tapes, prompting DeGeorge to raise the issue with the District Court.

On July 12, 2001, at a settlement conference before Magistrate Judge Joan G. Margolis, DeGeorge raised the issue of RFC's refusal to produce e-mails or back-up tapes. The parties agree that RFC told Magistrate Judge Margolis that it "was going to engage a vendor" to retrieve the emails. The parties understood at the July 12, 2001 conference that RFC would produce e-mails with the assistance of a vendor.

On or about July 25, 2001, EED apparently informed counsel for RFC that it would take "a couple of weeks" for it to print out the e-mails and transmit them to counsel for review. RFC, in turn, informed DeGeorge that day that it would begin producing responsive e-mails on a rolling basis starting on August 6, 2001. It represented that the e-mails would take "a few weeks" to produce. At this point, discovery was set to close on August 1, 2001, with jury selection to begin on September 5, 2001.

RFC did not begin producing e-mails on August 6, 2001, as it had promised. Instead, it informed DeGeorge on August 9, 2001, that it was continuing work on the production of e-mails and that "so far, most [of the e-mail printouts it had received from EED are] completely unrelated to the case."

By August 15, 2001, DeGeorge still had not received any production of e-mails from RFC. Accordingly, it raised the matter in a conference call with [trial] Judge Arterton on that date. RFC informed Judge Arterton that it had encountered technical difficulties, but that it expected to complete production "in the next couple of weeks." Judge Arterton ordered that production of the e-mails be completed by August 20, 2001.

RFC did not produce a single e-mail between August 15 and August 20, 2001. Instead, it informed DeGeorge on August 21, 2001, that EED was just beginning to print out e-mails due to additional "technical problems" and that responsive e-mails would be forthcoming "over the next couple of days."

On August 24, 2001, RFC produced 126 e-mails dating from January 1998 through early August 1998, and 2 e-mails from September 1998. There were no e-mails produced from October to December 1998—the critical factual time period.

DeGeorge immediately inquired as to the reason there were no e-mails from the end of 1998. RFC responded that "[i]f there were no responsive e-mails for 10/98–12/98 . . . it was either because there were no responsive e-mails from that date or because they did not exist on the accessible back-up tapes." On August 27, 2001, RFC confirmed that it had been "unable to retrieve October [to] December 1998 e-mails for production from RFC's back-up tapes."

On August 29, 2001, RFC produced 30 additional responsive e-mails retrieved from back-up tapes, none of which were from October to December 1998.

On September 1, 2001, DeGeorge again asked RFC to produce the back-up tapes so that it could investigate why no e-mails had been produced from the critical time period. On September 3, 2001, RFC agreed to provide the back-up tapes on the condition that any e-mails DeGeorge's vendor was able to retrieve be sent to RFC for review rather than to DeGeorge. The next morning, after initially rejecting the condition, DeGeorge agreed to RFC's terms in an e-mail sent at 11:17 a.m. In that e-mail, DeGeorge requested that the tapes be made available the next morning at jury selection. RFC did not produce the tapes at jury selection; instead, it sent them by overnight courier on September 5, 2001, so that DeGeorge did not receive them until the morning of September 6, 2001— three days before trial was to begin.

Although RFC turned over the back-up tapes, it refused to answer DeGeorge's questions regarding what type of tapes had been produced and their technical characteristics—information DeGeorge sought to assist its vendor in reading the tapes. Instead, RFC took the position that it had fulfilled its discovery obligations by producing the tapes, and that DeGeorge's vendor should just try to figure it out as RFC's vendor had done. DeGeorge brought RFC's recalcitrance to the attention of the District Court in a telephone conference held that day (September 6, 2001), during which RFC agreed to answer DeGeorge's questions.

The next day—September 7, 2001—DeGeorge asked RFC to ask its vendor why it could not retrieve anything from the October [to] December 1998 tapes. RFC responded that "the reason no e-mails were produced for 10–12/98 from the back-up tapes you received was either due to the fact that some of the tapes were physically damaged or corrupted or some tapes did not have e-mail on them at all."

Within four days of obtaining the tapes, "working a normal eight hour day," DeGeorge's vendor had located 950,000 e-mails on the November and December 1998 tapes. By September 13, 2001, the vendor had begun forwarding printed e-mails to RFC's counsel for review and production. Because of time pressure, the parties agreed that RFC would produce all of the 4,000 e-mails that DeGeorge's vendor had been able to print out; RFC did so in court on September 14, 2001. Ultimately, thirty of the 4,000 e-mails were responsive, though none appear to be damaging to RFC.

On September 18, 2001, DeGeorge moved for sanctions, asking Judge Arterton to instruct the jury that "it should presume the emails from October to December of 1998, which have not been produced, would have disproved RFC's theory of the case." The next day, during oral argument on the motion, RFC's counsel described RFC's retention of EED as follows:

> I believe that as early as mid-June we began contacting Electronic Evidence Discovery, Inc., who is our vendor that helped us retrieve the e-mails. And as we represented to the magistrate on [July 12th], we were getting help doing this.

In response to Judge Arterton's question regarding why RFC had not produced the back-up tapes earlier, RFC's counsel stated:

> It was a decision that we made internally that we endeavored to work with a world class vendor to achieve this—to achieve a result that would be satisfactory both for DeGeorge and for the Court, and we have yet to see that they would have been able to do any better.

Replying to Judge Arterton's question regarding why RFC had not turned over back-up tapes created in early 1999 so as to insure that all of the December 1998 e-mails were captured, RFC's counsel told the District Court that RFC had produced back-up tapes from "as late as February of 99 and January of 99." In fact, however, RFC had not produced any 1999 back-up tapes.

In an oral ruling the next morning (September 20, 2001), Judge Arterton denied DeGeorge's motion. She held that, to obtain an adverse inference charge, a party must show that "[1] the party with control over the evidence had an obligation to preserve it at the time it was destroyed; [2] the party that destroyed the evidence had a sufficiently culpable state of mind; and [3] some evidence suggest[s] that a document or documents relevant to substantiating [the claim of the party seeking sanctions] would have been included among the destroyed files." RFC did not dispute that it had an obligation to preserve and produce the e-mails; accordingly, Judge Arterton focused on the latter two prongs of the analysis.

With respect to the second prong, Judge Arterton found * * * that DeGeorge was not entitled to an adverse inference instruction because it had not established that RFC acted with "bad faith" or "gross negligence." She gave two reasons for this conclusion. First, she found that RFC's explanation that it decided to use an outside vendor to retrieve the e-mails rather than turn over the back-up tapes was "neither implausible nor unreasonable," and it was that decision that led to much of the delay. Second, although she recognized that

> subsequent acts by RFC, including representation that e-mails would be produced, without mentioning the absence of any from the critical time period, a missed Federal Express deadline for sending backup tapes so they could be forwarded to DeGeorge's vendors, and resis-

tance to responding to technical questions about the tapes, suggests a somewhat purposeful sluggishness on RFC's part,

she found that these acts would not have resulted in the unavailability of the evidence absent the "compressed timeline both parties were operating under."

Judge Arterton also held that DeGeorge had failed to establish that the e-mails would be helpful to it, as it "ha[d] not identified anything, apart from the nonproduction itself, suggesting that [the unproduced e-mails] would likely have been harmful to RFC."

Mindful that the e-mails had not been destroyed but rather not timely produced, Judge Arterton noted that:

> Should material evidence surface that is adverse to RFC after trial from the eventual disclosure of these e-mails, it might be the basis for post-trial motions, since it would obviously appear to fit within the category of being newly discovered and unavailable at the time of trial.

That day (September 20, 2001) was the last day evidence was presented in the case. The following Monday, September 24, 2001, the jury heard closing arguments, received the charge, and reached a verdict in favor of RFC for $96.4 million. * * *

On appeal, DeGeorge argues that (1) the District Court erred in holding (a) that it was required to establish "bad faith" or "gross negligence" to show that RFC acted with a sufficiently culpable state of mind so as to warrant sanctions, and (b) that it was required to show that the e-mails would have been harmful to RFC; and (2) the District Court's denial of its motion for sanctions was based on a "clearly erroneous view of the evidence." DeGeorge asks us to vacate the judgment of the District Court and remand for a new trial.

II. Discussion

A. The Nature of the Alleged Breach of a Discovery Obligation

* * *

Rule 37(b)(2) of the Federal Rules of Civil Procedure provides, in relevant part, that if a party fails to obey a discovery order, the court "may make such orders in regard to the failure as are just," including, but not limited to, "[a]n order that ... designated facts shall be taken as established for the purposes of the action in accordance with the claim of the party obtaining the order." Fed.R.Civ.P. 37(b)(2)(A). * * *

Even in the absence of a discovery order, a court may impose sanctions on a party for misconduct in discovery under its inherent power to manage its own affairs. *See generally Chambers v. NASCO, Inc.*, 501 U.S. 32, 43 (1991) ("It has long been understood that certain implied powers must necessarily result to our Courts of justice from the nature of their institution, powers which cannot be dispensed with in a Court, because they are necessary to the exercise of all others.'').

Where, as here, the nature of the alleged breach of a discovery obligation is the non-production of evidence, a district court has broad discretion in fashioning an appropriate sanction, including the discretion to delay the start of a trial (at the expense of the party that breached its obligation), to declare a mistrial if trial has already commenced, or to proceed with a trial and give an adverse inference instruction. In the instant case, however, DeGeorge chose not to seek a delay of the trial or a mistrial, but rather sought only an adverse inference instruction. Accordingly, we will not disturb the District Court's denial of DeGeorge's motion unless the District Court abused its discretion in failing to give the requested instruction.

B.   The District Court's Denial of DeGeorge's Motion

We review a district court's decision on a motion for discovery sanctions for abuse of discretion. "A district court would necessarily abuse its discretion if it based its ruling on an erroneous view of the law or on a clearly erroneous assessment of the evidence." In the instant case, DeGeorge contends that, in denying its motion for sanctions, the District Court both made errors of law and based its ruling on a clearly erroneous view of the evidence.

1.   The legal standard for an adverse inference instruction

As the District Court correctly held, a party seeking an adverse inference instruction based on the destruction of evidence must establish (1) that the party having control over the evidence had an obligation to preserve it at the time it was destroyed; (2) that the records were destroyed "with a culpable state of mind"; and (3) that the destroyed evidence was "relevant" to the party's claim or defense such that a reasonable trier of fact could find that it would support that claim or defense. Similarly, where, as here, an adverse inference instruction is sought on the basis that the evidence was not produced in time for use at trial, the party seeking the instruction must show (1) that the party having control over the evidence had an obligation to timely produce it; (2) that the party that failed to timely produce the evidence had "a culpable state of mind"; and (3) that the missing evidence is "relevant" to the party's claim or defense such that a reasonable trier of fact could find that it would support that claim or defense.

RFC did not dispute in its opposition to DeGeorge's motion that it (1) had an obligation to preserve and timely produce the back-up tapes. Accordingly, the only issues before the District Court were (2) whether RFC acted "with a culpable state of mind" in failing to timely produce the e-mails and (3) whether the missing e-mails are "relevant" to DeGeorge's claim or defense such that a reasonable trier of fact could find that they would support that claim or defense.

a. The proper legal standard for determining whether RFC acted "with a culpable state of mind"

* * *

The sanction of an adverse inference may be appropriate in some cases involving the negligent destruction of evidence because each party should bear the risk of its own negligence. As Magistrate Judge James C. Francis, IV aptly put it,

> [The] sanction [of an adverse inference] should be available even for the negligent destruction of documents if that is necessary to further the remedial purpose of the inference. It makes little difference to the party victimized by the destruction of evidence whether that act was done willfully or negligently. The adverse inference provides the necessary mechanism for restoring the evidentiary balance. The inference is adverse to the destroyer not because of any finding of moral culpability, but because the risk that the evidence would have been detrimental rather than favorable should fall on the party responsible for its loss.

Turner v. Hudson Transit Lines, Inc., 142 F.R.D. 68, 75 (S.D.N.Y. 1991). *See generally Kronisch v. United States,* 150 F.3d 112, 126 (2d Cir. 1998) (stating that an adverse inference instruction serves the remedial purpose, "insofar as possible, of restoring the prejudiced party to the same position he would have been in absent the wrongful destruction of evidence by the opposing party").

* * * [T]he District Court * * * explicitly analyzed only whether RFC acted in "bad faith" or with "gross negligence." It is therefore unclear whether the District Court applied the proper legal standard. Ordinarily, we would remand for clarification of this issue, but, in view of our analysis of the remaining issues in this case, such clarification is unnecessary.

b. The proper legal standard for determining whether De-George adduced sufficient evidence that the missing e-mails are "relevant"

Although we have stated that, to obtain an adverse inference instruction, a party must establish that the unavailable evidence is "relevant" to its claims or defenses, * * * our cases make clear that "relevant" in this context means something more than sufficiently probative to satisfy Rule 401 of the Federal Rules of Evidence.[3] Rather, the party seeking an adverse inference must adduce sufficient evidence from which a reasonable trier of fact could infer that "the destroyed [or unavailable] evidence would have been of the nature alleged by the party affected by its destruction." Courts must take care not to "hold the prejudiced party to too strict a standard of proof regarding the likely contents of the destroyed [or unavailable] evidence," because doing so "would subvert the purposes

---

3. Rule 401 provides:"Relevant evidence" means evidence having any tendency to make the existence of any fact that is of consequence to the determination of the action more probable or less probable than it would be without the evidence.

of the adverse inference, and would allow parties who have destroyed evidence to profit from that destruction."

Where a party destroys evidence in bad faith, that bad faith alone is sufficient circumstantial evidence from which a reasonable fact finder could conclude that the missing evidence was unfavorable to that party. Similarly, a showing of gross negligence in the destruction or untimely production of evidence will in some circumstances suffice, standing alone, to support a finding that the evidence was unfavorable to the grossly negligent party. Accordingly, where a party seeking an adverse inference adduces evidence that its opponent destroyed potential evidence (or other-wise rendered it unavailable) in bad faith or through gross negligence (satisfying the "culpable state of mind" factor), that same evidence of the opponent's state of mind will frequently also be sufficient to permit a jury to conclude that the missing evidence is favorable to the party (satisfying the "relevance" factor).[4]

A party seeking an adverse inference instruction need not, however, rely on the same evidence to establish that the missing evidence is "relevant" as it uses to establish the opponent's "culpable state of mind." * * *

In this case, the District Court stated that the only evidence De-George had adduced "suggesting that [the unproduced e-mails] would likely have been harmful to RFC" was the nonproduction itself. It also stated, however, that RFC's actions after it retained EED, "including representation that e-mails would be produced, without mentioning the absence of any from the critical time period, a missed Federal Express deadline for sending backup tapes so they could be forwarded to De-George's vendors, and resistance to responding to technical questions about the tapes, suggest a somewhat purposeful sluggishness on RFC's part."

It is unclear why the District Court did not consider RFC's acts evincing "purposeful sluggishness" as supportive of DeGeorge's claim that the e-mails were likely harmful to RFC. Just as the intentional or grossly negligent destruction of evidence in bad faith can support an inference that the destroyed evidence was harmful to the destroying party, so, too, can intentional or grossly negligent acts that hinder discovery support such an inference, even if those acts are not ultimately responsible for the unavailability of the evidence (i.e., even if those acts do not satisfy the "culpable state of mind" factor because they did not cause the destruction or unavailability of the missing evidence). Thus, if any of RFC's acts that hindered DeGeorge's attempts to obtain the e-mails was grossly negligent

---

4. Although the issue of whether evidence was destroyed with a "culpable state of mind" is one for a court to decide in determining whether the imposition of sanctions is warranted, whether the materials were in fact unfavorable to the culpable party is an issue of fact to be determined by the jury. Accordingly, a court's role in evaluating the "relevance" factor in the adverse inference analysis is limited to insuring that the party seeking the inference had adduced enough evidence of the contents of the missing materials such that a reasonable jury could find in its favor.

or taken in bad faith,[5] then it could support an inference that the missing e-mails are harmful to RFC.

———————

Because the District Court used the wrong legal standard in denying DeGeorge's motion, its decision was "based on an erroneous view of the law." Accordingly, the District Court abused it discretion in denying DeGeorge's motion.

2. The District Court's Factual Findings

DeGeorge also challenges the District Court's factual findings on bad faith and gross negligence. The District Court found that RFC's failure to timely produce the e-mails was neither in bad faith nor grossly negligent because (1) RFC's explanation that it decided to use an outside vendor to retrieve the e-mails rather than turn over the back-up tapes was "neither implausible nor unreasonable" and it was that decision that led to much of the delay; and (2) although RFC's subsequent actions evinced a "purposeful sluggishness," those acts would not have resulted in the unavailability of the evidence absent the "compressed timeline both parties were operating under." DeGeorge argues that these findings were clearly erroneous because (1) there was no explanation as to why e-mails from the back-up tapes were produced for January through September 1998 but not from October through December of 1998; and (2) RFC's actions amounted to more than "purposeful sluggishness."

It appears to us that, in the press of deciding this motion in the midst of trial, the District Court overlooked some evidence that could support a finding that RFC acted in bad faith or was grossly negligent. For example, the District Court did not appear to consider, in finding that RFC's explanation regarding its retention of EED was "neither implausible or unreasonable," the timing of the decision to retain EED. According to RFC's in-house counsel, "RFC retained EED in mid-June 2001," after he had determined that "RFC did not have the internal resources necessary to retrieve [the e-mails from the back-up tapes] in the permitted time frame." RFC first informed DeGeorge that it had been unable to retrieve e-mails from the back-up tapes in early July 2001—weeks after it retained EED. When DeGeorge brought the issue to the attention of Magistrate Judge Margolis at the July 12, 2001 conference, RFC told both the Magistrate Judge and DeGeorge that it would seek a vendor's assistance in retrieving the e-mails. In its September 19, 2001 brief to the District Court opposing DeGeorge's motion for sanctions, RFC stated that it "formally" retained EED on July 14, 2001, and it attached a contract

——————————

5. It appears that the District Court did not consider whether RFC's "purposefully sluggish" acts were grossly negligent or taken in bad faith, because it had already decided that those acts did not cause RFC's failure to timely produce the e-mails. Rather, the District Court found that the reason RFC did not produce the e-mails was that it hired a vendor that was unable to retrieve them.

between RFC and EED purportedly executed on that date as exhibit 3 to that brief.

This evidence raises a number of questions. For example, if RFC determined in mid-June that it lacked the resources to retrieve the e-mails and therefore retained EED to assist it in the task at that time, its early July 2001 statement to DeGeorge that it was unable to retrieve e-mails was presumably based not only on its own inability to retrieve the e-mails, but also on its inability to retrieve the e-mails with the assistance of EED. If so, RFC's decision to continue to use EED's services in an effort to retrieve the e-mails may not have been reasonable. If, on the other hand, RFC did not obtain EED's assistance before it told DeGeorge in early July that it had been unable to retrieve e-mails from the back-up tapes, it should explain (1) why it delayed telling DeGeorge of its inability to retrieve messages until weeks after its in-house lawyer determined that it could not do so, and (2) why it failed to obtain outside assistance as soon as it determined it could not retrieve e-mails on its own.

In a similar vein, it is unclear whether the District Court considered the reasonableness of RFC's continued reliance on EED throughout months of apparently fruitless attempts to retrieve the critical e-mails, in light of the ability of DeGeorge's vendor to identify and begin to retrieve those e-mails in just four days. The explanation for this apparent discrepancy in competence offered by EED Project Manager Christopher Mashburn—namely, that DeGeorge's vendor had a "head start" because of technical information supplied by RFC—is thoroughly unconvincing. The "technical information" RFC supplied DeGeorge in response to DeGeorge's questions consisted merely of the identification of the software used, the identification of the type and basic parameters of the tapes, and the fact that the tapes included back-ups from both servers and workstations. This basic information should have been readily available to EED from RFC's technical personnel, and, accordingly, there is no reason to believe that DeGeorge's vendor had any more of a "head start" than EED had.

The record also contains a number of at least careless, if not intentionally misleading, statements by RFC both to DeGeorge and to the District Court regarding the effort to retrieve the e-mails, the character of which statements may not have been fully apprehended by the District Court. For example, in light of the sworn statement by RFC's in-house counsel that "RFC retained EED in mid-June," RFC's statement at the July 12, 2001 conference to the effect that it intended to hire a vendor, coupled with its failure to inform the Magistrate Judge that it had already "retained" that vendor weeks earlier and its careful use of the word "formally" to describe its purported "retention" of EED in July 2001, suggests a deliberate attempt to mislead both DeGeorge and the District Court. Similarly, RFC's counsel told the District Court during argument on DeGeorge's motion for sanctions that it had produced back-up tapes through early 1999, when in fact it had produced only back-up tapes through December 1998.

In addition to our doubts over whether the District Court fully considered all of the evidence, we are uncertain whether the District Court appreciated that as a discovery deadline or trial date draws near, discovery conduct that might have been considered "merely" discourteous at an earlier point in the litigation may well breach a party's duties to its opponent and to the court. In the circumstances presented here—i.e., trial was imminent and RFC had repeatedly missed deadlines to produce the e-mails—RFC was under an obligation to be as cooperative as possible. Viewed in that light, RFC's "purposefully sluggish" acts—particularly its as-yet-unexplained refusal to answer basic technical questions about the tape until prompted to do so by the District Court—may well have constituted sanctionable misconduct in their own right.

Despite these doubts, we need not and do not decide whether the District Court's factual findings were clearly erroneous, because the District Court will have to reevaluate those findings in the context of the proper legal standard.

C.   Our Instructions on Remand

* * * DeGeorge should be given an opportunity to renew its motion for sanctions, with the benefit of discovery—including, but not necessarily limited to, reexamination of the back-up tapes and appropriate depositions of RFC's affiants—and, if appropriate, an evidentiary hearing before the District Court. Upon consideration of any such motion, the District Court should vacate the judgment and order a new trial if DeGeorge establishes that RFC acted with a sufficiently culpable state of mind (as described above) and that DeGeorge was prejudiced by the failure to produce the e-mails. Presumably, DeGeorge would attempt to establish prejudice by pointing to specific e-mails that it would have used at trial; if so, the District Court should consider the likelihood that the newly produced e-mails would have affected the jury's verdict, in light of all of the other evidence adduced at trial.

If the District Court finds that RFC acted with a culpable state of mind, but that DeGeorge was not prejudiced, it should consider whether lesser sanctions, including, but not limited to, awarding DeGeorge the costs of its motion for sanctions and this appeal, are warranted. Moreover, although it is now our holding that, absent a showing of prejudice, the jury's verdict should not be disturbed, the District Court should also consider whether, as a sanction for discovery abuse, RFC should also forfeit post-judgment interest for the time period from the date of the entry of judgment until the entry of the District Court's decision on remand. Finally, if the District Court concludes that RFC's failure to timely produce the e-mails was not caused by acts taken with "a culpable state of mind," it should separately consider whether RFC's acts of "purposeful sluggishness" nevertheless warrant the imposition of sanctions. District courts should not countenance "purposeful sluggishness" in discovery on the part of parties or attorneys and should be prepared to impose sanctions when they encounter it.

III. Conclusion

In sum, we hold that:

(1) where, as here, the nature of the alleged breach of a discovery obligation is the non-production of evidence, a District Court has broad discretion in fashioning an appropriate sanction, including the discretion to delay the start of a trial (at the expense of the party that breached its obligation), to declare a mistrial if trial has already commenced, or to proceed with a trial with an adverse inference instruction;

(2) discovery sanctions, including an adverse inference instruction, may be imposed upon a party that has breached a discovery obligation not only through bad faith or gross negligence, but also through ordinary negligence;

(3) a judge's finding that a party acted with gross negligence or in bad faith with respect to discovery obligations is ordinarily sufficient to support a finding that the missing or destroyed evidence would have been harmful to that party, even if the destruction or unavailability of the evidence was not caused by the acts constituting bad faith or gross negligence; and

(4) in the instant case, the District Court applied the wrong standard in deciding DeGeorge's motion for sanctions.

Accordingly, we vacate the order of the District Court denying De-George's motion for sanctions and remand with instructions to permit DeGeorge to renew its motion for discovery sanctions.

STEVENSON v. UNION PACIFIC RR CO.

354 F.3d 739 (8th Cir. 2004)

HANSEN, CIRCUIT JUDGE

This case arises out of a car-train grade crossing accident in which Frank Stevenson was injured and his wife was killed. In this diversity lawsuit against the Union Pacific Railroad Company ("Union Pacific" or "the Railroad"), a jury awarded damages to Mr. Stevenson and Rebecca Harshberger as Administratrix of Mary Stevenson's estate on claims of negligence. * * *

I.

On November 6, 1998, a Union Pacific train struck the Stevensons' vehicle as it crossed the tracks on Highway 364 in Vanndale, Arkansas. Mrs. Stevenson died as a result of the collision, and Mr. Stevenson suffered severe injuries and has no memory of the accident. Mr. Stevenson and the administratrix of his wife's estate filed this action alleging that the accident was caused by Union Pacific's negligence. Later, they amended their complaint to include additional negligence claims and to add Operation Lifesaver, Inc. ("Operation Lifesaver") as a defendant, asserting that it made negligent and fraudulent misrepresentations concerning the safety of the crossing. The district court granted partial summary judgment, dismissing several negligence claims, including allegations concerning the speed of the train. The district court also granted Operation Lifesaver's motion to dismiss for failure to state a claim.

The plaintiffs filed a motion for sanctions on the ground that Union Pacific had destroyed evidence, namely, a voice tape of conversations between the train crew and dispatch at the time of the accident and track maintenance records from before the accident. Union Pacific argued that sanctions were not justified because it destroyed the documents in good faith pursuant to its routine document retention policies. The district court granted the motion following a three-day evidentiary hearing. The district court imposed sanctions of an adverse inference instruction regarding the destroyed evidence and an award of costs and attorneys' fees incurred as a result of the spoliation of evidence.

Prior to trial, the plaintiffs filed a motion in limine, seeking to prohibit Union Pacific from calling witnesses to explain that it destroyed the tape and track maintenance records pursuant to its routine document retention policies. The district court granted the motion and, at the outset of trial, orally instructed the jury that the voice tape and track inspection records "were destroyed by the railroad and ... should have been preserved," and that the jurors "may, but are not required to, assume that the contents of the voice tapes and track inspection records would have been adverse, or detrimental, to the defendant." The district court thus permitted the plaintiffs to immediately reference the destroyed material and the fact that Union Pacific willfully destroyed it, but denied Union Pacific any opportunity to offer its routine document retention policy as an innocent explanation for its destruction of the evidence.

* * * At the close of trial, over Union Pacific's renewed objection, the district court repeated the spoliation instruction to the jury: "You may, but are not required to, assume that the contents of the voice tape and track inspection records would have been adverse, or detrimental, to the defendant." * * *

The jury returned a general verdict in favor of the plaintiffs, awarding Mr. Stevenson $2,000,000 in damages and awarding the estate $10,000 for funeral and ambulance expenses. The district court entered judgment on these amounts and also awarded the plaintiffs $164,410.25 in costs and attorneys' fees on the sanctions order. Union Pacific appeals, asserting that * * * the district court abused its discretion in giving the adverse inference instruction, and that the district court abused its discretion by ordering attorneys' fees as sanctions. * * *

II

* * *

B. Sanctions

Both prior to the filing of the lawsuit and during its pendency, Union Pacific destroyed two types of evidence—the tape of any recorded voice radio communications between the train crew and dispatchers on the date of the accident and all track maintenance records close in time to the accident. The district court imposed sanctions for this conduct under its inherent power by giving an adverse inference instruction, refusing to permit testimony to rebut the adverse inference, and imposing an award of attorneys' fees.

"We review a district court's imposition of sanctions under its inherent power for an abuse of discretion." *Dillon v. Nissan Motor Co.*, 986 F.2d 263, 267 (8th Cir. 1993). A court's inherent power includes the discretionary "ability to fashion an appropriate sanction for conduct which abuses the judicial process." Our interpretation of Supreme Court authority concerning a court's inherent power to sanction counsels that a finding of bad faith is not always necessary to the court's exercise of its inherent power to impose sanctions. The Union Pacific argues that the sanctions were an abuse of discretion because it did not engage in bad faith conduct by destroying evidence pursuant to document retention policies. We will consider the extent to which a finding of bad faith is necessary separately below with regard to each type of sanction employed. * * *

1. The Adverse Inference Instruction

* * *

The district court imposed this sanction of an adverse inference instruction after concluding that Union Pacific destroyed the voice tape in bad faith, and that Union Pacific destroyed the track maintenance records in circumstances where it "knew or should have known that the documents would become material" and "should have preserved them." The district court reached these conclusions after discussing * * * (1) whether the record retention policy is reasonable considering the facts and circumstances surrounding those documents, (2) whether lawsuits or complaints have been filed frequently concerning the type of records at issue, and (3) whether the document retention policy was instituted in bad faith.

* * * We have never approved of giving an adverse inference instruction on the basis of prelitigation destruction of evidence through a routine document retention policy on the basis of negligence alone. Where a routine document retention policy has been followed in this context, we now clarify that there must be some indication of an intent to destroy the evidence for the purpose of obstructing or suppressing the truth in order to impose the sanction of an adverse inference instruction.

The facts here are as follows. The accident occurred on November 6, 1998. The Stevensons filed this lawsuit on September 20, 1999, and mailed their requests for production of the voice tape on October 25, 1999. By that time, Union Pacific had long since destroyed the voice tape from the November 6, 1998, accident by recording over it in accordance with the company's routine procedure of keeping voice tapes for 90 days and then reusing the tapes. The district court found that although Union Pacific's voice tape retention policy was not unreasonable or instituted in bad faith, it was unreasonable and amounted to bad faith conduct for Union Pacific to adhere to the principle in the circumstances of this case.

In support of its bad faith determination, the district court found that Union Pacific had been involved in many grade crossing collisions and knew that the taped conversations would be relevant in any potential litigation regarding an accident that resulted in death and serious injury. * * * The district court listened to available samples of this type of voice tape and found that they generally contain evidence that is discoverable and useful in developing a case. Additionally, the district court found that Union Pacific had preserved such tapes in cases where it was helpful to Union Pacific's position. The district court also found that the plaintiffs were prejudiced by the destruction of this tape because there are no other records of comments between the train crew and dispatch contemporaneous to the accident. The district court thus held that sanctions were justified and that an adverse inference instruction was an appropriate sanction for the destruction of the voice tape.

After considering the record and the particular circumstances of this case, we conclude that, while this case tests the limits of what we are able to uphold as a bad faith determination, the district court did not abuse its discretion by sanctioning Union Pacific's prelitigation conduct of destroying the voice tape. The district court's bad faith determination is supported by Union Pacific's act of destroying the voice tape pursuant to its routine policy in circumstances where Union Pacific had general knowledge that such tapes would be important to any litigation over an accident that resulted in serious injury or death, and its knowledge that litigation is frequent when there has been an accident involving death or serious injury. While these are quite general considerations, an important factor here is that a voice tape that is the only contemporaneous recording of conversations at the time of the accident will always be highly relevant to potential litigation over the accident. We conclude that this weighs heavier in this case than the lack of actual knowledge that litigation was imminent at the time of the destruction. Additionally, the record indicates that Union Pacific made an immediate effort to preserve other types of evidence but not the voice tape, and the district court noted that Union Pacific was careful to preserve a voice tape in other cases where the tape proved to be beneficial to Union Pacific. The prelitigation destruction of the voice tape in this combination of circumstances, though done pursuant to a routine retention policy, creates a sufficiently strong inference of an intent to destroy it for the purpose of suppressing evidence of the facts surrounding the operation of the train at the time of the accident.

There must be a finding of prejudice to the opposing party before imposing a sanction for destruction of evidence. The requisite element of prejudice is satisfied by the nature of the evidence destroyed in this case. While there is no indication that the voice tape [that was] destroyed contained evidence that could be classified as a smoking-gun, the very fact that it is the only recording of conversations between the engineer and dispatch[er] contemporaneous with the accident renders its loss prejudicial to the plaintiffs. We find no abuse of discretion in the district court's decision to sanction the Railroad through an adverse inference instruction for its prelitigation destruction of the voice tape.

As to the track maintenance inspection records, the Union Pacific demonstrated that its policy is to destroy them after one year and replace them with the new inspection records. These records generally note defects that appear at a crossing on the day of its inspection and list the name of the person who inspected the track on that particular day, but they would not show the exact condition of the tracks on the day of the accident. The Stevensons requested the production of track maintenance records for two years prior to the accident. Union Pacific made no effort to preserve these documents from its routine document destruction policy.

The district court said it was not persuaded that the document retention policy was instituted in bad faith, but "[a]s with the voice tape, however, [Union Pacific] knew or should have known that the documents would become material and should have preserved them." The "knew or should have known" language indicates a negligence standard, and as noted earlier, we have never approved of giving an adverse inference instruction on the basis of negligence alone. Even if the district court intended its findings to be the equivalent of a bad faith determination, we conclude that the findings regarding the prelitigation destruction of track maintenance records do not amount to a showing of bad faith and that the district court abused its discretion in giving the adverse inference instruction in relation to the destruction of all track maintenance records up to two years prior to the accident.

There is no showing here that Union Pacific knew that litigation was imminent when, prior to any litigation, it destroyed track maintenance records from up to two years prior to the accident pursuant to its document retention policy. Additionally, maintenance records would only be relevant to potential litigation to the extent that they were relatively close in time to the accident and defective track maintenance was alleged to be the cause of the accident. Even then, track maintenance records are of limited use. While they may reveal defects in the track that existed at the time of the last inspection, they do not show the exact condition of the track at the time of the collision. The district court weighed heavily the fact that the Union Pacific knew that litigation is possible when there has been a serious accident but did not consider whether, when the prelitigation destruction was occurring, there had been any notice in this case of potential litigation or that the track maintenance would be an issue or an alleged cause of the accident. It appears that Union Pacific was not on notice that the track maintenance records should be preserved until it received the October 1999 request for production of documents, and the condition of the track was not formally put into issue until the second amendment to the complaint in May 2000. Thus, any bad faith determination regarding the prelitigation destruction of the track maintenance records is not supported by the record, and any adverse inference instruction based on any prelitigation destruction of track maintenance records would have been given in error.

Union Pacific continued destroying track maintenance records after this lawsuit was initiated. We find no abuse of discretion in the district court's decision to impose sanctions for the destruction of track maintenance records after the commencement of litigation and the filing of the plaintiffs' request for production of documents on October 25, 1999. At the time the plaintiffs requested the production of the track maintenance records, the records from October and November 1998 (closest in time to the accident and thus most relevant) would have been available, but Union Pacific made no effort to preserve them. Although Union Pacific's counsel did not send the discovery request to the claims agent, Mr. Fuller, until November 17, 1999, even then the records from November 1998 would have been available and could have been preserved, but they were not.

At the sanctions hearing, Union Pacific claimed innocence under its routine document retention policy and a lack of knowledge because the proper agents did not know that the records were relevant or where they were kept. * * * The district court did not credit the Railroad's claimed lack of knowledge because of its specific knowledge of and participation in this litigation, the actual notice of the document request, and the relevance of track maintenance documents to the pending litigation because they could have revealed the Railroad's extent of knowledge about the track conditions at the time of the accident. After the specific document request for track maintenance records, Union Pacific cannot rely on its routine document retention policy as a shield. Sanctioning the ongoing destruction of records during litigation and discovery by imposing an adverse inference instruction is supported by either the court's inherent power or Rule 37 of the Federal Rules of Civil Procedure, even absent an explicit bad faith finding, and we conclude that the giving of an adverse inference instruction in these circumstances is not an abuse of discretion.

2. Refusal to Allow Rebuttal

Union Pacific argues that even if the district court did not abuse its discretion by giving the adverse inference instruction as a sanction for the destruction of evidence in this case, the district court abused its discretion by not permitting it to offer a reasonable rebuttal to the inference. We agree.

* * * A permissive inference is subject to reasonable rebuttal. *See Lamarca v. United States,* 31 F.Supp.2d 110, 128 (E.D.N.Y. 1999) ("An adverse inference that the missing evidence is harmful can be rebutted by an adequate explanation of the reason for non-production."). While the district court need not permit a complete retrial of the sanctions hearing during trial, unfair prejudice should be avoided by permitting the defendant to put on some evidence of its document retention policy and how it

affected the destruction of the requested records as an innocent explanation for its conduct. Absent this opportunity, the jury is deprived of sufficient information on which to base a rational decision of whether to apply the adverse inference, and an otherwise permissive inference easily becomes an irrebuttable presumption.

The district court's timing of the instruction in this case also contributes to our finding of unfair prejudice by the exclusion of reasonable rebuttal testimony. At the very outset of trial, the district court informed the jury that the Railroad had destroyed evidence that should have been preserved, and the plaintiffs referred to this destruction throughout the trial. We see no need to unduly emphasize the adverse inference at the outset of trial, especially where there is no finding that the evidence destroyed was crucial to the case. No doubt the evidence destroyed was relevant and its destruction prejudiced the plaintiffs' discovery efforts, but in previous cases where we have sustained a sanction of precluding evidence completely or settling a disputed matter of fact (thus permitting no rebuttal), the offending party had destroyed the one piece of crucial physical evidence in the case. No such finding exists here.

* * *

COMMENTARY

a. What Degree of Culpable Conduct Is Required to Warrant Sanctions for Spoliation?

Culpable conduct falls along a sliding scale as follows: mere negligence, gross negligence, recklessness, bad faith, and intentional misconduct. Most courts consider two major factors when determining whether to impose sanctions and, if so, what sanctions are most appropriate. The first factor is the degree of culpability, and the second is prejudice to the innocent party.[1] Other factors include the degree of interference with the judicial process, whether a lesser sanction will remedy the harm, whether sanctions are necessary to deter similar conduct, and whether sanctions will unfairly punish an innocent party for spoliation committed by an attorney.

Just as culpable conduct is defined along a sliding scale, so is the range of sanctions that a court can impose. Those sanctions (from least to most severe) include: fines,[2] cost-shifting, burden shifting, preclusion of evidence, adverse inferences,[3] and default judgments. Most courts are careful to impose the least severe sanctions commensurate with the wrongdoing.

A sharp split of authority exists between the Eighth Circuit, which requires "a finding of intentional destruction indicating a desire to suppress

---

1. *See* Shira A. Scheindlin & Kanchana Wangkeo, *Electronic Discovery Sanctions in the Twenty–First Century*, 11 Mich. Telecomm. & Tech. L. Rev. 71, 94 (2004).

2. *See United States v. Philip Morris USA, Inc.,* 327 F. Supp. 2d 21 (D.D.C. 2004) (sanction of $2.75 million for spoliation).

3. *See MOSAID Techs. Inc. v. Samsung,* 348 F. Supp. 2d 332 (D.N.J. 2004) (imposing an adverse inference instruction and a $566,839.97 fine, *inter alia,* for failure to turn-off the auto-delete function of Samsung's e-mail system).

the truth," and the Second Circuit, in which mere negligence will meet the culpability standard. As discussed below, courts in other circuits line up on various points on the culpability spectrum.

"Bad faith," which appears to be synonymous with intent, is uniformly required to be found before a sanction can be imposed in the Fifth, Seventh, and Tenth Circuits.[4] However, the increasing prevalence and importance of e-discovery has led to a clear trend away from the "mens rea" or "scienter" approach of these circuits.

District court decisions in the Fourth, Ninth, Eleventh, and D.C. Circuits have directly followed or have leaned toward the Second Circuit's view that negligence is sufficient to establish culpability for spoliation. For example, Ninth Circuit decisions addressing dismissal as a sanction for spoliation have required a finding of "willfulness, fault, or bad faith."[5] However, at least one district court has found gross negligence to be sufficient for an adverse inference instruction.[6] More recently, that same court expressly adopted the Second Circuit's rule that negligence is sufficient to satisfy the culpability factor for spoliation.[7]

Other district courts in the Third, Fourth, and Eleventh Circuits have held that negligence is sufficient to establish culpability.[8] The same is true of a district court for the District of Columbia, which also embraced Second Circuit precedent.[9]

Perhaps the most distinctive approach to culpability is that of the First Circuit, which leaves the entire question of a spoliation finding to the factfinder with no required finding of any particular degree of culpability.

---

4. *See, e.g., Condrey v. Suntrust Bank of Georgia*, 431 F.3d 191, 203 (5th Cir. 2005) ("The Fifth Circuit permits an adverse inference against the destroyer of evidence only upon a showing of 'bad faith' or 'bad conduct.' "); *United States v. Esposito*, 771 F.2d 283, 286 (7th Cir. 1985) ("destruction must have been in bad faith"); *Aramburu v. Boeing Co.*, 112 F.3d 1398, 1407 (10th Cir. 1997) (requiring bad faith before imposing adverse inference); *Bryant v. Nicholson*, No. 07 Civ. 0183, 2008 WL 465270, at *5 (N.D. Tex. Feb. 21, 2008) (bad faith required for spoliation); *Rodgers v. Lowe's Home Ctrs., Inc.*, No. 05 Civ. 0502, 2007 WL 257714, at *5 (N.D. Ill. Jan. 30, 2007) ("mere negligence is not enough, for it does not sustain the inference of consciousness of a weak case") (quotation omitted).

5. *See Leon v. IDX Sys. Corp.*, 464 F.3d 951, 958 (9th Cir. 2006); *Anheuser-Busch, Inc. v. Natural Beverage Distribs.*, 69 F.3d 337, 348 (9th Cir. 1995).

6. *See UMG Recordings, Inc. v. Hummer Winblad Venture Partners (In re Napster, Inc. Copyright Litig.)*, 462 F. Supp. 2d 1060, 1078 (N.D. Cal. 2006).

7. *See World Courier v. Barone*, No. 06 Civ. 3072, 2007 WL 1119196, at *2 (N.D. Cal. Apr. 16, 2007) ("[T]he 'mental culpability' factor is satisfied where the party acted 'knowingly or ... negligently.' ") (*quoting Residential Funding*, 306 F.3d at 108). *Accord Housing Rts. Ctr. v. Sterling*, No. 03 Civ. 859, 2005 WL 3320739, at *7–8 (C.D. Cal. Mar. 2, 2005) (following *Residential Funding*).

8. *See, e.g., Brown v. Chertoff*, 563 F. Supp. 2d 1372, 1381 (S.D. Ga. 2008) (negligence is enough to find spoliation); *CentiMark Corp. v. Pegnato & Pegnato Roof Mgmt.*, No. 05 Civ. 708, 2008 WL 1995305, at *10 (W.D. Pa. May 6, 2008) ("[W]hile it is not entirely clear whether the Court of Appeals for the Third Circuit ... require[s] at least some bad faith, several courts within the Third Circuit have found that it does not, and have found that even negligent destruction of evidence is sufficient to give rise to the spoliation inference."); *Samsung Elec. Co. v. Rambus Inc.*, 439 F. Supp. 2d 524, 540 (E.D. Va. 2006), *rev'd on other grounds*, 523 F.3d 1374 (Fed. Cir. 2008) ("both negligent and willful destruction can constitute spoliation"); *Teague v. Target Corp.*, No. 06 Civ. 191, 2007 WL 1041191, at *2 (W.D.N.C. Apr. 4, 2007) (" 'culpable state of mind' could include ... ordinary negligence.").

9. *See Mazloum v. District of Columbia Metro. Police Dep't*, 530 F. Supp. 2d 282, 293 (D.D.C. 2008) (following *Residential Funding*).

Rather, the proponent of an adverse inference need only show that its opponent "knew of (a) the claim (that is, the litigation or the potential for litigation), and (b) the document's potential relevance to that claim," and "a trier of fact may (but need not) infer from a party's obliteration of a document relevant to a litigated issue that the contents of the document were unfavorable to that party."[10]

b. What Steps Must Be Taken to Avoid a Finding of Negligence?

No magic software or approved methodology exists that will be certain to eliminate any risk of the negligent loss of, or failure to produce, relevant evidence. However, attorneys and their clients must keep abreast of advances in technology affecting preservation, search, and retrieval methods.

3. Prejudice

GREYHOUND LINES, INC. v. WADE
485 F.3d 1032 (8th Cir. 2007)

BENTON, CIRCUIT JUDGE

Greyhound Lines, Inc. sued Robert N. Wade and Archway Cookies, LLC (collectively Archway). In August 2000, an Archway truck driven by Wade rear-ended a Greyhound bus operated by Debra Johnson on Interstate 80 in Nebraska. After a bench trial, the district court apportioned fault at 85 percent to Archway and 15 percent to Greyhound. Archway appeals, asserting the court erred in refusing sanctions * * *.

I.

At the time of the collision, due to mechanical failure, the Greyhound bus was traveling below the posted minimum speed, in the right lane, hazard lights flashing, as the driver tried to reach the nearest off-ramp. The bus had an electronic control module (ECM) that stored information, including speed, starts, stops, and the time and type of a mechanical failure. Ten days after the accident, Greyhound removed the ECM and retrieved the information. The ECM indicated that a speed-sensor failure caused the bus's slow speed. Greyhound then sent the ECM to the engine manufacturer, who erased the information before this case was filed. Archway requested sanctions against Greyhound for spoliation of evidence, and misleading and false discovery responses. The district court denied Archway's motions.

This court reviews the imposition of sanctions for an abuse of discretion. The district court, familiar with the case and counsel, receives substantial deference in determining sanctions. If the court bases its ruling on "an erroneous view of the law or on a clearly erroneous assessment of the evidence," the court abuses its discretion.

---

10. *Testa v. Wal–Mart Stores, Inc.*, 144 F.3d 173, 177 (1st Cir. 1998).

Archway contends that Greyhound deserves sanctions for destroying the ECM data and giving evasive and misleading responses in discovery. According to Archway, Greyhound had a duty to preserve the ECM data because litigation was likely, and the ECM data detailed the bus's operation before the accident. Archway believes that by failing to retain the ECM data, Greyhound prevented identifying when and where the bus first had problems. As to the discovery responses, Archway alleges that Greyhound's initial interrogatory responses identified a "vapor lock" as the mechanical impairment, although Greyhound knew it was a speed-sensor failure. Archway claims that three months before trial, it learned about the ECM data and the speed-sensor failure.

A spoliation-of-evidence sanction requires "a finding of intentional destruction indicating a desire to suppress the truth." "Intent is rarely proved by direct evidence, and a district court has substantial leeway to determine intent through consideration of circumstantial evidence, witness credibility, motives of the witnesses in a particular case, and other factors."

Before, during and after trial, the district court reviewed Archway's spoliation claims, each time denying sanctions. Archway argues that because litigation was likely, Greyhound had a duty to preserve the ECM data. The ultimate focus for imposing sanctions for spoliation of evidence is the intentional destruction of evidence indicating a desire to suppress the truth, not the prospect of litigation. Thus, the district court did not err in finding spoliation had not occurred. Additionally, although some material was not preserved, the ECM data identified the specific mechanical defect that slowed the bus, and several bus passengers testified how the bus acted before the collision. "There must be a finding of prejudice to the opposing party before imposing a sanction for destruction of evidence"

As to the discovery responses, the district court found that Greyhound's answers were responsive and that Archway was not prejudiced by untimely disclosure. Because Archway received responsive answers months before trial, the district court properly refused discovery sanctions.

The district court did not base its determinations on an erroneous view of the law or the evidence, and did not abuse its discretion by refusing sanctions against Greyhound.

* * *

ZUBULAKE v. UBS WARBURG LLC "ZUBULAKE V"
229 F.R.D. 422 (S.D.N.Y. 2004)

SCHEINDLIN, DISTRICT JUDGE

[The facts and background of this case are fully set forth in Chapter II.B, *supra*. Judge Scheindlin found as follows:]

Early on in this litigation, UBS's counsel—both in-house and outside—instructed UBS personnel to retain relevant electronic information. Notwithstanding these instructions, certain UBS employees deleted relevant e-mails. Other employees never produced relevant information to counsel. As a result, many discoverable e-mails were not produced to Zubulake until recently, even though they were responsive to a document request propounded on June 3, 2002. In addition, a number of e-mails responsive to that document request were deleted and have been lost altogether.

Counsel, in turn, failed to request retained information from one key employee and to give the litigation hold instructions to another. They also failed to adequately communicate with another employee about how she maintained her computer files. Counsel also failed to safeguard backup tapes that might have contained some of the deleted e-mails, and which would have mitigated the damage done by UBS's destruction of those e-mails.

* * *

Second, Zubulake argues that the e-mails that *were* produced, albeit late, "are brand new and very significant to Ms. Zubulake's retaliation claim and would have affected [her] examination of every witness . . . in this case." Likewise, Zubulake claims, with respect to the newly produced e-mails from Kim and Tong's active files, that UBS's "failure to produce these e-mails in a timely fashion precluded [her] from questioning any witness about them." These arguments stand unrebutted and are therefore adopted in full by the Court. Accordingly, UBS is ordered to pay the costs of any depositions or re-depositions required by the late production.

Third, UBS is ordered to pay the costs of this motion.[102]

[The Court concluded as follows:]

UBS failed to preserve relevant e-mails, even after receiving adequate warnings from counsel, resulting in the production of some relevant e-mails almost two years after they were initially requested, and resulting in the complete destruction of others. For that reason, Zubulake's motion is granted and sanctions are warranted. UBS is ordered to:

1.   Pay for the re-deposition of relevant UBS personnel, limited to the subject of the newly-discovered e-mails;

2.   Restore and produce relevant documents from Varsano's August 2001 backup tape;

3.   Pay for the re-deposition of Varsano and Tong, limited to the new material produced from Varsano's August 2001 backup tape; and

4.   Pay all "reasonable expenses, including attorney's fees," incurred by Zubulake in connection with the making of this motion.

---

102.   Fed. R. Civ. P. 37(b)(2).

In addition, I will give the following instruction to the jury that hears this case:

You have heard that UBS failed to produce some of the e-mails sent or received by UBS personnel in August and September 2001. Plaintiff has argued that this evidence was in defendants' control and would have proven facts material to the matter in controversy.

If you find that UBS could have produced this evidence, and that the evidence was within its control, and that the evidence would have been material in deciding facts in dispute in this case, you are permitted, but not required, to infer that the evidence would have been unfavorable to UBS.

In deciding whether to draw this inference, you should consider whether the evidence not produced would merely have duplicated other evidence already before you. You may also consider whether you are satisfied that UBS's failure to produce this information was reasonable. Again, any inference you decide to draw should be based on all of the facts and circumstances in this case.

* * *

COMMENTARY

Prejudice or harm from spoliation occurs when the requesting party is, as a practical matter, unable to obtain production of relevant information that would have helped its case because the information was destroyed in violation of a legal duty to preserve. However, it is self-evident that it can be challenging at best to demonstrate the relevance of information that is no longer available to be examined because it was destroyed.

In some situations, it may be possible to demonstrate the prejudicial effect of spoliation by means of information that was preserved and produced in discovery and that in one way or another shows the likely relevance and impact of the information that was destroyed. In other cases, it may be possible to extract the lost information from other sources, albeit at great expense and with the aid of computer forensics; for example, where a witness deleted e-mails from a laptop, they may be recoverable by forensic examination of the computer's hard drive. Courts may appoint an independent expert to ensure that all steps are being taken to recover missing information. For example, in a case where the defendant failed to comply with a preservation order and overwrote certain backup tapes subject to the order, the court recognized that "[h]ow much has been lost, and the extent of prejudice to the plaintiffs from the loss cannot be determined at this time" and appointed an independent expert to determine whether appropriate efforts were underway to retrieve the e-mail lost from the destroyed backup tapes.[11]

In many situations, however, it is not possible either to determine the likely contents of the destroyed information or extract it from another source

---

11. *Keir v. UnumProvident Corp.*, No. 02 Civ. 8781, 2003 WL 21997747, at *13 (S.D.N.Y. Aug. 22, 2003).

through no fault of the requesting party. Accordingly, courts will presume prejudice under certain circumstances. For example, where the culpability of the spoliator is egregious, prejudice is presumed. "Some misconduct may prove to be so 'contumacious' that the entry of a default judgment is warranted to preserve the integrity of the judicial process."[12]

Courts have recognized the inherent problem or at least the irony in requiring a party to show prejudice from spoliation when the opposing party has destroyed the means of doing so. To require too specific a showing would reward the spoliator. Thus, courts have often lowered the bar, for example, where "[t]he substantial and complete nature of the destruction of the evidence contained in the recorded telephone conversations and hard drives destroyed . . . justifies a finding of prejudice."[13]

Generally, where prejudice is demonstrated or presumed, courts will look to remedial sanctions to put the requesting party back in the position it would have been in had the spoliation not occurred. The degree of prejudice or harm will always impact the nature and degree of sanctions. The more severe the prejudice, the more likely it will be that the court will impose a severe sanction such as an adverse inference. Where the prejudice is very great, the assessment of the spoliator's culpability becomes less important. It is fair to say that the appropriate sanction turns on the facts of each case, both with respect to culpability and prejudice.

> Our case-by-case approach to the failure to produce relevant evidence seems to be working. Such failures occur along the continuum of fault ranging from innocence through the degrees of negligence to intentionality. . . . [I]t makes little sense to confine promotion of [the remedial purpose of spoliation sanctions] to cases involving only outrageous culpability, where the party victimized by the spoliation is prejudiced irrespective of whether the spoliator acted with intent or gross negligence.[14]

B. RULE 37(e)—GOOD FAITH OPERATION OF AN ELECTRONIC INFORMATION SYSTEM

DOE v. NORWALK COMMUNITY COLLEGE

248 F.R.D. 372 (D.Conn. 2007)

HALL, DISTRICT JUDGE

I. INTRODUCTION

The plaintiff, Jane Doe, brings this action against Norwalk Community College ("NCC") and the Board of Trustees, Connecticut Community Colleges ("Board") (collectively, the "defendants"), as well as against

---

12. *Danis v. USN Commc'ns, Inc.*, No. 98 C 7482, 2000 WL 1694325, at *34 (N.D. Ill. Oct. 23, 2000) (quoting *Barnhill v. United States*, 11 F.3d 1360, 1368 (7th Cir. 1993)).

13. *E*TRADE Secs., LLC v. Deutsche Bank AG*, 230 F.R.D. 582, 592 (D. Minn. 2005).

14. *Reilly v. Natwest Mkts. Group, Inc.*, 181 F.3d 253, 267–68 (2d Cir. 1999) (internal quotation marks omitted).

Ronald Masi in his individual capacity. In her Amended Complaint Doe alleges violations of Title IX of the Education Amendments of 1972, 20 U.S.C. §§ 1681–1688. Doe also asserts state law claims of negligent retention and supervision and negligent infliction of emotional distress.

Doe has filed a Motion for Sanctions for Discovery Misconduct and Spoliation of Evidence against the college defendants. * * *

II. FACTS

On November 22, 2004, Doe filed her Complaint initiating this lawsuit * * *. On March 1, 2006, Doe moved to compel the inspection of certain electronic records possessed by NCC, and a hearing was held on the motion before Magistrate Judge Holly Fitzsimmons on April 26, 2006. At the hearing, Dorran Delay of DataTrack Resources, LLC, a forensic computer firm retained by Doe to inspect NCC's computer records, testified regarding his qualifications to perform the inspection. On July 20, 2006, the court granted Doe's Motion to Compel, thereby permitting Delay to perform the inspection.

On August 15 and August 18, 2006, Delay carried out the inspection of certain NCC computers, which he memorialized in memoranda dated September 11 and October 3, 2006. Doe subsequently submitted two affidavits, written by Delay, as part of her Motion for Sanctions. In response to Delay's first affidavit, NCC's Information Technology Technician, Wyatt Bissell, submitted an affidavit as well. Their findings will be discussed below, where relevant.

This court scheduled a hearing on Doe's Motion for Sanctions, to take testimony from the computer experts regarding their results. At the hearing held on June 26, 2007 ("Hearing I"), Delay as well as Bissell were examined by counsel on both sides; additionally, the defendants presented the testimony of Mr. Olsen, the systems manager for Connecticut Community Colleges. On July 5, 2007, the court heard further testimony from Bissell and Delay ("Hearing II"), and also held Oral Argument regarding some of the remaining legal and factual issues involved in this Motion for Sanctions.

III. DISCUSSION

A. Spoliation of Evidence

Doe seeks an adverse evidentiary inference with regard to electronic files which she claims the defendants destroyed. * * * This sanction serves a threefold purpose of (1) deterring parties from destroying evidence; (2) placing the risk of an erroneous evaluation of the content of the destroyed evidence on the party responsible for its destruction; and (3) restoring the party harmed by the loss of evidence helpful to its case to where the party would have been in the absence of spoliation. * * *

A party seeking an adverse inference based on spoliation must establish "(1) that the party having control over the evidence had an obligation to preserve it at the time it was destroyed; (2) that the records were destroyed with a culpable state of mind; and (3) that the destroyed evidence was relevant to the party's claim or defense such that a reasonable trier of fact could find that it would support that claim or defense."

Doe claims that "the hard drives of key witnesses in this case were scrubbed" or "completely wiped of data." Such assertions are based on the conclusions of Delay, who inspected NCC's computer records using special forensic software. Delay explained in his affidavit and at the Hearing that Seaborn's computer had been replaced in December 2004, one month after Doe filed her lawsuit, and that Seaborn's old computer "was totally devoid of data; it appears to have had its data wiped."[3]

Additionally, Delay found the Microsoft Outlook PST files, which house electronic mailboxes, of four individuals had inconsistencies "that indicate that data has been altered, destroyed or filtered." For example, Professor Skeeter's PST file contained no Deleted Items and only one Sent Item and the Inbox and Sent Items contained data starting August 2004, "even though other activity is present starting in 2002." Doe has also presented evidence that the retention policy issued by the State Library, which provides for a two-year retention with respect to electronic correspondence, governs NCC retention, and that this policy was not followed with respect to the hard drives of the computers of faculty members who left the college.

* * *

Bissell * * * testified that, although he was familiar with the State Librarian's document retention policy, NCC did not follow it because, according to him, it did not apply to "normal computer usage" and transitory email messages did not need to be maintained. Additionally, the defendants argue that "evidence discussing Defendant Masi contained in various backup servers as well as computers from NCC faculty and staff were turned over to the plaintiff," thus presenting "powerful evidence" that the defendants did not destroy all emails or documents regarding Masi. The defendants claim that they provided Doe with "approximately six emails" referencing Masi, one of which was written by someone who claims Masi "was always touching me." Although the defendants rely on the fact that this email was written more than three months prior to Doe's filing of her lawsuit, the court finds that because this email postdates the incident with Masi by six months, it does not respond to Doe's argument that certain evidence was destroyed "that would support the plaintiff's claim that NCC had actual notice of Masi's conduct" prior to the incident of which she complained.

1. Duty to Preserve

The court finds that Doe has established the first prong of the adverse inference instruction, that the party having control over the evidence had an obligation to preserve it at the time it was destroyed. Such an

---

3. According to Delay, wiping is a "process that overwrites existing data on the hard drive, making this information unrecoverable." * * *

obligation to preserve evidence "usually arises when a party has notice that the evidence is relevant to litigation but also on occasion in other circumstances, as for example when a party should have known that the evidence may be relevant to future litigation." In this case, the defendants argue that the duty to preserve did not arise until well after Doe filed her lawsuit in November 2004, perhaps when Doe had indicated her need for the electronic discovery in her Rule 26(f) Report, dated February 18, 2005.

The court strongly disagrees with the defendants. * * * [T]he court finds that the duty to preserve certainly arose no later than September 2004, when Doe's counsel sent the defendants a demand letter indicating Doe's intention to sue NCC. In fact, the court believes the duty to preserve had arisen by February 13, 2004, when a meeting was held between Dean Fisher, Professor Skeeter and Professor Seaborn regarding the Doe incident, which indicates to the court that, as of that date, NCC was aware of Doe's allegations of sexual assault by Masi. At that time, even if Doe had not yet filed her lawsuit, the defendants should have known that any documents, including e-mails and hard drives, related to Professor Masi could potentially be relevant to future litigation.* * *

"The duty to preserve attached at the time that litigation was reasonably anticipated." *Zubulake*, 220 F.R.D. at 217. At that time, the defendants "must suspend [their] routine document retention/destruction policy and put in place a 'litigation hold' to ensure the preservation of relevant documents." However, NCC did not do so. Indeed, the defendants admit that they "scrubbed" Masi's hard drive "pursuant to normal NCC practice." Even if the court assumes the duty to preserve generally arose in September 2004, it finds that the defendants should not have "scrubbed" Masi's computer after his resignation because of the state criminal investigation against him.

* * *

With respect to the destruction of electronic data, the defendants cite to newly-promulgated Rule 37(e) of the Federal Rules of Civil Procedure, which states: "Absent exceptional circumstances, a court may not impose sanctions under these rules on a party for failing to provide electronically stored information lost as a result of the routine, good-faith operation of an electronic information system." Fed.R.Civ.P. 37(e). However, the Commentary to that Rule indicates that, "[w]hen a party is under a duty to preserve information because of pending or reasonably anticipated litigation, intervention in the routine operation of an information system is one aspect of what is often called a 'litigation hold.' " *Id.* at Advisory Committee Notes to 2006 Amendment. Thus, in order to take advantage of the good faith exception, a party needs to act affirmatively to prevent the system from destroying or altering information, even if such destruction would occur in the regular course of business. Because the defendants failed to suspend it at any time, the court finds that the defendants cannot take advantage of Rule 37(e)'s good faith exception.

In addition, as the Commentary to Rule 37(e) indicates, the Rule only applies to information lost "due to the 'routine operation of an electronic information system'—the ways in which such systems are generally designed, programmed, and implemented to meet the party's technical and business needs." This Rule therefore appears to require a routine system in order to take advantage of the good faith exception, and the court cannot find that the defendants had such a system in place. Indeed, testimony at the Hearings revealed that, after NCC shifted over to the Hartford server in August 2004, emails were backed up for one year; however, emails pre-dating this transfer were only retained for six months or less. Thus, the defendants did not appear to have one consistent, "routine" system in place, and Bissell admitted at Hearing II that the State Librarian's policy was not followed. Counsel for the defendants also indicated at Oral Argument that he was not aware that the defendants did anything to stop the destruction of the backup tapes after NCC's obligation to preserve arose.[9]

* * *

2. Culpable State of Mind

As for the second prong of a spoliation of evidence claim, a culpable state of mind is established by ordinary negligence. Indeed, because this court has found that a duty to preserve exists, and that the defendants breached that duty, "[o]nce the duty to preserve attaches, any destruction of documents is, at a minimum, negligent." *Zubulake*, 220 F.R.D. at 220.

However, the court finds more: it finds the defendants' failure to place a litigation hold and to preserve emails and hard drives relevant to Doe's allegations in this case to be at least grossly negligent, if not reckless. *Chan v. Triple 8 Palace, Inc.*, 2005 WL 1925579, at *7 ("[T]he utter failure to establish any form of litigation hold at the outset of litigation is grossly negligent. That is what occurred here: the defendants systematically destroyed evidence because they had never been informed of their obligation to suspend normal document destruction policies.").

The defendants claim that everything that happened was the result of a neutral retention system with limited resources. However, as discussed above, there is no evidence that the defendants did anything to stop the routine destruction of the backup tapes after NCC's obligation to preserve arose. Moreover, with respect to Delay's findings regarding the PST files, while the defendants explain that the reason for the deleted emails was because email storage space (mailbox) was limited to only 50 megabytes maximum of space, according to Delay space was not a reason for the

---

9. The court finds the defendants' argument that they had no choice but to continue the routine deletion of the backup server, because the plaintiff in this case is a Jane Doe plaintiff and they would otherwise have had to reveal her identity, to be unavailing. As the court offered at Oral Argument, the defendants could at least have conferred with Doe's counsel regarding this question of how to send a systemwide communication on document retention without revealing Doe's real name. Alternatively, they could have instructed employees, most especially IT employees, to cease deletion or scrubbing of electronic data.

limited activity in Professors Schwab, Skeeter and Verna's mailboxes. Further, it is inexplicable how there could not be one mention of Masi or Doe in Schwab's PST file, when there are 500 other communications that surround the date of the incident. The court finds that this indicates selective destruction, evidencing intentional behavior.

Delay also found what appeared to have been evidence tampering— that is, several files were accessed and deleted within minutes of Delay's investigation, and two documents were deleted from Dellamura's files about a month after the Doe incident that had "sexual harassment" in their titles. He also found significant activity on Professor's Seaborn's computer only a few days before his investigation—indeed, he found that 122 emails were sent or received at 8:43 a.m. on August 11, 2006, and that it appeared that files were copied into that computer at that time. Delay also found other activity occurred on Seaborn's computer on the morning of his investigation. Bissell testified that it was not likely another user than Seaborn had accessed her computer on those days, even if it was during summer vacation, because NCC did not know the ID's and passwords of each staff member; moreover, the defendants point to the fact that none of the 122 emails of August 11, 2006, involved Masi or the incidents in this case. While this last point may go to the third prong, the court credits the testimony of Delay, experienced in computer forensics, who concluded that Seaborn's PST file was manipulated in the time period after Doe filed her lawsuit, when the defendants were "unquestionably on notice of [their] duty to preserve." *Zubulake*, 220 F.R.D. at 221. According to Delay, the large amount of activity all at once is uncommon and when he typically examines computers, there is no activity on the day of his investigation.

Moreover, the court finds at least gross negligence, if not more, in the defendants' replacing Seaborn's computer in December 2004, one month after this lawsuit was filed. Regardless of the fact that the entire business department at NCC may have received new computers, the defendants were involved in this litigation and Seaborn was one of its key players. Thus, they had a clear obligation to preserve Seaborn's old computer rather than decommissioning it or reimaging and reissuing it, as Bissell testified at Hearing II. At the very least, they should have kept track of what was done with her old computer.

3. Relevance

Finally, to establish the third prong of a spoliation of evidence claim, that the destroyed evidence is "relevant" to a party's claims, that party "must adduce sufficient evidence from which a reasonable trier of fact could infer that the destroyed [or unavailable] evidence would have been of the nature alleged by the party affected by its destruction." However, because "holding the prejudiced party to too strict a standard of proof regarding the likely contents of the destroyed evidence would subvert the prophylactic and punitive purposes of the adverse inference, the level of proof that will suffice to support an inference in favor of the innocent party on a particular issue must be less than the amount that would suffice to survive summary judgment on that issue."

* * *

As discussed above, Doe has demonstrated that the defendants' failure to preserve hard drives and emails of certain key players in Doe's lawsuit was at a minimum grossly negligent. Therefore, no other proof of relevance is necessary, and Doe is entitled to an adverse inference instruction.

However, if the court were to only find the defendants to be negligent, Doe must demonstrate that the destroyed evidence would have been relevant and favorable to her. "In the absence of bad faith or gross negligence by the alleged spoliator, the relevance element can be established if the moving party submits extrinsic evidence tending to demonstrate that the missing evidence would have been favorable to it." "Doe has supplied some proof that the missing evidence was likely to be favorable to her: she has submitted an affidavit from R.M., in which R.M. states that she sent Seaborn an email in 2004 "complaining about what happened to Jane Doe in this case . . . [and] that the college could have stopped Masi after my complaint but did nothing." That email has been destroyed. Doe also has evidence of a missing file, entitled "Masi–POL. doc," which Delay found referenced but unrecoverable on Dellamura's computer. Thus, while not required to in light of the court's finding of at least gross negligence, Doe has shown that the destroyed evidence was favorable to her allegations.

Therefore, the court finds that Doe has established the elements of an adverse inference based on spoliation: the defendants had an obligation to preserve the evidence at the time it was destroyed; the defendants' failure to preserve evidence was at a minimum grossly negligent; and even if the defendants' conduct was simple negligence, Doe has established the relevance of the missing evidence. The court thus finds that Doe is entitled to an adverse inference jury instruction with respect to the destroyed evidence.

B. Costs

Doe is entitled to an award of the costs that she incurred with this motion. See *Zubulake v. UBS Warburg LLC,* 229 F.R.D. 422, 437 (S.D.N.Y. 2004). "Such a monetary award may be appropriate to punish the offending party for its actions or to deter the litigant's conduct, sending the message that egregious conduct will not be tolerated." *Chan,* 2005 WL 1925579, at *10 (Internal quotation marks omitted). Such an award also "serves the remedial purpose of making the opposing party whole for costs incurred as a result of the spoliator's wrongful conduct." *Id.* * * * In this case, Doe expended resources to retain Mr. Delay to perform the forensic investigation of NCC's computers, and those costs are compensable.

* * *

COMMENTARY

Doe may be compared with *Escobar v. City of Houston*, where the plaintiffs alleged that the defendant City had failed to preserve the records of electronic communications by the Houston Police Department in the twenty-four hours after the shooting death of a minor, Eli Escobar.[15] The plaintiffs alleged that they had provided notice to the City of their wrongful death claim within sixty days after the shooting and that the electronic communications were likely to discuss events that occurred after the minor had been shot. Police department policy was to keep transmissions for ninety days. The plaintiffs, therefore, argued that the destruction of these communications violated the City's preservation obligation. The plaintiffs sought spoliation sanctions in the form of an adverse inference instruction.

The City argued that the plaintiffs' notice of claim did not specifically request all electronic communications, that it was unaware that the plaintiffs sought the electronic communications, and that it preserved all evidence it *believed* to be relevant. "In the Fifth Circuit, a severe sanction for spoliation, including an adverse inference instruction, requires a showing of bad faith." The record did not provide a basis for an adverse inference instruction because there was no showing that relevant electronic communications were destroyed or that the destruction occurred in bad faith. Absent proof of relevance, or bad faith, the routine and automatic destruction of the police department's electronic communications was not sanctionable. Moreover,

> under Rule 37[e] of the Federal Rules of Civil Procedure, if the electronic communications were destroyed in the routine operation of the HPD's computer system, and if there is no evidence of bad faith in the operation of the system that led to the destruction of the communications, sanctions are not appropriate.

Escobar demonstrates that, absent a duty to preserve and absent bad faith, Rule 37(e) offers independent protection from sanctions when ESI is destroyed in the routine operation of an electronic information system.

1. What Constitutes Bad Faith?

In re Krause provides an example of a decision in which a party's destruction of relevant ESI was found to be in bad faith.[16] Krause was an adversary proceeding instituted by the Government and joined in by a trustee to, among other things, recover assets from the debtor (Krause). Both the trustee and the Government sought sanctions against Krause for violation of a preliminary injunction and discovery orders. The court found that, after the duty to preserve had attached, Krause installed and ran a wiping software and that after Krause's computers had crashed and while the adversary proceeding was pending and document requests had been served, installed and resumed the operation of the wiping software in the restoration process. These findings led the court to the "inescapable conclusion" that Krause "willfully and intentionally destroyed" ESI.

---

15. *See* No. 04–1945, 2007 WL 2900581, at *17 (S.D. Tex. Sept. 29, 2007).

16. 367 B.R. 740 (D. Kan. 2007).

Krause also rejected any argument that the debtor could rely on Rule 37(e):

> Nor can Krause claim that his use of GhostSurf 2006 was a good faith "routine operation" of his computers. With the 2006 amendments to the Federal Rules of Civil Procedure, a party enjoys a safe harbor from sanctions where electronic evidence is "lost as a result of the routine, good-faith operation of an electronic information system."
>
> * * *
>
> The undisputed evidence established that Krause's hard drives were far from being at full capacity thus making it improbable that electronic information was being overwritten or deleted by routine operation of his computers. Just as a litigant may have an obligation to suspend certain features of a "routine operation," the Court concludes that a litigant has an obligation to suspend features of a computer's operation that are not routine if those features will result in destroying evidence. Here, that obligation required Krause to disable the running of the wiping feature of GhostSurf as soon as the preservation duty attached. And it certainly obligated Krause to refrain from reinstalling GhostSurf when his computers crashed and he restored them.

Evidence adduced from salvaged ESI demonstrated to the *Krause* court that the destroyed ESI would have been relevant, that the ability of the Government and the trustee to proceed had been significantly harmed, and that the court should infer that the destroyed ESI was relevant. The court entered, among other things, a partial default judgment against the debtor.

Krause adds gloss to Rule 37(e) in two respects. *First*, it suggests that automatic deletion by the "routine operation" of a computer system cannot occur unless that system is at full capacity. *Second*, it requires a litigant to suspend "nonroutine" operations—which would appear to fall outside the scope of Rule 37(e).

2. Interpreting Terms Used in Rule 37(e)

- **"Absent exceptional circumstances** ..." Perhaps this is an attempt to restore the factor of prejudice to the requesting party's case.

- **"... a court may not impose sanctions under these rules** ..." A judge always has inherent authority or contempt powers.[17]

- **"... on a party** ..." This phrase explicitly excludes the non-party served with a *subpoena duces tecum* for ESI under Rule 45.

- **"... for failing to provide electronically stored information lost as a result of the routine, good-faith operation** ..." What is a routine, good-faith operation?

- **"... of an electronic information system."** What is an electronic information system? Does it include the human beings who run it?

When first proposed, Rule 37(e) was looked to as a "safe harbor" from discovery sanctions that might arise from the routine deletion of information from computer systems. From the Committee Note to the case law cited and

---

17. *See, e.g., Leon v. IDX Sys.,* 464 F.3d 951, 958 (9th Cir. 2006).

the commentaries quoted, it becomes obvious that Rule 37(e) affords no certain protection against sanctions. Indeed, it has been rarely relied on (either pro or con) and its sparse language raises serious questions about its reach and scope. The one common thread is that the Rule does not excuse a party from rule-based sanctions for a failure to comply with a preservation obligation.

In *Oklahoma ex rel. Edmondson v. Tyson Foods, Inc.,* the court addressed the adequacy of the plaintiff's privilege logs as well as the adequacy of the plaintiff's responses to interrogatories.[18] While the court did not otherwise mention Rule 37(e) in the course of its rulings, it did give this admonition:

> The Court notes that although no formal preservation order has been entered herein, the obligation of the parties to preserve evidence, including ESI, arises as soon as a party is aware the documentation may be relevant. The Court further advises the parties that they should be very cautious in relying upon any "safe harbor" doctrine as described in new Rule 37[e].

C. DEFAULT JUDGMENTS, DISMISSAL, AND ADVERSE INFERENCES[19]

COMMENTARY

1. When Is a Default Judgment or Dismissal Sanction Appropriate for Spoliation?

A district court may order a default judgment or a dismissal, either pursuant to Rule 37(b)(2), which authorizes a court to assess a sanction for violation of a discovery order, or pursuant to the court's inherent power to protect its integrity and prevent abuses of the judicial process. When evaluating the propriety of dismissal or default as a discovery sanction, a court should consider: (1) the degree of actual prejudice to the other party; (2) the amount of interference with the judicial process; (3) the culpability of the litigant; (4) whether the court warned the party in advance that default or dismissal of the action would be a likely sanction for noncompliance; and (5) the efficacy of lesser sanctions.[20]

2. When Is an Adverse Inference Jury Instruction Appropriate?

Under the "adverse inference rule," when a party has relevant evidence within its control that it fails to produce, that failure may permit a court to instruct the jury that it may infer that the missing evidence is unfavorable to the party who could have produced the evidence and did not. No inference can be drawn from the failure to produce evidence not in a party's control.

When a party has destroyed relevant evidence, a "spoliation inference" arises to the effect that the destroyed evidence would have been unfavorable

---

18. No. 05 Civ. 329, 2007 WL 1498973, at *1 (N.D. Okla. May 17, 2007).

19. For a detailed discussion of bad behavior by both client and counsel leading a court to impose a default judgment and significant attorneys' fees see *Metropolitan Opera Ass'n, Inc. v. Local 100, Hotel Employees and Restaurant Employees Int'l Union*, 212 F.R.D. 178 (S.D.N.Y. 2003).

20. *See Procter & Gamble Co. v. Haugen*, 427 F.3d 727, 738 (10th Cir. 2005).

to the position of the offending party. A party seeking an adverse inference based on spoliation allegations must "adduce sufficient evidence from which a reasonable trier of fact could infer that the destroyed or unavailable evidence would have been of the nature alleged by the [aggrieved] party...."[21] The bottom line is that the fact-specific balancing approach provides courts with the necessary flexibility to impose whatever type of sanction the court deems appropriate.

3. What Sanctions, If Any, Should Be Awarded for the Following:

Defendant used "Window Washer" disk scrubbing software on the hard drive of his laptop the day before the hard drive was to be turned over to a forensic expert. The defendant also performed mass deletions of electronic files on his laptop. There is no other source of the information that was contained on the hard drive. What sanctions would you award? If the answer is an adverse inference instruction, draft such an instruction.

D. MONETARY SANCTIONS

DOCTOR JOHN'S, INC. v. CITY OF SIOUX CITY, IOWA

486 F. Supp. 2d 953 (N.D. Iowa 2007)

BENNETT, DISTRICT JUDGE

By order dated May 1, 2007, the court dismissed this case in its entirety, with prejudice, upon the parties' settlement and Stipulation Of Dismissal. However, the court stated in the order dismissing the case that it would retain jurisdiction over the question of whether or not sanctions should be imposed upon the City for destruction, during the pendency of litigation, of relevant records, which consisted of recordings of closed sessions of the City Council concerning the ordinances challenged in this case. Thereafter * * * the court held a conference with counsel for the parties * * * to discuss the remaining sanctions question * * * [and] also received a letter from counsel for the City clarifying changes made to the City's policy regarding retention of recordings of closed sessions of the City Council. * * *

A first year law student should have—and most would have—known that a party must retain documents or records that are likely to be relevant in pending litigation. The City's claim that it was simply following state law in destroying key evidence is laughable and frivolous. No state or federal statute, rule, or common law allows a party to destroy critical evidence during the pendency of litigation, and the City policy that permitted destruction of certain documents after a specified period of time certainly did not require destruction of such documents.

Indeed, both state and federal law require just the opposite, retention of evidence potentially relevant to pending or reasonably anticipated

---

21. *Residential Funding Corp. v. Degeorge Financial Corp.*, 306 F.3d 99, 109 (2d Cir. 2002) (quotations omitted).

litigation. *See, e.g., Dillon v. Nissan Motor Co., Ltd.*, 986 F.2d 263, 268 (8th Cir. 1993) ("[T]he destruction of evidence that a party knew or should have known was relevant to imminent litigation certainly justifies a sanction under the court's inherent power comparable to the Rule 37 sanctions."); see also *Silvestri v. Gen. Motors Corp.*, 271 F.3d 583, 591 (4th Cir. 2001) ("The duty to preserve material evidence arises not only during litigation but also extends to that period before litigation when a party reasonably should know that the evidence may be relevant to anticipated litigation.") * * * *Zubulake v. UBS Warburg LLC*, 220 F.R.D. 212, 216 (S.D.N.Y.2003) ("The duty to preserve attached at the time that litigation was reasonably anticipated.").

Thus, the City's failure to preserve the tape recordings of the City Council's closed-session meetings, and the consequential destruction of critical evidence in this case, was clearly and unquestionably improper conduct.

Moreover, the court has the inherent power to sanction such improper conduct subject to review for abuse of discretion. * * * A court's inherent power includes the discretionary "ability to fashion an appropriate sanction for conduct which abuses the judicial process." *Chambers v. NASCO, Inc.*, 501 U.S. 32, 44–45 (1991). * * * Thus, the court must determine whether and what sanctions are appropriate for the City's improper destruction of records in this case.

The Eighth Circuit Court of Appeals has recognized that, under a court's inherent power to sanction parties, "a finding of bad faith is not always necessary to the court's exercise of its inherent power to impose sanctions." * * * [H]owever, * * * a finding of "bad faith" is required to impose sanctions in the form of an adverse inference instruction or award of attorney fees to the opposing party. * * * Consequently, this court will assume that a finding of "bad faith" is required to impose other monetary sanctions.

Here, a substantial monetary sanction against the City is easily justified by the City's outrageous conduct in failing to preserve the key evidence of recordings of closed-session meetings. That conduct was of a kind that "abuses the judicial process" * * * because it went to the very heart of the plaintiff's ability to prove the City's motivation in passing the challenged ordinances. Moreover, the circumstances give rise to a powerful inference of intentional destruction indicating a desire to suppress the truth, notwithstanding the City's contention that the records were destroyed pursuant to a document retention policy.

More specifically, as noted above, the contention that the document retention policy mandated by state law excused destruction of the records in question is laughable and frivolous, because that policy plainly did not require the destruction of any documents, and certainly did not authorize the destruction of records pertinent to pending litigation. Moreover, purported adherence to the policy by destroying records that the policy did not mandate for destruction was unreasonable and amounted to bad faith conduct where litigation was pending. Indeed, this case seems to this court to fall well within, not to test the limits of, conduct that constitutes bad faith destruction of documents, where the City had not simply been made aware of the circumstances giving rise to a potential lawsuit, but was in the throes of litigating a lawsuit over the constitutionality of its sex shop ordinances at the time that it destroyed records of closed sessions in which the City Council considered those ordinances. Moreover, while the City destroyed these records, the City went out of its way to provide evidence and even to generate new evidence to try to justify the ordinances long after they were passed, enjoined, and partially struck down. Finally, the recordings of the closed sessions in question here were the only contemporaneous evidence of the motives of the decision makers at the time certain decisions were made, and as such—where the motives of the decision makers were plainly at issue—the evidence was highly relevant to pending litigation.

To the same extent and for essentially the same reasons that the court finds that the City's conduct in destroying the records in question was in "bad faith," the court also finds that such conduct was prejudicial to the plaintiff. Again, the City's motive in passing the challenged ordinances was a critical element of the plaintiff's proof, and the City's destruction of contemporaneous recordings of closed sessions of City Council meetings in which the ordinances were discussed patently prejudiced the plaintiff's ability to prove that critical element.

In this case, the court finds that a monetary sanction in the amount of $50,000 is warranted for the City's destruction of plainly relevant records.

On the other hand, because of the City's ill-conceived, illegal, and unconstitutional actions in targeting and attempting to trample the plaintiff's First Amendment rights, the taxpayers have already paid dearly, to the tune of over $600,000. No matter how you fry it, that's a ton of Sneaky's chicken. Also, notwithstanding various City Council Members' attempts to save face by claiming that the City would have ultimately prevailed in this litigation—just how those City Council Members became such enlightened, sophisticated, and prophetic federal constitutional scholars remains a prodigious mystery—the City and Doctor John's have worked diligently to reach a settlement. In so doing, both sides engaged in substantial compromise from their equally unreasonable legal positions. Moreover, the City Council has voluntarily and wisely changed its record retention policy to prevent the destruction of such evidence in the future during pending litigation. Thus, having recognized the error of its ways, the City moved swiftly to correct its mistake.

Balancing all of these factors, the court finds that the scales of justice tip ever so slightly in favor of declining to impose sanctions against the City for destruction of relevant records. Any similar litigation misconduct in the future, however, will be dealt with severely, in light of the City's "get out of jail free" card here.

COMMENTARY

Sanctions against a spoliator may include reimbursement of attorney fees, monetary penalties against the party or attorney, and recovery of discovery costs.

Did the court's action in *Doctor John's* fail to serve the remedial purposes of discovery sanctions?

Although the defendant's bad faith destruction of documents warranted $50,000 in sanctions, the court found that countervailing factors weighed "ever so slightly" in favor of declining to impose that sanction. If, as the court determined, the defendant's bad faith conduct prejudiced the plaintiff's ability to prove its case, did the court's failure to impose sanctions effectively penalize the plaintiff?

While reimbursement of attorneys' fees and monetary penalties may constitute a sanction, pursuant to Rule 26 (g)(3), it is not entirely clear that shifting of discovery costs should be considered a sanction. A court has the power to apportion the costs of discovery pursuant to Rule 26(c)(1)(B) and Rule 26(c)(2), which provide that a court may "specify the terms" for discovery or disclosure and may "on just terms" order that "a party or person provide or permit discovery." Do you agree that the shifting of costs can be viewed as "a term" upon which discovery is permitted rather than a sanction?[22]

E.   SANCTIONING A PARTY/SANCTIONING COUNSEL

QUALCOMM INC. v. BROADCOM CORP.

No. 05 Civ. 1958, 2008 WL 66932 (S.D. Cal. Jan. 7, 2008)

MAJOR, MAGISTRATE JUDGE

At the conclusion of trial, counsel for Broadcom Corporation ("Broadcom") made an oral motion for sanctions after Qualcomm Incorporated ("Qualcomm") witness Viji Raveendran testified about emails that were not produced to Broadcom during discovery. The trial judge, United States District Court Judge Rudi M. Brewster, referred the motion to this Court * * *. On May 29, 2007, Broadcom filed a written motion requesting that the Court sanction Qualcomm for its failure to produce tens of thousands of documents that Broadcom had requested in discovery. * * *

After hearing oral argument and reviewing Judge Brewster's Order on Remedy for Finding of Waiver ("Waiver Order") and Order Granting Broadcom Corporation's Motion for Exceptional Case Finding and for an Award of Attorney's Fees (35 U.S.C. § 285) ("Exceptional Case Order"), this Court issued an Order to Show Cause Why Sanctions Should Not be

---

22. *See, e.g., Zubulake IV*, 220 F.R.D. at 222 (requiring defendant to pay costs incurred by plaintiff in taking additional discovery that resulted from defendant's failure to produce certain information in a timely manner).

Imposed against Qualcomm's retained attorneys ("OSC"). Specifically, this Court ordered * * * all * * * attorneys who signed discovery responses, signed pleadings and pretrial motions, and/or appeared at trial on behalf of Qualcomm to appear and show cause why sanctions should not be imposed for their failure to comply with this Court's orders.

On October 3, 2007, nineteen attorneys filed declarations and briefs responsive to the OSC. Qualcomm filed a brief and four declarations. * * * Having considered all of the written and oral arguments presented and supporting documents submitted, and for the reasons set forth more fully below, the Court GRANTS IN PART and DENIES IN PART Broadcom's motion for sanctions against Qualcomm, REFERS TO THE STATE BAR OF CALIFORNIA six attorneys, and SANCTIONS Qualcomm and six of its retained lawyers.

BACKGROUND

A. The Patent Infringement Case

Qualcomm initiated this patent infringement action on October 14, 2005, alleging Broadcom's infringement of Qualcomm patent numbers 5,452,104 (the "104 patent") and 5,576,767 (the "767 patent") based on its manufacture, sale, and offers to sell H.264–compliant products. Qualcomm sought injunctive relief, compensatory damages, attorneys' fees and costs. On December 8, 2006, Broadcom filed a First Amended Answer and Counterclaims in which it alleged (1) a counterclaim that the 104 patent is unenforceable due to inequitable conduct, and (2) an affirmative defense that both patents are unenforceable due to waiver. Broadcom's waiver defense was predicated on Qualcomm's participation in the Joint Video Team ("JVT") in 2002 and early 2003. The JVT is the standards-setting body that created the H.264 standard, which was released in May 2003 and governs video coding.

B. Evidence of Qualcomm's Participation in the JVT

Over the course of discovery, Broadcom sought information concerning Qualcomm's participation in and communications with the JVT through a variety of discovery devices.

* * *

In response to Broadcom's request for JVT documents, Qualcomm, in a discovery response signed by attorney Kevin Leung, stated "Qualcomm will produce non-privileged relevant and responsive documents describing QUALCOMM's participation in the JVT, if any, which can be located after a reasonable search." Similarly, Qualcomm committed to producing "responsive non-privileged documents that were given to or received from standards-setting body responsible for the ISO/IEC MPEG–4 Part 10 standard, and which concern any Qualcomm participation in setting the ISO/IEC MPEG–4 Part 10 standard." When asked for "the facts and circumstances of any and all communications between Qualcomm and any standards setting body relating to video technology, including . . . the JVT

..., " Qualcomm responded that it first attended a JVT meeting in December 2003 and that it first submitted a JVT proposal in January 2006. In response to Interrogatory No. 13, Qualcomm stated that it submitted four proposals to the JVT in 2006 but had no earlier involvement. This response included the statement that "Qualcomm's investigation concerning this interrogatory is ongoing and Qualcomm reserves the right to supplement its response to this interrogatory as warranted by its investigation." Kevin Leung signed both of these interrogatory responses.

Qualcomm's responses to Broadcom's Rule 30(b)(6) deposition notices were more troubling. Initially, Qualcomm designated Christine Irvine as the corporation's most knowledgeable person on the issue of Qualcomm's involvement in the JVT. Although attorney Leung prepared Irvine for her deposition, Qualcomm did not search her computer for any relevant documents or emails or provide her with any information to review. Irvine testified falsely that Qualcomm had never been involved in the JVT. Broadcom impeached Irvine with documents showing that Qualcomm had participated in the JVT in late 2003. Qualcomm ultimately agreed to provide another Rule 30(b)(6) witness.

Qualcomm designated Scott Ludwin as the new representative to testify about Qualcomm's knowledge of and involvement in the JVT. Leung prepared and defended Ludwin at his deposition. Qualcomm did not search Ludwin's computer for any relevant documents nor take any other action to prepare him. Ludwin testified falsely that Qualcomm only began participating in the JVT in late 2003, after the H.264 standard had been published. In an effort to impeach him (and extract the truth), Broadcom showed Ludwin a December 2002 email reflector list from the Advanced Video Coding ("AVC") Ad Hoc Group that listed the email address viji@ qualcomm.com.[2] Although Ludwin did not recognize the document, Broadcom utilized the document throughout the litigation to argue that Qualcomm had participated in the JVT during the development of the H.264 standard.

As the case progressed, Qualcomm became increasingly aggressive in its argument that it did not participate in the JVT during the time the JVT was creating the H.264 standard. This argument was vital to Qualcomm's success in this litigation because if Qualcomm had participated in the creation of the H.264 standard, it would have been required to identify its patents that reasonably may be essential to the practice of the H.264 standard, including the 104 and 767 patents, and to license them royalty-free or under non-discriminatory, reasonable terms. Thus, participation in the JVT in 2002 or early 2003 during the creation of the H.264 standard

---

2. The document is an "Input Document to JVT" entitled "Ad Hoc Report on AVC Verification Test." The report discusses a meeting set to take place on Awaji Island. *Id.* Annex A to the document is entitled a "list of Ad Hoc Members." It includes Raveendran's email address, viji@ qualcomm.com, and identifies her as a member of list avc_ce. While the document is not an email sent to or from Raveendran, it indicates that a Qualcomm employee was receiving JVT/AVC reports in 2002. This document became critical to Broadcom as it was the only evidence in Broadcom's possession indicating the truth—that Qualcomm had been actively involved in the JVT and the development of the H.264 standard in 2002.

would have prohibited Qualcomm from suing companies, including Broadcom, that utilized the H.264 standard. In a nutshell, the issue of whether Qualcomm participated in the JVT in 2002 and early 2003 became crucial to the instant litigation.

C.   Trial and Decision Not to Produce avc_ce Emails

Trial commenced on January 9, 2007, and throughout trial, Qualcomm argued that it had not participated in the JVT in 2002 and early 2003 when the H.264 standard was being created. In his opening statement, Qualcomm's lead attorney, James Batchelder, stated:

> Later, in May of 03, the standard is approved and published. And then Qualcomm, in the fall of 2003, it begins to participate not in JVT because it's done. H.264 is approved and published. Qualcomm begins to participate in what are called professional extensions, things that sit on top of the standard, additional improvements.

While preparing Qualcomm witness Viji Raveendran to testify at trial, attorney Adam Bier discovered an August 6, 2002 email to viji@ qualcomm.com welcoming her to the avc_ce mailing list. Several days later, on January 14, 2007, Bier and Raveendran searched her laptop computer using the search term "avc_ce" and discovered 21 separate emails, none of which Qualcomm had produced in discovery. The email chains bore several dates in November 2002 and the authors discussed various issues relating to the H.264 standard. While Raveendran was not a named author or recipient, the emails were sent to all members of two JVT email groups (jvt-experts and avc_ce) and Raveendran maintained them on her computer for more than four years. The Qualcomm trial team decided not to produce these newly discovered emails to Broadcom, claiming they were not responsive to Broadcom's discovery requests. The attorneys ignored the fact that the presence of the emails on Raveendran's computer undercut Qualcomm's premier argument that it had not participated in the JVT in 2002. The Qualcomm trial team failed to conduct any investigation to determine whether there were more emails that also had not been produced.

Four days later, during a sidebar discussion, Stanley Young argued against the admission of the December 2002 avc_ce email reflector list, declaring: "Actually, there are no emails—there are no emails . . . there's no evidence that any email was actually sent to this list. This is just a list of email . . . addresses. There's no evidence of anything being sent." None of the Qualcomm attorneys who were present during the sidebar mentioned the 21 avc_ce emails found on Raveendran's computer a few days earlier.

During Raveendran's direct testimony on January 24th, attorney Lee Patch pointedly did not ask her any questions that would reveal the fact that she had received the 21 emails from the avc_ce mailing list; instead, he asked whether she had "any knowledge of having read" any emails from the avc_ce mailing list. But on cross-examination, Broadcom asked the right question and Raveendran was forced to admit that she had received emails from the avc_ce mailing list. Immediately following this admission, in response to Broadcom's request for the emails, and despite the fact that he had participated in the decision three days earlier not to produce them, Patch told the Court at sidebar:

> It's not clear to me [the emails are] responsive to anything. So that's something that needs to be determined before they would be produced . . . I'm talking about whether they were actually requested in discovery. . . . I'm simply representing that I haven't seen [the emails], and [whether Broadcom requested them] hasn't been determined.

Over the lunch recess that same day, Qualcomm's counsel produced the 21 emails they previously had retrieved from Raveendran's email archive.

On January 26, 2007, the jury returned unanimous verdicts in favor of Broadcom regarding the non-infringement of the 104 and 767 patents, and in favor of Qualcomm regarding the validity and non-obviousness of the same. The jury also returned a unanimous advisory verdict in favor of Broadcom that the 104 patent is unenforceable due to inequitable conduct and the 104 and 767 patents are unenforceable due to waiver.

On March 21, 2007, Judge Brewster found (1) in favor of Qualcomm on Broadcom's inequitable conduct counterclaim regarding the 104 patent, and (2) in favor of Broadcom on Broadcom's waiver defense regarding the 104 and 767 patents. On August 6, 2007, Judge Brewster issued a comprehensive order detailing the appropriate remedy for Qualcomm's waiver. After a thorough overview of the JVT, the JVT's policies and guidelines, and Qualcomm's knowledge of the JVT and evidence of Qualcomm's involvement therein, Judge Brewster found:

> by clear and convincing evidence that Qualcomm, its employees, and its witnesses actively organized and/or participated in a plan to profit heavily by (1) wrongfully concealing the patents-in-suit while participating in the JVT and then (2) actively hiding this concealment from the Court, the jury, and opposing counsel during the present litigation.

Judge Brewster further found that Qualcomm's "counsel participated in an organized program of litigation misconduct and concealment throughout discovery, trial, and post-trial before new counsel took over lead role in the case on April 27, 2007." Based on "the totality of the evidence produced both before and after the jury verdict," and in light of these findings, Judge Brewster concluded that "Qualcomm has waived its rights to enforce the 104 and 767 patents and their continuations, continuations-in-part, divisions, reissues, or any other derivatives of either patent."

Also on August 6, 2007, Judge Brewster granted Broadcom's Motion for an Award of Attorneys' Fees pursuant to 35 U.S.C. § 285. Judge Brewster found clear and convincing evidence that Qualcomm's litigation misconduct, as set forth in his Waiver Order, justified Qualcomm's payment of all "attorneys' fees, court costs, expert witness fees, travel expenses, and any other litigation costs reasonably incurred by Broadcom" in the defense of this case. On December 11, 2007, Judge Brewster adopted this court's recommendation and ordered Qualcomm to pay Broadcom $9,259,985.09 in attorneys' fees and related costs, as well as post-judgment interest on the final fee award of $8,568,633.24 at 4.91 percent accruing from August 6, 2007.

D.   Qualcomm's Post–Trial Misconduct

Following trial, Qualcomm continued to dispute the relevancy and responsiveness of the 21 Raveendran emails. Qualcomm also resisted Broadcom's efforts to determine the scope of Qualcomm's discovery violation. By letter dated February 16, 2007, Bier told Broadcom "[w]e continue to believe that Qualcomm performed a reasonable search of Qualcomm's documents in response to Broadcom's Requests for Production and that the twenty-one unsolicited emails received by Ms. Raveendran from individuals on the avc_ce reflector are not responsive to any valid discovery obligation or commitment." In response to Broadcom's request that Qualcomm conduct additional searches to determine the scope of Qualcomm's discovery violation, Bier stated in a March 7, 2007 letter, we "believe your negative characterization of Qualcomm's compliance with its discovery obligation to be wholly without merit" but he advised that Qualcomm agreed to search the current and archived emails of five trial witnesses using the requested JVT, avc_ce and H.264 terms. Bier explained that Qualcomm has "not yet commenced these searches, and [does] not yet know the volume of results we will obtain." Throughout the remainder of March 2007, Bier repeatedly declined to update Broadcom on Qualcomm's document search.

But, on April 9, 2007, James Batchelder and Louis Lupin, Qualcomm's General Counsel, submitted correspondence to Judge Brewster in which they admitted Qualcomm had thousands of relevant unproduced documents and that their review of these documents "revealed facts that appear to be inconsistent with certain arguments that [counsel] made on Qualcomm's behalf at trial and in the equitable hearing following trial." Batchelder further apologized "for not having discovered these documents sooner and for asserting positions that [they] would not have taken had [they] known of the existence of these documents."

As of June 29, 2007, Qualcomm had searched the email archives of twenty-one employees and located more than forty-six thousand documents (totaling more than three hundred thousand pages), which had been requested but not produced in discovery. Qualcomm continued to produce additional responsive documents throughout the summer.

DISCUSSION

As summarized above, and as found by Judge Brewster, there is clear and convincing evidence that Qualcomm intentionally engaged in conduct designed to prevent Broadcom from learning that Qualcomm had participated in the JVT during the time period when the H.264 standard was being developed. To this end, Qualcomm withheld tens of thousands of emails showing that it actively participated in the JVT in 2002 and 2003 and then utilized Broadcom's lack of access to the suppressed evidence to repeatedly and falsely aver that there was "no evidence" that it had participated in the JVT prior to September 2003. Qualcomm's misconduct in hiding the emails and electronic documents prevented Broadcom from correcting the false statements and countering the misleading arguments.

A. Legal Standard

The Federal Civil Rules authorize federal courts to impose sanctions on parties and their attorneys who fail to comply with discovery obligations and court orders. Rule 37 authorizes a party to file a motion to compel an opponent to comply with a discovery request or obligation when the opponent fails to do so initially. Fed.R.Civ.P. 37(a). If such a motion is filed, the rule requires the court to award reasonable attorney's fees to the prevailing party unless the court finds the losing party's position was "substantially justified" or other circumstances make such an award unjust. Depending upon the circumstances, the court may require the attorney, the client, or both to pay the awarded fees. If the court grants a discovery motion and the losing party fails to comply with the order, the court may impose additional sanctions against the party. Fed.R.Civ.P. 37(b). There is no requirement under this rule that the failure be willful or reckless; "sanctions may be imposed even for negligent failures to provide discovery."

The Federal Rules also provide for sanctions against individual attorneys who are remiss in complying with their discovery obligations:

> Every discovery request, response or objection made by a party . . . shall be signed by at least one attorney. The signature of the attorney . . . constitutes a certification that to the best of the signer's knowledge, information, and belief, formed after a reasonable inquiry, the request, response, or objection is: consistent with the rules and law, not interposed for an improper purpose, and not unreasonable or unduly burdensome or expensive.

Fed.R.Civ.P. 26(g)(2). "[W]hat is reasonable is a matter for the court to decide on the totality of the circumstances." * * *

If an attorney makes an incorrect certification without substantial justification, the court must sanction the attorney, party, or both and the sanction may include an award of reasonable attorney's fees. Fed.R.Civ.P. 26(g)(3). If a party, without substantial justification, fails "to amend a prior response to discovery as required by Rule 26(e)(2)," the court may prevent that party from using that evidence at trial or at a hearing and impose other appropriate sanctions, including the payment of attorney's fees. Fed.R.Civ.P. 37(c)(1). * * * In addition to this rule-based authority, federal courts have the inherent power to sanction litigants to prevent abuse of the judicial process. * * * Sanctions are appropriate in response to "willful disobedience of a court order . . . or when the losing party has acted in bad faith, vexatiously, wantonly, or for oppressive reasons." When a court order is violated, a district court considering the imposition of sanctions must also examine the risk of prejudice to the complying party and the availability of less drastic sanctions.

* * *

C. Sanctions

The Court's review of Qualcomm's declarations, the attorneys' declarations, and Judge Brewster's orders leads this Court to the inevitable conclusion that Qualcomm intentionally withheld tens of thousands of decisive documents from its opponent in an effort to win this case and gain a strategic business advantage over Broadcom. Qualcomm could not have achieved this goal without some type of assistance or deliberate ignorance from its retained attorneys. Accordingly, the Court concludes it must sanction both Qualcomm and some of its retained attorneys.

1. Misconduct by Qualcomm

Qualcomm violated its discovery obligations by failing to produce more than 46,000 emails and documents that were requested in discovery and that Qualcomm agreed to produce. * * * Qualcomm has not established "substantial justification" for its failure to produce the documents. In fact, Qualcomm has not presented any evidence attempting to explain or justify its failure to produce the documents. Despite the fact that it maintains detailed records showing whose computers were searched and which search terms were used * * * Qualcomm has not presented any evidence establishing that it searched for pre-September 2003 JVT, avc_ce, or H.264 records or emails on its computer system or email databases. Qualcomm also has not established that it searched the computers or email databases of the individuals who testified on Qualcomm's behalf at trial or in depositions as Qualcomm's most knowledgeable corporate witnesses; in fact, it indicates that it did not conduct any such search. The fact that Qualcomm did not perform these basic searches at any time before the completion of trial indicates that Qualcomm intentionally withheld the documents. This conclusion is bolstered by the fact that when Qualcomm "discovered" the 21 Raveendran emails, it did not produce them and did not engage in any type of review to determine whether there were additional relevant, responsive, and unproduced documents. The conclusion is further supported by the fact that after trial Qualcomm did not conduct an internal investigation to determine if there were additional unproduced documents; but, rather, spent its time opposing Broadcom's efforts to force such a search and insisting, without any factual basis, that Qualcomm's search was reasonable.

Qualcomm's claim that it inadvertently failed to find and produce these documents also is negated by the massive volume and direct relevance of the hidden documents. As Judge Brewster noted, it is inexplicable that Qualcomm was able to locate the post-September 2003 JVT documents that either supported, or did not harm, Qualcomm's arguments but were unable to locate the pre-September 2003 JVT documents that hurt its arguments. Similarly, the inadvertence argument is undercut by Qualcomm's ability to easily locate the suppressed documents using fundamental JVT and avc search terms when forced to do so by Broadcom's threat to return to court. Finally, the inadvertence argument also is belied by the number of Qualcomm employees and consultants who received the emails, attended the JVT meetings, and otherwise knew about the information set forth in the undisclosed emails. It is inconceivable that Qualcomm was unaware of its involvement in the JVT and of the existence of these documents.

Assuming[,] *arguendo*, that Qualcomm did not know about the suppressed emails, Qualcomm failed to heed several warning signs that should have alerted it to the fact that its document search and production were inadequate. The first significant concern should have been raised in connection with the Rule 30(b)(6) depositions of Christine Irvine and Scott Ludwin. Both individuals testified as the Qualcomm employee most knowledgeable about Qualcomm's involvement in the JVT. But, Qualcomm did not search either person's computer for JVT documents, did not provide either person with relevant JVT documents to review, and did not make any other efforts to ensure each person was in fact knowledgeable about Qualcomm's JVT involvement. These omissions are especially incriminating because many of the suppressed emails were to or from Irvine. If a witness is testifying as an organization's most knowledgeable person on a specific subject, the organization has an obligation to conduct a reasonable investigation and review to ensure that the witness does possess the organization's knowledge. Fed.R.Civ.P. 30(b)(6).[6] * * * An adequate investigation should include an analysis of the sufficiency of the document search and, when electronic documents are involved, an analysis of the sufficiency of the search terms and locations. In the instant case, a reasonable inquiry should have included using the JVT, avc and H.264 search terms and searching the computers of Raveendran, Irvine, Ludwin (and other Qualcomm employees identified in the emails discovered on the computers of these witnesses). This minimal inquiry would have revealed the existence of the suppressed documents.

* * *

---

6. Qualcomm's self-serving statements that "outside counsel selects . . . the custodians whose documents should be searched" and the paralegal does not decide "what witnesses to designate to testify on behalf of the company" (Glathe Decl. at 1) does not relieve Qualcomm of its obligations. Qualcomm has not presented any evidence establishing what actions, if any, it took to ensure it designated the correct employee, performed the correct computer searches, and presented the designated employee with sufficient information to testify as the corporation's most knowledgeable person. Qualcomm also has not presented any evidence that outside counsel knew enough about Qualcomm's organization and operation to identify all of the individuals whose computers should be searched and determine the most knowledgeable witness. And, more importantly, Qualcomm is a large corporation with an extensive legal staff; it clearly had the ability to identify the correct witnesses and determine the correct computers to search and search terms to use. Qualcomm just lacked the desire to do so.

Qualcomm had the ability to identify its employees and consultants who were involved in the JVT, to access and review their computers, databases and emails, to talk with the involved employees and to refresh their recollections if necessary, to ensure that those testifying about the corporation's knowledge were sufficiently prepared and testified accurately, and to produce in good faith all relevant and requested discovery. * * * Qualcomm chose not to do so and therefore must be sanctioned.

2. Attorneys' Misconduct

The next question is what, if any, role did Qualcomm's retained lawyers play in withholding the documents? The Court envisions four scenarios. First, Qualcomm intentionally hid the documents from its retained lawyers and did so so effectively that the lawyers did not know or suspect that the suppressed documents existed. Second, the retained lawyers failed to discover the intentionally hidden documents or suspect their existence due to their complete ineptitude and disorganization. Third, Qualcomm shared the damaging documents with its retained lawyers (or at least some of them) and the knowledgeable lawyers worked with Qualcomm to hide the documents and all evidence of Qualcomm's early involvement in the JVT. Or, fourth, while Qualcomm did not tell the retained lawyers about the damaging documents and evidence, the lawyers suspected there was additional evidence or information but chose to ignore the evidence and warning signs and accept Qualcomm's incredible assertions regarding the adequacy of the document search and witness investigation.

Given the impressive education and extensive experience of Qualcomm's retained lawyers, the Court rejects the first and second possibilities. It is inconceivable that these talented, well-educated, and experienced lawyers failed to discover through their interactions with Qualcomm any facts or issues that caused (or should have caused) them to question the sufficiency of Qualcomm's document search and production. Qualcomm did not fail to produce a document or two; it withheld over 46,000 critical documents that extinguished Qualcomm's primary argument of non-participation in the JVT. In addition, the suppressed documents did not belong to one employee, or a couple of employees who had since left the company; they belonged to (or were shared with) numerous, current Qualcomm employees, several of whom testified (falsely) at trial and in depositions. Given the volume and importance of the withheld documents, the number of involved Qualcomm employees, and the numerous warning flags, the Court finds it unbelievable that the retained attorneys did not know or suspect that Qualcomm had not conducted an adequate search for documents.

The Court finds no direct evidence establishing option three. Neither [of the parties] party nor the attorneys have presented evidence that Qualcomm told one or more of its retained attorneys about the damaging emails or that an attorney learned about the emails and that the knowledgeable attorney(s) then helped Qualcomm hide the emails. While knowledge may be inferred from the attorneys' conduct, evidence on this issue is limited due to Qualcomm's assertion of the attorney-client privilege.[8]

Thus, the Court finds it likely that some variation of option four occurred; that is, one or more of the retained lawyers chose not to look in the correct locations for the correct documents, to accept the unsubstantiated assurances of an important client that its search was sufficient, to ignore the warning signs that the document search and production were inadequate, not to press Qualcomm employees for the truth, and/or to encourage employees to provide the information (or lack of information) that Qualcomm needed to assert its non-participation argument and to succeed in this lawsuit. These choices enabled Qualcomm to withhold hundreds of thousands of pages of relevant discovery and to assert numerous false and misleading arguments to the court and jury. This conduct warrants the imposition of sanctions.

a. Identity of Sanctioned Attorneys

* * *

Attorneys Leung, Mammen and Batchelder are responsible for the initial discovery failure because they handled or supervised Qualcomm's discovery responses and production of documents. The Federal Rules impose an affirmative duty upon lawyers to engage in discovery in a responsible manner and to conduct a "reasonable inquiry" to determine whether discovery responses are sufficient and proper. In the instant case, a reasonable inquiry should have included searches using fundamental terms such as JVT, avc_ce or H.264, on the computers belonging to knowledgeable people such as Raveendran, Irvine and Ludwin. * * * Had Leung, Mammen, Batchelder, or any of the other attorneys insisted on reviewing Qualcomm's records regarding the locations searched and terms utilized, they would have discovered the inadequacy of the search and the suppressed documents. Similarly, Leung's difficulties with the Rule 30(b)(6) witnesses, Irvine and Ludwin, should have alerted him (and the supervising or senior attorneys) to the inadequacy of Qualcomm's document production and to the fact that they needed to review whose computers and databases had been searched and for what. Accordingly, the Court finds that the totality of the circumstances establish that Leung, Mammen and Batchelder did not make a reasonable inquiry into Qual-

---

8. Qualcomm asserted the attorney-client privilege and decreed that its retained attorneys could not reveal any communications protected by the privilege. Several attorneys complained that the assertion of the privilege prevented them from providing additional information regarding their conduct. This concern was heightened when Qualcomm submitted its self-serving declarations describing the failings of its retained lawyers. Recognizing that a client has a right to maintain this privilege and that no adverse inference should be made based upon the assertion, the Court accepted Qualcomm's assertion of the privilege and has not drawn any adverse inferences from it. However, the fact remains that the Court does not have access to all of the information necessary to reach an informed decision regarding the actual knowledge of the attorneys. As a result, the Court concludes for purposes of this Order that there is insufficient evidence establishing option three.

comm's discovery search and production and their conduct contributed to the discovery violation.[10]

Attorneys Bier, Mammen and Patch are responsible for the discovery violation because they also did not perform a reasonable inquiry to determine whether Qualcomm had complied with its discovery obligations. When Bier reviewed the August 6, 2002 email welcoming Raveendran to the avc_ce email group, he knew or should have known that it contradicted Qualcomm's trial arguments and he had an obligation to verify that it had been produced in discovery or to immediately produce it. If Bier, as a junior lawyer, lacked the experience to recognize the significance of the document, then a more senior or knowledgeable attorney should have assisted him. To the extent that Patch was supervising Bier in this endeavor, Patch certainly knew or should have recognized the importance of the document from his involvement in Qualcomm's motion practice and trial strategy sessions.

Similarly, when Bier found the 21 emails on Raveendran's computer that had not been produced in discovery, he took the appropriate action and informed his supervisors, Mammen and Patch. Patch discussed the discovery and production issue with Young and Batchelder. While all of these attorneys assert that there was a plausible argument that Broadcom did not request these documents, only Bier and Mammen actually read the emails. Moreover, all of the attorneys missed the critical inquiry: was Qualcomm's document search adequate? If these 21 emails were not discovered during Qualcomm's document search, how many more might exist? The answer, obviously, was tens of thousands. If Bier, Mammen, Patch, Young or Batchelder had conducted a reasonable inquiry after the discovery of the 21 Raveendran emails, they would have discovered the inadequacy of Qualcomm's search and the suppressed documents. And, these experienced attorneys should have realized that the presence on Raveendran's computer of 21 JVT/avc_ce emails from 2002 contradicted Qualcomm's numerous arguments that it had not participated in the JVT during that same time period. This fact, alone, should have prompted the attorneys to immediately produce the emails and to conduct a comprehensive document search.

Finally, attorneys Young, Patch, and Batchelder bear responsibility for the discovery failure because they did not conduct a reasonable inquiry

---

10. Leung's attorney represented during the OSC hearing that Leung requested a more thorough document search but that Qualcomm refused to do so. If Leung was unable to get Qualcomm to conduct the type of search he deemed necessary to verify the adequacy of the document search and production, then he should have obtained the assistance of supervising or senior attorneys. If Mammen and Batchelder were unable to get Qualcomm to conduct a competent and thorough document search, they should have withdrawn from the case or taken other action to ensure production of the evidence. *See* The State Bar of California, Rules of Professional Conduct, Rule 5–220 (a lawyer shall not suppress evidence that the lawyer or the lawyer's client has a legal obligation to reveal); Rule 3–700 (a lawyer shall withdraw from employment if the lawyer knows or should know that continued employment will result in a violation of these rules or the client insists that the lawyer pursue a course of conduct prohibited under these rules). Attorneys' ethical obligations do not permit them to participate in an inadequate document search and then provide misleading and incomplete information to their opponents and false arguments to the court.

into Qualcomm's discovery production before making specific factual and legal arguments to the court. Young decided that Qualcomm should file a motion for summary adjudication premised on the fact that Qualcomm had not participated in the JVT until after the H.264 standard was adopted in May 2003. Given that non-participation was vital to the motion, Young had a duty to conduct a reasonable inquiry into whether that fact was true. And, again, had Young conducted such a search, he would have discovered the inadequacy of Qualcomm's document search and production and learned that his argument was false. Similarly, Young had a duty to conduct a reasonable inquiry into the accuracy of his statement before affirmatively telling the court that no emails were sent to Raveendran from the avc_ce email group. Young also did not conduct a reasonable (or any) inquiry during the following days before he approved the factually incorrect JMOL. A reasonable investigation would have prevented the false filing.

Patch was an integral part of the trial team—familiar with Qualcomm's arguments, theories and strategies. He knew on January 14th that 21 avc_ce emails had been discovered on Raveendran's computer. Without reading or reviewing the emails, Patch participated in the decision not to produce them. Several days later, Patch carefully tailored his questions to ensure that Raveendran did not testify about the unproduced emails. And, after Broadcom stumbled into the email testimony, Patch affirmatively misled the Court by claiming that he did not know whether the emails were responsive to Broadcom's discovery requests. This conduct is unacceptable and, considering the totality of the circumstances, it is unrealistic to think that Patch did not know or believe that Qualcomm's document search was inadequate and that Qualcomm possessed numerous, similar and unproduced documents.

Batchelder also is responsible because he was the lead trial attorney and, as such, he was most familiar with Qualcomm's important arguments and witnesses. Batchelder stated in his opening statement that Qualcomm had not participated in the JVT before late 2003. Despite this statement and his complete knowledge of Qualcomm's legal theories, Batchelder did not take any action when he was informed that JVT documents that Qualcomm had not produced in discovery were found on Raveendran's computer. He did not read the emails, ask about their substance, nor inquire as to why they were not located during discovery. And, he stood mute when four days later, Young falsely stated that no emails had been sent to Raveendran from the avc_ce email group. Finally, all of the pleadings containing the lie that Qualcomm had not participated in the JVT in 2002 or early 2003 were sent to Batchelder for review and he approved or ignored all of them. The totality of the circumstances, including all of the previously-discussed warning signs, demanded that Batchelder conduct an investigation to verify the adequacy of Qualcomm's document search and production. His failure to do so enabled Qualcomm to withhold the documents.

For all of these reasons, the Court finds that these attorneys did not conduct a reasonable inquiry into the adequacy of Qualcomm's document search and production and, accordingly, they are responsible, along with Qualcomm, for the monumental discovery violation.

b.   Identity of Non–Sanctioned Attorneys

* * *

The Court * * * declines to sanction * * * attorneys Kleinfeld and Tucker. These attorneys primarily monitored the instant case for its impact on separate Qualcomm/Broadcom litigation. However, for logistical reasons, both attorneys signed as local counsel pleadings that contained false statements relating to Qulacomm's non-participation in the JVT. Given the facts of this case as set forth above and in the declarations, the limitations provided by the referral, and the totality of the circumstances, the Court finds that it was reasonable for these attorneys to sign the pleadings, relying on the work of other attorneys more actively involved in the litigation.

* * *

3.   Imposed Sanctions

As set forth above, the evidence establishes that Qualcomm intentionally withheld tens of thousands of emails and that the Sanctioned Attorneys assisted, either intentionally or by virtue of acting with reckless disregard for their discovery obligations, in this discovery violation. The remaining issue, then, is what are the appropriate sanctions.

a.   Monetary Sanctions Against Qualcomm

* * *

The suppressed emails directly rebutted Qualcomm's argument that it had not participated in the JVT during the time the H.264 standard was being developed. As such, their absence was critical to Qualcomm's hope and intent of enforcing its patents against Broadcom (as well as presumably all other cellular companies utilizing the H.264 technology in their products). Because Broadcom prevailed at trial and in the post-trial hearings despite the suppressed evidence, it is reasonable to infer that had Qualcomm intended to produce the 46,000 incriminating emails (and thereby acknowledge its early involvement in the JVT and its accompanying need to disclose its intellectual property), the instant case may never have been filed. Even if Qualcomm did file this case, the hidden evidence would have dramatically undermined Qualcomm's arguments and likely resulted in an adverse pretrial adjudication, much as it caused the adverse post-trial rulings. Accordingly, Qualcomm's failure to produce the massive number of critical documents at issue in this case significantly increased the scope, complexity and length of the litigation and justifies a significant monetary award.

The Court therefore awards Broadcom all of its attorneys' fees and costs incurred in the instant litigation. * * * Accordingly, for its monumental and intentional discovery violation, Qualcomm is ordered to pay $8,568,633.24 to Broadcom; this figure will be reduced by the amount actually paid by Qualcomm to Broadcom to satisfy the exceptional case award.

b. Referral to the California State Bar

As set forth above, the Sanctioned Attorneys assisted Qualcomm in committing this incredible discovery violation by intentionally hiding or recklessly ignoring relevant documents, ignoring or rejecting numerous warning signs that Qualcomm's document search was inadequate, and blindly accepting Qualcomm's unsupported assurances that its document search was adequate. The Sanctioned Attorneys then used the lack of evidence to repeatedly and forcefully make false statements and arguments to the court and jury. As such, the Sanctioned Attorneys violated their discovery obligations and also may have violated their ethical duties. *See e.g.*, The State Bar of California, Rules of Professional Conduct, Rule 5–200 (a lawyer shall not seek to mislead the judge or jury by a false statement of fact or law), Rule 5–220 (a lawyer shall not suppress evidence that the lawyer or the lawyer's client has a legal obligation to reveal or to produce). To address the potential ethical violations, the Court refers the Sanctioned Attorneys to The State Bar of California for an appropriate investigation and possible imposition of sanctions. Within ten days of the date of this Order, each of the Sanctioned Attorneys must forward a copy of this Order and Judge Brewster's Waiver Order to the Intake Unit, The State Bar of California, 1149 South Hill Street, Los Angeles, California 90015 for appropriate investigation.

c. Case Review and Enforcement of Discovery Obligations

The Court also orders Qualcomm and the Sanctioned Attorneys to participate in a comprehensive Case Review and Enforcement of Discovery Obligations ("CREDO") program. This is a collaborative process to identify the failures in the case management and discovery protocol utilized by Qualcomm and its in-house and retained attorneys in this case, to craft alternatives that will prevent such failures in the future, to evaluate and test the alternatives, and ultimately, to create a case management protocol which will serve as a model for the future.

Because they reviewed and approved the false pleadings, the Court designates the following [in-house] Qualcomm attorneys to participate in this process as Qualcomm's representatives: Alex Rogers, Roger Martin, William Sailer, Byron Yafuso, and Michael Hartogs (the "Named Qualcomm Attorneys"). Qualcomm employees were integral participants in hiding documents and making false statements to the court and jury. Qualcomm's in-house lawyers were in the unique position of (a) having unlimited access to all Qualcomm employees, as well as the emails and documents maintained, possessed and used by them, (b) knowing or being able to determine all of the computers and databases that were searched and the search terms that were utilized, and (c) having the ability to review all of the pleadings filed on Qualcomm's behalf which did (or should have) alerted them to the fact that either the document search was inadequate or they were knowingly not producing tens of thousands of relevant and requested documents. Accordingly, Qualcomm's in-house lawyers need to be involved in this process.

At a minimum, the CREDO protocol must include a ***detailed analysis*** (1) identifying the factors that contributed to the discovery violation (e.g., insufficient communication (including between client and retained counsel, among retained lawyers and law firms, and between junior lawyers conducting discovery and senior lawyers asserting legal arguments); inadequate case management (within Qualcomm, between Qualcomm and the retained lawyers, and by the retained lawyers); inadequate discovery plans (within Qualcomm and between Qualcomm and its retained attorneys)); etc.), (2) creating and evaluating proposals, procedures, and processes that will correct the deficiencies identified in subsection (1), (3) developing and finalizing a comprehensive protocol that will prevent future discovery violations (e.g., determining the depth and breadth of case management and discovery plans that should be adopted; identifying by experience or authority the attorney from the retained counsel's office who should interface with the corporate counsel and on which issues; describing the frequency the attorneys should meet and whether other individuals should participate in the communications; identifying who should participate in the development of the case management and discovery plans; describing and evaluating various methods of resolving conflicts and disputes between the client and retained counsel, especially relating to the adequacy of discovery searches; describing the type, nature, frequency, and participants in case management and discovery meetings; and, suggesting required ethical and discovery training; etc.), (4) applying the protocol that was developed in subsection (3) to other factual situations, such as when the client does not have corporate counsel, when the client has a single in-house lawyer, when the client has a large legal staff, and when there are two law firms representing one client, (5) identifying and evaluating data tracking systems, software, or procedures that corporations could implement to better enable inside and outside counsel to identify potential sources of discoverable documents (e.g. the correct databases, archives, etc.), and (6) any other information or suggestions that will help prevent discovery violations.

* * *

While no one can undo the misconduct in this case, this process, hopefully, will establish a baseline for other cases. Perhaps it also will establish a turning point in what the Court perceives as a decline in and deterioration of civility, professionalism and ethical conduct in the litigation arena. To the extent it does so, everyone benefits–Broadcom, Qualcomm, and all attorneys who engage in, and judges who preside over, complex litigation. If nothing else, it will provide a road map to assist counsel and corporate clients in complying with their ethical and discovery obligations and conducting the requisite "reasonable inquiry."

Editor's Note: Qualcomm and the sanctioned lawyers appealed Judge Major's order imposing sanctions. Judge Brewster vacated the order in part. 2008 WL 638108 (S.D. Cal. Mar. 5, 2008). Judge Brewster held that the six sanctioned attorneys could not be prevented by the attorney-client privilege from using client communications to defend themselves. (*See* footnote 8 of Judge Major's opinion, *supra*, addressing the lawyers' complaint that they were limited in their defense by their inability to use privileged information.) Judge Brewster declared: "The attorneys have a due process right to defend themselves under the totality of circumstances presented in this sanctions hearing where their alleged conduct regarding discovery is in conflict with that alleged by Qualcomm concerning performance of discovery responsibilities." Judge Brewster remanded the case as to the individual attorneys for another hearing. Importantly, however, the court did not question the appropriateness of sanctions against the lawyers if the facts were as Judge Major had found them to be. And the court affirmed the sanctions against Qualcomm.

COMMENTARY

1. Should a Party Be Sanctioned Where the Fault Lies With the Party's Counsel?

A court must not sanction a party where the fault lies with inattentive, inept, or incompetent counsel. Because sanctions are based on personal responsibility, where counsel alone is responsible, counsel alone should be sanctioned.[23]

2. Can Sanctions Be Imposed on a Party and Its Counsel Jointly and Severally?

In *In re Sept. 11th Liability Insurance Coverage Cases,* the court held an insurer was subject to sanctions for not timely producing relevant documents, including an existing printed copy of a policy as it existed in electronic form on the day of the occurrence and an attached endorsement affecting the additional insured status of litigants, as well as other requested materials.[24] The court found the insurer had deleted an electronic copy of the policy as it appeared in its computer records. The court also found the insurer's attorneys did not act inadvertently in allowing a printed copy of the policy to languish

---

23. *See Exact Software N. Am., Inc. v. Infocon, Inc.,* 479 F. Supp. 2d 702, 718–19 (N.D. Ohio 2006) (ordering hearing to determine whether counsel was at fault for discovery misconduct).

24. 243 F.R.D. 114 (S.D.N.Y. 2007).

in their files. The court imposed sanctions in the amount of $500,000 against the insurer and its attorneys jointly and severally, payable to the opposing party to defray the costs they unreasonably had incurred in wasted discovery proceedings. The court denied requests for more than five million dollars in sanctions because it was impossible to separate the time spent on particular issues affected by discovery abuses from other work on the same time entries.[25]

---

25. *See id.* at 132. *See also Phoenix Four, Inc. v. Strategic Res. Corp.*, No. 05 Civ. 4837, 2006 WL 2135798, at *2–3 (S.D.N.Y. Aug. 1, 2006) (sanctions in the amount of $45,162 to be paid equally by defendants and their law firm; defendants' share "may not be borne by their insurance carriers").

VI

PRIVILEGE ISSUES ARISING DURING
ELECTRONIC DISCOVERY

■ ■ ■

When lawyers produce information in response to a discovery demand, they must take care not to disclose the client's privileged information. Such a disclosure could constitute a waiver of the privilege and, under some circumstances, might result in a finding of subject matter waiver—meaning that the client must make a further production of all privileged communications on the same subject matter as the previously disclosed documents. Consequently, lawyers engage in pre-production review of documents to determine whether they are privileged.

While pre-production privilege review has always been necessary, the burdens of such review have skyrocketed for electronic discovery. Stories abound of teams of lawyers (junior to senior) reading e-mails for hours on end, to determine whether they contain privileged information.

The case below discusses the phenomenon of pre-production privilege review of electronic information. That case as well as the rest of the materials in this Chapter address ways in which the skyrocketing costs of pre-production privilege review can be limited.

A.   THE RISKS OF WAIVER AND THE COSTS OF PRE–PRODUCTION PRIVILEGE REVIEW OF ELECTRONIC DATA

HOPSON v. THE MAYOR AND CITY COUNCIL OF BALTIMORE

232 F.R.D. 228 (D. Md. 2005)

GRIMM, MAGISTRATE JUDGE

This case has been referred to me for resolution of all discovery disputes. Pending and ripe for a decision is the Plaintiffs' motion to compel Rule 33 and 34 discovery. Plaintiffs have asserted putative class claims and individual claims against the City of Baltimore ("The City") and the Baltimore City Police Department ("BCPD") alleging that BCPD engaged in racial discrimination against African American police officers

315

in connection with the administration of the disciplinary system for Baltimore police officers. It is alleged that the disparate impact and disparate treatment claims extend back to 1992, the commencement date for the misconduct that is the focus of the class claims.

When the court issued its scheduling order and discovery commenced, Plaintiffs promptly served interrogatories and document production requests on the Defendants. The Rule 34 requests were extensive and clearly sought both "hard copy" records as well as electronically stored records and data. Companion interrogatories included more than 15 specifically designed to discover the nature, extent, and location of electronically stored records, the Defendants' IT capabilities, the nature of archived data, e-mail, and records retention policies—in short, all of the computer generated information that is the subject of so much discussion these days.

Defendants answered, raising many objections to the discovery sought, including burdensomeness and expense. * * * One of the Defendants' concerns was the cost and burden of performing pre-production privilege review of the records sought by the Plaintiffs. * * * [T]he issues presented in this case prominently showcase challenges that recur in connection with the discovery of electronic data, * * * [and raise] significant unresolved issues relating to the nature of privilege review that must be performed by a party producing electronically stored information, whether non-waiver agreements entered into by counsel to permit post-production assertion of privilege are permissible, and effective for their intended purpose, as well as the application of principles of substantive evidence law related to the waiver of privilege by inadvertent production.

* * *

As noted in the Federal Judicial Center Manual for Complex Litigation:

> A responding party's screening of vast quantities of unorganized computer data for privilege prior to production can be particularly onerous in those jurisdictions in which inadvertent production of privileged data may constitute a waiver of privilege as to a particular item of information, items related to the relevant issue, or the entire data collection. Fear of the consequences of inadvertent waiver may add cost and delay to the discovery process for all parties. Thus, judges often encourage counsel to stipulate at the outset of discovery to a "nonwaiver" agreement, which they can adopt as a case-management order. Such agreements protect responding parties from the most dire consequences of inadvertent waiver by allowing them to "take back" inadvertently produced privileged materials if discovered within a reasonable period, perhaps thirty days from production.

Similarly, the recent report of the Judicial Conference Committee on Rules of Practice and Procedure to the Chief Justice of the United States and the Members of the Judicial Conference of the United States that forwarded proposed revisions to Federal Rules of Civil Procedure 16, 26, 33, 34, and 37, addresses this same issue:

> The problems that can result from efforts to guard against privilege waiver often become more acute when discovery of electronically stored information is sought. The volume of the information and the forms in which it is stored make privilege determinations more difficult and privilege review correspondingly more expensive and time-consuming, yet less likely to detect all privileged information. Inadvertent production is increasingly likely to occur. Because the failure to screen out even one privileged item may result in an argument that there has been a waiver as to all other privileged materials related to the same subject matter, early attention to this problem is more important as electronic discovery becomes more common. Under the proposed amendments to Rules 26(f) and 16, if the parties are able to reach an agreement to adopt protocols for asserting privilege and work-product protection claims that will facilitate discovery that is faster and at lower cost, they may ask the court to include such arrangements in a case-management or other order.

* * *

The changes recommended to Rules 16 and 26 encourage the party receiving the electronic discovery to agree not to assert waiver of privilege/work product protection against an opposing party that agrees to provide expedited production of electronically stored information without first doing a full-fledged privilege review. Similar agreements have been approved by a number of courts in the past.[10]

Although the use of "non-waiver" agreements presently may be growing * * * they certainly are not risk-free. Some commentators appear to be openly skeptical of their ability to insulate the parties from waiver, and even if they are enforceable as between the parties that enter into them, it is questionable whether they are effective against third-parties. *See Westinghouse Elec. Corp. v. Republic of the Philippines*, 951 F.2d 1414, 1426–27 (3d Cir. 1991) (agreement between litigant and DOJ that documents produced in response to investigation would not waive privilege does not preserve privilege against different entity in unrelated civil proceeding); *Bowne v. AmBase Corp.*, 150 F.R.D. 465, 478–79 (S.D.N.Y. 1993) (non-waiver agreement between producing party in one case not applicable to third party in another civil case).

* * *

* * * [T]here is a viable method of dealing with the practical challenges to privilege review of electronically stored information without running an unacceptable risk of subject-matter waiver. It lies with the

---

10. Not all courts have approved non-waiver agreements between counsel. *See Koch Materials Co. v. Shore Slurry Seal, Inc.*, 208 F.R.D. 109, 118 (D.N.J. 2002) (court declined to give effect to agreement between counsel that production of certain documents would not waive privilege protection because such agreements "could lead to sloppy attorney review and improper disclosure which could jeopardize clients' cases"). * * *

courts issuing scheduling orders under Fed. R. Civ. P. 16, protective orders under Fed. R. Civ. P. 26(c), or discovery management orders under Fed. R. Civ. P. 26(b)(2) that incorporate procedures under which electronic records will be produced without waiving privilege or work product that the courts have determined to be reasonable given the nature of the case, and that have been agreed to by the parties. * * * As will be seen, it is essential to the success of this approach in avoiding waiver that the production of inadvertently produced privileged electronic data must be at the compulsion of the court, rather than solely by the voluntary act of the producing party, and that the procedures agreed to by the parties and ordered by the court demonstrate that reasonable measures were taken to protect against waiver of privilege and work product protection.

* * *

In *Transamerica Computer Co. v. IBM*, 573 F.2d 646 (9th Cir. 1978), the Ninth Circuit held that IBM had not waived its privilege claims to records that erroneously had been produced in prior litigation involving different parties, because the production was in response to an accelerated discovery schedule that the trial court had imposed, and the disclosures had been unintentional. Notably, the court observed that in the earlier litigation, IBM had produced 17 million pages of documents during a court ordered production schedule that had "dramatically accelerated the document inspection program." The court noted that during this demanding production schedule, IBM had undertaken "herculean" efforts to review documents for privilege. Therefore, it had not been guilty of any want of diligence. Of greater importance, however, was the fact that the trial judge had ruled that "the inadvertent production of allegedly privileged material by either party would not constitute a waiver of that party's right to claim the attorney-client privilege, provided only that the party disclaiming waiver had continued to employ procedures reasonably designed to screen out privileged material."

In concluding that IBM had not waived its privilege claims by producing the documents in the earlier litigation, and therefore could not be compelled by Transamerica in the subsequent litigation to produce it, the Ninth Circuit declined to view the issue solely as one of inadvertent disclosure, but rather focused on the importance of the court's compulsion of the production of the documents under conditions that unavoidably resulted in disclosure of some privileged material. * * *

Also central to the court's ruling was its recognition that the production of some privileged material by IBM had occurred as a result of the trial court's discovery order:

> As the judicial officer directly in charge of supervising the discovery proceedings in that litigation ... [the trial judge] was in an ideal position to determine whether the timetable he himself had imposed was so stringent that, as a practical matter, it effectively denied IBM the opportunity to claim the attorney-client privilege for documents it was producing for inspection by CDC [in that litigation]. [Trans-

america] acknowledges that waiver cannot be directly compelled, and
. . . [the judge's] rulings recognize and we so hold, that neither can it
be indirectly compelled.

Finally, the court noted that the trial judge had further issued a
ruling "explicitly protecting and preserving all claims of privilege, provided only that the parties wishing to preserve privilege had engaged in
suitable screening techniques."

* * *

The *Transamerica* case and those that have followed it would allow
parties that have entered into an agreement to preserve privilege claims
with respect to production of electronically stored information to avoid
subsequent claims by third parties that the production waived the privilege, provided: (a) the party claiming the privilege took reasonable steps
given the volume of electronically stored data to be reviewed, the time
permitted in the scheduling order to do so, and the resources of the
producing party; (b) the producing party took reasonable steps to assert
promptly the privilege once it learned that some privileged information
inadvertently had been disclosed, despite the exercise of reasonable measures to screen for privilege and, importantly; (c) the production had been
compelled by court order that was issued after the court's independent
evaluation of the scope of electronic discovery permitted, the reasonableness of the procedures the producing party took to screen out privileged
material or assert post-production claims upon discovery of inadvertent
production of privileged information, and the amount of time that the
court allowed the producing party to spend on the production.

* * *

In this case the BCPD did file an affidavit intended to particularize
the unreasonable burden that would result from producing all of the
records sought by the Plaintiffs in their Rule 34 requests. However, it was
less complete than it should have been. It did identify the limited number
of information technology personnel available to conduct the search for
electronic records, and the competing demands on their services within
the police department, but it failed to estimate the number of hours that
would be required for them to conduct the requested review, or to
sufficiently demonstrate how this would impact adversely the fiscal and
operational capabilities of the police department. A party that seeks an
order from the court that will allow it to lessen the burden of responding
to allegedly burdensome electronic records discovery bears the burden of
particularly demonstrating that burden and of providing suggested alternatives that reasonably accommodate the requesting party's legitimate
discovery needs.

Second, as this case graphically demonstrates, it is no longer acceptable for the parties to defer good faith discussion of how to approach
discovery of electronic records * * *. Rather, as the * * * changes to Rule
16(f) make clear, counsel have a duty to take the initiative in meeting and

conferring to plan for appropriate discovery of electronically stored information at the commencement of any case in which electronic records will be sought. * * * At a minimum, they should discuss: the type of information technology systems in use and the persons most knowledgeable in their operation; preservation of electronically stored information that may be relevant to the litigation; the scope of the electronic records sought (i.e. e-mail, voice mail, archived data, back-up or disaster recovery data, laptops, personal computers, PDA's, deleted data) the format in which production will occur (will records be produced in "native" or searchable format, or image only; is metadata sought); whether the requesting party seeks to conduct any testing or sampling of the producing party's IT system; the burdens and expenses that the producing party will face based on the Rule 26(b)(2) factors, and how they may be reduced (i.e. limiting the time period for which discovery is sought, limiting the amount of hours the producing party must spend searching, compiling and reviewing electronic records, using sampling to search, rather than searching all records, shifting to the producing party some of the production costs); the amount of pre-production privilege review that is reasonable for the producing party to undertake, and measures to preserve post-production assertion of privilege within a reasonable time; and any protective orders or confidentiality orders that should be in place regarding who may have access to information that is produced.

It cannot be emphasized enough that the goal of the meeting to discuss discovery is to reach an agreement that then can be proposed to the court. The days when the requesting party can expect to "get it all" and the producing party to produce whatever they feel like producing are long gone. In many cases, such as employment discrimination cases or civil rights cases, electronic discovery is not played on a level field. The plaintiff typically has relatively few electronically stored records, while the defendant often has an immense volume of it. In such cases, it is incumbent upon the plaintiff to have reasonable expectations as to what should be produced by the defendant.

In this case, the Plaintiffs filed voluminous and detailed Rule 33 and 34 discovery requests that clearly identified their interest in discovering electronically stored information. The Defendants' immediate response should have been to invite the Plaintiffs to meet to discuss a reasonable discovery plan. Instead, objections first were raised, many of them boilerplate and conclusory, in the Defendants' answers to the discovery requests. The Plaintiffs responded with multiple written communications outlining their objections to the Defendants responses. When impasse was not overcome, the Plaintiffs * * * served a motion to compel. Only when that motion was fully briefed was it filed with the court. An expedited hearing was held, but even so, months had passed from the commencement of discovery while the dispute festered. Such delay is no longer acceptable, and it is the duty of the parties to initiate the negotiation process if the court has not ordered it. As I ordered during the hearing, the meeting that should have occurred months ago will be held within 30 days. A follow-up hearing with the court will be scheduled at which time a reasonable electronic discovery plan will be ordered.

One of the issues the parties were ordered to discuss was the nature of privilege review the Defendants would undertake, both pre-and post-production. The Defendants were advised that they bore the burden of demonstrating with particularity the need for less than full pre-production privilege review, as well as of proposing reasonable alternatives. I advised the parties that at the follow-up hearings, I would issue an order that compelled production of electronic records within a specific time that is reasonable. I also stated that I would independently determine, using the Rule 26(b)(2) factors, the amount of electronic discovery that would be permitted; whether less than full privilege review was reasonable given the extent of electronic discovery allowed and the time to do so and, if full privilege review was not feasible, whether the procedures agreed to by counsel are reasonable. If so, I will issue an order approving them that includes language that compliance with the approved procedures will not result in the waiver of any privilege or work product claim for any inadvertently produced privileged material. As I stated during the hearing, the issuance of such an order is essential to protecting against subject matter waiver of attorney-client privileged or work product protected information. * * *

B. AGREEMENTS BETWEEN THE PARTIES TO CONTROL THE COST OF PRE–PRODUCTION PRIVILEGE REVIEW OF ELECTRONIC DATA

As the court noted in *Hopson*, parties often enter into arrangements to control the risks of waiver when privileged electronic data is disclosed during discovery. These arrangements can cover inadvertent disclosure, or can more broadly cover even intentional disclosures. Generally speaking there are two kinds of agreements: "claw back" and "quick peek." The 2006 Advisory Committee Note to Rule 26 discusses the costs of pre-production privilege review of electronic data, as well as the use of "claw back and quick peek" agreements:

> Parties may attempt to minimize these costs and delays by agreeing to protocols that minimize the risk of waiver. They may agree that the responding party will provide certain requested materials for initial examination without waiving any privilege or protection—sometimes known as a "quick peek." The requesting party then designates the documents it wishes to have actually produced. This designation is the Rule 34 request. The responding party then responds in the usual course, screening only those documents actually requested for formal production and asserting privilege claims as provided in Rule 26(b)(5)(A). On other occasions, parties enter agreements—sometimes called "clawback agreements"—that production

without intent to waive privilege or protection should not be a waiver so long as the responding party identifies the documents mistakenly produced, and that the documents should be returned under those circumstances. Other voluntary arrangements may be appropriate depending on the circumstances of each litigation. In most circumstances, a party who receives information under such an arrangement cannot assert that production of the information waived a claim of privilege or of protection as trial-preparation material.

Although these agreements may not be appropriate for all cases, in certain cases they can facilitate prompt and economical discovery by reducing delay before the discovering party obtains access to documents, and by reducing the cost and burden of review by the producing party.

The way these agreements often work in practice is that the disclosing party takes a "first cut" of the material and removes all the data that is clearly privileged upon a cursory review—for example, e-mails from or to counsel. The rest of the material is then produced, and if it turns out on further review that it is privileged, it is returned. Such agreements limit the multiple levels of intensive review of all the electronic data that would otherwise be required for pre-production privilege review. If a party has signed such an agreement, it waives any argument that a disclosure of privileged information by the other side is a waiver.[1]

There are a number of factors, however, that limit the utility of "claw back" and "quick peek" agreements. Most important, they provide protection only in the proceeding in which they are entered. As the *Hopson* court noted, an agreement between two parties in one litigation does not estop a third party, in a subsequent litigation, from arguing that a waiver occurred by disclosure of the privileged information in the previous matter. As the court also noted, parties have sought greater enforceability by asking the court to "so order" the agreement between the parties—but there was doubt under common law (before the enactment of Rule 502, *infra*) that even those orders would be binding against those who were not parties to the litigation in which the order was entered.

Another limitation on such agreements is obvious—the parties must agree. Where the discoverable electronic data on both sides is relatively equal, then all parties have an incentive to enter such an agreement. But where one side has most of the data—*e.g.*, an employment discrimination case brought by a fired employee, where all the e-mails are on the employer's server—then the party with few (if any) documents may not be inclined to limit the costs of the adversary's pre-production privilege review. (One factor that may still provide an incentive is if the party has an interest in *expedited* discovery; if there is no non-waiver agreement in

---

1. *See, e.g., Prescient Partners, L.P. v. Fieldcrest Cannon, Inc.*, No. 96 Civ. 7590, 1997 WL 736726 (S.D.N.Y. Nov. 26, 1997) (enforcing a confidentiality agreement and refusing to find a waiver from an inadvertent disclosure of privileged information).

effect, then the court is very likely to allow the party with custody of the data greater time to conduct a full pre-production privilege review).

Drafting Project: Draft a clawback or quick peek agreement that would be acceptable to both sides in a case in which one corporation sues another for patent infringement. Is it necessary to specify the kind of information that is covered, e.g., e-mails, spreadsheets, etc. Do you need a clause specifying how the receiving party is to act when it receives information that is apparently privileged? Do you need to specify that the receiving party is not allowed to keep a copy of the material or to use it in any way?

C.   WHAT PRECAUTIONS SHOULD BE EMPLOYED?

VICTOR STANLEY, INC. v. CREATIVE PIPE, INC.

250 F.R.D. 251 (D. Md. May 29, 2008)

GRIMM, MAGISTRATE JUDGE

The plaintiff, Victor Stanley, Inc. ("VSI" or "Plaintiff") filed a motion seeking a ruling that five categories of electronically stored documents produced by defendants Creative Pipe, Inc. ("CPI") and Mark and Stephanie Pappas ("M. Pappas", "S. Pappas" or "The Pappasses") (collectively, "Defendants") in October, 2007, are not exempt from discovery because they are within the protection of the attorney-client privilege and work-product doctrine, as claimed by the Defendants. VSI argues that the electronic records at issue, which total 165 documents, are not privileged because their production by Defendants occurred under circumstances that waived any privilege or protected status. * * * Defendants acknowledge that they produced all 165 electronic documents at issue to VSI during Rule 34 discovery, but argue that the production was inadvertent, and therefore that privilege/protection has not been waived. * * * For the reasons that follow, I find that all 165 electronic documents are beyond the scope of the attorney-client privilege and work-product protection because assuming, arguendo, that they qualified as privileged/protected in the first instance * * * the privilege/protection was waived by the voluntary production of the documents to VSI by Defendants.

Background Facts

The following facts are not subject to dispute. The Defendants' first Rule 34 response was a "paper production," not ESI, made in May 2007. Plaintiff objected to its sufficiency, and following a hearing, the court ordered the parties' computer forensic experts to meet and confer in an effort to identify a joint protocol to search and retrieve relevant ESI responsive to Plaintiff's Rule 34 requests. This was done and the joint protocol prepared. The protocol contained detailed search and information retrieval instructions, including nearly five pages of keyword/phrase search terms. It is noteworthy that these search terms were aimed at locating responsive ESI, rather than identifying privileged or work-product protected documents within the population of responsive ESI. After the protocol was used to retrieve responsive ESI, Defendants reviewed it to locate documents that were beyond the scope of discovery because of privilege or work-product protection. Counsel for Defendants had previously notified the court on March 29, 2007, that individualized privilege review of the responsive documents "would delay production unnecessarily and cause undue expense." To address this concern, Defendants gave their computer forensics expert a list of keywords to be used to search and retrieve privileged and protected documents from the population of documents that were to be produced to Plaintiff. However, Defendants' counsel also acknowledged the possibility of inadvertent disclosure of privileged/protected documents, given the volume of documents that were to be produced, and requested that the court approve a "clawback agreement" fashioned to address the concerns noted by this court in *Hopson v. Mayor of Baltimore*, 232 F.R.D. 228 (D. Md. 2005) [set forth at the beginning of this Chapter]. * * * However, on April 27, 2007, Defendants' counsel notified the court that because Judge Garbis recently had extended the discovery deadline by four months, Defendants would be able to conduct a document-by-document privilege review, thereby making a clawback agreement unnecessary. Accordingly, Defendants abandoned their efforts to obtain a clawback agreement and committed to undertaking an individualized document review.

* * *

After receiving Defendants' ESI production in September, 2007, Plaintiff's counsel began their review of the materials. They soon discovered documents that potentially were privileged or work-product protected and immediately segregated this information and notified counsel for Defendants of its production, following this same procedure each time they identified potentially privileged/protected information. Defendants' Counsel, Mr. Schmid, responded by asserting that the production of any privileged or protected information had been inadvertent. Defendants also belatedly provided Plaintiff with a series of privilege logs, purportedly identifying the documents that had been withheld from production pursuant to Fed. R. Civ. P. 26(b)(5).

* * *

Thus, according to the Plaintiff, the Defendants have waived any claim to attorney client privilege or work-product protection for the 165 documents at issue because they failed to take reasonable precautions by performing a faulty privilege review of the text-searchable files and by failing to detect the presence of the 165 documents, which were then given to the Plaintiff as part of Defendants' ESI production. As will be seen, under either the Plaintiff's or Defendants' version of the events, the Defendants have waived any privilege or protected status for the 165 documents in question.

Applicable Law

* * * [C]ourts have taken three different approaches when deciding whether the inadvertent production to an adversary of attorney client privileged or work-product protected materials constitutes a waiver. Under the most lenient approach there is no waiver because there has not been a knowing and intentional relinquishment of the privilege/protection; under the most strict approach, there is a waiver because once disclosed, there can no longer be any expectation of confidentiality; and under the intermediate one, the court balances a number of factors to determine whether the producing party exercised reasonable care under the circumstances to prevent against disclosure of privileged and protected information, and if so, there is no waiver. [The court rejects the most lenient approach as inconsistent with Fourth Circuit case law.] Under the strict approach, there is no legitimate doubt that Defendants' production of the 165 asserted privileged/protected documents waived the attorney-client privilege and work-product protection. Even under the intermediate test, however, the result would be the same.

The intermediate test requires the court to balance the following factors to determine whether inadvertent production of attorney-client privileged materials waives the privilege: (1) the reasonableness of the precautions taken to prevent inadvertent disclosure; (2) the number of inadvertent disclosures; (3) the extent of the disclosures; (4) any delay in measures taken to rectify the disclosure; and (5) overriding interests in justice. The first of these factors militates most strongly in favor of a finding that Defendants waived the privilege in this case.

Assuming that the Plaintiff's version of how Defendants conducted their privilege review is accurate, the Defendants obtained the results of the agreed-upon ESI search protocol and ran a keyword search on the text-searchable files using approximately seventy keywords selected by M. Pappas and two of his attorneys. Defendants, who bear the burden of proving that their conduct was reasonable for purposes of assessing whether they waived attorney-client privilege by producing the 165 documents to the Plaintiff, have failed to provide the court with information regarding: the keywords used; the rationale for their selection; the qualifications of M. Pappas and his attorneys to design an effective and reliable search and information retrieval method; whether the search was a simple keyword search, or a more sophisticated one, such as one employing Boolean proximity operators; or whether they analyzed the results of the search to assess its reliability, appropriateness for the task, and the quality of its implementation. While keyword searches have long been recognized as appropriate and helpful for ESI search and retrieval, there are well-known limitations and risks associated with them, and proper selection and implementation obviously involves technical, if not scientific knowledge. See, e.g., *The Sedona Conference Best Practices Commentary on the Use of Search & Information Retrieval Methods in E–Discovery*, 8 Sedona Conf. J. 189, 194–95, 201–02 ("[A]lthough basic keyword searching techniques have been widely accepted both by courts and parties as sufficient to define the scope of their obligation to perform a search for responsive documents, the experience of many litigators is that simple keyword searching alone is inadequate in at least some discovery contexts. This is because simple keyword searches end up being both over-and under-inclusive in light of the inherent malleability and ambiguity of spoken and written English (as well as all other languages).'').

Further, the Defendants' attempt to justify what was done, by complaining that the volume of ESI needing review and time constraints presented them with no other choice is simply unpersuasive. Defendants were aware of the danger of inadvertent production of privileged/protected information and initially sought the protections of a non-waiver agreement * * *. Had they not voluntarily abandoned their request for a court-approved non-waiver agreement, they would have been protected from waiver. Instead, they advised the court that they did not need this protection and elected to do a document-by-document privilege review. According to Defendants version of the facts, when they undertook an individualized review of the nontext-searchable ESI and determined that they could only review the title pages, they neither sought an extension of time from the court to complete an individualized review nor reinstated their request for a court-approved non-waiver agreement, despite their awareness of how it would have provided protection against waiver. In these circumstances, Defendants' protests that they did their best and that their conduct was reasonable rings particularly hollow.

The remaining factors to be assessed under the intermediate test may be quickly disposed of. The Defendants produced 165 asserted privileged/protected documents to the Plaintiff, so this case does not present an instance of a single document slipping through the cracks. Further, the court's in camera review of the documents reflects that many of them are email and other communications between the Defendants and their various attorneys, as well as draft discovery responses, documents relating to settlements in unrelated litigation, comments from M. Pappas to counsel regarding discovery responses, and email correspondence between M. Pappas and Ms. Turner, the ESI forensic expert retained by Defendants. Thus, the disclosures were substantive—including numerous communications between defendants and their counsel. As noted by other district courts within the Fourth Circuit, any order issued now by the court to attempt to redress these disclosures would be the equivalent of closing the barn door after the animals have already run away. And, while the precise dates of the disclosures of the documents at issue are not clear from the record—since the Defendants made a series of ESI productions over a several week period—it is noteworthy that the Defendants did not discover the disclosure, but rather the Plaintiff made the discovery and notified the Defendants that potentially privileged/protected ESI had been produced. Therefore, this is not an instance in which a party inadvertently produced privileged information to an adversary, discovered the disclosure promptly, and then took immediate steps to inform the adversary that they had received the information inadvertently, thus demanding that it be returned.

While Defendants' counsel did assert privilege and inadvertent production promptly after being notified by the Plaintiff of the production of possible privileged/protected information, the more important period of delay in this case is the one-week period between production by the Defendants and the time of the discovery by the Plaintiff of the disclosures—a period during which the Defendants failed to discover the disclosure. Finally, the Defendants have pointed to no overriding interests in justice that would excuse them from the consequences of producing privileged/protected materials. The Plaintiff is blameless, but the Defendants are not, having failed to take reasonable precautions to prevent the disclosure of privileged information, including the voluntary abandonment of the non-waiver agreement that the Plaintiff was willing to sign. Every waiver of the attorney-client privilege produces unfortunate consequences for the party that disclosed the information. If that alone were sufficient to constitute an injustice, there would never be a waiver. The only "injustice" in this matter is that done by Defendants to themselves. Accordingly, even under the intermediate test, the Defendants are not insulated from waiver.

* * *

Conclusion

For the reasons stated, the court finds that the Defendants waived any privilege or work-product protection for the 165 documents at issue by disclosing them to the Plaintiff. Accordingly, the Plaintiff may use these documents as evidence in this case, provided they are otherwise admissible. In this regard, the Plaintiff has only sought use of the documents themselves, and the court has not been asked to rule, and accordingly does not, that there has been any waiver beyond the documents themselves.

COMMENTARY

Under recently-enacted Rule 502 (discussed *infra*) a court will find that a mistaken disclosure is not a waiver if the disclosing party took reasonable steps to prevent the disclosure and engaged in reasonably prompt measures to rectify the error once it was discovered. Reasonableness will of course depend on the circumstances; proper use of word searching may be a sufficient step.

Under the fault-based view of inadvertent waiver, there will be cases where the lawyer's work is so sloppy and inattentive that a mistaken disclosure will result in a forfeiture. In *S.E.C. v. Cassano*, the SEC was proceeding against investors for insider trading.[2] The case was brought in New York but was handled by the Boston office of the SEC. A discovery protocol allowed all of the unprivileged SEC electronic and hardcopy documents to be sent to New York, where defense counsel reviewed them (a process known as the "reading

---

2.   189 F.R.D. 83 (S.D.N.Y. 1999).

room"), and then an SEC paralegal on the premises would copy whatever documents defense counsel selected, and send those documents to counsel within a month. Combing through the information, defense counsel found a smoking gun document—an SEC staff memorandum, clearly privileged. He asked the paralegal if she could provide a copy of the document immediately so that he could take it with him that day. The paralegal telephoned SEC counsel in Boston, who immediately agreed to the unusual request, without checking the document number against the privilege log. A few weeks later, the SEC discovered its gaffe and sought an order requiring defense counsel to return the document. The court held that the SEC's actions in response to defense counsel's request to photocopy the memorandum were so careless as to surrender any claim that it took reasonable steps to ensure its confidentiality; hence the privilege as to the document was forfeited. The court noted that inadvertent production will constitute a forfeiture of the privilege only if the producing party's conduct was "so careless as to suggest that it was not concerned with the protection of the asserted privilege." The court declared that the

> circumstances of the request clearly should have suggested to the SEC attorney that defense counsel had found what they regarded as gold at the end of the proverbial rainbow. Any attorney faced with such a request in comparable circumstances should have reviewed the document immediately, if only to find out what the other side thought so compelling.... Yet the SEC attorney authorized production of this document, sight unseen.

SEC counsel was also found delinquent in failing to promptly discover the inadvertent disclosure of the privileged memorandum.

In re Sealed Case is an example of the "strict liability" view of inadvertent disclosure.[3] There, the court held that the inadvertent disclosure of a few privileged documents in the course of a massive discovery response not only constituted a waiver of the privilege with respect to the documents, but also worked a subject matter waiver. As a result, the client was forced to make a further production of *all* previously privileged documents covering the subject matter of the inadvertently disclosed documents. The court reasoned that the privilege was costly to the search for truth, and therefore that privileged information must be guarded "like the crown jewels." The problem with this draconian rule is that it increases the costs of discovery and hence the costs of legal services; lawyers are likely to spend inordinate amounts of time ensuring that privileged material does not slip through—the cost adds up when there are seven levels of review of millions of e-mails, all to protect against a finding of waiver. This is not an efficient discovery model, in economic terms. Moreover, parties might fight tooth and nail during discovery over materials— questionably privileged, no matter how inconsequential, if a court might find it later on to be privileged, with the consequence being a subject matter waiver. Thus the D.C. Circuit view on inadvertent waiver leads to an increase in the number of privilege issues that a court will have to hear. Rule 502, discussed immediately below, explicitly rejects the strict liability view of *In re Sealed Case*.

---

3.   877 F.2d 976 (D.C. Cir. 1989).

In some state jurisdictions, there is no risk of inadvertent waiver. These jurisdictions hold that waiver of the privilege must be intentional. So it does not matter how negligent the disclosure in these jurisdictions is—the disclosing party has the right to get it back.[4]

D. LEGISLATIVE SOLUTION TO LIMIT THE COSTS OF REVIEW OF ELECTRONIC DATA FOR PRIVILEGE: FEDERAL RULE OF EVIDENCE 502

The costs of privilege review, in order to avoid the consequences of waiver, can rise to the millions of dollars. Concerned about the rising costs of electronic discovery and privilege review, the Judiciary Committee of the House of Representatives asked the Judicial Conference Advisory Committee on Evidence Rules ("the Advisory Committee") to prepare a rule that will provide some protection against these costs, by providing a more liberal, and a uniform, rule on waiver. That rule is discussed immediately below.

Introduction

The suggestion for the proposal of a rule dealing with waiver of attorney-client privilege and work product was presented in a January 23, 2006 letter from F. James Sensenbrenner, Jr., then-Chair of the House Committee on the Judiciary. In the letter, Congressman Sensenbrenner urged the Judicial Conference to proceed with rulemaking that would

- protect against the forfeiture of privilege where a disclosure in discovery is the result of an innocent mistake; and

- permit parties, and courts, to protect against the consequences of waiver by permitting disclosures of privileged information between the parties to a litigation.

Congressman Sensenbrenner noted the impact on litigation costs of reviewing for privilege and work product protection the enormous volume of materials in cases involving electronic discovery. He noted the concern that any disclosure could waive the privilege not only with regard to a particular document but for all other documents dealing with the same subject matter. He also observed that, while parties may make agreements limiting forfeiture of privilege, such agreements do not provide adequate assurance against waiver of the privilege in other proceedings. He added:

A federal rule protecting parties against forfeiture of privileges in these circumstances could significantly reduce litigation costs and delay and markedly improve the administration of justice for all participants.

---

4. *See, e.g.,* Rule 193.3(d) of the Texas Rules of Civil Procedure.

The task of drafting a proposed rule responding to Congressman Sensenbrenner's request was referred to the Judicial Conference Advisory Committee on Evidence Rules, which prepared proposed Rule 502, recognizing that unlike other rules of evidence, privilege rules must be directly enacted by Congress.

Rule 502 was approved by the Judicial Conference and thereafter approved by both Houses of Congress on unanimous consent. It was signed by the President on September 19, 2008.

PROBLEMS ADDRESSED BY RULE 502

Rule 502 does not attempt to deal comprehensively with either attorney-client privilege or work product protection. It also does not purport to cover all issues concerning waiver or forfeiture of either the attorney-client privilege or work product protection. The Rule covers issues of scope of waiver, inadvertent disclosure, selective waiver by disclosure to a federal office or agency, and the controlling effect of court orders and agreements.

Rule 502 provides the following protections against waiver of privilege or work product:

- *Limitations on Scope of Waiver:* Subdivision (a) provides that if a waiver is found, it applies only to the information disclosed, unless a broader waiver is made necessary by the holder's misleading use of privileged or protected communications or information.

- *Protections Against Inadvertent Disclosure:* Subdivision (b) provides that an inadvertent disclosure of privileged or protected communications or information, when made at the federal level, does not operate as a waiver if the holder took reasonable steps to prevent such a disclosure and employed reasonably prompt measures to retrieve the mistakenly disclosed communications or information.

- *Confidentiality Orders Binding on Non–Parties:* Subdivision (d) provides that if a federal court enters an order providing that a disclosure of privileged or protected communications or information does not constitute a waiver, that order is enforceable against all persons and entities in any federal or state proceeding. This provision allows parties in an action in which such an order is entered to limit the cost of preproduction privilege review.

- *Confidentiality Agreements:* Subdivision (e) provides that parties in a federal proceeding can enter into a confidentiality agreement providing for mutual protection against waiver in that proceeding. While those agreements bind the signatory parties, they are not binding on non-parties unless incorporated into a court order.

- *Disclosures Made in State Proceedings of Communications or Information Subsequently Offered in a Federal Proceeding:* Subdivision (c) provides that if privileged or protected communications or information are disclosed in a state proceeding, then admissibility in a subsequent federal proceeding is determined by the law that is most protective against waiver.

The Text of Rule 502 of the Federal Rules of Evidence

Rule 502. Attorney–Client Privilege and Work Product; Limitations on Waiver

The following provisions apply, in the circumstances set out, to disclosure of a communication or information covered by the attorney-client privilege or work-product protection.

(a) Disclosure made in a federal proceeding or to a federal office or agency; scope of a waiver.—When the disclosure is made in a federal proceeding or to a federal office or agency and waives the attorney-client privilege or work-product protection, the waiver extends to an undisclosed communication or information in a federal or state proceeding only if:

(1) the waiver is intentional;

(2) the disclosed and undisclosed communications or information concern the same subject matter; and

(3) they ought in fairness to be considered together.

(b) Inadvertent disclosure.—When made in a federal proceeding or to a federal office or agency, the disclosure does not operate as a waiver in a federal or state proceeding if:

(1) the disclosure is inadvertent;

(2) the holder of the privilege or protection took reasonable steps to prevent disclosure; and

(3) the holder promptly took reasonable steps to rectify the error, including (if applicable) following Fed. R. Civ. P. 26(b)(5)(B).

(c) Disclosure made in a state proceeding.— When the disclosure is made in a state proceeding and is not the subject of a state-court order concerning waiver, the disclosure does not operate as a waiver in a federal proceeding if the disclosure:

(1) would not be a waiver under this rule if it had been made in a federal proceeding; or

(2) is not a waiver under the law of the state where the disclosure occurred.

(d) Controlling effect of a court order.—A federal court may order that the privilege or protection is not waived by disclosure connected with the litigation pending before the court—in which event the disclosure is also not a waiver in any other federal or state proceeding.

(e) Controlling effect of a party agreement.—An agreement on the effect of disclosure in a federal proceeding is binding only on the parties to the agreement, unless it is incorporated into a court order.

(f) Controlling effect of this rule.— Notwithstanding Rules 101 and 1101, this rule applies to state proceedings and to federal court-annexed and federal court-mandated arbitration proceedings, in the circumstances set out in the rule. And notwithstanding Rule 501, this rule applies even if state law provides the rule of decision.

(g) Definitions.—In this rule:

1) "attorney-client privilege" means the protection that applicable law provides for confidential attorney-client communications; and

2) "work-product protection" means the protection that applicable law provides for tangible material (or its intangible equivalent) prepared in anticipation of litigation or for trial.

E. ETHICAL QUESTIONS INVOLVED IN RECEIVING MISTAKENLY DISCLOSED PRIVILEGED INFORMATION

IN RE NITLA S.A. DE C.V.

92 S.W.3d 419 (Tex. 2002)

PER CURIAM

The issue here is whether the trial court abused its discretion when it refused to disqualify Nitla's counsel, who had reviewed privileged documents that the trial court ordered the opposing party to produce. The court of appeals issued mandamus, ordering the trial court to disqualify Nitla's counsel. However, in so doing, the court of appeals misapplied the law and thus abused its discretion. Accordingly, we granted Nitla's motion for rehearing, and we now conditionally grant a writ of mandamus and direct the court of appeals to vacate its order.

Nitla, a Mexican pharmaceutical company, sued Bank of America (BOA) in 1996. Nitla claimed that BOA misappropriated over $24 million of Nitla's funds on deposit. During discovery, Nitla asked BOA to produce certain documents. BOA resisted and asserted the attorney-client and work-product privileges. After an in camera inspection and a hearing, the trial court identified numerous documents that it determined BOA should produce. BOA asked the trial court to stay production until BOA decided whether to seek emergency relief in the court of appeals. Rather than issue an order, the trial court requested additional briefing and scheduled another hearing. The trial court also indicated it would order BOA to produce any nonprivileged documents at that time.

At the second hearing, after considering the additional briefing and oral arguments, the trial court ordered BOA to produce the previously identified documents. BOA again asked the trial court to stay production, arguing that if Nitla's counsel reviewed the documents, BOA would be irreparably harmed. Moreover, BOA argued that if Nitla's counsel reviewed the documents and the court of appeals determined them privileged, Nitla's counsel could be disqualified. Nevertheless, the trial court granted, in part, Nitla's motion to compel production. The trial court next handed the documents, which were under the trial court's control, directly to Nitla's counsel. This enabled Nitla's counsel to review the documents before BOA could seek mandamus relief.

Later that same day, BOA notified Nitla by fax that it still believed all the tendered documents were privileged. BOA also asked Nitla not to review or distribute the documents, because BOA would seek mandamus relief. However, Nitla's counsel relied on the trial court's order and reviewed the documents.

After BOA filed for mandamus relief, the court of appeals abated the proceeding to allow the trial court's new judge to reconsider his predecessor's decision. After another hearing, the trial court again overruled BOA's objection that the documents were privileged. However, the trial court ordered Nitla to return the documents to BOA pending appellate review. Nitla complied with this order. BOA then reurged its mandamus petition in the court of appeals, and the court of appeals held that most of the documents were privileged.

BOA then moved to disqualify Nitla's counsel, alleging that Nitla's counsel "disregarded their ethical and professional obligations to gain an unfair advantage" when they reviewed the privileged documents. BOA also argued that the *Meador* factors support disqualification. See *In re Meador*, 968 S.W.2d 346, 351–52 (Tex. 1998) (discussing six factors a trial court should consider when deciding whether to disqualify an attorney who receives privileged information outside the normal course of discovery).

After a hearing, the trial court denied BOA's motion to disqualify. Even though the trial court found that Nitla had extensively reviewed the documents and that BOA had "clean hands," the trial court denied the disqualification motion because it found: (1) Nitla's counsel did not act unprofessionally or violate any disciplinary rules; (2) Nitla's counsel did not obtain the documents wrongfully, but rather, after a judicial proceeding; and (3) no competent evidence showed that Nitla's counsel had developed its trial strategy based on the documents. Moreover, the trial court determined that it had less severe measures available to prevent Nitla from using the privileged information to gain unfair advantage.

BOA sought mandamus relief from the trial court's order denying disqualification. The court of appeals reviewed the trial court's decision under *Meador*. The court of appeals determined that, although two *Meador* factors supported the trial court's order, two other *Meador* factors overwhelmingly supported disqualification. The court of appeals then concluded that the trial court could have reached only one decision under

Meador—to disqualify Nitla's counsel. Therefore, the court of appeals conditionally issued the writ.

* * * Nitla contends that the trial court correctly refused to disqualify Nitla's counsel, because BOA did not prove the disqualification grounds with specificity and did not prove it would suffer actual harm. Furthermore, Nitla argues, the court of appeals misapplied *Meador* and improperly substituted its own judgment for the trial court's judgment. In response, BOA claims that the court of appeals correctly applied *Meador*. BOA asserts: Nitla improperly reviewed the documents when it knew BOA intended to seek appellate relief; Nitla's actions irreparably harmed BOA; and there is no evidence that disqualification would harm Nitla. Therefore, BOA argues, the court of appeals properly issued mandamus against the trial court. We disagree.

* * *

"Disqualification is a severe remedy." It can result in immediate and palpable harm, disrupt trial court proceedings, and deprive a party of the right to have counsel of choice. In considering a motion to disqualify, the trial court must strictly adhere to an exacting standard to discourage a party from using the motion as a dilatory trial tactic. This Court often looks to the disciplinary rules to decide disqualification issues. However, the disciplinary rules are merely guidelines—not controlling standards— for disqualification motions. Even if a lawyer violates a disciplinary rule, the party requesting disqualification must demonstrate that the opposing lawyer's conduct caused actual prejudice that requires disqualification. And, under appropriate circumstances, a trial court has the power to disqualify a lawyer even if he has not violated a specific disciplinary rule.

In *Meador*, we acknowledged that there are undoubtedly some situations when a party's lawyer who reviews another party's privileged information must be disqualified, even though the lawyer did not participate in obtaining the information. However, we did not articulate a brightline standard for disqualification in such situations. Instead, we determined that a trial court must consider the importance of our discovery privileges along with all the facts and circumstances to decide "whether the interests of justice require disqualification." We then identified six factors a trial court should consider when a lawyer receives an opponent's privileged materials. However, we emphasized that "these factors apply only when a lawyer receives an opponent's privileged materials outside the normal course of discovery."

Here, the trial court determined that Nitla's counsel did not violate a disciplinary rule. Consequently, the disciplinary rules provide no guidance. Moreover, Nitla's counsel received the documents directly from the trial court in a discovery hearing. Thus, the six *Meador* factors do not apply. We have not defined a precise standard for disqualification in such circumstances. Nevertheless, the trial court referred to the appropriate guiding principles when it denied BOA's motion to disqualify.

In disqualification cases, our analysis begins with the premise that disqualification is a severe measure that can result in immediate harm, because it deprives a party of its chosen counsel and can disrupt court proceedings. Consequently, when a party receives documents from a trial court, and a reviewing court later deems the documents privileged, the party moving to disqualify opposing counsel must show that: (1) opposing counsel's reviewing the privileged documents caused actual harm to the moving party; and (2) disqualification is necessary, because the trial court lacks any lesser means to remedy the moving party's harm.

We conclude that the trial court correctly applied these principles. Thus, we hold that the trial court did not abuse its discretion when it denied BOA's motion to disqualify Nitla's counsel. At the disqualification hearing, the trial court focused on whether BOA proved it suffered actual prejudice. BOA argued that the mere fact that Nitla had extensively reviewed the privileged documents demonstrated prejudice to BOA. However, BOA could not show that Nitla's trial strategy had significantly changed after reviewing the documents. Indeed, BOA could only demonstrate that reviewing the documents might have enabled Nitla's counsel to identify four new witnesses to depose, and that this additional testimony could potentially harm BOA. Recognizing that disqualification is a severe measure, the trial court determined that less severe measures, such as quashing depositions, could cure BOA's alleged harm. Accordingly, the trial court concluded that disqualification was neither a necessary nor an appropriate remedy.

The court of appeals, in contrast, abused its discretion when it conditionally issued mandamus and ordered the trial court to disqualify Nitla's counsel. The court of appeals recognized that Nitla's counsel did not obtain the documents through any wrongdoing. Nonetheless, it explicitly applied the *Meador* factors and determined that some factors supported the trial court's order whereas others did not. In so doing, the court of appeals misapplied the law.

Accordingly, we grant Nitla's motion for rehearing. * * * [W]e conditionally grant a writ of mandamus and direct the court of appeals to vacate its order.

COMMENTARY

You are minding your own business and your adversary sends you a CD in response to a discovery request. You put it up on your computer, and as you toggle through, you see an email from the CEO of the adversary to litigation counsel, which reports a fact that indicates a major weakness in the adversary's case. Do you amend your pleadings? Send the information to your expert? Call the adversary? Return the information? Disqualify yourself because now you know about privileged information? Of course, if you have signed a confidentiality agreement, it will ordinarily require you, like your adversary, to return all apparently privileged information immediately. But what if there is no agreement in place?

The 2006 amendments to the Federal Rules provide some guidance for parties who receive what appears to be mistakenly disclosed privileged information. Rule 26(b)(5)(B) provides that assuming there is no confidentiality agreement in place if a receiving party is *notified* of the mistaken disclosure by the adversary, then the receiving party "must promptly return, sequester, or destroy the specified information and any copies it has; must not use or disclose the information until the claim [i.e., whether it is privileged information at all and whether the privilege has been waived] is resolved." The receiving party is allowed to go to court under seal to get a determination of whether the information is protected.

What happens if you look at the information, do not think that it is privileged, and send it to IT to be put in all the spreadsheets being prepared for the litigation or send it to your expert who plugs the information into her calculations, and then you get a call from the other side claiming privilege? In that case, Rule 26(b)(5)(B) requires the receiving party "to take reasonable steps to retrieve the information if the party disclosed it before being notified." But shouldn't the receiving party be entitled to some recompense for the cost of retrieving the information and unringing all the bells that have been rung? Rule 26 does not explicitly provide for any remedy to the receiving party—but a court would certainly have discretion to order some reimbursement as a condition of preserving the privileged information. Moreover, the burden on the receiving party can be taken into account in the fairness analysis of whether to find that the privilege has been waived. If retrieving the information would be cost-prohibitive for the receiving party, a court might be justified in finding that the party who made the mistaken disclosure has waived the privilege.

Note that Rule 26 does not require the receiving party to tell the adversary that it appears to have mistakenly disclosed privileged information. But Rule 4.4(b) of the ABA Model Rules of Professional Conduct imposes an ethical obligation on the receiving party to notify the adversary of the mistake:

> (b) A lawyer who receives a document relating to the representation of the lawyer's client and knows or reasonably should know that the document was inadvertently sent shall promptly notify the sender.

The Commentary to Model Rule 4.4(b) elaborates on the supposed need for this rule:

> [2] Paragraph (b) recognizes that lawyers sometimes receive documents that were mistakenly sent or produced by opposing parties or their lawyers. If a lawyer knows or reasonably should know that such a document was sent inadvertently, then this Rule requires the lawyer to promptly notify the sender in order to permit that person to take protective measures. Whether the lawyer is required to take additional steps, such as returning the original document, is a matter of law beyond the scope of these Rules, as is the question of whether the privileged status of a document has been waived. * * * For purposes of this Rule, document includes e-mail or other electronic modes of transmission subject to being read or put into readable form.

[3] Some lawyers may choose to return a document unread, for example, when the lawyer learns before receiving the document that it was inadvertently sent to the wrong address. Where a lawyer is not required by applicable law to do so, the decision to voluntarily return such a document is a matter of professional judgment ordinarily reserved to the lawyer.

In light of the obligations imposed on the receiving party by Rule 26 and Model Rule 4.4(b), one might wonder: What happened to the adversary system? Why can't the receiving party take full advantage of the mistakes of her adversary?

†